Raggett
on
HTML 4

Raggett
on
HTML 4

second edition

Dave Raggett
Jenny Lam
Ian Alexander
Michael Kmiec

Addison-Wesley

Harlow, England • Reading, Massachusetts • Menlo Park, California
New York • Don Mills, Ontario • Amsterdam • Bonn • Sydney • Singapore
Tokyo • Madrid • San Juan • Milan • Mexico City • Seoul • Taipei

© Addison Wesley Longman 1998

Addison Wesley Longman Limited
Edinburgh Gate
Harlow
Essex CM20 2JE
England

and Associated Companies throughout the World.

Cover designed by odB Design and Communication, Reading, UK
and printed by Riverside, Reading, UK
Cover illustration by Jenny Lam
Typeset by 43
Printed and bound in the United States of America

First printed 1997

ISBN 0-201-17805-2

British Library Cataloguing-in-Publication Data
A catalogue record for this book is available from the British Library

PREFACE

This book provides a detailed and lively description of the Web publishing language HTML 4, written for both the novice and the advanced user. We hope that it is intelligently presented and enjoyable to read.

HTML 4 is the latest version of the Web's publishing language: it follows on from HTML 3.2, which was a much simpler specification. HTML 4 comes from the World Wide Web Consortium ('W3C'), an international organization founded in 1994 to further the evolution of the World Wide Web. Both Netscape and Microsoft are members of W3C: they are publicly committed to the implementation of HTML 4 on their browsers. HTML 4 is on its way to becoming a truly cross-industry standard useful to a wide and international audience.

New features for HTML 4

Many entirely new features of HTML 4 are explained in this book:

- Tables are more sophisticated.

- Forms have been modified to help visually impaired readers who use speech generation software to read Web pages.

- Style sheets are fully supported by HTML 4; their use is now an integral part of the process of designing a Web site.

- With a view to making the Web truly international, HTML 4 encourages publishing in a variety of human languages.

- Frames have now been formally incorporated into the specification.

- The new OBJECT tag at last provides a standard way of incorporating many kinds of multimedia application.

About the authors

Dave Raggett

Jenny Lam

Ian Alexander

Michael Kmiec

Dave Raggett

Dave Raggett is the lead architect for HTML 4 on assignment from Hewlett-Packard Laboratories. He works with the World Wide Web Consortium where he continues to pursue a major role in HTML's development.

Jenny Lam

Jenny Lam is a technical writer who specializes in explaining science and technology at layman level. In an age of cyberspace and virtual men, Jenny remains down-to-earth by combining writing with her career as a full-time housewife and mother.

Ian Alexander

Ian Alexander is a systems engineer specializing in requirements engineering. He divides his time between writing, training, research and consultancy. When not otherwise engaged he collects natural patterns for his Web site.

Michael Kmiec

Michael Kmiec is an applications developer who uses C, C++, Java and a bit of Tao to make things work.

Overall structure

The book starts by explaining the basic concepts of the Web for the layman. It then goes on to give an inside story of how HTML came about, embarking on an interesting historical account of the language. There follows a chapter which tells you how to compose your first HTML document and also introduces you to the technical terms and concepts needed to understand the later and more technical chapters in the book.
We cover:

- Simple mark-up of paragraphs and headings including how to apply a style to give text a color on the screen or display text in a special font and size.

- Character mark-up including subscripts, superscripts, bold text, emphasized text and other effects.

- Lists: simple bulleted lists, numbered lists, lists within lists, lists with customized bullets.

- Hypertext links, including a layman's explanation of what they are and how to construct them, how to link to a particular place in the document rather than to the beginning.

- Style sheets: an introduction to using the CSS style sheet language to control color and font, background texture and position on the 'page'. The CSS language is very easy to use: if you have some experience of desk top publishing then simple use of CSS should be no problem.

- Graphics: inserting photographs, illustrations and other artwork into Web pages. There is a discussion of graphics formats and notes on which are applicable under what circumstances: GIF, JPEG and PNG.

- Tables, including design principles, merging table cells, automatic alignment, fancy borders and more.

- Frames: how to structure a Web site to keep individual documents simple and maintainable, how to provide decent navigation tools, how to combine text with graphics, and, not least, how to support older browsers.

- Multimedia on the Web: the use of the new standard `OBJECT` tag to insert animation clips, music and sound bites, and much else besides.

An explanation of the characters in the cartoons in this book.

Adrian Anorak

Adrian is always in his head, he lives in the virtual world of the Internet, which consists of a world-wide web of interlinked nodes, represented here by a lily pond.

Prunella

Prunella is Adrian's aunt. She treats Adrian as the small boy she embarrassingly once knew, and probably still thinks he is.

Lily Pond

Virtual pond in Prunella's garden, representing the waters of Cyberspace. The water-lily leaves are nodes on the web.

Fred Frog

Fred lives in the pond, hopping from leaf to leaf. He is of course a virtual frog, unlike Adrian who only imagines he is virtual (well, maybe . . .) Fred is naturally derisive (Brrrekk!)

- Scripts to support a range of simple animation and navigation purposes. We deal with the HTML involved in client-side scripting far enough to help readers understand what they can achieve, and when they will need to make the investment in server-side programming.

- Appendices consisting of convenient reference material, an entertaining and informative glossary, and a look behind the scenes at the Cyberia Café.

Thanks to . . .

Our thanks to Fred Volans for livening up the book with her wonderful cartoons.

We would also like to thank Karen Mosman and Nicky McGregor for their valued efforts in diplomacy and negotiation, also Kathryn Esplin who did the copy-editing, and Louise Wilson who coordinated the production of this book.

Thanks also go to Grandpa and Grandma Lam for distracting children, guinea-pigs, rabbits and birds at critical moments, a service which cannot be underestimated in its value. And to Sabina for constant support and the best coffee in the world.

CONTENTS

10 Tables   165

11 Forms   197

1
INTRODUCTION TO THE WORLD WIDE WEB

Included in this chapter is information on:

- How the World Wide Web works
- How the World Wide Web is different from the Internet
- Java, Scripting and SGML – a layperson's explanation
- How the Web has been made accessible for people with disabilities
- How style sheets can improve Web documents

Summary

HTML is the publishing language for the World Wide Web. Behind the scenes, every document you see on the Web – whether covering the national news, giving information about university courses, selling books or describing a local cat show – is written using HTML. But why is HTML necessary? Why is a browser needed to display HTML documents, and what is the role of the server? These questions, as well as simple descriptions of Java, scripting, multimedia and other Web-associated technologies, form the subject of this chapter.

1.1 Simple use of the Web

From your home in the United Kingdom, in the small English town of Chipping Sodbury, you decide to find out what entertainment there is in Bath, the famous city only 15 miles away. A company publishes *What's On in Bath* online, and you have read that this is available on http://www.bath.info.uk/ as a series of Web 'pages' on the Internet. You decide to take a look. You switch on your computer and start it up in the usual way. Just as you might click on an icon to start up your desktop publishing package, so you click on the icon to load your World Wide Web browser. The browser is a piece of software that allows you to display certain kinds of information from the Internet.

Your modem, which connects your computer to the telephone line in the street via an ordinary household telephone socket, makes a series of electronic beeps as it dials up the nearest Internet point of presence and puts you onto the 'Net. Via the interface provided by your Web browser, you can now enter the Internet address, otherwise known as the URL, or Uniform Resource Locator, of the file containing the front page of *What's On in Bath*. As with all other information on the Web, this would start with 'http://', for example:

```
http://www.bath.avon.uk/
```

HTTP (HyperText Transfer Protocol) is the name of the Web's own transmission protocol. Web pages are sent over the Internet to your computer courtesy of HTTP.

Protocols
A protocol consists of salutations exchanged between computers: 'good morning', 'be with you in a tick', 'file coming down the line now' and so on. Each service on the Internet has its own protocol: its own personal way of sending files around the system. The protocol for the Web is HTTP. File Transfer Protocol (FTP) is another common protocol of which you may have heard.

The difference between the Web and the Internet

Do not make the rather common mistake of confusing the Web with the Internet itself: the Internet simply provides the medium for the Web to run on, just as a telephone line provides the medium for telephone conversations. What the Web does is provide the technology for publishing, sending and obtaining information over the expanse of the Internet. How the Internet actually works may be a matter of interest, but the Web user does not need to know about it in any detail.

This fictitious home page would have perhaps a photo showing the famous Roman Baths on the first page, together with a short paragraph introducing the town, and a menu of icons that call up specific information on Bath's museums, parks, bus-tours and so on. These icons provide hypertext links for you to click on-screen 'buttons', enabling you to home-in on the information you want. Hypertext links are in many ways the most important feature of the Web. In the case of our imaginary Web pages, clicking on hypertext buttons mostly displays data that is held on computers somewhere in Bath itself. Sometimes, however, a hypertext link may fetch a file from somewhere quite different on the Internet. If you click on the title of a play taking place in Bath, information about the performing company may be fetched across the Internet from a computer thousands of miles away in the United States. From that point on, you might be able to call up pages that tell you about other plays by the same company. With the Web, you can depart on your own private 'tour' of information on a chosen subject whenever the inclination takes you. This is by virtue of the hypertext links that span the globe.

You can also pay for goods and services over the Web. You could, for example, decide to order some tickets for a play by filling in a form displayed on a 'page' of an online magazine. You might buy a $20.00 seat for '*As You Like It*' at the Bath Playhouse and then pay by credit card. The example below is taken from a different application on the Web. You can see now what a Web page looks like.

You can see on-screen buttons to click on: these are the hypertext links. There are two types: underlined words and pictures. These buttons serve to

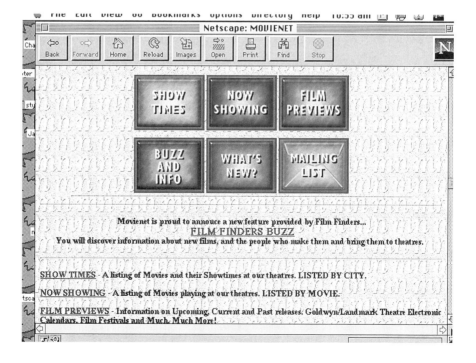

fetch up new information across the Internet. Also, you can see the title of the page and a URL at the bottom of the screen telling you from where the information originated.

Looking at this screen and other pages from the Web, you can see that the Web provides the following:

- A means for publishing online information. The Web enables you to lay out text and graphics of the 'pages' on the screen, and to insert titles, photos, captions and so on.

- A means for retrieving online information via hypertext links, at the click of a button. You can also use Web search programs to find the information you want.

- An interface for looking at information retrieved. This is done by virtue of a Web browser.

A Web page may also contain forms for conducting commercial transactions across the Internet and include other applications; for example, spreadsheets, video clips, sound clips and so on.

The Web is, therefore, simultaneously a means of online publishing, a way of accessing, storing and retrieving information, as well as a means of sending, acquiring and querying data across the Internet. Most importantly, the Web allows the use of hypertext links that can take you to any computer on the Internet. All these functions work by using the hardware: the wires, the cables, the computers, the satellite links that are used to send information from computer to computer using Internet protocols.

Before the Web, the Internet was largely the domain of computer nerds and others who delighted in the abstract and concise. Interfaces to early Internet applications required almost mathematical precision to operate, and programs such as FTP and Telnet were purely command-driven. Later, when file-retrieval services such as WAIS and Gopher became popular on the Internet, these had the advantage of being menu-driven, but still were rather cumbersome.

Although the Internet still was using interfaces suitable for the more technically inclined, software for home and office markets long ago departed from command-driven applications. The idea of a graphical interface using Windows, which originated from work at Xerox PARC (Palo Alto Research Center) in the 1970s, was popularized in the early 1980s, primarily through Apple Computer Inc.'s Macintosh computer. IBM Corp.'s Personal Computer and other manufacturers' PC-compatible machines followed suit with the introduction of Microsoft Corp.'s MS-Windows operating system a few years later. At the same time, windowing systems were introduced to the UNIX workstation market, which is now dominated by the X-11 interface. It has, however, taken until the middle 1990s to introduce a simple and reliable user interface for accessing information over the Internet. The Web's popularity has doubtless been in part because it offers a simple point-and-click interface, which immediately makes it more accessible to a much wider range of users. Another important factor must have been email, which, as it has gained popularity, has made the idea of sending information across networked computers that much more acceptable.

What is a URL?

This is a much-simplified explanation for the novice.

Given the fact that there are vast numbers of Web servers, the question remains of how can HTTP possibly locate just the file you want from somewhere on the Internet. The answer is through the use of the URL, the Uniform Resource Locator. This is rather like the telephone number of a computer on the Internet, together with information appended to specify the exact file to be sent to your machine. Taking the URL for our fictitious Web pages in Bath, we can see the general pattern that URLs adopt. Look at

```
http://www.bath.avon.uk
```

more closely.

'http' is the name of the Web protocol used to access the data across the Internet.

'www.bath.avon.uk' is the Internet name or the domain name of the computer on which the information is stored. The 'www' indicates that this is a World Wide Web server. 'uk' is the country code for the United Kingdom.

To be more specific about the file you want from the server in question, you add to the URL a path and a file name. For example:

```
http://www.bath.avon.uk/time_tables/buses.html
```

which would point to a file called 'buses.html' in a directory called 'time_tables'. We can imagine that 'buses.html' contains bus timetables for the city of Bath, which can be conveniently called up on your screen.

URLs can specify files to be accessed using protocols other than 'http'. A URL beginning with 'ftp://' points to a file to be fetched using FTP – the File Transfer Protocol. Meanwhile, a file beginning with 'mailto://' links to an application which allows you to send an email message to a pre-defined address, and 'news://' points to a USENET newsgroup and uses the Network Transfer Protocol to transfer data.

There are various conventions when it comes to URLs. Take the letters '.com' for instance. These mean 'company' as in: 'http://www.microsoft.com'.

Non-profit organizations may use '.org' and educational establishments use '.edu'. Similarly, there are codes for countries. A URL may end in '.us' for the United States, '.fr' for France, '.au' for Australia and so on. Some of the conventions for URLs are listed in Appendices E and F.

How are email addresses different from URLs? Email addresses follow a different format: name@name.name.domain. For example: tiptoes@hawks. uni.edu.

The string of letters following the @ sign identifies the machine to which the mail will be sent, whereas the name of the person who will receive the mail is given directly before the @ sign. There may be more than one person logging on to the machine to read mail. That is why the name of the person becomes important in an email address.

1.2 The Web in the context of the Internet

The Internet is a vast network of interconnected computers. Just as AT&T, France Telecom, British Telecom, and other countrywide or regional telephone networks now are joined together to form a global telephone system, so it is with the Internet. The many thousands of computer networks that make up the Internet are joined together on a global scale, so that any Internet computer can communicate with any other.

How can your computer know how to find someone else's computer on the other side of the world? Just as each telephone in the world has its own unique telephone number, so each computer connected to the Internet has its own computer number. This is known as its IP, or Internet Protocol, address. However, because IP addresses consist of long series of numbers that are cumbersome to remember and type, you rarely come across them in everyday Internet use; most people prefer to use the parallel system of naming computers. This is the system of Internet host names, sometimes called Internet addresses or even domain names. Whereas a computer on the Internet may have an IP address such as 17.254.0.63, it may have a more manageable Internet host or domain name such as www.drizzle.org. Servers consult a globally distributed directory to map each host name onto the corresponding IP address.

Once you are connected to the Internet, you can theoretically 'dial' anywhere you want. This gives you tremendous freedom. The cost of Internet access remains the same regardless of whether or not you talk to a computer in Australia, England, the United States, or in the next town. This is because you pay only for the time spent on the line to your nearest Internet point of presence. And, just as when you make a phone call to another country, you are hardly aware that your voice is traveling along foreign telephone lines, so it is, theoretically, with the Internet. Although data sent from a computer linked to a network in an office in Paris may travel across constituent networks *en route* to Los Angeles, as a user, you do not have to worry about the path it takes. The only evidence you have that the requested information comes from far away is when a part of the Internet system is in heavy use and you have to wait.

The French system Minitel is used in ways similar to the Web

It is interesting to note that the French have been using a public system of information access for a number of years, which, in many ways, has occupied the same niche as the Web, although not nearly so sophisticated nor as versatile. Called Minitel, the system consists of hardware in the form of a computer, keyboard and modem originally given away free to subscribers of France Telecom, the national French telephone company. Minitel is very easy to use and is extremely popular – most homes have one. Minitel has existed as a household 'pet' for more than 10 years. Using your Minitel, you dial up on the Minitel online service, and then proceed through a number of menus to book yourself a seat on a train, read the latest recipe for *la mousse au chocolat à l'anglaise*, inspect your bank balance, book hotel rooms and so on.

1.3 Basic components of the Web

The basic components of the Web are shown in the following illustration. They are:

- **Web servers**, which are computers that hold information for distribution over the Internet. In the example application in the diagram, one Web server might hold the text and graphics of the online magazine *What's On in Bath*, and another server might hold information on which seats are available for a particular concert. The magazine would be formatted using the Web's own publishing language, HTML (HyperText Mark-up Language). The data on available seats and their price would be held in a database with links to specific forms that are published using HTML.

- **Servers**, which can be PCs, Macintosh systems or UNIX workstations: it is the server software that makes them special, rather than the computer itself. That said, servers need to be fairly up-market machines. Servers do need to be left on all the time, so that people can access the information on them whenever they want. Another important point about servers: they are relatively difficult to set up. If you are a non-technical person who wants to publish on the Web, the best thing to do is to rent some space on someone else's server.

- **Web clients**, which can be PCs, Macintoshes and other computers that are connected to the Internet and which can retrieve information from Web servers. A Web client is the computer on your desk. PCs, Macintoshes, UNIX workstations and even simple terminals can run client software. Different client software is marketed (or is given away free) for different platforms. Thus, Mosaic has both a Macintosh and a PC implementation.

- **HTTP protocol**, which is used to transmit files between servers and clients. When you click on a hypertext link or fill out a form in a Web document, the results need to be sent across the Internet as quickly as possible, and then to be understood by a server at the other end. Instructions such as 'send me this file' or 'get me that image' are carried by the Web communications protocol, HTTP. This protocol is the 'messenger' that fetches files to and from servers, and then delivers results to your computer every time you click with a request. HTTP has its counterparts in other Internet services: FTP, file transfer protocol, and Gopher are protocols that obtain different sorts of information from across the Internet.

- **Browser** software, which is needed by a Web client for displaying text, images, video clips and so on. This is supplied under the umbrella name 'browser', of which Mosaic, Microsoft Corp.'s Internet Explorer and Netscape Communications Corp.'s Navigator and Communicator browsers are probably the best-known examples. Browser software gives you the ability to scan information retrieved from Web servers, as you would browse through a book. It also gives you facilities for saving and printing information obtained on the Web.

Simplified view of components of the Web.

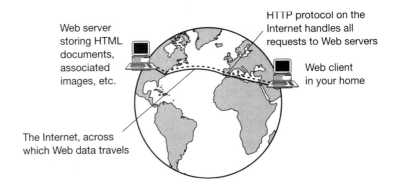

Web server storing HTML documents, associated images, etc.

HTTP protocol on the Internet handles all requests to Web servers

Web client in your home

The Internet, across which Web data travels

A key point that helped make the Web successful is that it is multi-platform. What this means is that it does not matter what kind of computer you are using; you can still view information published on other, usually incompatible, machines. Thus, a PC user can access information published on a Macintosh; a Macintosh can access information published by a PC; UNIX users will find that they are compatible with everyone. The trick is that each computer in its own way can assimilate HTML. What happens when an HTML document gets to its destination is up to the computer on the receiving end. It can display paragraphs in Helvetica 20-point type if it pleases, and headings in Times 14-point bold type, if that is the font available. Whereas the document is transmitted computer-to-computer in a standard format, individual browsers may display it quite differently, depending on the capabilities of the hardware and software in the computer on the receiving end.

1.4 A universally understood publishing language: HTML

To publish information for global distribution on the World Wide Web, you need a universally understood publishing language, a kind of mother tongue, which all computers on the Web can potentially understand. You also need a commonly understood communications protocol for sending published information 'down the wire' from computer to computer. This should enable users to download information to their machine at the click of a button, and also to send back information (your address, a credit card number, a query to a database and so on) with little effort.

The publishing language used by the Web is called HTML (HyperText Mark-up Language). Using HTML, you can specify which parts of your text are to be headings, paragraphs, bulleted lists, and which parts are to be rendered in bold-face type, in italicized type and so on. You can use HTML to insert tables into documents, to write equations, to import images and to format fill-out forms for querying databases at a distance. (Some of these features are specific to HTML 3 and are not supported by earlier versions of HTML.) The HTML language itself is very flexible and not difficult to use, although, as with all tasks associated with computing, patience is a necessary virtue for authoring hypertext. Part of the Web's appeal is that almost anyone with a reasonable PC, Macintosh or UNIX computer can publish information without being unduly technical. Judging by the variety of publishers on the Web today, HTML is within the grasp of many. A simple example of HTML can be seen at the beginning of Chapter 3.

1.5 The HTTP protocol

A long-distance jump
⟨A HREF = "http://www.norge.org/ docs/norse.html "⟩

The initial protocol for the Web was very, very simple. The client sent a request: 'GET this filename' and the other end sent back the file and closed the connection. And that was it. There was no content type to tell you what kind of file was being sent. No status code. Just the file. The client therefore had to guess what it had been given and this developed into a fine art. First, the browser would look at the file extension to see if there were any clues, such as .GIF or .HTML, and then it would look at the beginning of the file in case the first few bytes gave the game away – all rather precarious.

Then along came MIME, a kind of multimedia extension to email. This was soon adapted to HTTP so that now, when you receive a file, you actually have a status code and a content type. This content type tells you whether or not the file is text/HTML, video/MPEG, image/GIF and so on, which gives the browser a chance to call up the correct viewers to display the file. The burden of finding out what kind of file it was has now moved to the server. On UNIX and DOS, servers still play this game of 'guess the file format'; whereas on the Macintosh, this is stored as part of the file itself.

The HTTP we use today is the product of collaboration between CERN and a group at the National Center for Supercomputer Applications (NCSA) at the University of Illinois at Champaign-Urbana. Innovations since that time included security features such as Netscape's secure socket layer (SSL), and more recently, the ability to keep open the connection to the server so that the server can make multiple requests. The World Wide Web Consortium is looking into ways of improving this protocol, and into methods of text compression that enable information on the Web to arrive at its destination much quicker.

1.6 More than just text and pictures on the Web

The Web is expanding not only in terms of how much information it holds, but also in terms of the variety of information it holds. The figure below illustrates this general trend. On the left-hand side, you can see the Web as it started, predominantly as a medium for publishing information in textual form, and then it progressed to include photos, diagrams and so

More variety on the Web. From being a simple text-based system, the Web now supports a variety of media.

• First graphics
• X-bit map and X-pix map formats
• GIF format

• Java and HotJava – programs sent over the Web
• Plug-ins become increasingly popular and supported
• Sophisticated forms in HTML
• Better tables in HTML
• Division of browser windows into multiple areas
• Rifts between browser writers

• Style sheets implemented
• Scripting for HTML widespread
• Multi-column layout on screen
• Many tools for automatic generation of HTML

| 1992 | 1993 | 1994 | 1995 | 1996 | 1997 |

• Text based Web
• Crude mechanism for querying on key words
• No graphics
• No nested lists

• Simple tables
• JPEG supported
• MPEG video files supported but slow downloading
• Sun's AV audio and QuickTime audio format files can be sent over the Web, but downloading is slow

• Java matures
• Style sheets partially implemented
• Revisions to HTML

on. Toward the right-hand side of our diagram, we show the latest features at the time of writing: the introduction of plug-in modules, the Java programming language that enables all manner of small applications to be sent down the wire and used within Web applications, and so on.

Many of the new features of HTML are associated with this departure away from the simple document and toward a Web which combines text, graphics, video, audio, applications such as spreadsheets, front ends to databases, virtual reality applications and all sorts of other 'objects'.

Java

At the time of writing, Java is a very popular buzzword. Java is a programming language that enables programmers to write small applications that are sent over the Web and then executed on the client. It is an object-oriented language related to the C language. What is so special about Java is that programs can be sent to any machine with the right browser to understand them; furthermore, the code will run safely without any risk of adversely affecting the client.

From the user's point of view, Web documents suddenly become much cleverer. It is as though your browser automatically creates features, such as the ability to run a spreadsheet or to play a piece of animation, right in front of your eyes, without you having to load any extra software. The code required to do such tricks is compiled into a special binary format and executed by a Java interpreter in your machine. Java applications are called 'applets' (which means 'small applications' – it would be another thing entirely to send full-blown application software over the Web) and are small pieces of code that rely on libraries of Java 'classes' in the browser.

These libraries indicate that the browser has a certain amount of processing knowledge resident in the browser itself: the browser knows how to create a window, respond to events, paint things within a window, draw text within a window and so on. The applets arriving across the Web capitalize on this knowledge and use the library routines to do something useful, such as displaying a simple spreadsheet or a piece of animated graphics.

But, what happens if the applet calls upon a class that is not available at the client end? In such cases, the class has to be fetched over the Internet, a process that indeed may be rather slow. For this reason, it is best to limit the number of these 'additional' classes.

Scripts for HTML

Scripts are small programs, which are transparent to the user and which go on 'behind the scenes' fine-tuning Web pages in one way or another. The author can write a script in one of several available scripting languages. Scripts themselves may have one of several functions. The classic function is rendering a form to seem 'smart' so that it interacts with you as you fill it in. Thus, you might arrange for a script to check each form field in turn to make sure it is properly filled in, and then to advise you if you have mistakenly left out some critical piece of information.

BBScript was invented by Microsoft and is an adapted version of Visual Basic; JavaScript is a Netscape scripting language and Sun has tcl.

In the future, scripts may be used to create various special effects, such as animation. The later chapter in this book on Scripting examines some of the current and upcoming uses for scripting. Scripts can also be used to tailor components of a particular program, such as a spreadsheet program. In this instance, application software developers will supply off-the-shelf components for a program. Let us suppose that the components are for a spreadsheet program; with a script, you can easily integrate off-the-shelf components into the application, a feat that would have previously required many programmer hours to compile. But with the hypothetical script you have written, this almost seamless integration happens in much the same way as it does with Visual Basic; here, the components are written in a kind of systems language and then, the script enables off-the-shelf components to be integrated into the application itself. If scripts are half as good as they promise, they can save many a programmer's headache.

The idea of the Internet media type

If HTML can have all sorts of items embedded in it – pieces of animation to be played by your browser, small programs to run on your computer, and even music – then surely the browser must have some way of knowing what kind of beast is coming down the line. A browser can sense what type a file is and therefore it can know what to do with it by using the *Internet media type*. The Internet media type is a code sent with the file. The browser uses this code to work out what software is needed to interpret and display the data. Some examples include the following: the Internet media type for an HTML document is text/HTML: for a JPEG image, the Internet media type is image/JPEG.

Once the media type has been recognized and the correct software called up to deal with the file, the information in the file can be displayed embedded in the document; that is, it is displayed in an area of the document as though it were simply part of it. Another way of looking at this is that information can be 'plugged in' to a document. Indeed, the phrase 'plug-in' is commonly used to describe downloading embedded files that are not in HTML, and which require software at the browser end to come to the rescue and display them.

A browser may allow, for example, a PDF (Portable Document Format) file to appear down the wire. The browser sees that this has an Internet media type Application/PDF. It then calls up the Adobe Acrobat reader to display the PDF file. Once the media type is known, the browser loads the correct application software and interprets the file.

1.7 HTML and its relationship to SGML

Early work on representing documents focused on rendering instructions needed to print the documents. Work by IBM on GML (Generalized Mark-up Language) focused on an alternative approach, whereby standard document structures such as headers, paragraphs, lists and so on were marked up by tags inserted into document text. The emphasis on document structure rather than on rendering instructions, made it dramatically easier to move documents from one system to another whether for display on simple terminals, line printers or sophisticated typesetting machinery.

This work led to the Standard Generalized Mark-up Language, which is an international standard ISO 8879:1986. SGML enables you to define a grammar for marked-up documents that defines the ways in which tags can be inserted into documents. For instance, list items only make sense in the context of a list, and table cells only make sense in the context of a table. SGML's formal way of describing the grammar is called the Document Type Definition.

Global hypertext makes worse the problem in moving documents from one system to another; for example, we have Macintosh systems, PCs, a variety of UNIX boxes, simple terminals and even speech I/O devices for the visually impaired. SGML proved ideally suited for this application. Tim Berners-Lee chose SGML to define the HTML document format for the World Wide Web. HTML is formally an application of SGML. The HTML

Document Type Definition (DTD) formally defines the set of HTML tags and the ways that they can be inserted into documents.

To the uninitiated, DTDs may seem rather intimidating. This book tries to act as a guiding hand to explain the HTML mark-up language and how to apply it so that it creates documents for Web publishing. HTML is not a static document format, but is evolving rapidly from its simple beginnings as conceived by Tim Berners-Lee.

1.8 The Web for people with disabilities

One of the areas in which the World Wide Web Consortium (W3C) has shown great interest is how to make the Web accessible to the blind. In the case of HTML, this has involved two things in particular, discussed below.

First of all, the IMG tag for inserting images (as explained in our chapter *Graphics on the Web*) is to be superseded by an entirely different tag (OBJECT), which enables the browser to display textual mark-up as an alternative when a visual image appears on the screen.

Suppose you have a photograph as part of your Web pages. Browsers will usually display the photograph as the author intended. A browser used by a blind or visually impaired person will, however, be set up to display a paragraph or two of descriptive text instead of the photograph. This text must be included by the author for the benefit of text-only browsers and may contain hypertext links, itemized lists and all kinds of other mark-up. Seeing such text, the browser will read aloud the words to the user and even use appropriate intonation for bold, emphasized text and so on.

By including textual mark-up as an alternative to images, the blind or visually impaired Web user is in a far better position than previously. The still-popular IMG tag allows only very limited alternative text in lieu of images and thus puts it out of favor with those who rely on speech generation.

Second of all, the W3 Consortium is encouraging authors to separate the *structural* aspects of their documents from those aspects of the documents that are merely to do with *layout*. Once this has been done, the software that enables the text to be synthesized and read aloud to the blind or visually impaired user has got an easier job to do. Think about it: if a page is marked up solely in terms of headings, paragraphs, lists, and other structural items, then it becomes much simpler to understand the HTML and to render the content into speech. But the moment that extraneous information about font size, alignment of text, margin width, color and so on is mixed in with the general mark-up, then translating that mark-up into a spoken equivalent becomes much harder.

An ardent enthusiast when it comes to making the Web available to the blind is Dr T.V. Raman. A clear and original thinker, Raman – himself blind – has contributed widely to discussions and negotiations with browser vendors on the subject of Web access for people with disabilities, and also is an active participant at the Math Working Group. He has also written the Emacspeak Speech Interface, which is a full-fledged, speech-output system that enables the blind and visually impaired to access the Web with a line-mode browser within a UNIX environment.

1.9 Math and HTML

Math plug-in
A new plug-in for math should be ready by August 1997. This is a simple-to-use piece of software which allows easy publishing of mathematical and scientific expressions on the Web. It is written by Dave Raggett under the auspices of the World Wide Web Consortium.

This book you may notice, does not cover how to mark up math on the Web. In this book's previous edition, math was inserted as a chapter in its own right with the happy anticipation that math soon would become part of the HTML standard. Unfortunately, that never happened, and, although certain browsers have implemented the math spec as it stood, for the main, math on the Web is still in the wizards' pot; to be sure, there is no end of disagreement on the recipe.

Just as HTML has its own Working Group, so does Math. The HTML Math group includes representatives from companies who produce special software for typing and editing mathematical formulae on computers; examples of such software are Waterloo Maple and Wolfram. There are also representatives from scientific publishers such as Reed-Elsevier Ltd, as well as the American Mathematical Society. Each has its own view of the correct way to do things, and Dave Raggett of the World Wide Web Consortium, who did the original HTML Math proposal, has his own ideas, too.

Given the widely disparate views of group members, evolving a standard for marking up math on the Web is a challenge, indeed. None-theless, the Math Working Group eventually hopes to come up with a proposal for concrete notation of HTML math, with the initial deployment via *plug-ins*, which is add-on software that enables browsers to cope with math notation. Meanwhile, mathematicians, physicists, chemists and other scientists are finding it very difficult to use ordinary HTML to express mathematical formulae and scientific expressions.

It is strange to think that the Web originally evolved for the benefit of physicists to facilitate communication of ideas and papers.

1.10 HTML and style sheets

Both Netscape and Microsoft are at last implementing style sheets for Web pages.

Chapter 9 in this book explains how to use style sheets, and throughout this book you will see references as to how to use the style sheet language, CSS (Cascading Style Sheets) to obtain the layout effects you want.

Cascading Style Sheets potentially gives the user nearly as much control over the look and feel of material as would a conventional desktop publishing package, and so, it relieves HTML of the burden of non-standard extensions, rendering HTML available for its proper role of structuring information. World Wide Web Consortium members Håkon Lie and Bert Bos, with contributions from Chris Lilley, Dave Raggett and others developed CSS. Microsoft is implementing CSS on its Internet Explorer browser.

2
A HISTORY
OF HTML

Included in this chapter is information on:

- How the World Wide Web began
- The events and circumstances that led to the World Wide Web's current popularity
- How HTML has grown from its conception in the early 1990s

Summary

HTML has had a life-span of roughly seven years. During that time, it has evolved from a simple language with a small number of tags to a complex system of mark-up, enabling authors to create all-singing-and-dancing Web pages complete with animated images, sound and all manner of gimmicks. This chapter tells you something about the Web's early days, HTML, and about the people, companies and organizations who contributed to HTML+, HTML 2, HTML 3.2 and finally, HTML 4.

This chapter is a short history of HTML. Its aim is to give readers some idea of how the HTML we use today was developed from the prototype written by Tim Berners-Lee in 1992. The story is interesting – not least because HTML has been through an extremely bumpy ride on the road to standardization, with software engineers, academics and browser companies haggling about the language like so many Ministers of Parliament debating in the House of Commons.

1989: Tim Berners-Lee invents the Web with HTML as its publishing language

The World Wide Web began life in the place where you would least expect it: at CERN, the European Laboratory for Particle Physics in Geneva, Switzerland. CERN is a meeting place for physicists from all over the world, where highly abstract and conceptual thinkers engage in the contemplation of complex atomic phenomena that occur on a minuscule scale in time and space. This is a surprising place indeed for the beginnings of a technology which would, eventually, deliver everything from tourist information, online shopping and advertisements, financial data, weather forecasts and much more to your personal computer.

Tim Berners-Lee is the inventor of the Web. In 1989, Tim was working in a computing services section of CERN when he came up with the concept; at the time he had no idea that it would be implemented on such an enormous scale. Particle physics research often involves collaboration among institutes from all over the world. Tim had the idea of enabling researchers from remote sites in the world to organize and pool together information. But far from simply making available a large number of research documents as files that could be downloaded to individual computers, he suggested that you could actually link the text in the files themselves. In other words, there could be cross-references from one research paper to another. This would mean that while reading one research paper, you could quickly display part of another paper that holds directly relevant text or diagrams. Documentation of a scientific and mathematical nature would thus be represented as a 'web' of information held in electronic form on computers across the world. This, Tim thought, could be done by using some form of hypertext, some way of linking documents together by using buttons on the screen, which you simply clicked on to jump from one paper to another. Before coming to CERN, Tim had already worked on document production and text processing, and had developed his first hypertext system, 'Enquire', in 1980 for his own personal use.

Tim's prototype Web browser on the NeXT computer came out in 1990.

Through 1990: The time was ripe for Tim's invention

The fact that the Web was invented in the early 1990s was no coincidence. Developments in communications technology during that time meant that, sooner or later, something like the Web was bound to happen. For a start, *hypertext* was coming into vogue and being used on computers. Also, Internet users were gaining in the number of users on the system: there was an increasing audience for distributed information. Last, but not least, the new domain name system had made it much easier to address a machine on the Internet.

Hypertext

Although already established as a concept by academics as early as the 1940s, it was with the advent of the personal computer that hypertext came out of the cupboard. In the late 1980s, Bill Atkinson, an exceptionally gifted programmer working for Apple Computer Inc., came up with an application called *Hypercard* for the Macintosh. Hypercard enabled you to construct a series of on-screen 'filing cards' that contained textual and graphical information. Users could navigate these by pressing on-screen buttons, taking themselves on a tour of the information in the process. Hypercard set the scene for more applications based on the filing card idea. Toolbook for the PC was used in the early 1990s for constructing hypertext training courses that had 'pages' with buttons which could go forward or backward or jump to a new topic. Behind the scenes, buttons would initiate little programs called scripts. These scripts would control which page would be presented next; they could even run a small piece of animation on the screen. The application entitled Guide was a similar application for UNIX and the PC.

Hypercard and its imitators caught the popular imagination. However, these packages still had one major limitation: hypertext jumps could only be made to files on the same computer. Jumps made to computers on the other side of the world were still out of the question. Nobody yet had implemented a system involving hypertext links on a global scale.

The domain name system

By the middle 1980s, the Internet had a new, easy-to-use system for naming computers. This involved using the idea of the domain name. A domain name comprises a series of letters separated by dots, for example:

'www.bo.com' or 'www.erb.org.uk'. These names are the easy-to-use alternative to the much less manageable and cumbersome IP address numbers.

A program called Distributed Name Service (DNS) maps domain names onto IP addresses, keeping the IP addresses 'hidden'. DNS was an absolute breakthrough in making the Internet accessible to those who were not computer nerds. As a result of its introduction, email addresses became simpler. Previous to DNS, email addresses had all sorts of hideous codes such as exclamation marks, percent signs and other extraneous information to specify the route to the other machine.

Choosing the right approach to create a global hypertext system

To Tim Berners-Lee, global hypertext links seemed feasible, but it was a matter of finding the correct approach to implementing them. Using an existing hypertext package might seem an attractive proposition, but this was impractical for a number of reasons. To start with, any hypertext tool to be used worldwide would have to take into account that many types of computers existed that were linked to the Internet: Personal Computers, Macintoshes, UNIX machines and simple terminals. Also, many desktop publishing methods were in vogue: Hewlett-Packard's SGML, Interleaf, LaTex, Microsoft Word, and Troff among many others. Commercial hypertext packages were computer-specific and could not easily take text from other sources; besides, they were far too complicated and involved tedious compiling of text into internal formats to create the final hypertext system.

What was needed was something very simple, at least in the beginning. Tim demonstrated a basic, but attractive way of publishing text by developing some software himself, and also his own simple protocol – HTTP – for retrieving other documents' text via hypertext links. Tim's own protocol, HTTP, stands for HyperText Transfer Protocol. The text format for HTTP was named HTML, for HyperText Mark-up Language; Tim's hypertext implementation was demonstrated on a NeXT workstation, which provided many of the tools he needed to develop his first prototype. By keeping things very simple, Tim encouraged others to build upon his ideas and to design further software for displaying HTML, and for setting up their own HTML documents ready for access.

Tim bases his HTML on an existing internationally agreed upon method of text mark-up

The HTML that Tim invented was strongly based on SGML (Standard Generalized Mark-up Language), an internationally agreed upon method for marking up text into structural units such as paragraphs, headings, list items and so on. SGML could be implemented on any machine. The idea was that the language was independent of the formatter (the browser or other viewing software) which actually displayed the text on the screen. The use of pairs of tags such as <TITLE> and </TITLE> is taken directly from SGML, which does exactly the same. The SGML elements used in Tim's HTML included P (paragraph); H1 through H6 (heading level 1 through heading level 6); OL (ordered lists); UL (unordered lists); LI (list items) and various others. What SGML does not include, of course, are hypertext links: the idea of using the anchor element with the HREF attribute was purely Tim's invention, as was the now-famous 'www.name.name' format for addressing machines on the Web.

Basing HTML on SGML was a brilliant idea: other people would have invented their own language from scratch but this might have been much less reliable, as well as less acceptable to the rest of the Internet community. Certainly the simplicity of HTML, and the use of the anchor element A for creating hypertext links, was what made Tim's invention so useful.

September 1991: Open discussion about HTML across the Internet begins

Far from keeping his ideas private, Tim made every attempt to discuss them openly online across the Internet. Coming from a research background, this was quite a natural thing to do. In September 1991, the WWW-talk mailing list was started, a kind of electronic discussion group in which enthusiasts could exchange ideas and gossip. By 1992, a handful of other academics and computer researchers were showing interest. Dave Raggett from Hewlett-Packard's Labs in Bristol, England, was one of these early enthusiasts, and, following electronic discussion, Dave visited Tim in 1993. There, in Tim's tiny room in the bowels of the sprawling buildings of CERN, the two engineers further considered how HTML might be taken from its current beginnings and shaped into something more appropriate for mass consumption. Trying to anticipate the kind of features that users really would like, Dave looked through magazines, newspapers and other printed media to get an idea of what sort of HTML features would be important when that same information was published online. Upon return to England, Dave sat down at his keyboard and resolutely composed HTML+, a richer version of the original HTML.

Late 1992: NCSA is intrigued by the idea of the Web

Meanwhile on the other side of the world, Tim's ideas had caught the eye of Joseph Hardin and Dave Thompson, both of the National Center for

Supercomputer Applications, a research institute at the University of Illinois at Champaign-Urbana. They managed to connect to the computer at CERN and download copies of two free Web browsers. Realizing the importance of what they saw, NCSA decided to develop a browser of their own to be called *Mosaic*. Among the programmers in the NCSA team were Marc Andreessen – who later made his millions by selling Web products – and the brilliant programmer Eric Bina – who also became rich, courtesy of the Web. Eric Bina was a kind of software genius who reputedly could stay up three nights in succession, typing in a reverie of hacking at his computer.

December 1992: Marc Andreessen makes a brief appearance on WWW-talk

Early Web enthusiasts exchanged ideas and gossip over an electronic discussion group called WWW-talk. This was where Dave Raggett, Tim Berners-Lee, Dan Connolly and others debated how images (photographs, diagrams, illustrations and so on) should be inserted into HTML documents. Not everyone agreed upon the way that the relevant tag should be implemented, or even what that tag should be called. Suddenly, Marc Andreessen appeared on WWW-talk and, without further to-do, introduced an idea for the IMG tag by the Mosaic team. It was quite plain that the others were not altogether keen on the design of IMG, but Andreessen was not easily redirected. The IMG tag was implemented in the form suggested by the Mosaic team on its browser and remains to this day firmly implanted in HTML. This was much to the chagrin of supporters back in academia who invented several alternatives to IMG in the years to come. Now, with the coming of HTML 4, the OBJECT tag potentially replaces IMG, but this is, of course, some years later.

March 1993: Lou Montulli releases the Lynx browser version 2.0a

Lou Montulli was one of the first people to write a text-based browser, Lynx. The Lynx browser was a text-based browser for terminals and for computers that used DOS without Windows. Lou Montulli was later recruited to work with Netscape Communications Corp., but nonetheless remained partially loyal to the idea of developing HTML as an open standard, proving a real asset to the HTML working group and the HTML Editorial Board in years to come. Lou's enthusiasm for good, expensive wine, and his knowledge of excellent restaurants in the Silicon Valley area were to make the standardization of HTML a much more pleasurable process.

Early 1993: Dave Raggett begins to write his own browser

While Eric Bina and the NCSA Mosaic gang were hard at it hacking through the night, Dave Raggett of Hewlett-Packard Labs in Bristol was working part-time on his Arena browser, on which he hoped to demonstrate all sorts of newly invented features for HTML.

April 1993: The Mosaic browser is released

In April 1993, version 1 of the Mosaic browser was released for Sun Microsystems Inc.'s workstation, a computer used in software development running the UNIX operating system. Mosaic extended the features specified by Tim Berners-Lee; for example, it added images, nested lists and fill-out forms. Academics and software engineers later would argue that many of these extensions were very much ad hoc and not properly designed.

Late 1993: Large companies underestimate the importance of the Web

Dave Raggett's work on the Arena browser was slow because he had to develop much of it single-handedly: no money was available to pay for a team of developers. This was because Hewlett-Packard, in common with many other large computer companies, was quite unconvinced that the Internet would be a success; indeed, the need for a global hypertext system simply passed them by. For many large corporations, the question of whether or not any money could be made from the Web was unclear from the outset. There was also a misconception that the Internet was mostly for academics. In some companies, senior management was assured that the telephone companies would provide the technology for global communications of this sort, anyway. The result was that individuals working in research labs in the commercial sector were unable to devote much time to Web development. This was a bitter disappointment to some researchers, who gratefully would have committed nearly every waking moment toward shaping what they envisioned would be *the* communications system of the future.

Dave Raggett, realizing that there were not enough working hours left for him to succeed at what he felt was an immensely important task, continued writing his browser at home. There he would sit at a large computer that occupied a fair portion of the dining room table, sharing its slightly sticky surface with paper, crayons, Lego bricks and bits of half-eaten cookies left by the children. Dave also used the browser to show text flow around images, forms and other aspects of HTML at the First WWW Conference in Geneva in 1994. The Arena browser was later used for development work at CERN.

May 1994: NCSA assigns commercial rights for Mosaic browser to Spyglass, Inc.

In May 1994, Spyglass, Inc. signed a multi-million dollar licensing agreement with NCSA to distribute a commercially enhanced version of Mosaic. In August of that same year, the University of Illinois at Champaign-Urbana, the home of NCSA, assigned all future commercial rights for NCSA Mosaic to Spyglass.

May 1994: The first World Wide Web conference is held in Geneva, with HTML+ on show

Although Marc Andreessen and Jim Clark had commercial interests in mind, the rest of the World Wide Web community had quite a different attitude: they saw themselves as joint creators of a wonderful new technology, which certainly would benefit the world. They were jiggling with excitement. Even quiet and retiring academics became animated in discussion, and many seemed evangelical about their new-found god of the Web.

At the first World Wide Web conference organized by CERN in May 1994, all was merry with 380 attendees – who mostly were from Europe but also included many from the United States. You might have thought that Marc Andreessen, Jim Clark and Eric Bina surely would be there, but

At the World Wide Web conference in Geneva. Left to right: Joseph Hardin from NCSA, Robert Cailliau from CERN, Tim Berners-Lee from CERN and Dan Connolly (of HTML 2 fame) then working for Hal software.

A panel discussion at the Geneva conference. Kevin Altis from Intel, Dave Raggett from HP Labs, Rick 'Channing' Rodgers from the National Library of Medicine.

they were not. For the most part, participants were from the academic community, from institutions such as the World Meteorological Organization, the International Center for Theoretical Physics, the University of Iceland and so on. Later conferences had much more of a commercial feel, but this one was for technical enthusiasts who instinctively knew that this was the start of something big.

During the course of that week, awards were presented for notable achievements on the Web; these awards were given to Marc Andreessen, Lou Montulli, Eric Bina, Rob Hartill and Kevin Hughes. Dan Connolly, who proceeded to define HTML 2, gave a slide presentation entitled *Interoperability: Why Everyone Wins*, which explained why it was important that the Web operated with a proper HTML specification. Strange to think that at least three of the people who received awards at the conference were later to fly in the face of Dan's idea that adopting a cross-company uniform standard for HTML was essential.

Dave Raggett had been working on some new HTML ideas, which he called HTML+. At the conference it was agreed that the work on HTML+ should be carried forward to lead to the development of an HTML 3 standard. Dave Raggett, together with CERN, developed Arena further as a proof-of-concept browser for this work. Using Arena, Dave Raggett, Henrik Frystyk Nielsen, Håkon Lie and others demonstrated text flow around a figure with captions, resizable tables, image backgrounds, math and other features.

The conference ended with a glorious evening cruise on board a paddle steamer around Lake Geneva with *Wolfgang and the Werewolves* providing Jazz accompaniment.

September 1994: The Internet Engineering Task Force (IETF) sets up an HTML working group

In early 1994, an Internet Engineering Task Force working group was set up to deal with HTML.

The Internet Engineering Task Force is the international standards and development body of the Internet and is a large, open community of network designers, operators, vendors and researchers concerned with the evolution and smooth operation of the Internet architecture. The technical work of the IETF is done in working groups, which are organized by topic into several areas; for example, security, network routing, and applications. The IETF is, in general, part of a culture that sees the Internet as belonging to The People. This was even more so in the early days of the Web.

The feelings of the good 'ole days of early Web development are captured in the song, *The Net Flag*, which can be found 'somewhere on the Internet'. The first verse runs as follows:

The people's web is deepest red,
And oft it's killed our routers dead.
But ere the bugs grew ten days old,
The patches fixed the broken code.

Chorus:

So raise the open standard high
Within its codes we'll live or die
Though cowards flinch and Bill Gates sneers
We'll keep the net flag flying here.

In keeping with normal IETF practices, the HTML working group was open to anyone in the engineering community: any interested computer scientist could potentially become a member and, once on its mailing list, could take part in email debate. The HTML working group met approximately three times a year, during which time they would enjoy a good haggle about HTML features present and future, be pleasantly suffused with coffee and beer, striding about plush hotel lobbies sporting pony tails, T-shirts and jeans without the slightest care.

July 1994: HTML specification for HTML 2 is released

During 1993 and early 1994, lots of browsers had added their own bits to HTML; the language was becoming ill-defined. In an effort to make sense of the chaos, Dan Connolly and colleagues collected all the HTML tags that were widely used and collated them into a draft document that defined the breadth of what Tim Berners-Lee called HTML 2. The draft was then circulated through the Internet community for comment. With the patience of a saint, Dan took into account numerous suggestions from HTML enthusiasts far and wide, ensuring that all would be happy with the eventual HTML 2 definition. He also wrote a Document Type Definition for HTML 2, a kind of mathematically precise description of the language.

November 1994: Netscape is formed

During 1993, Marc Andreessen apparently felt increasingly irritated at simply being *on* the Mosaic project rather than in charge of it. Upon graduating, he decided to leave NCSA and head for California where he met Jim Clark, who was already well known in Silicon Valley and who had money to invest. Together they formed Mosaic Communications, which then became Netscape Communications Corp. in November, 1994. What they planned to do was create and market their very own browser.

The browser they designed was immensely successful – so much so in fact, that for some time to come, many users would mistakenly think that Netscape invented the Web. Netscape did its best to make sure that even those who were relying on a low-bandwidth connection – that is, even those who only had a modem-link from a home personal computer – were able to access the Web effectively. This was greatly to the company's credit.

Following a predictable path, Netscape began inventing its own HTML tags as it pleased without first openly discussing them with the Web community. Netscape rarely made an appearance at the big International WWW conferences, but it seemed to be driving the HTML standard. It was a curious situation, and one that the inner core of the HTML community felt they must redress.

Late 1994: The World Wide Web Consortium forms

The World Wide Web Consortium was formed in late 1994 to fulfill the potential of the Web through the development of open standards. They had a strong interest in HTML. Just as an orchestra insists on the best musicians, so the consortium recruited many of the best-known names in the Web community. Headed up by Tim Berners-Lee, here are just some of the players in the band today (1997):

- Dave Raggett on HTML; from the United Kingdom.

- Arnaud le Hors on HTML; from France.

- Dan Connolly on HTML; from the United States.

- Henrik Frystyk Nielsen on HTTP and on enabling the Web to go faster; from Denmark.

Members of the World Wide Web Consortium at the MIT site. From left to right are Henrick Frystyk Neilsen, Anselm Baird-Smith, Jay Sekora, Rohit Khare, Dan Connolly, Jim Gettys, Tim Berners-Lee, Susan Hardy, Jim Miller, Dave Raggett, Tom Greene, Arthur Secret, Karen MacArthur.

- Håkon Lie on style sheets; from Norway. He is located in France, working at INRIA.

- Bert Bos on style sheets and layout; from the Netherlands.

- Jim Miller on investigating technologies that could be used in rating the content of Web pages; from the United States.

- Chris Lilley on style sheets and font support; from the United Kingdom.

The W3 Consortium is based in part at the Laboratory of Computer Science at Massachusetts' Institute of Technology in Cambridge, Massachusetts, in the United States; and in part at INRIA, the *Institut National de Recherche en Informatique et en Automatique*, a French governmental research institute. The W3 Consortium is also located in part at Keio University in Japan. You can look at the Consortium's Web pages on 'www.w3.org'.

The consortium is sponsored by a number of companies that directly benefit from its work on standards and other technology for the Web. The member companies include Digital Equipment Corp.; Hewlett-Packard Co.; IBM Corp.; Microsoft Corp.; Netscape Communications Corp.; and Sun Microsystems Inc., among many others.

Through 1995: HTML is extended with many new tags

During 1995, all kinds of new HTML tags emerged. Some, like the BGCOLOR attribute of the BODY element and FONT FACE, which control stylistic aspects of a document, found themselves in the black books of the academic engineering community. 'You're not supposed to be able to do things like that in HTML,' they would protest. It was their belief that such things as text color, background texture, font size and font face were definitely outside the scope of a language when their only intent was to specify how a document would be organized.

March 1995: HTML 3 is published as an Internet Draft

Dave Raggett had been working for some time on his new ideas for HTML, and at last he formalized them in a document published as an Internet Draft in March, 1995. All manner of HTML features were covered. A new tag for inserting images called FIG was introduced, which Dave hoped would supersede IMG, as well as a whole gambit of features for marking up math and scientific documents. Dave dealt with HTML tables and tabs, footnotes and forms. He also added support for style sheets by including a STYLE tag and a CLASS attribute. The latter was to be available on every element to encourage authors to give HTML elements styles, much as you do in desktop publishing.

Although the HTML 3 draft was very well received, it was somewhat difficult to get it ratified by the IETF. The belief was that the draft was too large and too full of new proposals. To get consensus on a draft 150 pages long and about which everyone wanted to voice an opinion was optimistic – to say the least. In the end, Dave and the inner circle of the HTML community decided to call it a day.

Of course, browser writers were very keen on supporting HTML 3 – in theory. Inevitably, each browser writer chose to implement a different subset of HTML 3's features as they were so inclined, and then proudly proclaimed to support the standard. The confusion was mind-boggling, especially as browsers even came out with *extensions* to HTML 3, implying to the ordinary gent that *normal* HTML 3 was, of course, already supported. Was there an official HTML 3 standard or not? The truth was that there was not, but reading the computer press you might never have known the difference.

March 1995: A furor over the HTML Tables specification

Dave Raggett's HTML 3 draft had tackled the tabular organization of information in HTML. Arguments over this aspect of the language had continued for some time, but now it was time to really get going. At the 32nd meeting of the IETF in Danvers, Massachusetts, Dave found a group from the SGML brethren who were up in arms over part of the tables specification because it contradicted the CALS table model. Groups such as the US Navy use the CALS table model in complex documentation. After long negotiation, Dave managed to placate the CALS table delegates and altered the draft to suit their needs. HTML tables, which were not in HTML originally, finally surfaced from the HTML 3 draft to appear in HTML 3.2. They continue to be used extensively for the purpose of providing a layout grid for organizing pictures and text on the screen.

August 1995: Microsoft's Internet Explorer browser comes out

Version 1.0 of Microsoft Corp.'s Internet Explorer browser was announced. This browser was eventually to compete with Netscape's browser, and to evolve its own HTML features. To a certain extent, Microsoft built its business on the Web by extending HTML features. The ActiveX feature made Microsoft's browser unique, and Netscape developed a plug-in called Ncompass to handle ActiveX. This whole idea whereby one browser experiments with an extension to HTML only to find others adding support to keep even, continues to the present.

In November 1995, Microsoft's Internet Explorer version 2.0 arrived for its Windows NT and Windows 95 operating systems.

September 1995: Netscape submits a proposal for frames

By this time, Netscape submitted a proposal for frames, which involved the screen being divided into independent, scrollable areas. The proposal was implemented on Netscape's Navigator browser before anyone really had time to comment on it, but nobody was surprised.

November 1995: The HTML working group runs into problems

The HTML working group was an excellent idea in theory, but in practice things did not go quite as expected. With the immense popularity of the Web, the HTML working group grew larger and larger, and the volume of associated email soared exponentially. Imagine one hundred people trying to design a house. 'I want the windows to be double-glazed,' says one. 'Yes, but shouldn't we make them smaller, while we're at it,' questions another. Still others chime in: 'What material do you propose for the frames – I'm not having them in plastic, that's for sure'; 'I suggest that we don't have windows, as such, but include small, circular port-holes on the Southern elevation...' and so on.

You get the idea. The HTML working group emailed each other in a frenzy of electronic activity. In the end, its members became so snowed under with email that no time was left for programming. For software engineers, this was a sorry state of affairs, indeed: 'I came back after just three days away to find over 2000 messages waiting,' was the unhappy lament of the HTML enthusiast.

Anyway, the HTML working group still was losing ground to the browser vendors. The group was notably slow in coming to a consensus on a given HTML feature, and commercial organizations were hardly going to sit around having tea, pleasantly conversing on the weather whilst waiting for the results of debates. And they did not.

November 1995: Vendors unite to form a new group dedicated to developing an HTML standard

In November, 1995 Dave Raggett called together representatives of the browser companies and suggested they meet as a small group dedicated to standardizing HTML. Imagine his surprise when it worked! Lou Montulli from Netscape, Charlie Kindel from Microsoft, Eric Sink from Spyglass, Wayne Gramlich from Sun Microsystems, Dave Raggett, Tim Berners-Lee and Dan Connolly from the W3 Consortium, and Jonathan Hirschman from Pathfinder convened near Chicago and made quick and effective decisions about HTML.

November 1995: Style sheets for HTML documents begin to take shape

Bert Bos, Håkon Lie, Dave Raggett, Chris Lilley and others from the World Wide Web Consortium and others met in Versailles near Paris to discuss the deployment of Cascading Style Sheets. The name Cascading Style Sheets implies that more than one style sheet can interact to produce the final look of the document. Using a special language, the CSS group advocated that everyone would soon be able to write simple styles for HTML, as one would do in Microsoft Word and other desktop publishing software packages. The SGML contingent, who preferred a LISP-like language called DSSSL – it rhymes with whistle – seemed out of the race when Microsoft promised to implement CSS on its Internet Explorer browser.

November 1995: Internationalization of HTML Internet Draft

Gavin Nicol, Gavin Adams and others presented a long paper on the internationalization of the Web. Their idea was to extend the capabilities of

HTML 2, primarily by removing the restriction on the character set used. This would mean that HTML could be used to mark up languages other than those that use the Latin-1 character set to include a wider variety of alphabets and character sets, such as those that read from right to left.

December 1995: The HTML working group is dismantled

Since the IETF HTML working group was having difficulties coming to consensus swiftly enough to cope with such a fast-evolving standard, it was eventually dismantled.

February 1996: The HTML ERB is formed

Following the success of the November, 1995 meeting, the World Wide Web Consortium formed the HTML Editorial Review Board to help with the standardization process. This board consisted of representatives from IBM, Microsoft, Netscape, Novell, Softquad and the W3 Consortium, and did its business via telephone conference and email exchanges, meeting approximately once every three months. Its aim was to collaborate and agree upon a common standard for HTML, thus putting an end to the era when browsers each implemented a different subset of the language. The bad fairy of incompatibility was to be banished from the HTML kingdom forever, or one could hope so, perhaps.

Dan Connolly of the W3 Consortium, also author of HTML 2, deftly accomplished the feat of chairing what could be quite a raucous meeting of the clans. Dan managed to make sure that all representatives had their say and listened to each other's point of view in an orderly manner. A strong chair was absolutely essential in these meetings.

In preparation for an ERB meeting, specifications describing new aspects of HTML were made electronically available for ERB members to read. Then, at the meeting itself, the proponent explained some of the rationale behind the specification, and then dearly hoped that all who were present also concurred that the encapsulated ideas were sound. Questions such as, 'should a particular feature be included, or should we kick it out,' would be considered. Each representative would air his point of view. If all went well, the specification might eventually see daylight and become a standard. At the time of writing, the next HTML standard, code-named *Cougar*, has begun its long journey in this direction.

The BLINK tag was ousted in an HTML ERB meeting. Netscape would only abolish it if Microsoft agreed to get rid of MARQUEE; the deal was struck and both tags disappeared. Both of these extensions have always been considered slightly goofy by all parties. Many tough decisions were to be made about the OBJECT specification. Out of a chaos of several different tags – EMBED, APP, APPLET, DYNSRC and so on – all associated with embedding different types of information in HTML documents, a single `OBJECT` tag was chosen in April, 1996. This `OBJECT` tag becomes part of the HTML standard, but not until 1997.

April 1996: The W3 Consortium working draft on Scripting comes out

Based on an initial draft by Charlie Kindel, and, in turn, derived from Netscape's extensions for JavaScript, a W3C working draft on the subject of Scripting was written by Dave Raggett. In one form or another, this draft should eventually become part of standard HTML.

July 1996: Microsoft seems more interested than first imagined in open standards

In April 1996, Microsoft's Internet Explorer became available for Macintosh and Windows 3.1 systems.

Thomas Reardon had been excited by the Web even at the second WWW conference held in Darmstadt, Germany in 1995. One year later, he seemed very interested in the standardization process and apparently wanted Microsoft to do things the right way with the W3C and with the IETF. Traditionally, developers are somewhat disparaging about Microsoft, so this was an interesting turn of events. It should be said that Microsoft did, of course, invent tags of their own, just as did Netscape. These included the remarkable `MARQUEE` tag that caused great mirth among the more academic HTML community. The `MARQUEE` tag made text dance about all over the screen – not exactly a feature you would expect from a serious language concerned with structural mark-up such as paragraphs, headings and lists.

The worry that a massive introduction of proprietary products would kill the Web continued. Netscape acknowledged that vendors needed to push ahead of the standards process and innovate. They pointed out that, if users like a particular Netscape innovation, then the market would drive it to become a de facto standard. This seemed quite true at the time and, indeed, Netscape has innovated on top of that standard again. It's precisely this sequence of events that Dave Raggett and the World Wide Web Consortium were trying to avoid.

December 1996: Work on 'Cougar' is begun

The HTML ERB became the HTML Working Group and began to work on 'Cougar', the next version of HTML with completion late Spring, 1997, eventually to become HTML 4. With all sorts of innovations for the disabled and support for international languages, as well as providing

Dave Raggett, co-editor of the HTML 4 specification, at work composing at the keyboard at his home in Boston.

style sheet support, extensions to forms, scripting and much more, HTML 4 breaks away from the simplicity and charm of HTML of earlier years!

January 1997: HTML 3.2 is ready

Success! In January 1997, the W3 Consortium formally endorsed HTML 3.2 as an HTML cross-industry specification. HTML 3.2 had been reviewed by all member organizations, including major browser vendors such as Netscape and Microsoft. This meant that the specification was now stable and approved of by most Web players. By providing a neutral forum, the W3 Consortium had successfully obtained agreement upon a standard version of HTML. There was great rejoicing, indeed. HTML 3.2 took the existing IETF HTML 2 standard and incorporated features from HTML+ and HTML 3. HTML 3.2 included tables, applets, text flow around images, subscripts and superscripts.

One might well ask why HTML 3.2 was called HTML 3.2 and not, let's say, HTML 3.1 or HTML 3.5. The version number is open to discussion just as much as is any other aspect of HTML. The version number is often one of the last details to be decided.

3
SIMPLE TUTORIAL AND INTRODUCTION TO HTML 4

Included in this chapter is information on:

- Creating your own simple HTML document
- Basic HTML terminology
- The formal structure of an HTML 4 document

Summary

HTML was originally developed by Tim Berners-Lee when he first devised the World Wide Web. Developed as an application of a standard method of textual mark-up called SGML, Tim aimed for a way of marking up text that was simplicity itself. The first HTML had no more than a dozen tags and certainly was easy to use. The simplicity of HTML was indeed critical to the widespread development of the World Wide Web.

Although many formats (such as the RTF format used by Word and the MIF format used by FrameMaker) interlace information about layout and page presentation with the structural description of the document, HTML concentrates purely on the latter. Although new tags concerned with presentation such as font and color have in a sense polluted HTML, it still remains predominantly a mark-up language concerned with describing a document in terms of its structural components.

This chapter introduces HTML as a language for structural mark-up and demonstrates how style sheets can be used to take care of font, color and other stylistic issues.

3.1 Introduction

What is a text editor?
This is a piece of software that programmers use to edit their code. It differs from a word processing package or desktop publishing package in that it does not insert usually invisible formatting codes into the text to organize it into paragraphs, lists, tables and so on. The text you type into an editor is saved without anything else added.

You will have gathered from Chapter 1 that HTML is the Web's own publishing language. To see samples of HTML on your screen, switch to viewing the 'source' of any page on the Web (most browsers have an option SOURCE under the VIEW menu for doing this), and you will see the HTML that gave rise to the page in question. The HTML consists of a number of codes or 'tags' that the author has used to mark up the various components of the document – its paragraphs, headings, tables and so on – and also to insert graphics and hypertext links. Common tags you might spot in the source of a Web page are `<P>` for 'paragraph', `<H1>` for 'heading1' and `<UL>` for 'unordered list'.

It is only when the document is processed by a browser that such codes 'come alive' and trigger various browser formatting routines which, in turn, give rise to a properly presented document. A browser knows that `<P>` marks the beginning of a new paragraph; that `<B>` signals bold text, and will display emboldened words accordingly. HTML is not like an ordinary WYSIWYG editor over which you have precise control regarding screen layout and printing; in HTML, different browsers will display your document in different ways. A text-only browser will, for example, display a document differently from one that displays graphics. The Netscape and Microsoft browsers will display documents slightly differently from each other.

3.2 Step-by-step guide: Entering text and displaying it on a browser

Having understood what HTML is, you are now in the perfect position to start creating your own HTML documents. This section shows you how to create two small HTML documents, test them, and then play with them to create your own effects on the screen. The instructions should work for recent installations of Microsoft Internet Explorer and Netscape's Navigator browsers using the Windows operating system or on the Macintosh. Readers who have other browsers or configurations should get the general idea of what to do, even though the specifics will be different.

A really simple HTML document

HTML generators
What about packages that generate HTML for you? You can do this to understand how HTML works so that you can fine-tune the output of such packages, using HTML to its full potential, style sheets and all. There are a number of excellent HTML editors; some are mentioned at the end of this chapter.

This first example involves using an editor to write the file, and then loading it into a browser to prove it works. You will need the following:

• A browser such as Microsoft's Internet Explorer or Netscape's Navigator or Communicator

• A text editor

If you do not have a text editor, as such, you can use a desktop publishing package and save the file as *text-only* (as opposed to the usual desktop publishing format).

Proceed as follows:

• Load the text editor.

• Open a new file.

• Into this new file, enter this small HTML document, below:

```
<TITLE>Small document<TITLE/>
<P> This is a very small HTML document with a single paragraph of
text
```

• Save the file. Choose a filename ending in .htm (for PC users) or .html (for Macintosh and UNIX users) when you save it. Take note of exactly where you save it so that you can easily load it when the time comes. Do not close the file yet, but leave it on the screen.

• Make the text editor window smaller so that it occupies approximately less than half of the screen.

• Load your browser.

• Make the browser window smaller so that it occupies more or less the other half of the screen to the editor window, in the fashion shown below:

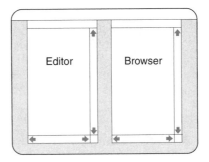

- To select, click anywhere in the browser window.
    - With Netscape, select Open and then click the browse button.
    - With Internet Explorer, select Open File from the browser menu (do *not* select Open Location).

- Click through the directories or folders until you see your HTML file.

- To open, click on the HTML file. The browser should then interpret your HTML document, with the results displayed in the browser window.

Playing with the HTML file and seeing the results

Once you have the source code of your HTML document in one window and the results displayed in the other window, you can have some fun.

- To select, click anywhere in the editor window.

- Edit the source code to change the text: try adding some more text or placing a couple of words in bold. You do this by inserting a <B> in the mark-up where the bold should begin and </B> where you want it to end.

- Save the edited HTML file.

- To select the browser application, click anywhere in the browser window.

- To re-load the source code, click on the RELOAD button. You should see the document displayed with any extra text or edits added.

A more complicated HTML document with style sheet

This example[1] is designed to introduce you to further aspects of mark-up, including style sheets. Once you have this example working, you can play with the color, font and alignment of text to your heart's content. The style-sheet part is boxed simply to distinguish it from the rest of the mark-up.

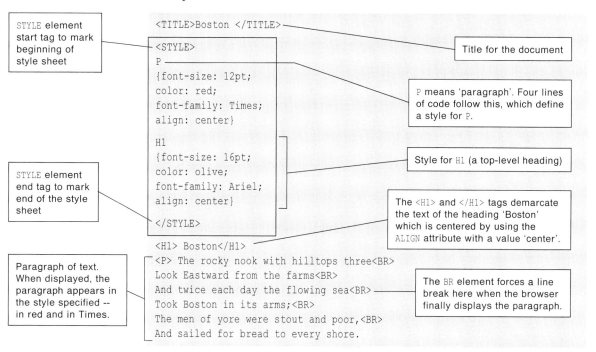

STYLE element start tag to mark beginning of style sheet

STYLE element end tag to mark end of the style sheet

Paragraph of text. When displayed, the paragraph appears in the style specified -- in red and in Times.

```
<TITLE>Boston </TITLE>
<STYLE>
P
{font-size: 12pt;
color: red;
font-family: Times;
align: center}

H1
{font-size: 16pt;
color: olive;
font-family: Ariel;
align: center}

</STYLE>
<H1> Boston</H1>
<P> The rocky nook with hilltops three<BR>
Look Eastward from the farms<BR>
And twice each day the flowing sea<BR>
Took Boston in its arms;<BR>
The men of yore were stout and poor,<BR>
And sailed for bread to every shore.
```

Title for the document

P means 'paragraph'. Four lines of code follow this, which define a style for P.

Style for H1 (a top-level heading)

The <H1> and </H1> tags demarcate the text of the heading 'Boston' which is centered by using the ALIGN attribute with a value 'center'.

The BR element forces a line break here when the browser finally displays the paragraph.

The result should look something like this:

Boston
The rocky nook with hilltops three
Look Eastward from the farms
And twice each day the flowing sea
Took Boston in its arms;
The men of yore were stout and poor,
And sailed for bread to every shore.

[1] This is the first verse of a ballad by Ralph Waldo Emerson about his native city of Concord, Massachusetts.

On Microsoft's Internet Explorer browser you see the colored text and the correct font style and size. Netscape's browser should now also show the font correctly according to the style sheet.

Here is the mark-up explained in a bit more detail:

- `<TITLE>` and `</TITLE>` are the start and end tags for the `TITLE` element and are used to give a title to the piece we are writing. Every HTML document must have a title. This is not the same as a heading that appears on the screen, but is rather for internal use.

- `<H1>` and `</H1>` are tags to give a heading to the poem to appear displayed on the screen. The **ALIGN** attribute has been used to set the heading's position on the page. The value for the **ALIGN** attribute in this case is 'center' (UK readers, note the US spelling).

- All text within the boundaries of the `<STYLE>` and `</STYLE>` tags consists of a small Web style sheet. You can see that the style allocated to the heading specifies 16-point Arial type, centered on the page and colored Olive. The notation for composing style sheets is explained in Chapter 9.

- `<P>` is the tag for a paragraph. In the style sheet you will see that paragraphs should be rendered in Times 12-point type, colored white (to contrast with the navy blue background) and centrally aligned.

You can play with the HTML and change the color of the text. Try substituting 'blue' for 'red' to produce blue text, or 'yellow' for 'olive'. Or you could change the point sizes in the style sheet. Edit the source, save the file, refresh the browser window and see the result.

3.3 More on HTML syntax

This section explains what are HTML tags and attributes, and how to write them; it also explains where you should put spaces in the syntax and in which instances you should use upper-case letters rather than lower-case letters.

Start tags and end tags

You will notice that the `<TITLE>` and `</TITLE>` tags are found in pairs, as are `<H1>` and `</H1>` and `<STYLE>` and `</STYLE>`. This is usual in HTML. These tags mark up the structural parts of a document; generally, a *start tag* marks the beginning of such a part, whereas an *end tag* marks the end of it. The end tag differs from the start tag only in that it has a slash '/' included following the opening bracket. The symbols '<', '>' and '</' are called

delimiters since they are essentially parameters that define, or delimit, your mark-up.

Some tags, such as <P> for 'paragraph', do not need a complementary end tag, although you may put one in if you want. The end tag can be left out, as the browser infers its presence. Other elements must not have an end tag, for example, IMG. The more common elements that do not need an end tag are listed in Table 3.1. The common elements that must not have an end tag are listed in Table 3.2.

Table 3.1 Some of the common HTML elements which do not need an end tag.

Element name
P (paragraph)
LI (list item)
OPTION
DT, DD
HEAD
BODY
HTML

Table 3.2 Some of the common HTML 3 elements which *must* not have an end tag.

Element name
HR (horizontal rule)
IMG (inline figure)
BR (break)
COL (in tables)
META (in HTML body)
LINK
BASE
ISINDEX

Spaces in tags

Can you put spaces inside tags? The answer is quite subtle. The following are *not* allowed:

1. < TITLE > You cannot insert a space between the start tag and the element name, or after the element name and before the end tag.

2. < TITLE> You cannot insert a space between the start tag and the element name, even though there is no space between the element name and the end tag.

Whereas, these *are* allowed:

3.   `<TITLE>`   Notice there is no space between the start tag and element name and between the element name and the end tag.

4.   `<TITLE >`   Notice there is no space between the start tag and element name, but there is a space between the element name and the end tag. This is allowed.

As a rule, you can insert a space after the element name (as in example number 4) but the browser will not process a tag that has a space inserted before (as in example number 1 and number 2). Keep it simple and do not put in spaces at all.

Lower- or upper-case for tag names

You may use either lower-case characters or upper-case characters for tag names, or you may use a combination of both. In this book, we use upper-case characters for tag names for consistency.

The syntax for HTML attributes

The general syntax for including attributes in HTML follows the same pattern each time:

```
<TAGNAME ATTRIBUTE=value>
```

Or, you may use a slight variant:

```
<TAGNAME ATTRIBUTE="value">
```

If the attribute value consists entirely of letters, digits, periods (full stops) or hyphens, then that value does not need to be placed in quotation marks. If, however, it contains characters other than those mentioned, then placing the attribute in quotation marks is essential.

It is quite legitimate to omit a space before or after the '=' sign.

```
<H1 ALIGN=center>
```

You can insert a space before and after the '=' and the browser is also quite happy:

```
<H1 ALIGN = center>
```

It is also alright to insert a space before the '=' and no space after, or vice versa:

```
<H1 ALIGN= center>
<H1 ALIGN =center>
```

Multiple spaces are, however, *not* allowed, as shown below:

```
<H1 ALIGN  =  center>
```

Implied attribute values

In HTML, you use such tags as:

```
<UL COMPACT>
<UL PLAIN>
<TABLE BORDER>
```

You may also use various other constructs that appear to be different from the usual attribute-value pair format. In the DTD or document type definition (a tight definition of HTML that encapsulates the rules of the language), these are actually a shortened form for fuller forms such as `<UL COMPACT=compact>`. It is recommended that you do not use the full form because it may confuse browsers. The SGML mechanism behind this is too technical to be included in a discussion at this level.

More than one attribute in a tag

URLs
Be reminded that URLs are case sensitive. Make sure they are entered correctly when you include them in hypertext links.

You may need to include more than one attribute-value pair in a tag. This is certainly allowed. Here is an example:

```
<IMG SRC="owl.gif" ALT="The Owl playing his guitar">
```

The attribute **SRC** has a value that corresponds to the image that will be displayed. So much is obvious. However, what happens if your browser cannot display graphics? Should this be the case, the attribute **ALT** gives an alternative textual description of the picture. This idea is particularly useful for visually impaired people who may have a computer that will read aloud a description of a picture, or print it in Braille, rather than display the picture.

Note: Some attribute values (for example `SRC`, `HREF`, `ALT1`) allow entities in them, for example `ALT="Voulez vous du caf&eacute?"`.

Upper- or lower-case characters for attributes and their values

It does not matter which case you choose; even using both cases is acceptable. Spelling is, of course, very important so that 'centre' will not work where 'center' is required.

3.4 A more formal explanation of HTML terms and concepts

HTML is an application of SGML, or Standard Generalized Mark-up Language, an ISO standard for document description and designed for text interchange. Many of the concepts and terms used to formally discuss HTML are taken directly from SGML ideas. We recommend *Practical SGML* by Eric van Herwijnen as an introduction to the subject.

Tags contain element names

When you mark up an HTML document, you are essentially structuring it into a number of *elements*. Paragraphs are elements, as are tables, forms, lists and images. To mark up an element, insert a start tag to indicate its beginning and an end tag to indicate its end. A browser will usually employ a different formatting routine to display the elements of each different kind.

Each element has an *element name*. The element name for a paragraph element is P; that for a list item is LI; that for a top-level heading is H1. Element names are not case sensitive; although, in this book we adopt the convention of placing all element names in upper-case characters. You can type them using lower-case characters or you can even use both upper- and lower-case characters, if you like.

Rules about the order of elements in a document

HTML mark-up cannot occur arbitrarily and must conform to the HTML document grammar. This grammar describes the tags that can be used, and the legitimate order in which they can be inserted into a document. This idea is explained briefly in Chapter 1, which discusses the relationship between SGML (Standard Generalized Mark-up Language) and HTML.

The content model

The content model relates to which elements can be included within a given element in the document. For example, when marking up a table, the

TH (table header cell) element has a content model that includes text, lists, mathematical symbols, notation and formulae, graphics and so on. What this means is that within any TH element, you can include text, lists, the mathematical elements described above, graphics and many other elements. The content model tells you that all of these things are allowed in the cell of a table.

Permitted context

The permitted context meanwhile relates to the context in the document in which an element can be used. For example, TH elements (that is, table header cells) can only be used in the context of a table row, TR. This makes perfect sense, as it would be surprising if you could place a table cell in, let's say, a title or a heading, or in an ordinary paragraph. The context for TH elements is never a paragraph, heading or list; it is always a table row.

Block-level elements versus character-level elements

There are two groups of elements: block-level elements and character-level elements. A working definition of these two groups is as follows: A block-level element is one which, when inserted into a document, has the effect of automatically terminating the preceding paragraph and throwing a paragraph break. For example, when you insert a figure in a paragraph using the block-level element OBJECT, the paragraph preceding the OBJECT element is terminated prior to OBJECT beginning. Tables, forms and lists are just some of the items inserted into a document by using block-level elements.

Character-level elements behave differently from block-level elements. Character-level elements include text itself, character entities, various font-style and character-emphasis elements, and the proposed MATH element (you can put a math equation in a line of text). They also include hypertext links and inline graphics with the IMG element. All of these things form part of the text flow within a paragraph.

Some block-level elements have further structures within them. For example, a definition list contains pairs of terms and their corresponding definitions; a table starts with a caption followed by a list of rows; a figure starts with a caption followed by a figure description, and then a credit. Throughout this book we will use the terms block-level element and character-level element to indicate where a given element can occur, or to describe what an element can contain. In other words, the ideas of block- and character-level elements will appear in the descriptions of content model and permitted context. Some common block-level and character-level elements are shown in Tables 3.3 and 3.4, respectively.

Table 3.3 Some common block-level elements.

P	Paragraph
TABLE	Table
FORM	Form
H1...H6	Headings
ADDRESS	Address
DIV	Division
PRE	Preformatted text
BLOCKQUOTE	Longer quotations in the text
NOTE	Note
BR	Line break
FN	Footnote (HTML 3 not yet implemented)
UL	Unordered list
DL	Definition list
CAPTION	Caption
OL	Ordered list
FIG	Figure (HTML 3 not yet implemented)
HR	Horizontal rule

Note: You can have a look at the reference card provided at the back of this book to see what the status is for each of these elements. Remember different elements are implemented on different browsers and some HTML 3 elements are merely proposed at the time of writing.

Table 3.4 Some common character-level elements.

ABBREV	Abbreviation in text
ACRONYM	Acronym in text
AU	Author, for example of a poem or book
CITE	Citation. Sections tagged as citations are typically rendered in italics
CODE	A sample of computer code as might be included in online computer manuals
DEL	Delete text (for legal documents). Shown with strike-through
DFN	Definition of term
EM	Emphasis, which most browsers will render as italics
INS	Inserted text (for legal documents)
KBD	Text to be entered at the keyboard (for use in computer manuals)
Q	Short quotation. Typically quotation marks are added by the browser using the correct punctuation for the language in which the text is displayed. HTML 3 – not yet widely implemented
STRONG	Strong emphasis
VAR	Variable (for use in on-screen computer manuals)
TT	Teletype font: a fixed-pitch typewriter font
U	Underlined

Table 3.4 (*cont.*).

S (STRIKE)	Strike-through. The text should be displayed with a horizontal line through it, for showing changes in the text, or for use in legal documents
BIG	Text to be displayed using a bigger font if possible
SMALL	Text to be displayed in a smaller font if possible
SUB	Subscript
B	Bold
I	Italic
BLINK	Causes characters to 'flash' on the screen
SUP	Superscript
A	Anchor element (for hypertext)
IMG	Image (for inline images as opposed to block-level images inserted using FIG)

The character set used for a document

One question you may want to ask yourself is whether or not the document is to be written in English, German, Swedish, Portuguese or another language, based on Roman letters. Or, alternatively, if it is it to be written in Arabic, Russian or Hindi, or another language that uses a completely different character set. Whatever the case may be, the browser must know which character set is involved so that it can display the document properly. Chapter 17 gives some information on this subject.

3.5 Including symbols and accented characters in documents

Numeric entities
There is also a parallel system of numeric entities. These are strings of numbers, as opposed to characters, and represent symbols. Numeric entities always start with the '#' symbol. Examples are &#42 which is used to display an asterisk and &#36 which is used to display a dollar sign. We recommend that you do not use numeric entities with HTML 4.

When you write an HTML document, usually you concentrate on typing the text of the document and inserting the various tags and attributes. However, certain symbols and special characters cannot be entered directly at the keyboard (they simply are not there or they would be confused with symbols used in mark-up) and so have to be inserted 'manually'. For example, suppose you want to include a character such as å in an HTML document. You can specify such characters by using the appropriate character entities. A character entity is a sequence of characters, which codes a specific symbol. For example, Ê is specified as an upper-case E with a circumflex accent; the entity é is specified as a lower-case e with an acute accent. The browser sees the character entity and displays the symbol accordingly, as shown: <P>Vous voulez du café? is rendered: Vous voulez du café? The character entities that you can use in HTML 4 documents are given in Appendix B.

3.6 Non-breaking space characters, hyphens and spaces

Entity names
All entity names should be followed by a semicolon ';' even though, in theory, this is not required. In practice, the semicolon is needed by browsers which otherwise may not display the entity correctly.

Certain characters are meant to have a special meaning within the context of an HTML document. In particular, two characters may be interpreted by the browser to have specific effects in text formatting. These are as follows below:

- **The space character**. This is interpreted as a word space in all contexts except PRE for preformatted text, where it is treated as a non-breaking space.

  The character entities   and   denote respectively an en space and an em space. An en space is equal to one half of the point size of the current font; an em space is equal to the full point size of the current font. For fixed-pitch fonts, the browser can treat the en space as equivalent to a single-space character, and the em space as equivalent to two space characters. They are not yet widely used.

Character entities
Character entities are case sensitive. Do not make the mistake of altering the case. For example, Â is Â, but â is â. A list of character entities is given at the back of this book.

- **Non-breaking space** ( ). This is treated in the same way as the space character, except that the browser should never break the line at this point. By placing   you ensure that a word stays together and does not break between one line of text and the line directly below it.

See also the NOBR element, which is a Netscape extension, and also its associated element WBR, both documented in Chapter 4.

A hyphen is displayed on the screen as a hyphen symbol in all circumstances and browsers may insert a break in the line as though it were a normal word space. A hyphenated word may, therefore, be split between syllables.

There are a number of special entities used in HTML 4 and these are the following: © for a copyright symbol, ® for Registration mark, &tm; for Trade Mark, ­ for a soft hyphen, and &cbsp; for conditional breaking space. Netscape extensions to HTML 2.0 include ® and ©.

3.7 Formal structure of an HTML 4 document

Our document example at the start of this chapter was purposely simple. It could have been even simpler; in fact, the simplest legal HTML document consists of a TITLE element and nothing else. In this section we look at the formal structure of an HTML document and acquaint the reader with the associated concepts.

Formally, each document starts with an HTML element, which contains a HEAD element followed by a BODY element. The HTML code below shows the structure of a document as seen in these terms. The head of a document relates to information about the document as a whole and specifies general links from the document to others. The document head is like the header in a memo; for example, it tells you what the document is, who authored it, its expiry date, to what other documents it is related, and all sorts of other meta-information.

Meanwhile, the body of the document contains elements that are text, images, hypertext links, tables, lists and so on. It is, in fact, the main part of the document itself.

3.8 The HTML 4-compliant document

Every conforming HTML 4 document must start with the `<!DOCTYPE>` declaration that is needed to distinguish HTML 4 documents from other versions of HTML. Documents should start with a `<!DOCTYPE>` declaration followed by an HTML element containing a `HEAD` and then a `BODY` element. The minimal HTML 4 document thus looks like:

```
<!DOCTYPE HTML PUBLIC "-//W3C//DTD HTML 4.0 Draft//EN">
<HTML>
<HEAD>
<TITLE>The title for your document </TITLE>
... other head elements
</HEAD>
<BODY>
... document body
```

In practice, you can generally omit `<HTML>`, `<HEAD>` and `<BODY>` and their equivalent end tags. This is because the browser software will be able to recognize the head and body elements even though the tags may be missing. The mystery is explained in that the browser, upon recognizing elements it knows are not allowed to be in the document head, can nevertheless deduce that the head has ended and the body begun. That said, you cannot use elements that follow the document head in the wrong order. All the elements associated with the document head must be at the start of the document, and you cannot suddenly insert an element associated with the document head in the document body.

However, in actual use, HTML frequently does break these rules, because text often appears before the document head. Although browsers do their best to cope, it is important to ensure that you do not compound the problem. To test your documents, you can go to certain test pages on the Internet. You then click on the version of HTML you would like to test and then submit your document URL. Errors are sent back to you in one form or another.

4
MARKING UP PARAGRAPHS AND HEADINGS

Included in this chapter is information on:

- Performing simple paragraph mark-up and other block-level elements
- Controlling line breaks and hyphenation
- Marking up quotations in the text

Summary
HTML 4 includes simple block-level elements that you can use to mark up paragraphs and headings. The following are covered in this chapter:

- `P` for paragraphs
- `H1` to `H6` for headings

- `PRE` for preformatted text

- `DIV` for dividing text into sections with similar layout

- `BLOCKQUOTE` for quoted text

`WBR` and `NOBR` are *not* in HTML 4; these remain proprietary tags although they are widely supported by browsers. However, the non-breaking space entity ` ` *is* in HTML 4.

You will note that the `STYLE` attribute, available on all of the above, can now be used to specify a style for the element in terms of font, color, background and so on.

Tabs have not yet made it into the standard, nor have footnotes. The CSS style sheet group of the World Wide Web Consortium will address these features during the next year or so.

4.1 Introduction

In Chapter 3, you saw how to write a simple HTML document and how to load it into a browser. This chapter takes things a step further, explaining in greater detail about marking up complex paragraphs, quotations and

Simple heading element created with `<H2>`

Text flows around left-aligned picture

Italic text by using `<I>`

Bündner Oberland

JPEG image inserted with `IMG` element

Also Known by: *Bündner Oberland (German), Graubünden, Grisions*

Bold text by using `<B>`

Origin: The Tavet or Nalps Sheep achieved general recognition around the turn of this century, when scientists recognized a direct descendent of the Turf Goat in this ancient breed which was already widespread in the Stone Age. The Tavet Sheep had at this time regressive conditions already, and the last pure Tavet Sheep died because of inbreeding symptoms in 1954, despite efforts to maintain it.

Current Situation: In the Bündner Oberland, in Somvitg, in Tavetsch and above all in Vrin and in Medels some original animals have remained, for their breeders withstood cross-breeding with outside breeds. From the Medels sheep, also horned and similar to the Tavet sheep, the foundation Pro Specie Rara has built up herd book breeding from the year 1984, with breeders groups in all of eastern Switzerland. It is now designated as the Bündner Oberland Sheep.

What you can do with very simple HTML: quite a lot. This page is done by simple paragraphs flowing round an image and is perfectly effective.

Simple paragraphs by using `<P>`

headings in HTML. It also covers using the DIV element to divide up your document into sections that are rendered in particular ways; for example, you may want introductory paragraphs of a document that are displayed in large text to be formatted in a different color.

4.2 Paragraph mark-up

Trouble with gaps between paragraphs?
The Netscape browser occasionally fails to insert a gap between consecutive paragraphs. To remedy the matter try including the </P> end tag in your mark-up. There is a bug in the browser which shows up in certain (limited) circumstances – it is most generally the case that </P> does *not* need to be included.

The paragraph is a fundamental structural unit of an HTML document. Paragraphs are block-level elements, which means to say that they can include any of the 20 or so character-level elements you will find described in the next chapter. Within a paragraph you can tag the text to embolden it, to make words appear italicized, to make them appear larger or smaller than usual, or to appear as subscripts, superscripts and so on. The possibilities are endless.

Each paragraph must begin with the familiar <P> start tag. All text up to the next tag is then considered by the browser to be part of the same paragraph and you can simply type paragraph after paragraph in succession. You do not need to insert your own line breaks between paragraphs, as the browser does this for you. Paragraphs do not need an end tag, which some HTML authors still do not realize. Of course, you *can* insert an end tag if you like, but this is not really necessary. You can always omit the end tag, as the browser is clever enough to infer the paragraph's end from context.

Here are three simple paragraphs:

```
<P>Poems are made of words. <P>The poet chooses certain words rather than
others and places them in a particular order; the words combine to
produce an effect on those who read them. <P>It is clear that some study
of a poet's choice and use of words is essential if we are to understand
the way poetry works.
```

These paragraphs are displayed as:

> Poems are made of words.
>
> The poet chooses certain words rather than others and places them in a particular order; the words combine to produce an effect on those who read them.
>
> It is clear that some study of a poet's choice and use of words is essential if we are to understand the way poetry works.

Although it is common for people to try to do so, you cannot put in extra space by inserting 'blank' paragraph tags between lines. If you try to insert additional paragraph tags between lines in an attempt to get your text to look like this:

```
First line
Second line
```

the browser will render the text as if the additional paragraph tags simply were not there. If you do want more (or less) space between paragraphs, the best way to accomplish this is to allocate a style to the paragraph, an idea we will come to later.

Word-wrap

Normally, a paragraph will be wrapped around from one line to the next, as happens in most word processing packages. As the window in which the paragraph is displayed becomes narrower, so the lines are wrapped more frequently to accommodate them; as the window is expanded, so the lines are wrapped less frequently.

Controlling line breaks

There are various ways of controlling line breaks in HTML. One of the simplest is the <BR> element, which comes in handy for creating short lines of text in a paragraph. This tends to be used a great deal for poetry on the Web, for example:

```
I sing of a maiden<BR>That is makeless;<BR>
King of kings<BR>To her son she ches.<BR>
He came all so still,<BR>There his mother was,<BR>
As dew in April<BR>That falleth on the grass
```

This text is rendered in HTML as the following:

```
I sing of a maiden
That is makeless;
King of kings
To her son she ches.
He came all so still,
There his mother was,
As dew in April
That falleth on the grass
```

NOBR and WBR
Neither NOBR nor WBR is in the HTML 4 standard.

Netscape 2.0 uses the NOBR element to mark up sections of text that must not be broken. The browser will not insert a line break between the start tag <NOBR> and the end tag </NOBR>, as word wrap is essentially switched off.

If, for example, you want to keep text on the same line, you can do the following:

> Where are the songs of spring? Ay, Where are they?

In the example above, the `<NOBR>` element is used. The result is a long unbroken line of text that will not wrap even when the window is made smaller. Now, if you know where you would *like* to break the line (that is, if it *has* to be broken), then you can use Netscape's `WBR` (WordBREak) element. For example, we suggest to the browser that, if necessary, it can break the line after the word 'spring':

```
<NOBR>Where are the songs of spring? <WBR>Ay, Where are they?
</NOBR><BR>
Think not of them, thou hast thy music too
```

This is rendered appropriately, below:

> Where are the songs of spring? Ay, Where are they?
> Think not of them, thou hast thy music too

Or, less appropriately, in a narrow window, below:

> Where are the songs of spring?
> Ay, Where are they?
> Think not of them, thou hast thy music too

`WBR` corresponds to a conditional space. Conditional breaking spaces behave as ordinary spaces, but indicate a good place to break the line.

Preventing a word from being split between lines

HTML 4 gives you the option of using a non-breaking space entity ` ` to ensure that the line is *not* broken at a crucial point in the text. You simply insert the entity at the point where you want the non-breaking space to be. For example:

```
Rolled round in earth's diurnal course
```

If the words 'diurnal course' fall at the end of a line, they will not be split apart. The use of ` ` is implemented by Netscape and Microsoft. Note that, although it is not necessary for the SGML standard, it is always recommended in HTML documents.

Hyphens

The ­ entity
The ­ entity is part of HTML 4, but, because it is harder to implement than you might think, browser companies may take time to support it.

The HTML entity is ­ which defines a soft hyphen. A soft hyphen indicates a place that is usually invisible, but is a good point to break the word if necessary. For example:

```
hyphen&shy;ated
```

will appear as:

hyphenated

or, at the end of a line, it may be split onto the next:

hyphen-
ated

A hard hyphen, by contrast, is a visible hyphen that joins two parts of a word. For English documents, browsers will assume that a hard hyphen is a good place to break, regardless of whether or not the word-wrap feature is switched on.

Setting the font and color for paragraph text

FONT FACE
FONT FACE is in the HTML 4 standard although you are advised to use a style sheet to specify the font if possible.

Once upon a time, the browser chose the font for you, but people were not altogether happy. Then along came FONT FACE, a popular (but non-standard) method for the document author to specify the color and typeface to be used by the browser when it came to putting up text on the screen.

But in the computer world, nothing stays still for long. It is no surprise, then, that FONT FACE is now being superseded by something quite different – namely, font-family, font-size, font-weight and other properties that are newly available with Web style sheets. If you look in Section 9.5 you will see how easy it is to design a style that can be applied to certain paragraphs, to a single paragraph, or to the whole document. Using this simple idea, you can very quickly specify the color of the text and the font:

```
<P STYLE= {font-family : OldCentury, Sherwood, serif; font-size: 10 pt}>
The undivided nave and chancel, built in the 12th century are an
interesting example of a complete church of that period ... the windows
are the early lancets, remarkable for their wide concave splays, and a
stringcourse runs round the cream walls above and below them.
```

which we hope comes out like this:

> The undivided nave and chancel, built in the
> 12th century are an interesting example of
> a complete church of that period ... the
> windows are the early lancets, remarkable
> for their wide concave splays, and a
> stringcourse runs round the cream walls
> above and below them.

If the browser on the receiving end just has not got OldCentury installed, then this is not a problem. With the CSS style-sheet language, you can give several alternatives for the font, in the hopeful anticipation that at least one of them will work. Chapter 9 tells all.

Paragraph alignment

Justified text
We asked a well-known Web developer why no browser to our knowledge had implemented justified text. 'Too lazy' was his simple, economical reply.

Paragraphs can be aligned with the **ALIGN** attribute, which is used to specify the horizontal alignment of the text, or with the **align** property of Web style sheets. The **ALIGN** attribute is more universally understood by browsers.

- `<P ALIGN=left>` means that the paragraph is rendered by the browser as flush left. This is the default alignment and is used if the **ALIGN** attribute is not inserted into the mark-up.

- `<P ALIGN=center>` means that the paragraph is centered.

- `<P ALIGN=right>` means that the paragraph is flush right.

The ultimate shape that a paragraph assumes on the screen is also a function of window size.

Paragraphs in conjunction with images: Control of text flow

You probably are familiar with the idea of text flow in desktop publishing packages. Many desktop publishing packages have options that control text flow around frames, with the possibility of either flowing text around an image in a frame or pushing it under the frame. The **CLEAR** attribute can be used to produce similar effects in HTML, as shown at the top of the next page. Text flows around the first image, but not the second.

... his organic yet electrifying style captures that sense of internal bewilderment and excitement which so characterize his early works and is still vivid today in these unique pieces. The unique  combination of strength of colour matches with beauty of line to give a sense of the unexpected, of the intimate and of the musical. On show now at the Roxborough Gallery, we recommend that you visit 'Jam for Tea' before the exhibition finishes at the end of the month.

... his organic yet electrifying style captures that sense of internal bewilderment and excitement which so characterize his early works and is still vivid today in these unique pieces. The unique  combination of strength of colour matches with beauty of line to give a sense of the unexpected, of the intimate and of the musical. On show now at the Roxborough Gallery, we recommend that you visit 'Jam for Tea' before the exhibition finishes at the end of the month.

Suppose you choose to place an image that is positioned to the right of the display window, as shown below. To get this kind of effect and to ensure that the next paragraph always begins below the image, you can use the **CLEAR** attribute `BR CLEAR=right`:

... his organic yet electrifying style captures that sense of internal bewilderment and excitement which so characterize his early works and is still vivid today in these unique pieces.

The unique combination of strength of colour matches with beauty of line to give a sense of the unexpected, of the intimate and of the musical. On show now at the Roxborough Gallery, we recommend that you visit 'Jam for Tea' before the exhibition finishes at the end of the month.

```
<IMG SRC=painting.gif ALIGN=right>...his organic yet electrifying style
captures that sense of internal bewilderment and excitement which so
characterize his early works and is still vivid today in these unique
pieces.
<BR CLEAR=right>
<P>The unique combination of strength of color matches with beauty of
line to give a sense of the unexpected, of the intimate and of the
musical. On show now at the Roxborough Gallery, we recommend that you
visit 'Jam for Tea' before the exhibition finishes at the end of the
month.
```

The BR element acts to move the rendering position down until the margin is clear of the right-aligned obstructing image. If the image had been left-aligned, you would have used BR CLEAR=left. If there were images on the left and the right margins then you would have used BR CLEAR=all.

Indented paragraphs

It is now possible to indent paragraphs. You invent a style for paragraphs that exploits the very useful **indent** property available in the new Web style sheet language. See Chapter 9, page 158.

Headings

Headings are easy to insert in HTML and, although you probably will only want to use up to level 3 headings, HTML defines six heading levels. A heading element simply tells the browser what kind of heading you would like: the browser determines all the font changes, paragraph breaks before and after, and any white space necessary to render it on the screen.

The heading elements are H1, H2, H3, H4, H5, and H6, with H1 being the highest (or most important) level, and H6 being the least important.

Heading elements have the same content model as paragraphs; that is, text and character-level mark-up such as character emphasis and inline images. This means, for example, that you can place an image in a heading.

Examples of the six heading levels

These are the six heading levels as they were rendered on the Netscape browser. The headings were marked up quite simply as:

```
<H1>Major Rumple</H1>
<H2>Captain Haddock</H2>
<H3>Lieutenant Klein</H3>
<H4>Sergeant-Major Jones</H4>
<H5>Lance-Corporal Smith</H5>
<H6>Abbie-the-Cat</H6>
```

Major Rumple

Captain Haddock

Lieutenant Klein

Sergeant-Major Jones

Lance-Corporal Smith

Abbie-the-Cat

Font and color used for headings

The font and color used for headings is now under your control. Blue Arial lettering or gorgeous OldCentury in purple are extravagances now possible without resorting to the wonders of the GIF image. Now that style sheets are here, fun headings can be done without importing a graphic when you want something different. The result will be that headings load much faster. By using a small style sheet (see the example in Chapter 3 or look in Chapter 9 on Style Sheets for more detail), you can work wonders.

Heading alignment

Headings are usually rendered flush left. The **ALIGN** attribute can be used to specify the horizontal alignment:

- ALIGN=left which renders the heading flush left (the default)

- ALIGN=center which does as you would expect and centers the heading on the screen

- ALIGN=right which renders the heading flush right

Numbering headings

Footnotes
Part of the HTML 3.0 proposal, footnotes have not been implemented. To move the idea forward until it becomes a standard will take some time.

The numbering of headings is something that people need, and yet it has not been implemented. It will come, but it will not happen quickly.

Dave Raggett proposed some ideas for numbering of headings with style sheets but browser vendors saw it as a low priority. Numbering of headings is unlikely to be possible in HTML until 1998.

Other attributes that can be used with headings

These include the following:

- **NOWRAP**, which is used when you do not want the browser to automatically wrap lines. You can switch off word-wrap for a header element and then use BR to insert line breaks.

- **CLEAR**, which allows you to control whether or not a heading is to be placed alongside of or below a graphic or table in the margin.

4.3 Preformatted text

Preformatted text, which is specified using the <PRE> and </PRE> tags, is rendered using a fixed-pitched font. In preformatted text, white-space characters (principally space, line-feed and carriage-return characters) and also <BR> tags are treated literally. This means that when you author text, each space you insert is depicted on the screen exactly when the text is displayed. This is in contrast to other tags for which repeated white-space characters are collapsed to a single-space character; the browser introduces line breaks automatically.

One of the things you find on the Web is lyrics of songs. Almost invariably, these are written using preformatted text. Preformatted text is a simple way of ensuring that indents and line breaks are in the right place. The text and white space in the PRE element come out more or less exactly as you inserted them. It's a bit of a giveaway that the result is rendered in a fixed-width font such as Courier, but this is not important for those who simply want the lyrics of songs rather than an especially beautiful presentation. Here's the first verse of the chorus in Carl Orff's *Carmina Burana*, which no doubt is somewhere on the Web:

```
<PRE>
O fortuna
Velut luna
stratu variabilis
semper crescis
aut decrescis
vita detestabilis
nunc obdurat
et tunc curat
ludo mentis aciem
egestatem,
potestatem
dissolvit ut glaciem.
</PRE>
```

It comes out just as you type it in:

```
O fortuna
Velut luna
Stratu variabilis
Semper crescis
aut decrescis
vita detestabilis
nunc obdurat
et tunc curat
ludo mentis aciem
egestatem,
potestatem
dissolvit ut glaciem.
```

In preformatted text, carriage-returns and line-feeds within the text are rendered as a move to the beginning of the next line, with the exception of line breaks immediately following the starting <PRE> tag, or immediately preceding the ending </PRE> tag. The browser should ignore these remarks.

The <P> tag should be avoided in preformatted text, but browsers usually treat these tags as line breaks. Block-level elements such as headers, lists and TABLE should be avoided in preformatted text.

Anchor elements for hypertext links may be included in preformatted text, as well as character-level elements and FORM elements.

Attributes used with the PRE element are **ID**, **LANG**, **CLEAR** and **CLASS**. The **LANG** attribute is explained in Chapter 17 on Internationalization of the Web; **CLASS** is explained in Chapter 9 and **ID** in Chapter 7.

We suggest that, although you may change font color or font size, with PRE you should stick to a fixed-width font. Do not try to combine PRE with Helvetica, Times or another of your favorite fonts. PRE should be rendered in something such as Courier.

4.4 Quotations with the Q and BLOCKQUOTE elements

Tabs in HTML?
Not at the moment. Tabs are being handled in style sheets. The proposal is to use the ASCII TAB character and to allow people to define a tab.

HTML needs to cater to two kinds of quotations: simple, inline quotations that are a few words long, and longer quotations that are several lines of extended quotations.

Short, inline quotations can be included with the character-level element Q, which is part of HTML 4 (see Chapter 5). The effects of Q can be more than simply placing the relevant characters in quotes. First, the browser should select the correct quotation marks for the language. Then, in instances in which the browser is being used by the visually impaired, the quote can be read aloud with a different intonation, so as to render a richer connotation to what is being heard. HTML 4 includes the **HREF** attribute on Q to allow a link to the source of the quotation.

The BLOCKQUOTE element is for marking up larger quotations that the browser treats as block-like elements. Browsers should display BLOCKQUOTE text as perhaps italicized text with the borders slightly indented. For example:

> *'The only way to boil eggs is to rapidly lower them into fast-boiling water and then to cook for exactly nine minutes'*
>
> Cecil Chou de Gratin

4.5 The DIV element to give a section or chapter a uniform style

DIV was in HTML 3.0 as a proposed element; now, it finally appears in HTML 4. The word DIV was borrowed from the Text Encoding Initiative (TEI), which was a several-year project between the humanities and the computer sciences to mark up a variety of literary material. The DIV element is used for structuring documents. It is used to provide a means of giving different styles to 'containers' such as chapters, sections, appendices, abstracts and so on. DIV has a general content type, which means that it can include a series of elements, such as paragraphs, tables, lists or headings. From a stylistic point of view, the browser can then treat these as a single unit. For example, an 'abstract' could have its paragraphs and tables displayed in a font different from those in a 'chapter'. A 'sidebar' could have its paragraphs enclosed in a border, and so on.

One of the most common uses of DIV is aligning a whole series of paragraphs, headings or other elements as left, right or center. In other words, let us suppose you want something such as the following below:

```
<DIV ALIGN=right>
...
...
</DIV>
```

All elements between the DIV start and end tags will be aligned to the right. Thus, paragraphs, lists, tables, and so on will all be right-aligned between the start and finish of DIV.

Examples of the use of DIV are given in Chapter 9 on Style Sheets, to which the reader is encouraged to refer.

4.6 ADDRESS

This is a rather old element, which is a little vague in its use. The ADDRESS element is intended to contain information about the author of the document, such as name and address. It can also be used for including 'mailto' links, special links that start an email program on some servers and let the user send email to the Web page owner. The most general way of providing your email address is inside the ADDRESS element. An example:

```
<ADDRESS>
The Editor<BR>
45, Bridge Street,<BR>
Acton-in-the-Woods<BR>
Berkshire<BR>
RG56 34T<BR>
Tel: +144 (123) 456 789
</ADDRESS>
```

Centering text with CENTER

HTML's CENTER element enables you to center items on the page. Unlike the ALIGN paragraph attribute, for example, <P ALIGN=center>, the <CENTER>...</CENTER> attribute applies to all text, headings and other mark-up included within it. Formally, it is a shorthand for <DIV ALIGN=center>...</DIV>, to which it is equivalent and indeed the approved way to center text. For example:

```
<CENTER>Madam,<BR>I'<BR>m &quot;Adam&quot;</CENTER>
```

which is rendered in HTML as the following:

> Madam,
> I'
> m 'Adam'

Note that the approved way to center text in HTML is to use <DIV ALIGN=center></DIV>, or the ALIGN attribute in headers (<H3 ALIGN=center>) or paragraphs.

A proprietary tag outside the HTML 4 standard: the MARQUEE element for animating text

Microsoft's Internet Explorer supports the MARQUEE tag as an HTML extension. The popularity of Java for animating text may reduce the enthusiasm for doing the job in HTML.

MARQUEE animates text in the manner of a marquee advertising a theatrical performance on Broadway. MARQUEE is a zippy feature whose designers have really let down their hair – at least, judging by the number of attributes MARQUEE contains, most of which are unique to the element.

We will try to cover them briefly; if anything makes the case for a tightly controlled standard, this is it.

`<MARQUEE ALIGN=top>` makes the scrolling text align with the top of the marquee. Other values are middle and bottom.

`BEHAVIOR=scroll` is the default. The text scrolls on to the display (from the left) and then scrolls off it (to the right).

`BEHAVIOR=slide` scrolls in and sticks there.

`BEHAVIOR=alternate` bounces back and forth.

`BGCOLOR=Fuchsia` lets you specify the background color for the marquee. See Appendix D for details of how to name colors.

`DIRECTION=right` makes the text scroll from right to left instead of the usual left to right.

`HEIGHT` and `WIDTH` let you size the marquee either in pixels or as a percentage of the screen height or width, respectively. For example,

```
<MARQUEE HEIGHT=50% WIDTH=80%>
```

`SCROLLAMOUNT` sets the size of the step in pixels from one redrawing of the marquee text to the next. If you make it large, the marquee effectively seems to move more quickly but also in a rather jerky fashion.

`SCROLLDELAY` sets the delay in milliseconds before the marquee starts its next cycle.

`HSPACE` and `VSPACE` set the left/right and top/bottom margins respectively in pixels, for example, `HSPACE=5`.

For example:

```
<MARQUEE BGCOLOR=lime
BEHAVIOR=alternate
SCROLLAMOUNT=3
SCROLLDELAY=50
HEIGHT=40%
VSPACE=20
LOOP=666>A programmer's approach to HTML.
</MARQUEE>
```

5
CHARACTER
EMPHASIS

Included in this chapter is information on:

- Using *font-style elements* that indicate how text is to be presented on the screen; for example, bold, italic, underline, strike-through.
- Using *phrase-style elements* that are similar to font-style elements, but which are associated with a specific function. For example, phrase-style elements include the KBD element for text the user keys in at a particular point; the CODE element indicates that the text is a piece of computer code.
- Using special *text-level elements* to control font size, color and typeface.

Summary

HTML 4 includes a variety of character-level elements:

Font-style elements

TT	fixed-width teletype-style font
I	italic text
B	bold text
U	underlined text (recently deprecated)
STRIKE (S)	strike-through (recently deprecated)
BIG	big text
SMALL	small text
SUP	superscript
SUB	subscript

Phrase-style elements

EM	emphasized text
STRONG	strongly emphasized text
DFN	definition of term
CODE	computer code
SAMP	display characters exactly as typed in
KBD	text to be entered at keyboard (in computer documentation)
VAR	variable name (in computer documentation)
CITE	for citing references

Special character-level elements

BASEFONT	the base font for the document (deprecated but in widespread use)
BR	line break
FONT	font face, size and color (deprecated but in widespread use)
Q	inline quotes
SPAN	associating a style with phrase or short section of text

5.1 Introduction

In Chapter 3, we explained that there were two kinds of HTML elements: block-level and character-level. Block-level elements include paragraphs, headings, preformatted text and many other elements that commonly end with a paragraph break. The browser throws a break after each block-level element.

Character-level elements, meanwhile, are used to mark up text *within* block-level elements. They are generally used to mark up individual letters, words, phrases or sentences.

This chapter deals with elements at the character level. It covers how to mark up bold text, italicized text, subscript text, superscript text, and so on within 'parent' elements on the page.

5.2 Font-style elements

Font-style elements directly affect the way that text is rendered in terms of *look* – whether bold, underlined etc. Phrase-style elements by contrast, specify logical, or functional, mark-up.

The B element for bold text

Boldface type is widely used to distinguish items under discussion, and for many kinds of emphasis. Since HTML provides specific tags for headings (such as <H3> ... </H3>) and many other document structures, you should consider whether or not the boldface tag is what you really want. For example, shown below is the HTML:

```
Come all you <B>sailors bold</B> and draw near!
```

which is rendered as the following:

> Come all you **sailors bold** and draw near!

The BIG element for a larger font

The <BIG> tag specifies that the font used for the enclosed text should be larger than usual. See also the character-level tag, <SMALL>, which has the opposite properties. For example, shown below is the HTML:

```
<BIG>O</BIG>nce upon a time,
```

which is rendered as the following:

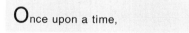

The I element for italic text

An italicized typeface is useful for many purposes; conventionally, it is employed to draw the reader's attention toward a word or a short phrase, which is used differently than the reader might have expected. For example, shown below is the HTML:

```
... but it was during the <I>Italian Renaissance</I> that ...
```

which is rendered as the following:

> ... but it was during the *Italian Renaissance* that ...

The STRIKE or S element to strike-through characters

STRIKE is now deprecated
This element, along with other font style elements, is being phased out in favor of style-sheet control of font characteristics.

The character tag <STRIKE> is particularly useful in legal documents in which it is necessary to show the reader that text has been struck from the record. For example:

```
<STRIKE>mistake</STRIKE> message
```

which is rendered as the following:

> ~~mistake~~ message

If you don't want to use STRIKE, you may choose the SPAN element (which marks up a particular phrase). You can then give a style to the SPANned text; for example, one that displays text to be 'greyed', crossed out, or otherwise changed. Greyed text can be accomplished by simply changing the font color to grey, and the CSS style sheet language does include a **strikeout** property. See Chapter 9.

The SMALL element for small print

The SMALL print character tag specifies that the font used for the enclosed text should be smaller than usual. See also the <BIG> print character tag, above. For example:

```
Whereas <SMALL>whispered</SMALL> conversation seems sibilant.
```

which is rendered as the following:

> Whereas <small>whispered</small> conversation seems sibilant.

The SUB element for subscripts

Using a subscript character tag <SUB> is necessary in many mathematical, scientific, and engineering fields. For example:

```
pH = -Log<SUB>10</SUB>[H]<SUP>+</SUP>
```

which is rendered as the following:

$$pH = -Log_{10}[H]^{+}$$

The SUP element for superscripts

Using a superscript character tag <SUP> is very useful for many scientific applications. For example:

```
e=mc<SUP>2</SUP>
```

which is rendered as the following:

$$e = mc^{2}$$

The TT element for a fixed-width, 'teletype-style' font

The 'teletype-style' font is very helpful when you want to show the reader that the text is typed. Since it is also a fixed-pitch font, it can be useful for simple character formatting. The tag in question is TT. Here is an example of its use:

```
<P>Jane typed: <TT>I am learning to type</TT> with Grandpa's Imperial.
```

which is rendered as the following:

Jane typed: `I am learning to type` with **Grandpa's Imperial.**

The U element for underlining text

U is deprecated This element is now (July 1997) deprecated from the HTML specification.

Underlining was formerly used in instances in which bold and italicized text now is more popular. Mechanical typewriters and line printers were able to underline text by overstriking text with the underline key. Since underlined text is difficult to read when the underscore crosses the descenders of letters p, q, g and so on, we can perhaps suggest that underlining ought to be a rare means of emphasis.

You can use underlining by employing the U tag, which is supported by Netscape and Internet Explorer browsers. Some browsers still may not support it for fear of confusion with link Anchors. For example:

```
<U>Potamogeton fluitans</U>
```

which is rendered as the following:

Potamogeton fluitans

Scientific (Linnean) names of species, as in this example, are nowadays usually printed in italicized text, so that using the character tag for an italic font <I>...</I> may be more appropriate and more likely to be supported by your readers' browsers than using the underlining tag.

5.3 Phrase-style tags

This section discusses phrase-style tags. These are associated not with a desired appearance of text on the screen, but with an intended purpose.

The EM and STRONG tags for emphasis

The <EM> and <STRONG> tags are used to emphasize text. For example:

```
I <EM>specially</EM> like <STRONG>dark</STRONG> chocolates.
```

Most browsers choose to render this example as something like the following:

I *specially* like **dark** chocolates.

<EM> typically is italicized text, although you should not assume this to be the case in all instances. <STRONG> typically is boldface text, but you should not assume this, either. A very simple screen handler with only one font option might instead render the example as shown below:

I _specially_ like *dark* chocolates.

Lynx, one of the best-known text-only browsers, ignores both `<EM>` and `<STRONG>`.

The `CITE` element for citing references

Citations are usually used to supply references in books, journals, and papers in sufficient detail to enable the reader to find them in a library. The citation attribute `<CITE>` differs from `<A HREF=...>` in that it does not create a hypertext link (which in line with Web philosophy would allow the reader to find the document simply by clicking on the link anchor). Citations are useful in enabling programs to collect references to documents, even if they are not available online. For example, shown below is the HTML for a citation from a printed book:

```
<CITE>Patanjali, Yoga Sutras, No. 2, India</CITE>
```

This is rendered as the following:

Patanjali, Yoga Sutras, No. 2, India

You can combine the use of `<CITE>` with `<A HREF=...>` to indicate that a link also is a formal or scientific document reference. For example, shown below is the HTML for a citation link:

```
<CITE>
    <A HREF="patanj.html">
        <IMG SRC="yogafrog.gif">
        Patanjali, Yoga Sutras, No. 2, India
    </A>
</CITE>
```

The `CODE` element for indicating computer code in the text

This program code tag indicates that the text is a piece of quoted computer program code, typically because you want to explain it or otherwise write about it. It is usually rendered in a fixed-pitch font as with `<TT>`, the obsolete `<PRE>`, and `<KBD>`, but its logical meaning is different. The use of the `<CODE>` tag enables filters to search for and extract the program code from documents for further processing. For example:

```
<CODE>For i=0 To MaxChars Do ProcessChar(i)</CODE>
```

which may be rendered as follows:

```
For i = 0 To MaxChars Do
ProcessChar(i)
```

The DFN element for definitions

The definition tag is intended to supply a defining instance of a term used elsewhere in a document. For example, the HTML:

```
<DFN>flaming means (inadvisably) attacking <I>ad hominem</I></DFN>
```

is rendered as follows:

```
flaming means (inadvisably)
attacking ad hominem
```

The KBD element for use in online documentation

The keyboard tag indicates text, which the user can type. It is more specific in meaning than <TT> and should be used in preference to it, if you want to indicate 'now it's your turn', rather than simply 'this is text'. Its purpose is primarily for use in instruction manuals. Here is a simple example:

```
<P>You should now enter:
<KBD>Run myprog dear computer </KBD>
<P> If the good fairy of computing is with you, your machine will behave
accordingly.
```

which is rendered as the following:

```
You should now enter:

Run myprog dear computer

If the good fairy of computing is
with you, your machine will
behave accordingly.
```

SAMP for displaying characters as they have been typed

The sample tag passes any characters enclosed within it to the display. This can be useful in instances in which the possibility exists that the browser might take other actions with the characters. SAMP is meant for samples of output from scripts or programs. For example, the HTML:

```
Then he said <SAMP>$@%#</SAMP> and Daisy gasped.
```

is rendered as the following:

```
Then he said $@%# and Daisy
gasped.
```

The VAR element for a named variable in online documentation

The VAR element indicates the name of a variable or placeholder in a quoted computer program or script (presumably indicated with the CODE element). For example, the HTML:

```
<VAR>Current_Account_Balance</VAR>
```

is rendered as the following:

```
Current_Account_Balance
```

5.4 Special text-level elements

This section discusses two tags that now are in HTML 4. Note that style sheets now offer a cleaner and more satisfactory way of specifying font. See Chapter 9.

The BASEFONT element for setting font size, color and face

BASEFONT is officially deprecated in HTML 4 In real life lots of people will continue to use BASEFONT. The idea is that authors should use style sheets to set font size, color and face. This will increasingly become the trend now that style sheets have been widely implemented on browsers.

This element is used to set the underlying font size for the text. This size then may be modified using FONT. BASEFONT is an empty element which means that an end tag is forbidden: you do not need to insert </BASEFONT> and, indeed, this is not allowed.

BASEFONT has an attribute **SIZE** that takes as its value an integer ranging from 1 to 7. The BASEFONT size applies to normal and preformatted text but not to headings, except where these are modified using the FONT element with a relative font size.

The default size is 3.

FONT FACE

FONT FACE is now deprecated in HTML 4. The font face is better controlled via style sheets, as in Chapter 9.

FONT FACE accepts a list separated by commas of font names in order of preference. This is used to search for an installed font with the corresponding name.

When would you use BASEFONT? A typical example is at the beginning of a document in a DIV element:

```
<P>An ordinary paragraph in an ordinary size.

<DIV> <BASEFONT SIZE=2> <P>From now on the document assumes a font size
which is somewhat large. All the paragraphs will use this font size until
you to decide to cancel it by inserting the DIV end tag.

<P>Even this paragraph will use the font size specified by BASEFONT.

</DIV>
```

which is rendered as the following:

An ordinary paragraph in an ordinary size

From now on the document assumes a font size which is somewhat large. All the paragraphs will use this font size until you to decide to cancel it by inserting the DIV end tag.

Even this paragraph will use the font size specified by BASEFONT.

Using BASEFONT more than once in a document may be confusing.

The FONT element to specify a local change to the font

This element, which requires both start and end tags, changes the font size, color and typeface for the enclosed text.

The size of the font can be specified with the **SIZE** attribute which takes an absolute value in the range 1 to 7. The digit 1 means that the browser should use the smallest available font; the digit 7 means that the browser should use the largest available font. The exact size of the font the browser uses depends on the configuration of the browser. So, for instance, <FONT SIZE=2> tells the browser to use the second-smallest font but whether or not this is 8 point, 10 point or another point size is left open to question.

If you prefix the SIZE attribute with a '+' or '-' sign, then the font size is calculated relative to the document's BASEFONT element. Let's say you specified <FONT SIZE=+2>. This would tell the browser to increase the font size by two points. Thus, if the BASEFONT were set to point size 3, the resulting font would be point size 5.

For example:

```
Little fingers need <FONT SIZE=+3>Big building blocks.</FONT>
```

which is rendered as the following:

Little fingers need Big
building blocks.

The following shows the effects of setting font to absolute sizes:

Size 7 is the largest available.

size=1 size=2 size=3 size=4 size=5
size=6 size=7

The following shows the effect of relative font sizes using a base font size of 3:

```
<BASEFONT size=3>
```

Size 3 + 4 = 7 so +3 and +4 are the same here.

size=-4 size=-3 size=-2 size=-1 size=+1 size=+2
size=+3 size=+4

The same thing with a base font size of 6:

```
<BASEFONT size=6>
```

Size 6 + 1 = 7 so +1, +2, +3 and +4 are all the same here.

size=-4 size=-3 size=-2 size=-1 size=+1
size=+2 size=+3 size=+4

The COLOR attribute of FONT is used to vary the color of the text, including headings. For example, you can write COLOR=Red or COLOR="c00000" using the RGB (Red Green Blue) format. See Appendix D for details of how to name colors.

Look at the following:

```
<H3><FONT COLOR = red>RED LETTER DAY</FONT></H3>
<P>Back to Black
```

On a browser you should see:

```
RED LETTER DAY
Back to Black
```

You should see 'RED LETTER DAY' in red and the rest of the text displays in the default color (usually black). Incidentally, the FONT element's closing tag </FONT> is mandatory, and you may get confusing errors if you omit it. On some browsers, the effect is to upset normal changes in font size, such as would happen when you switch back and forth between headings and paragraphs of text.

The FONT element has an attribute **FACE**, which can be used to specify Helvetica, Times, Courier or other fonts to be used in text. Before you use this attribute, however, do read the section on Fonts in Chapter 9. This explains how style sheets can be used to allocate a font to text on the screen. The style sheet mechanism is a better choice than using FONT; but, of course, style sheets are only implemented on the latest browsers.

Here is an example of FONT FACE:

```
<FONT FACE=Arial>Shiver the rabbit licked his friend Stripey the
guinea-pig</FONT>
```

This specifies that browsers should display the text in Arial if this is available to them, and if no local setting for typeface has been made. If the browser does not have Arial installed, it will use its default font to display the text.

The SPAN element for associating a style with a phrase

The SPAN element is for giving a phrase or a longer selection of text a particular display attribute such as, font, color, and size. Let us suppose you want to render text to appear in a different font, for example, italic. To do this, you can use the SPAN element in combination with the **CLASS** attribute. For example:

```
<P> As your modem communicates with the machine the other end, you will
hear a variety of unexpected noises including a loud clanging. All this
is quite normal.<SPAN CLASS=note> Customers who hear a distinct tweeting
sound for more than 15 seconds as their computers establish the server
connection are probably using an M3567-666t unit. These are no longer
supported. </SPAN>
```

which might (depending on how **note** was described in your style sheet) be rendered as follows, with italicized text perhaps in a color:

As your modem communicates with the machine the other end, you will hear a variety of unexpected noises including a loud clanging. All this is quite normal. *Customers who hear a distinct tweeting sound for more than 15 seconds as their computers establish the server connection are probably using an M3567-666t unit. These are no longer supported.*

All the text between `<SPAN CLASS=note>` and `</SPAN>` will assume the style specified in the style sheet as 'note'. This might be 'red text in italics', 'blue text in Gaslight 12-point font', or whatever else takes your fancy. The process of specifying a style such as 'note' in our example is covered in Chapter 9 on style sheets.

The Q element to mark up inline quotations (in place of " . . . " or ' . . . ')

Inline quotations are useful for short snippets of quoted text that you want to discuss without having to put them in block quotes (using `BLOCKQUOTE`) as entire paragraphs in their own right. You might also like to use them to distinguish technical words or phrases when they are introduced for the first time. (This makes it easy to search for such occurrences, for instance to make a cross-reference table.) Text within `<Q>...</Q>` tags typically is shown in English-language browsers by using double quotation marks ("...") alternating with single quotes ('...') when nesting of quotations occurs.

Displays for languages other than English may use different symbols, such as «...» in Spanish or "...". The language context is specified by the **LANG** attribute within an individual `<Q>` tag, or by separate `<LANG>...</LANG>` tags.

Here is an example of Q in use:

```
<Q lang = "en.uk"> <Q>Yoga is the stilling of the thought-waves of the
mind</Q>, recited Peter.</Q>
```

which is rendered as:

> " 'Yoga is the stilling of the thought-waves
> of the mind', recited Peter."

5.5 Combining tags

You can combine the use of tags in a sentence, as in the example shown
below:

```
<P>Here is some <B><I><U><TT>excessively NOISY script </B></I></U></TT>
```

Browsers will render the text as directed below, if at all possible:

> Here is some *excessively NOISY script*

Tags of various kinds can be freely mixed to combine effects.
Although such freedom can be very useful, mixing tags enables you to
construct confusingly marked-up texts. Best to keep things neat and
simple.

5.6 Elements rarely used but still in the HTML 4 specification

The ABBR element for abbreviations

Abbreviations are meant for standard phrases, which are not acronyms.
Again, the tag can be searched for, to help ensure that all jargon
used is properly explained. For example, shown below is the HTML:

```
<P>We had cucumber sandwiches, boiled eggs, cheese and pickle, <ABBR>etc.
etc.</ABBR> all provided by the Clever Catering Company, <ABBR>Ltd.
</ABBR>
```

This is rendered as:

> We had cucumber sandwiches, boiled
> eggs, cheese and pickle, *etc. etc.* all
> provided by the Clever Catering
> Company *Ltd*.

This tag eventually may make it into HTML 4, but it seems unlikely.

Acronyms with the `ACRONYM` element

TITLE with ACRONYM
By using the TITLE attribute available in ACRONYM, you can arrange for the browser to display the full text of an acronym on the screen at your reader's command. The reader points to the acronym with the mouse, and the full explanation of the acronym appears in a small 'balloon box' on the screen.

Acronyms are far too abundant in many documents nowadays, even or perhaps especially when they actually convey rather little technical information. The <ACRONYM> element, representing tags for acronyms, helps control the spread of undefined jargon, by making it easy to identify, locate, and describe all abbreviations in a document. For example, shown below is the HTML for an organization's acronym:

```
<ACRONYM>NASA</ACRONYM>
```

`DEL` for deleted text

The deleted text tag denotes that the enclosed text is formally deleted from a document. Browsers may render deleted text in strike-through form via the strike-through attribute (<S>), but are not obliged to do so. For example, shown below is the HTML:

```
Plaintiff shall be understood to mean <DEL>Mr</DEL> Mrs Jones.
```

This is rendered as:

> Plaintiff shall be understood to mean
> ~~Mr~~ Mrs Jones.

The `INS` element for inserted text

The inserted text tag marks the enclosed text as formally inserted into, for instance, a legal document (compare with <DEL> for deleted text). Browsers may use formatting such as underscore to indicate inserted text. Below is the HTML:

```
Plaintiffs shall be understood to mean <INS>Mr and</INS> Mrs Jones.
```

This is rendered as:

> Plaintiffs shall be understood to mean
> <u>Mr and</u> Mrs Jones.

6
MARKING UP LISTS

Included in this chapter is information on:

- Bulleted lists
- Numbered lists
- Definition lists

Summary

HTML 4 includes the list elements familiar to earlier HTML versions. The main difference is that now you can use style sheets to specify the kind of bullet you want, and also what their position will be with respect to the text. Style sheets also can be used to give lists a color, change the font, alter the line spacing, and so on. The list elements included in the HTML 4 standard are:

- OL   ordered (numbered) list
- UL   unordered (bulleted or simple) list
- LI   (list item)
- DL   (definition list)
- DT   (definition term)
- DD   (definition itself)

Stop press –
COMPACT goes out
COMPACT is now
deprecated – following
discussions between
engineers during late
Spring '97: it is now no
longer part of HTML 4.

The OL element specifies a numbered list. OL attributes are TYPE, START and COMPACT, and also the global ID, LANG, CLASS and DIR. The START element is used to initialize the sequence number, whereas TYPE specifies the numbering system. COMPACT specifies a condensed list layout, to take up less space on the screen. Each list item in a numbered list is specified with LI and this can take a VALUE attribute to set its number explicitly. There is no facility to carry through a numbering sequence from an earlier list or of skipping missing values in an intelligent way. To do this, you need to use explicit numbering with VALUE.

UL marks up unordered (simple bulleted) lists. Attributes are TYPE, this time to set the bullet type on all list items, and COMPACT which has the same effect as explained above. The global attributes ID, LANG, CLASS and DIR apply also to UL.

LI takes the attribute TYPE, also ID, LANG, CLASS and DIR. The TYPE attribute can be used to set the bullet type on individual list items.

The DL element defines a Definition List and can contain any number of DT-DD pairs, each couplet marking up a term to define and its corresponding definition. DD elements can hold block-level elements (excluding headings H1 to H6 and ADDRESS elements). The DL element has the COMPACT attribute and also the global attributes ID, LANG, CLASS and DIR.

LI, DT and DD do not need end tags; OL, UL and DL must have start and end tags.

6.1 Introduction

This chapter is devoted to the subject of marking up lists in HTML. Lists of shopping items, lists of birds seen out of kitchen windows, product lists and numbered instruction lists, lists for glossaries and lists of hypertext links. All these and more can be accomplished simply in HTML 4.

There are three kinds of lists involved:

1. Bulleted lists, for example:

```
<UL>
    <LI>a bullet point
    <LI>next bullet point
</UL>
```

which might be rendered:

- a bullet point
- next bullet point

2.   Numbered lists, for example:

```
<OL>
    <LI>first item
    <LI>next item
</OL>
```

which might be rendered:

1. First item
2. Next item

3.   Definition lists, which you see in glossaries, with each entry having a word or phrase on the left and a definition of that phrase on the right.

```
<DL>
<DT>Harebell<DD> Delicate violet blue flower shaped as a small bell
<DT>Bluebell <DD> Wild hyacinth found carpeting woods in spring
</DL>
```

which might be rendered:

Harebell   Delicate violet blue flower shaped as a small bell
Bluebell   Wild hyacinth found carpeting woods in spring

6.2 Bulleted lists

The UL element (which stands for 'Unordered Lists') creates a list with bullets. It is worth noting that you *cannot* switch off the bullets: there is no way of getting rid of them. Although HTML architects certainly have suggested that lists without bullets should be possible with UL, browser vendors show an unfortunate reluctance in this area.

One way to get around this problem is to use style sheets. The **list-style** property explained in Chapter 9 indeed allows for lists plain and simple, or with all kinds of bullets to your fancy.

When you insert a UL element, essentially you say to the browser: 'I want a list with bullets.' The UL element alone, however, does not say anything about individual list items. These are created with LI elements, any number of which may be included.

End tags
The UL element always needs a start and end tag. The LI element does not need one.

The global attributes associated with lists are ID, Chapter 7; LANG, Chapter 17; and CLASS and STYLE, Chapter 9.

The UL element meanwhile has two attributes: **TYPE** and **COMPACT**.

- The **TYPE** attribute tells the browser which sort of bullet to use; it can take the values disc, circle, and square.

- **COMPACT** is used to indicate that the list should be displayed in a more compact form on the screen.

Since an LI element can contain other elements, there is no reason why you cannot insert bold mark-up in a list item, anchor element or image. Arranging hypertext links as list items is common practice.

Creating a simple bulleted list

Here is a simple bulleted list:

```
<UL><B>Spices</B>
    <LI>Aniseed
    <LI>Bay
    <LI>Cardamom
</UL>
```

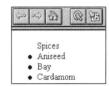

Specifying a bullet type

Values for bullet types
HTML 4 includes values for TYPE as:
- Disc
- Square
- Circle

Design your own bullets
If you want to instead insert your own customized bullet, then you can do so by using style sheets. Wonderful bullets of your own design can be inserted by using a property called **list-style-image**, explained in Chapter 9 on Style Sheets. This property takes as its value a URL, and with it you can specify the location of the (.gif) image to use for the bullet.

A limited range of bullet types – for example, squares, circles and spheroid discs can be specified within HTML:

```
<UL TYPE=square>
    <LI>cube
    <LI TYPE=disc>spheroid
</UL>
```

Changing the bullet type part way through a list

You can change the bullet type part way through a list. This is easily done by using the **TYPE** attribute for the item in question, as in the example above. If you want each and every list item to have the same kind of bullet, then you only need to include the **TYPE** attribute once in the UL element heading up the list.

Keeping lists compact

The **COMPACT** attribute advises browsers to display the list in a condensed style so that it takes up less space on the screen.

6.3 Numbered lists

The OL element (OL stands for Ordered List and is a programming term) creates a numbered list. A numbered list consists of one or more items, each of which needs to be marked up as an individual LI element. The browser automatically numbers these in sequence.

A numbered list usually starts with '1'. The **START** attribute can be used to specify an alternative start number, if required, so that the list can begin at, let us say, 5.

The default numbering style is 1, 2, 3, and so on; however, you may change this if you desire something fancier. For example, you may choose letters of roman numerals, or you may choose letters of the alphabet. You can, of course, select one style in one particular list and then select another style in another list, even within the same document. You might want, for example:

1	Cheese
2	Bread
3	Milk
A	Apple
B	Orange
C	Lemon
i,	Bullfinch
ii,	Greenfinch
iii,	Chaffinch

to be in the same document, which is certainly possible. You can also *nest* numbered lists such as you find in technical operating manuals. The result may look something like this:

1	Selecting a suitable position
2	Planting your Hucklebuckle tree
2.1	Digging a hole
2.2	Adding the compost
2.2.1	Watering

and so on. Note, though, that the treatment of lists with a second or third level of numbering is browser-specific. If you want complete control over the precise rendering of lists, a style sheet may well be the solution.

Here is an example of a nested numbered list and an idea of how it might be rendered on the screen:

```
<OL><B>Library Organization</B>
   <LI>Aeronautics
   <LI>Agriculture
      <OL>--- a nested list
         <LI>Agrobotany --- might appear as 2.1 or 2:a in some browsers
         <LI>Agroeconomics --- might appear as 2.2 or 2:b, etc.
         <LI>Agronomy
      </OL>
   <LI>Astronomy
</OL>
```

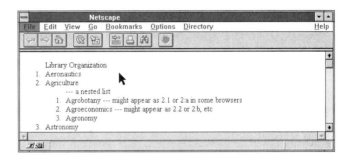

The numbering style

HTML 4 allows you to specify a numbering style for an ordered list by using the **TYPE** attribute. Notice, incidentally, that this very same attribute is also used in conjunction with bulleted lists. However, with unordered lists, the effect is that it alters the type of bullet and not the number of bullets for each list item. In the context of ordered lists, the **TYPE** attribute can take values as shown below:

Value	Description	Effect
1	Arabic numerals (default)	1, 2, 3
A	CAPITAL LETTERS	A, B, C
a	small letters	a, b, c
I	LARGE ROMAN NUMERALS	I, II, III, IV, V
i	small roman numerals	i, ii, iii, iv, v

Here is a simple example of a numbered list that starts at 5 and uses small roman numerals:

```
<OL TYPE=i START=5>
   <LI>fifth column
   <LI>sixth sense
   <LI>seventh seal
   <LI>eighth army
</OL>
```

v	fifth column
vi	sixth sense
vii	seventh seal
viii	eighth army

Changing the numbering sequence

By default, ordered lists begin at 1 (which may be shown as i, I, a, A, or 1 depending on the style in force), and increase from there. You can start the numbering at a different number by using the **START** attribute like this:

```
OL START=3
OL START=2
```

This sets the numbering of LI elements to start at 3 and 2, respectively. You can also interrupt the sequence within an ordered list, by modifying individual LI tags. Simply use the **VALUE** attributes to set the numerical values at the number you select. For example:

```
<OL START=3>
    <LI>Three, three, the rivals
    <LI>Four for the gospel-makers
    <LI VALUE=7>Seven for the symbols at your door
</OL>
```

This is rendered (depending on the browser's configuration) as:

```
3    Three, three, the rivals
4    Four for the gospel-makers
7    Seven for the symbols at your door
```

You could have written <LI VALUE=3> for the first item, but the **START** attribute is clearly preferable.

6.4 Definition lists

Definition lists are used to create glossaries or other lists with a heading for each entry. The definition list is defined by the DL element. Within the <DL> and </DL> tags are couplets of DT and DD elements which mark up:

- the term to be defined (given in the DT or 'definition terms' text)

- the definition itself (given as DD or 'definition list definition' text)

This is the structure of a definition list:

Definition lists
The idea of the definition list extends readily to explanation: you can use DL to show off goods on sale, to explain how things work, or to detail items mentioned in a news bulletin. Another use of DL is to set up dialogues, with each DT naming a speaker, and each DD containing a speech. An example is given in Appendix A.

```
<DL>
    <DT>Term
    <DD>Definition of Term
    ...
</DL>
```

Definition lists must be contained within <DL>...</DL>, but within this there is no need to use the closing tags </DT> and </DD>, as the definitions are satisfactorily bounded by the next item and by the closing </DL> tag. We suggest that you never use </DT> and </DD> at all.

You can use a list containing only DL and DT, creating the effect of a plain indented list. (A better solution is to specify an indented left margin in a style sheet.) Here is a simple definition list:

```
<DL><B>Some Famous Netizens</B>
    <DT>Dweeb<DD>Young excitable person,
        Who may mature into a <EM>Nerd</EM> or <EM>Geek</EM>
    <DT>Cracker<DD>Hacker on the Internet
    <DT>Nerd<DD>Male so into the Net that he forgets wife's birthday
</DL>
```

This is rendered (depending on the browser's configuration) as:

> ***Some Famous Netizens***
> Dweeb
>   Young excitable person, who may mature into a *Nerd* or *Geek*
> Cracker
>   Hacker on the Internet
> Nerd
>   Male so into the Net that he forgets wife's birthday

You can see that bold and emphasized text can be used in definition list terms which is allowed because DT, like LI, can contain a variety of other mark-up. You can place hypertext links and even images in a DT element.

Making definition lists more compact

You can use the attribute **COMPACT** with DL as with other kinds of list. It instructs browsers to attempt to save screen space by packing terms and definitions more tightly than usual. We cannot especially recommend you to use <DL COMPACT>, as its effect is bound to vary between browsers; and in any case, the definition format is not very suitable for squashing up.

The example illustrated here shows what Netscape does with <DL COMPACT> – instead of starting each DD on a new line, it is just tabbed a short distance on the same line as the DT term. This treatment, although correct and typical of what you can expect HTML browsers to do, is not especially readable. Some browsers may typeset the `DT` text differently from the `DD`, for example using boldface.

```
<DL COMPACT>
    <B>Shortlist</B>
    <DT>short<DD>small is beautiful
    <DT>sweet<DD>as the honeycomb
</DL>
```

This is rendered something like this:

Other browsers may use different fonts for `DT` and `DD`.

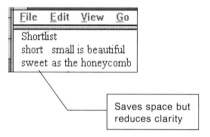

7
HYPERTEXT LINKS

Included in this chapter is information on:

- How hypertext links work
- Creating hypertext links to files elsewhere on the Internet
- Creating hypertext links to specific points in a document using **NAME** and **ID**
- Using URLs: basic and more technical information on their format
- Using the **TITLE**, **REV** and **REL** attributes

Summary

Hypertext links in HTML are accomplished by means of the familiar A (anchor) element. This now has a number of attributes as well as the global attributes: ID, CLASS, STYLE, LANG and DIR. Anchor elements cannot be nested (you cannot have an anchor element in another anchor element). They always need a start and end tag.

Attributes for A (the anchor element) are as follows:

- NAME – This allows you to associate a unique string with the link so that it can be targeted in the future by other hypertext jumps.

- HREF – This specifies a file by means of its URL. This is generally another HTML document.

- REL – This enables you to specify relationships to other resources. If several documents form part of a chapter, for example, then REL, can be used to indicate this relationship to be used in printing the collection of documents in a logical way.

- REV – This defines a reverse relationship. REV=made is sometimes used to identify the document author, either the author's email address with a mailto URL, or a link to the author's home page.

- TITLE – This can be used by the browser to create a pop-up box on the screen, giving some idea of where the hypertext link leads.

- AccessKey – This is a single character used as a shortcut to activate or give focus to the associated element (see Chapter 11 on Forms).

- SHAPE – This is to use with OBJECT (see Chapter 15 on OBJECT).

- COORDS – This is to use with OBJECT SHAPES (see Chapter 15 on OBJECT).

- TABINDEX – This indicates the position in tabbing order (see Chapter 11 on Forms).

- onClick – This is used in scripting (see Chapter 16 on Scripting).

- onMouseOver – This is used in scripting (see Chapter 16 on Scripting).

7.1 Introduction

One of the most important aspects of HTML is that it allows you to construct hypertext links between documents. The basic concept of cross-referencing information is centuries old, even predating the printing press. Indeed, in this sense, hypertext links have been around for a long time. Computer technology has now made it possible for readers to follow the links effortlessly, literally at the click of a button.

Hypertext links are what make the Web more than a collection of independent files. The ability to simply click on your mouse to a hypertext link to retrieve a file on the Web, on a different computer, in a different company, a different country – or, perhaps, even somewhere on your own machine – is what makes the Web so successful. It has altered the direction of several industries: software and computing; telecommunications, cable

TV and publishing; and now, the banking and financial industries, and credit card associations are struggling to understand the impact of the Web, thanks to the invention of global hypertext links.

Advice to beginners

Even if you plan to write only simple hypertext links, you will need a basic knowledge of the following:

- The use of filenames and directories/folders to organize files on disk. You need to know about these concepts because hypertext links reference information by naming the file and directory in which the information is found.

- The design principles for putting together a series of linked Web pages. Read Chapter 17, which not only gives you some advice on this subject, but also shows examples of how other people have tackled the problem.

7.2 Simple examples of hypertext links

Example 1: Tourist information online

We start our explanation of hypertext links on the Web with a very simple example. This partly consists of a fictitious, online Tourist Information leaflet about Boston. The idea is very simple: we want readers to be able to click on the words 'Boston Common' where they can jump to more information about Boston. This is how it is done: There are two files, which, for the sake of simplicity, are on the same computer and in the same directory. These are the following: a plain text file, 'boston.html', which contains general information on Boston marked up with HTML tags, and a second file called 'common.html', that contains information about the Boston Common. Here they are shown below:

boston.html

```
<P> If you are visiting Boston, you will no doubt want to come and see
the famous <A HREF="common.html"> Boston Common</A>, which is the oldest
park in the United States.
```

common.html

```
<P>Boston Common was purchased in 1634 to be used as grazing land for
cattle, goats and sheep. It lies near the fashionable area of Beacon Hill
and displays fine summer flowers. Not far from the Charles River, it is
centrally placed.
```

Stylistically, browsers render HTML code in different ways, so there are no hard and fast rules about how this code would appear to the user on the screen. The most common way for showing hypertext links is underlined, so this is how we have depicted the links in our own rendering below:

> If you are visiting Boston, you will no doubt want to come and see the famous Boston Common, which is the oldest park in the United States.

When you click on *Boston Common*, you see the file 'common.html' displayed thus:

> The Boston Common was purchased in 1634 to be used as grazing land for cattle, goats and sheep. It lies near the fashionable area of Beacon Hill and displays fine summer flowers. Not far from the Charles River, it is centrally placed.

The mark-up of the hypertext link is as follows:

```
<A HREF="common.html">Boston Common</A>
```

- The <A> tag is the anchor element start tag; </A> is the corresponding end tag. These tags are used to define a hypertext link.
- **HREF** is an attribute of the anchor element. The value it takes is the destination of the link, in this case the file 'common.html'.
- Boston Common is the *label* of the link: the words that will appear as a clickable hotword on the screen when the mark-up is displayed.

Example 2: Link to the *New York Times*

In Example 1, we chose to link to a file in the same directory and on the same computer, and such links certainly are not difficult to construct. However, it is more likely that you want to establish a link to a computer somewhere else on the Internet, which is inevitably more complicated. This is because you need to include in the value of the **HREF** attribute, information about its exact location on the many, many computers connected to the Internet.

In Example 2, we construct an imaginary link, which will extend from the current document you are writing to another file on the Web, the home page of the *New York Times*:

```
<P>My favorite newspaper is the <A HREF="http://www.nytimes.com/">New
York Times</A>.
```

which most browsers will render as follows:

> My favorite newspaper is the New York
> Times.

The anchor element is used again, and you will identify three parts to it:

- The **label** for the link. In this case, the label of the link is the *New York Times*. Note that the browser has rendered the link on the screen as underlined text.

- The **HREF** attribute to indicate the target of the link.

- The value for the **HREF** attribute. This long sequence of characters that starts with 'http:' is the URL, the Uniform Resource Locator. This tells the computer from which machine on the Internet the file should be retrieved, and even the directory in which it is contained. The URL is a kind of global network address and is explained in Chapter 1. If you are not familiar with URLs, you should now refer to Chapter 1.

More about URLs

A beginner's guide to URLs is given in Chapter 1; our aim here is to give you a little more information about them. Look at some examples of URLs:

```
http://www.lcs.mit.edu/
```

The Laboratory for Computer Science at MIT in Cambridge, Massachusetts.

```
http://www.hp.com/
```

Access HP, the home page for the Hewlett-Packard Company.

```
http://www.bath.ac.uk/
```

The University of Bath, in the United Kingdom.

```
http://www.sunday-times.co.uk/
```

The Sunday Times edition of the *The Times* newspaper of London, in the United Kingdom.

All these examples use HTTP, the HyperText Transfer Protocol, for retrieval and this explains the 'http:' prefix at the start of the URL. The part following the '//' is the host name for the computer that acts as the server for this URL. It is common for Web servers to have host names that start with 'www' although this is by no means universal. The last part of the host name gives you a clue as to what type of organization maintains the server. In the US, URLs for universities end in '.edu', whereas URLs for companies end in '.com'. Non-profit organizations typically use '.org'. Outside the US, it is common to see an abbreviation for the country name; for example you would use '.ca' for Canada, '.it' for Italy and '.uk' for the United Kingdom. Multinational corporations typically use the '.com' suffix because typically they are located in several countries. Country codes and suffixes are detailed in the appendices. Occasionally, you will see URLs for other kinds of protocols. For example:

```
ftp://ftp.netscape.com/
```

This is the FTP server for the Netscape Communications Company. The File Transfer Protocol (FTP), as explained in Chapter 1, is often used for computer software, such as free versions of Web browsers. FTP servers tend to have host names starting with 'ftp.'

Example 3: A Web page for a Cat Club

This third example again uses URLs. This time, the URLs are more specific and home-in on specific files found in particular directories of named machines on the Internet. The example also serves to illustrate how to construct a series of bulleted hypertext links as a list, a most popular method of presenting alternative paths for users. The elements used in our example are UL for 'unordered list' and LI for 'list item'. The element UL has the effect of telling the browser to insert a bullet automatically in front of each list item; H2 is a second-level heading; A is, of course, the anchor element.

This is the effect we want:

> **The Kenton and Preston Road Cat Fanciers Club**
> This Web page gives information on forthcoming events in August and September including shows, talks and meetings. Click on any item from the list below for information.
> - Dates for the next months
> - Cat shows in August and September
> - Entering your cat
> - Parking at cat shows
> - Maps of locations and useful phone numbers

Here is the HTML to do the job:

```
<H2>The Kenton and Preston Road Cat Fanciers Club</H2>
<P>This Web page gives information on forthcoming events in August and
September including shows, talks and meetings. Click on any item from the
list below for information.
```

```
<UL>
<LI><A HREF="http://kitten.rs.kenton.edu/cats/meet.html">Dates for the
next months</A>
<LI><A HREF="http://kitten.rs.kenton.edu/cats/shows.html">Cat shows in
August and September</A>
<LI><A HREF="http://kitten.rs.kenton.edu/cats/entering.html">Entering
your cat</A>
<LI><A HREF="http://kitten.rs.kenton.edu/kitten/parking.html">Parking at
cat shows</A>
<LI><A HREF="http://kitten.rs.kenton.edu/kitten/maps.html">Maps of
locations and useful phone numbers</A>
</UL>
```

Careful with quotes!
The value for `HREF` includes the characters '//', also '/' and ':'. The inclusion of these characters, and indeed any other characters that are not one of the following: letters, digits, periods (full stops to UK readers) or hyphens, necessitates the use of quotes around the attribute value.

Note straightaway the use of URLs in the hypertext links. For example:

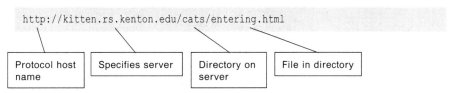

The author has placed the links in list elements, which is quite legitimate. You can equally place them in headings, credits, captions, table cells, and so on. Hypertext links can in fact be included in most elements (but not in math equations). They can be inserted within character emphasis elements and can include character emphasis themselves. Thus, a hypertext link which has been italicized is shown below:

```
<LI><A HREF="http://kitten.rs.kenton.edu/cats/meet.html">
<I>Dates for the next months</I></A>
```

This will appear shown accordingly on your screen. By and large, the principle behind HTML is to impose as few restrictions as possible on authors. This is done deliberately so that it is easy to translate documents generated by word processing packages into HTML. Note, however, that the hypertext links cannot themselves contain headings, lists, paragraphs or other block elements.

Relative URLs

HTTP and FTP support a more concise form of URLs in which the network address is expressed relative to the URL for the current document. This is particularly useful when you want to link to another file in the same directory or folder as the current document; it allows you to abbreviate the URL to just the filename of the target file. You do not have to write the full URL every time.

For instance, suppose there are two files: 'overview.html' and 'products.html' in the same directory. If you want to make a link from 'overview.html' to 'products.html', there is no need to spell out the complete URL for the file you want to link to: this can be inferred from the context.

The examples below illustrate this point. Below is a directory tree. The files contain information about cats and dogs presented as two sub-directories of Animals: this is called, quite simply, Dogs and Cats. Imagine you are writing about the dog, Treacle, in a file called 'treacle.html' (on the diagram) and want to link to his photo in 'pict1.gif' (also on the diagram). The link need not include the whole long URL for that file, but rather just specify where, *relative* to 'treacle.html', 'pict1.gif' is found. In the hypertext link in 'treacle.html', all you need to write is:

```
HREF="/DogPhotos/pict1.gif"
```

which reads: *go down a directory into DogPhotos, and then to pict1.gif.*

From 'treacle.html' to a photo of a cat:

```
HREF="../Cats/CatPhotos/pict2.gif"
```

which is: *go up to the parent directory, then into Cats, then into CatPhotos and finally into pict2.gif.*

To reference a dog photo, 'treacle.gif' from a file 'abbie.html' in Cats you would use:

```
HREF="../Dogs/DogPhotos/treacle.gif"
```

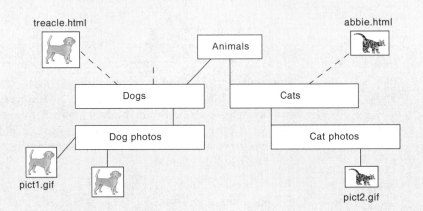

You can see that two dots '..' are used to mean 'the parent directory' and a slash '/' is used to mean 'the child directory'. This is UNIX notation, and a basic guide to UNIX will explain more. Note that DOS uses a backslash ('\') instead of a slash ('/'). This may be confusing, but that is the computer industry for you.

URLs use the UNIX convention for directories and paths

The rule is that the UNIX '/' is used to separate directory levels, regardless of whether or not the server is a UNIX box, a DOS or Windows PC, or a Macintosh. This means that you have to translate the DOS and Macintosh conventions to the UNIX slash when you want to write a file path as a URL. On DOS, this means that backslash ('\') becomes a slash ('/'), whereas, on the Macintosh, colon (':') becomes a slash ('/'). This sleight-of-hand is required so that browsers can always apply standard rules for interpreting relative URLs.

You also are not allowed spaces in filenames.

Macintosh users are in a pickle (as we British say) over filenames. Macintosh filenames often include spaces, which are not allowed in URLs. The trick is to replace them by the code '%20'; for example, the filename for this chapter on our Macintosh, 'Chapter 7 Hypertext links', is written as a URL shown below:

```
Chapter%207%20Hypertext%20links
```

Windows 95 also supports long filenames with spaces in them. The same trick applies as for the Macintosh: you must replace each space character by the code '%20'.

7.3 Links to a specific point in a document: NAME and ID

HTML 4 includes two attributes called **NAME** and **ID**, which can be associated with most elements. These attributes allow you to make hypertext leaps to *specific places* in documents, as opposed to the start of a file. When you activate an ordinary hypertext link, the new document is fetched and displayed, starting at the top: you are presented with the first 'page' of the document. **NAME** and **ID** allow the reader to travel to a particular point, say, halfway through the document, to a particular paragraph, heading or other element. The **NAME** attribute is older – it was one of the early features of HTML. The **ID** attribute comes out of the HTML 3.0 specification. It is recommended that you use **ID** simply because it is easier to incorporate into documents. On the other hand, not all browsers have implemented **ID** yet. Certainly, Microsoft Internet Explorer supports it, and Netscape Navigator is likely to do so in the near future. The choice is yours!

An example of the NAME attribute

Back when hypertext was in the early days of construction, the idea of jumping to specific places in files was already addressed. Tim Berners-Lee decided to use a **NAME** attribute for this purpose, and it is still in use today. We will show you how **NAME** works.

Take the following example: imagine a Web page on Garden Birds. A hypertext link saying, 'More on Finches' is shown ready to be clicked. You click on the link and behold, a new document appears displayed precisely at the point where Finches are discussed. It is ready for you to read about the delights of greenfinches, chaffinches and other European garden delights. How this is done is shown below:

In the current file, displayed:

```
<A HREF="birds.htm#Finches">More on finches</A>
```

This is a fairly straightforward hypertext link that references the file 'birds.html', but with the extra code #Finches added.

In the file you jump to:

```
<A NAME="Finches"><H2>Finches, Sparrows and Buntings</H2></A>
```

This is a long document on birds in general. Each heading in this file has been uniquely labeled in anticipation that a hypertext link will one day connect to it. Here you can see that the heading, 'Finches, Sparrows and Buntings' has the unique label Finches.

So, when you click on the hypertext link More on Finches in the original file, off goes the browser, 'Ah, yes, indeed, I need to display "birds.htm" and go straight to the part labeled with the character string Finch.' This indeed it does and duly rewards you with:

Finches, Sparrows and Buntings
These are a large group of seed-eating birds that are found worldwide. Some are quite tame and cheeky, particularly the House Sparrow and the Green Finch, both of which frequent gardens. The Chaffinch has been known to appear on tables in outdoor restaurants and finish off the crumbs. It is partial to jam scones and cream.

Note: Named anchors should be named with a text string, starting with a character from the set a to z or A to Z, and should never be exclusively numeric. A value for **NAME** such as '12' is not allowed, although 'bird33' is. Values for **NAME** are also case sensitive. No spaces are allowed before the '#' character.

A fishy example

This is another simple example of the **NAME** attribute. It concerns fish. The idea is to arrange that, if the reader clicks on Fish Lures, a list of possible lures to attract the attention of the Emerald Mullet appears on the screen.
In the source file we have:

```
<H3><A NAME=lures>Fish Lures</A></H3>
<P>The Emerald Mullet is quite friendly and will come and investigate any
bait within minutes. Observe and marvel but do not attempt to catch the
fish, for this mullet is both poisonous and very partial to toes.
```

In the target file we have:

```
<LI><A HREF="#lures">Minced meat, lamb chops, fish fingers, corned beef.
Hamburgers and hot dogs are <EM>not</EM> taken.</A>
```

The '#' character following a URL precedes the fragment identifier. For an external link, in other words, a link to a different file, you might have:

```
<LI><A HREF="../fishing/fish.html#lures">minced meat, lamb chops, fish
fingers</A>
```

ID **as a better alternative to** NAME

NAME is rather cumbersome to use; the way you need to insert an anchor element in the destination file is rather laborious. HTML needs a simpler way to specify headings, paragraphs, list items and so on as candidate destinations for hypertext links.
HTML 4 allows you to give almost any element an **ID**. Once you have done this, it is a matter of simply specifying that **ID** as part of a hypertext link and the browser will know where it should jump. You do not have to place an anchor element in the destination file.

ID **for jumping to files on other servers**

Can you jump to an **ID** from a file on a different server? You can. The URL notation used in specifying the destination of hypertext links allows for names of documents, their filenames and the server name as well as the # symbol to denote an **ID**. This means you can potentially jump to a particular paragraph in a document held on quite a different server, or a heading of a scientific paper that is held on a computer one thousand miles across the Web.

An example of the ID attribute

In this example, the reader sees a strange word highlighted and then thankfully realizes that this is defined in the online glossary. He or she clicks on it immediately to see the file containing the glossary itself displayed just at the right point. This trick is accomplished by first giving each entry in the glossary a unique **ID**, for example:

```
<P ID=rumple> A rumple is the fold of fur which many rabbits have under
their chins. Well-fed rabbits almost invariably have large rumples.
```

Then, in the text of the document:

```
<P>The rabbit soon settled down on the cushion with Tickles the
guinea-pig snuggling against her large white fluffy
<A HREF="glossary.html#rumple">rumple</A>
```

Clicking on the word 'rumple' in the text of the document takes you straight to the glossary definition of that word.

You could equally access the glossary files on distant servers – it is just a matter of including a URL together with a reference to the **ID**:

```
<A HREF="http://www.bump.com/animals/rabbits/glossary.html#rumple">
```

ID is also useful for scripting and for style sheets to attach properties to a specific HTML element.

Is it a redpoll or is it a linnet?
Online bird watching shows the use of ID

We now include a bird-watching example in which you jump to different birds in an online 'book' by clicking on the names of species. A link to a point within a document is done with a *fragment identifier*, which is the technical term for a piece of HTML that singles out a unique piece of the marked-up text. The fragment identifier is a way of tagging a place in a document so that hypertext links can jump straight there on future occasions.

For this example, you need to imagine the unlikely situation in which all the material on birds is held on a single file on a server. In reality, the file would be too large to be held on a single file on one server, of course. All you want to do is ensure that readers can click on a bird name in the text to jump to another part of the file, as required. If they click on Arctic Redpoll, the section on Arctic Redpolls is immediately displayed. If they click on

Twite, the section on Twites appears. Here is the HTML 4 code to do the job:

```
<H4 ID="Twt">Twite</H4>
Adult male and female dull brown above, with dark streaking; pale buff
below, shading to white on belly. In summer, male may show an indistinct
red patch. May be confused with <A HREF="#Lin">Linnet.</A>

<H4 ID="Lin">Linnet</H4>
The Linnet is a sociable bird that is found in open farmland. Do not
confuse the Linnet with the <A HREF="#Twt">Twite</A> which has a yellow
beak, rather than the black beak of the Linnet.

<H4 ID="Redp">Redpoll</H4>
Small dark finch. Adult male and female dark above, with blackish
streaking. Small black bib; small characteristic red patch on forehead.
See also <A HREF="#Arctic">Arctic Redpoll.</A>

<H4 ID="Arctic">Arctic Redpoll</H4>
Small pale finch. Underparts often white and fluffy in appearance. Small
black bib; red patch on forehead. Breeds on arctic tundra and willow
scrub.
```

Note that each bird name consists of an H4 element with its own special **ID**. Twite has got the **ID** 'twt', Redpoll's **ID** is 'Redp' and so on. Having got your **ID**s organized, you can use them in hypertext links all over the place, as required. So, let us imagine you want to include a link to the information on Twites. All you have to do is include:

```
<A HREF="#Twt">Twite</A>
```

at the appropriate point. To include a link to the section on Redpolls you write:

```
<A HREF="#Redp">Redpoll</A>
```

The # indicates a reference within a file. In this case, the expression "#Twt" says that the reference is to an item with an **ID** of "Twt". When the link is triggered, the browser finds the item with the matching **ID** and displays the file at that point. Most elements can be given **ID**s, but the most useful ones are probably captions of tables and figures, with the idea being that you can jump to these from other documents, as necessary. When authoring a document by hand it is generally a good idea to make identifiers understandable to yourself. Be warned that identifiers are case sensitive, so sec3 and SEC3 are different. Each **ID** must be unique within a document.

Technical notes on URLs

While URLs have been very effective, they do have some notable drawbacks. They are currently limited to US ASCII, making it impractical to create URLs in languages such as Arabic and Japanese.

URLs with accented characters

You can include accented Western European characters from the Latin-1 character set, using an escape mechanism. For example:

```
http://www.intermarche.fr/r%E9clame
```

for the file réclame (special offers). The '%' character acts as an escape code and is followed by two hexadecimal digits, in this case E9, which is Latin-1 for a lower case acute e. Note that host names cannot be treated in this way, so we were unable to use an acute e for the last character of the company name: *Intermarché*.

Escape codes

Some of the more common escape codes are:

%09	the horizontal tab character
%20	the space character (ASCII 32)
%25	the % character (ASCII 37)
%26	the & character
%2B	the + character
%3F	the ? character
%40	the @ character

Including a query string in a URL

URLs may be followed by a query string. This is indicated by a '?' character, as in:

```
http://www.acme.com/searchindex?special%20offers
```

Such queries are generally handled by the server, using special programs, typically invoked by CGI (Common Gateway Interface) scripts. As a hangover from the early days, '+' signs in query strings are interpreted as space characters. So if you want to include a '+' sign in a query string you will need to escape this as '%2B'. Sometimes you will see complex queries such as:

```
http://guidep.infoseek.com/WW/NS/Titles?qt=fly+fishing&col=NN
```

This is a simple example of HTML form data encoded as a URL query string. The query appears as one or more field attribute=value pairs, separated by '&' characters. The example is for an Infoseek Guide query, with the text 'fly fishing' (qt=fly+fishing), on the database of network news articles (col=NN). Note the use of '+' for the space between fly and fishing. Luckily, it is rarely necessary to include such complex URLs in hypertext links in actual documents.

7.4 Hypertext links using clickable graphics instead of text

As explained earlier in this chapter, a hypertext link contains a label. This is, in textual links, the word or phrase that you see on the screen ready to click. In HTML, this label can be a graphic rather than just text. You click on the graphic and the link is triggered.

Simple example of a graphic which, when clicked, triggers a hypertext link

The code below shows how a clickable graphic is generated. When the cursor is moved over the image, the browser senses that it lies over a clickable image and changes shape accordingly. Clicking the mouse button now summons up the file indicated by the **HREF** attribute. Here is the code:

```
<A HREF="/bug.html"><IMG SRC="/webfiles/images/bug.gif">Find out about
Joe the beetle</A>
```

and here is the result:

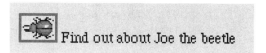

The link starts off with the anchor element start tag A, which includes the **HREF** attribute, to reference the file to be fetched when the link is triggered. In this case, this is a file called 'bug.html'. Within the confines of the anchor element is an IMG statement, which references the graphic to be displayed as the label for the link. Most browsers will draw a colored line around images to show you when they are part of a hypertext link.

Switching off the border

In the next example, you click on the cat to call up more information about her. If the image already invites you to click on it by the very nature of its appearance, the border is superfluous and gets in the way of the design.

You can switch off the border around the image by including the attribute BORDER=0. For example:

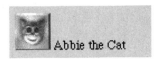

Here is the code to achieve this effect:

```
<P><A HREF="/cat.html"><IMG SRC="cat.gif" BORDER=0></A> Abbie the Cat
```

Using a small clickable graphic as the label for a link to a larger one

Next, the same idea, but with the hypertext link targeting a large graphic. This idea is commonly used on the Web for paintings and photographs, which take a long time to download. For example:

```
<A HREF=bluejay.jpeg><IMG href=bluejay.gif> Bluejay (500k Jpeg)</A>
```

You click on the small picture of the Blue Jay to see a nice, large photograph showing one greedily feeding at your bird table.

Setting the color of hypertext link labels

You can specify the color of the hypertext link labels by using the **TEXT** attribute, which belongs to the BODY element. Here are the opening chords of an HTML document for this purpose.

```
<BODY BGCOLOR="#000015" TEXT="#000020" LINK="#000050"
VLINK="#000050" ALINK="#000050"&>
```

These lines specify information as follows:

- **BGCOLOR** is the background color
- **TEXT** is the main text color; you can only have one color for this
- **LINK** is the normal color of a hypertext link prior to visiting
- **VLINK** is the color of a visited link
- **ALINK** is the color of an active or being visited link

You do not have to specify all of these; in fact, you can specify none at all. All five attributes are optional. What are these funny codes used to specify colors? Where do they come from and how do you know which one to choose? They are hexadecimal codes of RGB (Red-Green-Blue) values. Remember that graphics packages allow you to fiddle with the amount of red, green and blue components to produce the color of your choice. When you have generated a color you like, you can find out its equivalent hexadecimal value using the graphics package and then write it down. Note that the hexadecimal value will not always generate an identical color on all Web browsers, as the color codes are not 'gamma corrected'. Charts are available that tell you which code results in which color. Try searching on 'HTML' and 'color' to find one. Note that style sheets have properties to set the color and font for the labels of hypertext links – see Chapter 9.

7.5 Link semantics: REL and REV

People have been using hypertext on the Web in a fairly limited fashion, in the sense that they have concentrated on simple jumps from one place to another. There now are moves afoot to encourage people to link related documents more intelligently. In Adobe's Framemaker and other desktop publishing packages, individual documents can be combined into a larger entity such as a book; this can then be indexed, printed and accessed as a whole even though it consists of distinct parts held separately on disk. The same kind of idea may be applied to documents on the Web. Features are now in development that enable people to print out collections of related material in a seamless fashion, or to index several documents which are intrinsically related. Such links between information, which tell you something *about* the relationship between the two items, are called *semantic* links.

The two attributes **REV** and **REL** for anchor elements play a part in this idea of semantic links.

Imagine there are two documents, the source document (the one being currently read) and the destination document (at the end of a hypertext link):

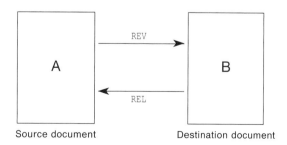

Source document   Destination document

The **REL** attribute describes the relationship that the destination document plays with respect to the source document. It might say, 'the destination document is the glossary of the current document', or 'the destination document is a section of the current chapter'.

The **REV** attribute can be used to define the reverse relationship. It could say 'the destination document is the document to which this glossary belongs', or 'the destination document is the chapter to which this section belongs'. You can see that a link from document A to document B (see diagram) with REV=relation expresses the same relationship as a link from B to A with REL=relation.

For example:

```
See also<A HREF=book.html REL="glossary">Glossary of terms</A> for more
explanation

This is chapter 4 of <A REL='book'> Guide to Famous Guinea-pigs of
England and Wales </A>
```

Following the precedent set by HTML 2.0, **REL** and **REV** can take a space-separated list of relationship values. Note that **REL** and **REV** are also used with the LINK element. **REL** and **REV** values are case sensitive.

7.6 Using the TITLE attribute

The anchor element has a **TITLE** attribute, which can be used to tell the browser something about the link before it is triggered. As the reader passes the cursor over the link, a pop-up box tells you succinctly where the link will take you. The words that appear in the pop-up box are precisely the words that you have given as the value of the **TITLE** attribute.

7.7 Where to go from here

This chapter concentrated on simple hypertext links. Here are the other related topics:

- Clickable images with hotzones (see Chapter 14 on Imagemaps).

- Use of the LINK element in HTML 4. This allows you to make references to other documents, style sheets, document author, and so on (see Chapter 13).

8
GRAPHICS
ON THE WEB

Included in this chapter is information on:

- Inserting graphics using the IMG element
- Borders, background colors and horizontal rules
- Using GIF, JPE, JPEG and PNG graphics formats
- Ensuring that your Web pages are accessible to people with disabilities

Summary

Simple graphics are inserted using the character-level IMG element. The OBJECT element, meanwhile, should be used to insert other media into the document (see Chapter 15). This can also be used for constructing image maps. The two graphics formats widely supported are GIF and JPEG. PNG will increasingly be supported.

Captions for images referenced with IMG are not in the HTML 4 specification, even though they were suggested in the HTML 3 proposal. Unfortunately, major browser vendors refused to implement captions, probably in their rush to get products out the door. HTML authors must therefore improvise on this front.

The following IMG element attributes are in the HTML 4 specification:

- **SRC** – A URL giving the address of the image – it is obligatory – you must include the source of the image with IMG.

- **ALT** – A string of text describing the image for the purpose of those unable to display graphics on their screen, or for the print-impaired who rely on a piece of software to read what is on the screen.

- **ALIGN** – Top, middle, bottom, left and right. These describe the positioning of the image relative to the current baseline. The default is bottom.

- **HEIGHT** and **WIDTH** – Numerical values are given to these attributes and are used to indicate the height and width of the image in pixels.

- **BORDER** – A number used to indicate the line border width in pixels. Used only when the IMG element is used as the label of a hypertext link; use BORDER=0 to suppress the border.

- **HSPACE** – A number used to indicate the horizontal gutter; in other words, the width of white space to the immediate left and right of the image. Specified in pixels with a default value giving the equivalent of the small gutter only.

- **VSPACE** – Similar to **HSPACE** but indicating the vertical gutter (the amount of white space above and below the image).

- **USEMAP** – This attribute is for handling client-side image maps (see Chapter 14).

- **ISMAP** – The presence of this attribute indicates that the image is a clickable image map. If the reader clicks on the image, this attribute causes the cursor location to be passed to the server.

- **STYLE** – Can be used to allocate the image a style to specify such things as the space around the image (rather like **VSPACE** and **HSPACE**), and also the background on which the image is displayed and the border around the image.

- **ID** – Can be used for marking the image with a unique identifier for the purpose of making it the target of a hypertext link (see Chapter 7).

- **LANG** – Can be used to set the language for the **ALT** attribute (see Chapter 17).

- **CLASS** – For applying a style to the image (see Chapter 9).

8.1 Introduction

This chapter looks at how to use HTML to insert all kinds of graphics into your Web pages: photos, pictures, diagrams, fancy bullets, beautiful backgrounds, and so on. All of this can be done with surprising ease, even by those who are not programmers at heart. Although we do not explain in great detail how to create the graphics files themselves, we do give a summary of the main ideas involved in taking your own design and preparing it for publication.

- If you want to insert Java applets, video clips, and other multimedia objects into your document, read Chapter 15.

- For a discussion of using images with 'hotzones' see Chapter 14 on Image maps. These are the kind of images in which the user can click on different parts of the image to elicit different responses. For example, let us suppose the screen shows a map of Europe, in which you can click on a particular country to find out the information it contains. Each country will have been set up as a 'hotzone' which, when clicked on, triggers a hypertext link.

In general, pictures, photos and artwork are placed on a Web page by means of the IMG tag. The IMG tag has been part of HTML for some time; in

In the beginning there was <IMG> for putting images on the Web. Then, as animation, sound chips and other applications appeared on the Web, a plethora of new tags were born. The trouble was that different browsers implemented different tags, resulting in incompatibility. HTML 4 simply has IMG and OBJECT.

fact, this has been true since the days of the Mosaic browser. Even at its inception, IMG was the source of great debate among the HTML community. Many computer engineers consider IMG to be badly designed with not enough thought put into it.

Various alternatives have been proposed, including the FIG element in HTML 3.0, as well as proprietary tags such as DYNSRC, EMBED and LOWRES, but IMG has continued unabashed. Now, in HTML 4, authors can at last benefit from the OBJECT element, which is primarily for inserting multimedia, Java applets and other mini-applications to be loaded into documents. OBJECT can equally reference ordinary graphics and it is quite likely that it will supersede IMG in the long run.

Why does IMG invite criticism?

IMG is an *empty element*, meaning that it cannot contain any other mark-up. When a graphic is inserted by using IMG, there is no way that more than a few words of descriptive text can be displayed to users who do not have graphical interfaces, such as to the print-impaired who rely on their browser to give spoken descriptions of displayed pictures. A better-designed IMG would have included the possibility of including whole paragraphs and other text mark-up to be displayed if, and only if, the browser did not render the graphics on the screen, as in the case of a non-graphical browser.

IMG gives no opportunity for authors to suggest alternative media. For example, let us suppose you want to say, 'If the browser supports MPEG files, then play this video; if it does not, then show this high-resolution image instead.' With IMG this kind of thing is impossible and with so many new media available on the Web, is a great shortcoming.

8.2 How IMG works

This section explains how IMG works by giving a number of examples. We cover the various IMG attributes associated with layout such as **ALIGN**, **VSPACE** and **HSPACE**, **BORDER** and so on. There is also a section on **ALT**, which is an attribute designed to allow authors to insert a small caption or other text which non-graphical browsers can display in lieu of the image.

Simple example

We begin with an example of an image inserted into a document using the tag in its simplest way.

Saving images with the rest of the document
Can you save a document with images in it so that you can then print it at a later time? At the time of writing, browser vendors have not made this easy. We can only hope.

```
<P>The World Wide Web Widows object that their husbands spend so much
time on the Web that they have taken up a kind of virtual existence on
the Internet. WWWWs are constantly seeking ways of sabotaging their
husband's curious obsession. For instance, one lady encouraged the
children's pet rabbit 'Bouncer' to nip through the keyboard cable, which
it did with great enjoyment. <IMG SRC="blackwidow.gif" ALT="the Web widow
spider"> Another wife directed a small child into the room and suggested
he play a tuneless song on a school recorder only inches away from her
husband's ear. As expected, the noise forced Daddy to abandon the virtual
world of cyberspace, but not for long. Having confiscated the offending
instrument, within seconds, he was back on the computer trying to
download a program from the Web which lets you play the recorder by
simply typing in at the keyboard. 'I don't think the music teacher would
approve,' said his wife. 'She wouldn't,' said her son.
```

Here is how this code might be rendered on the screen:

The World Wide Web Widows object that their husbands spend so much time on the Web that they have taken up a kind of virtual existence on the Internet. WWWWs are constantly seeking ways of sabotaging their husband's curious obsession. For instance, one lady encouraged the children's pet rabbit 'Bouncer' to nip through the keyboard cable, which it did with great enjoyment.

Another wife directed a small child into the room and suggested he play a tuneless song on a school recorder only inches away from her husband's ear. As expected, the noise forced Daddy to abandon the virtual world of cyberspace, but not for long. Having confiscated the offending instrument, within seconds, he was back on the computer trying to download a program from the Web which lets you play the recorder by simply typing in at the keyboard. 'I don't think the music teacher would approve,' said his wife. 'She wouldn't,' said her son.

In this simple example, the picture, 'blackwidow.gif', has been introduced rather arbitrarily in the middle of the paragraph. The browser tried to display the image on the same line, but it did not fit. For this reason, the image has been pushed to the next line, which was forced apart from the previous line to make room for the current line. This treatment of this image by the browser is easily explained when you realize that IMG is a *character-level* element.

Imagine you are typing in Word or another desktop publishing package. If your paragraph is set in 10-point Helvetica and you suddenly include a character that is set in 20-point Helvetica, it will push apart the lines of text. This happens because the larger font has created additional space in the leading – the white space between lines of text. For example, see below:

A character-level element is placed on the baseline of the text just like any other character. If the element is

excessively large, then it will force apart the lines of text by adding additional leading or white space between lines of text, shown above. If you insert a character that is smaller in size than the surrounding characters, then it will not distort the text in this way.

This is what happens when you include an image with IMG. The graphic is positioned along the line with the text, and, unless the image specified is very small, it will push apart the text to accommodate it. Luckily, there are many ways by which you can control the behavior of IMG, as the next group of examples demonstrates.

The idea of inline images

If you are a beginner, some concepts and terminology may be useful. You may have heard that the images inserted into the Web using the IMG element are said to be embedded or *inline*. What this means is that the images are inserted as part of the document rather than displayed in their own separate window, as are external images.

Inline images are retrieved automatically with the document when it is downloaded across the Internet. On the other hand, *external images* are displayed using a separate viewing program the browser initiates, and which must be specifically requested by triggering a hypertext link. When you save a Web document to a file, the inline images referenced by IMG are not saved: you only get the text of the document without the images incorporated.

How does a browser lay out a page with inline images? Inline images are treated rather like a word in a paragraph. This is because the IMG element itself is a character-level element, a concept explained in Chapter 3. As a consequence of this character-level status, an image referenced by IMG may appear in the middle of a paragraph, just like a word. If you specifically want an image to stand by itself, you may need to manipulate its position by using other elements such as BR (which breaks a line so that the image starts on a fresh line), a method which we explain in this chapter.

IMG has an empty content model, which means that it cannot include any other elements within its bounds. So, you cannot include a hypertext link within IMG nor can you include lists, paragraphs or any other HTML elements. That said, you can, of course, include IMG in other bits of HTML. You can, for example, insert an IMG in a list item (unfortunately, the bullet for the list item is also drawn because there is no way to switch bullets off in a UL list) and in a table cell.

How to control the image's position relative to the text

ALIGN may be phased out
With the coming of style sheets, the ALIGN attribute becomes redundant: style sheets provide properties to do the job instead. While waiting for style sheets to be properly established in the world of the Web, ALIGN remains, however, extremely useful.

In the next sequence of examples, you see how to use HTML to position the image where you want it and to control the amount of white space around the image. The ultimate way to position a graphic is to use a table as a layout grid. This idea is discussed later in this chapter and also in the chapter on Tables (see Chapter 10). For the moment, we discuss the simple use of IMG attributes to achieve layout effects.

First of all, you can alter how the text is positioned horizontally with respect to the image. Do you want the text to line up with the image bottom, start half-way up the image, or to be aligned with the image top? You control this by using the **ALIGN** attribute, demonstrated below. Positioning an image to line up with the text in these three different ways is done with ALIGN=bottom, ALIGN=middle and ALIGN=top. HTML 4 also provides ALIGN=left and ALIGN=right which are discussed in the section on text flow.

Hi there! I am a small rodent, delighted to make your acquaintance!

Hi there! I am a small rodent, delighted to make your acquaintance!

Hi there! I am a small rodent, delighted to make your acquaintance!

In the first case, Mr Chipmunk is positioned using <IMG SRC= chipmunk.gif ALIGN=bottom>. This is why the text appears lined up with the bottom of his picture. In the second case, the text lines up with the middle of his portrait (ALIGN=middle) and finally, Mr Chipmunk is positioned so that the text lines up with the top of his image (ALIGN=top).

Forcing a line break before a picture

The <BR> tag, explained in Chapter 4 on 'Paragraphs and Headings', is useful for forcing a line break so that the image is pushed onto the next line. You insert it immediately before the IMG tag:

The traditional ways of treating ornament, and traditional forms of ornament (derived, or not, from nature) are well worth study. There was a time, and perhaps not so very long ago, when art ran too smoothly in the tracks of tradition.

 inserted here

But we have long since got out of the ruts, and our danger now is of losing sight of the roads that once led to perfect ornament -- and may do so again.

Text flow around the image

The browser will automatically flow text around an image if the **ALIGN** attribute has a value of 'left' or 'right'. You can see this in the next two examples. In the first example, the image flows to the left of the text because the image is left-aligned; in the second case the image is right-aligned. The text flows automatically around an IMG element specified as left- or right-aligned: you have to do nothing.

… his organic yet electrifying style captures that sense of internal bewilderment and excitement which so characterize his early works and is still vivid today in these unique pieces. The unique  combination of strength of color matches with beauty of line to give a sense of the unexpected, of the intimate and of the musical. On show now at the Roxborough Gallery, we recommend that you visit 'Jam for Tea' before the exhibition finishes at the end of the month.

… his organic yet electrifying style captures that sense of internal bewilderment and excitement which so characterize his early works and is still vivid today in these unique pieces. The unique combination of strength of color matches with beauty of line to give a sense of the unexpected, of the intimate and of the musical. On show now at the Roxborough Gallery, we recommend that  you visit 'Jam for Tea' before the exhibition finishes at the end of the month.

In the next example, we have used a special combination of the <BR> tag and the **CLEAR** attribute (a) to make a break in the paragraph and (b) to force the line immediately after the break to start only once the left margin is clear of the image. The result is that the text continues on a fresh line after the image. A similar effect can be achieved using <BR CLEAR=right>.

The traditional ways of treating ornament, and traditional forms of ornament (derived, or not, from nature) are well worth study. There was a time, and perhaps not so very long ago, when art ran too smoothly in the tracks of tradition.

```
<IMG
SRC="pict.gif"
ALIGN=right>
<BR CLEAR=right>
inserted here
```

Right-aligned image

But we have long since got out of the ruts, and our danger now is of losing sight of the roads that once led to perfect ornament -- and may do so again.

The traditional ways of treating ornament, and traditional forms of ornament (derived, or not, from nature) are well worth study. There was a time, and perhaps not so very long ago, when art ran too smoothly in the tracks of tradition.

```
<IMG
SRC="pict.gif"
ALIGN=left>
<BR CLEAR=left>
inserted here
```

Left-aligned image

But we have long since got out of the ruts, and our danger now is of losing sight of the roads that once led to perfect ornament -- and may do so again.

```
<P>The traditional ways of treating ornament, and traditional forms of
ornament (derived, or not, from nature) are well worth study. There was a
time, and perhaps not so very long ago, when art ran too smoothly in the
tracks of tradition. <IMG SRC="pict.gif" ALIGN=right> <BR CLEAR=right>
But we have long since got out of the ruts, and our danger now is of
losing sight of the roads that once led to perfect ornament -- and may do
so again. <HR>
<P>The traditional ways of treating ornament, and traditional forms of
ornament (derived, or not, from nature) are well worth study. There was a
time, and perhaps not so very long ago, when art ran too smoothly in the
tracks of tradition. <IMG SRC="pict.gif" ALIGN=left> <BR CLEAR=left> But
we have long since got out of the ruts, and our danger now is of losing
sight of the roads that once led to perfect ornament -- and may do so
again. <HR>
```

The amount of space around an image

There are two ways to control the space around an image. The first and most widely used method is by using the two IMG attributes **VSPACE** and **HSPACE**, which stand for 'vertical space' and 'horizontal space'.

Dark chocolate, luscious cherries, beautiful cream and wondrous kirsch make this cake an irresistable treat. It was, however, in the late nineteenth and early 20th centuries that there was a proliferation of this cake, which must have been at its best when the black cherries were fresh off the bough, mouth-wateringly lush and perfect for consumption. Today cream is liberally applied to the Black Forest cake and eaten in quantity in German coffee shops. In the small village of Oettershagen, near Waldbroel, it was rumored that a Schwatzwaldkuchen was eaten by a sheep grazing past a picnic table. The story runs that even the sheep was in raptures of contentment, putting her nose into the cream and bleating softly before retiring for a nap in a nearby deck chair.

Space created by VSPACE=20

Space results because of HSPACE=30

```
<P><B>Dark chocolate</B>, luscious cherries, beautiful cream and wondrous
kirsch make this cake an irresistable treat. It was, however, in the late
nineteenth and early 20th centuries that there was a proliferation of
this cake, which must have been at its best when the black cherries were
fresh off the bough, mouth-wateringly lush and perfect for consumption.
<IMG SRC="blackwid.gif" ALIGN=left WIDTH=50 HEIGHT=50 VSPACE=20
HSPACE=30> Today cream is liberally applied to the Black Forest cake and
eaten in quantity in German coffee shops. In the small village of
Oettershagen, near Waldbroel, it was rumored that a Schwatzwaldkuchen was
eaten by a sheep grazing past a picnic table. The story runs that even
the sheep was in raptures of contentment, putting her nose into the cream
and bleating softly before retiring for a nap in a nearby deck chair.
```

The designer David Siegel uses a small, blank 'gif' image padded out by using **HSPACE** and **VSPACE** to insert white space in Web pages. This clever trick can be seen in action on the Web pages of company Verso at 'www.verso.com'.

The ALT attribute to provide text as alternative to the image

The **ALT** attribute is used in HTML 4 to supply a small amount of text that is used by text-only browsers in place of images. It is always essential to include a textual explanation of an image if at all possible, except in the case of bullets and other purely decorative features. You must put **ALT** text in quotes because it constitutes an attribute value that contains white space, and any value of this kind must be entered as a quote string:

```
<IMG SRC="guinea.gif" ALT="Drawing of Sniffy guinea-pig">
```

An **ALT** text can run onto several lines, but it will be rendered very simply on the screen. You cannot place any mark-up (that is, other HTML tags) in **ALT** text.

8.3 Telling the browser how big your image is for faster loading

A clever trick by David Siegel
If you have a linear sequence of Web pages with a lot of large graphics, here is a simple trick to ensure the pictures appear quickly. What you do is to place *all* the graphics on the first page, each only one pixel big. This is done by referencing each graphic with IMG, with HEIGHT and WIDTH set to '1'. A one-pixel graphic is a pin-prick of light; it is almost invisible. When the user presses the 'next page' icon, subsequent pages appear quickly complete with graphics already down-loaded. Behind the scenes the graphics are referenced on these pages with IMG set to the proper height and width. As the images were already on page 1 they are in the browser cache and appear almost instant-aneously.

The IMG element includes the **WIDTH** and **HEIGHT** attributes for specifying the size of an image in pixels. The idea is to give the browser some warning of the picture size being downloaded. That way, it can get ready and organize the layout of the page in preparation for the big moment when the images actually appear. Remember that the **WIDTH** and **HEIGHT** attributes are part of the HTML, and so, they travel relatively quickly across the Internet. The images, however, are sent separately and larger files are often subject to delay. At least when they arrive, the page is ready and waiting for the files to slot into position.

If you do not use **WIDTH** and **HEIGHT**, the browser has to lay out the page once the images appear, which takes longer.

It is possible to use these to control the actual size of the picture on the screen, but of course, there is no saying how a very large image will look once it has been made very small – probably not quite right. One of the problems is that the colors will come out strangely. If you are using true color, then the problem is partly cured, but with only 16 colors, the smaller image looks funny.

Going the other way around, that is, using **WIDTH** and **HEIGHT** to enlarge an image, similar problems occur. You have a process called smooth the image, which becomes tricky if you have fixed-palette colors, as it involves selecting colors that are in between the existing ones.

8.4 Borders around images

Introduction

If, and only if, an image is clickable, you can specify a border for it with the **BORDER** attribute. Originally, the **BORDER** attribute was a Mosaic extension passed on to Netscape. Those with a software engineering background have been quick to point out that, had style sheets been implemented by

Netscape *when they were needed*, the **BORDER** attribute, together with a clutch of other HTML extensions, would not have been necessary.

Some examples of borders. These were obtained from the Netscape browser.

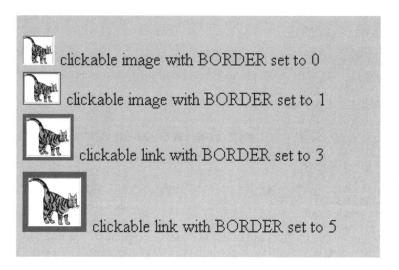

clickable image with BORDER set to 0

clickable image with BORDER set to 1

clickable link with BORDER set to 3

clickable link with BORDER set to 5

If you want to insert a border around an IMG element, you can also do so using the many Cascading Style Sheets properties. There is a choice of **border-width**, **border-style** and even **border-color**, as explained in Chapter 9. By default, images do not have borders.

Constructing simple clickable images

If you want to find out how to make an image into a simple hypertext link, read Chapter 7 on Hypertext links. The same chapter explains the idea of thumbnail images where you want to arrange that, on clicking a miniature of a large image on the Web, the full-size file is downloaded.

Implementation of BORDER in HTML 4

A border around a clickable image is inserted using the **BORDER** attribute. This takes a numerical value in pixels to indicate the width of the line to be drawn, for example BORDER=5. The number can be anything from 0 (no border) to 10 (a thick border).

How do you turn off the border? Specify BORDER=0, which you will see is very common. Borders are really a stylistic issue and better done with style sheets, which allow you to specify not only the thickness but also the rendering and color for the border (see Chapter 9).

8.5 Background textures for your Web pages

A background for your Web page is very easy to construct from a GIF or JPEG image. Backgrounds are an exciting part of design that afford great possibilities both for tasteful expression and also for indiscriminately colorful proclamations. A beautiful background of some elaborate Victorian design repeated several times across the screen may look gorgeous with emerald green text; but, can you read the information? Consider also that color-blindness is quite common.

The most common way of inserting a background for your Web pages is by using the **BACKGROUND** attribute of the BODY element. It is remarkably easy. All you do is write a statement (such as the example below)

```
BODY BACKGROUND=marble.gif
```

in the head of your document (many current Web documents make BODY BACKGROUND the first line after TITLE). As if by magic the GIF file is repeated across the screen by the browser (you do nothing) to add a subtle and complementary texture on which to superimpose your text. The smaller the image, the more repetitions.

Background textures. Many backgrounds are available free or at a small cost as Web clip art. You can download a square of your favorite background texture and incorporate it into your Web page.

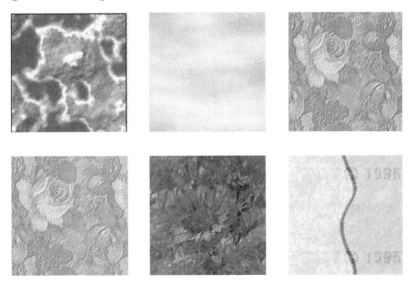

Any number of backgrounds are available over the Web ready-built. If you search on the words 'graphics' and 'backgrounds', you should come up with lots of references to these 'libraries' of GIF files. Every effect is available: marble, cumulus cloud, parchment, carpet, virtual recycled paper (most odd, that one), sandpaper, formica, cardboard, tree bark, and so on. The list of possibilities is as varied as taste allows. Make sure your backgrounds do not take too long to download. The smaller the graphic, the more repetitions there will be when the background is tiled. Small images arrive faster than larger ones – meaning that a large tile may take a long time to download. Larger images, which compress very well, are fine; flat, non-textured areas of color indeed do well on this count.

You can use flat colors to generate three-dimensional effects. For example, you might want to use three shades of grey for a bas-relief corporate logo in a pattern that repeats in wallpaper fashion. Bear in mind that the browser clips tiles when you resize the window. Make your own background effects. You can create your own background material. Scan in some paper with a nice texture and then clip it so that it is a perfect square, let us say, about an inch wide. Convert it to the appropriate GIF or JPEG format. You can also scan-in patterns to tile, but getting the edges to line up is difficult.

You can also set a simple color for the background with BODY BGCOLOR. For example:

```
BODY BGCOLOR="olive"
```

The names of colors – there are 16 in all to choose from – reflect current fashion in women's sportswear. See Appendix D for more information on how to specify color.

8.6 Placing a texture or color behind an image

The best way to do this is by using style sheets. It is possible to give a single image, say, a red background, by using the **background** property explained in Chapter 9, or to insert a special texture behind the image (also explained in that chapter).

Using the **padding** style sheet property to control the layout of an IMG image. In this case **padding** has been used to create an area of color around the image. Many other effects are possible.

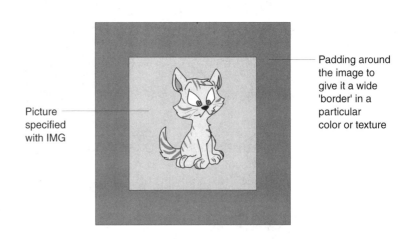

Picture specified with IMG

Padding around the image to give it a wide 'border' in a particular color or texture

If parts of the image are transparent (see the later section in this chapter on transparency), then the color or texture beneath the image will show through in those places. By using the **padding** property, you can place an image on a rectangle of color that is larger than the image itself, thus giving the image a border of color around it. The same can be done with background textures.

Style sheets also allow you to control text flow around an image, specify the margins around an image and much more. Refer to Chapter 9 for information on how to set up a style sheet to do this kind of thing.

8.7 Horizontal rules with HR

Horizontal rules across the page are accomplished with the HR element. This element has no content; that is, it cannot contain other elements, or any end tag. Netscape, in accordance with current fashion for all things three-dimensional, draws nicely sculptured rules, as shown below. Other browsers will draw horizontal rules differently. As the author, you have control over the width of the rule across the page and also over the thickness of the rule in terms of the line drawn.

The width across the page is controlled with the **WIDTH** attribute while the thickness of the line is a function of the **SIZE** attribute.

WIDTH is given as a percentage value:

```
<HR WIDTH=50%>
```

Horizontal alignment is given as either right-alignment, left-alignment or center-alignment:

```
<HR ALIGN=left>
<HR WIDTH=30% ALIGN=right>
<HR ALIGN=center>
```

Size is specified as a number in pixels, for example:

```
<HR SIZE=2>
<HR SIZE=4>
```

The default horizontal rule is always as wide as the page. With the **WIDTH** attribute, you can specify an exact width in pixels, or a relative width measured as a percentage of document width.

```
<HR NOSHADE>
```

If you really want a solid bar, the **NOSHADE** attribute lets you specify that you do not want three-dimensional shading of your horizontal rule.

Horizontal rules. The illustration shows various horizontal rules created with HR.

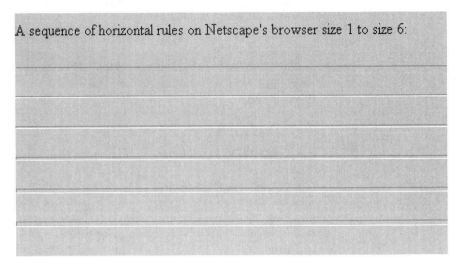

A sequence of horizontal rules on Netscape's browser size 1 to size 6:

8.8   Preparing graphics for the Web

Choosing a source of graphics

The basic choices are:

- Use an existing image. Note that the Web has a gigantic library of clip art.

- Draw a diagram using a vector-drawing program (one that concentrates on simple lines, polygons and fills).

- Paint an image using a paint package on your computer.

- Scan-in an image.

- Obtain the image using a digital camera.

Clip art for the Web

Although you may want to construct your own graphics, you may prefer to use existing icons, backgrounds and other decorative features available as clip art on the Web. Enthusiasts all over the world have carefully assembled pages full of GIF images and all you have to do is tune in, copy and paste. There seems to be every conceivable icon, every imaginable zany bullet, and every type of background design, just waiting for you to copy and paste. An enormous library of clip art is available across the Internet: it is just a matter of finding what you want. To do this, we recommend that you call up an Internet search program and then search on the keywords 'graphics' and 'icons', or perhaps on 'graphics' and 'backgrounds', or on similar combinations. All sorts of references to graphic material turn up. Delving into a list of referenced icon libraries, we found literally hundreds of icons at a single Web location, including 'hot dog', 'hula girl', 'champagne', 'valentine hearts' and 'silhouette of woman with mixing bowl'. Quite extraordinary.

To copy a graphic from a Web page, you generally click on it with the shift key held down, and, from the menu resulting, you choose 'Save As'. Choose a name and a place in which to save the graphic, and behold, it is copied onto your own hard disk. Check whether or not there are any copyright restrictions or whether any payment is involved; on the whole, there are not, because people actually want you to use their graphics. Look under the 'comments' associated with the image.

What if someone wants to use your own graphics images? You may not mind, but if you do, graphics formats such as GIF, PNG and JPEG have a facility for sticking text messages as part of the image data. Use this to include a copyright message and consider including an email address in the possibility that someone would like to reuse your image.

Using your own artwork

There is no reason why you should not use your own artwork for Web pages. You need a flatbed scanner, which is not cheap to buy; you may want to have the picture scanned-in at a service bureau in your area.

A selection of natural objects can be directly scanned-in – you do not need to stick to artwork – one of the authors used a scanner to take a 'photo' of his foot to use for a 'path to follow' icon for a Web page.

Once you have scanned-in an image, or have acquired one from some other source, the next step is to convert it to the correct image format. The formats widely used on the Web are GIF and JPEG. A new format called PNG (Portable Network Graphics – you pronounce it 'ping') will have built-in support on Internet Explorer 4.0. This format is likely to eventually take over from GIF and JPEG.

Notes on using photographs

To put a photograph on a Web page, first you have to scan it using a digital camera and then use an image-processing package to create a JPEG or GIF image on your computer. Practically all the popular packages can do this (see Chapter 18). Many cheap and effective scanners now exist; good models of flatbed scanners, such as those from Hewlett-Packard, cost a little more. Handheld scanners are inexpensive and often work remarkably well, though they cannot be as accurate as flatbeds, and the colors may be noticeably off. Digital scanners are more expensive than flatbed scanners, and currently may have very limited resolution. If you want very nice results, then use a conventional camera (35 mm or better), make a large, glossy print, and scan it in at high resolution. This produces an alarmingly large file (often several megabytes of image data).

Save the file to disk and load it into your image processor package. For simple needs, a cheap package like PaintShop Pro (also available in shareware) is quite effective. More subtle effects can be obtained with smart packages like CorelDraw or Adobe PhotoShop. The main things you need to do are the following:

- Correct the brightness and contrast so that the image works well on the screen.

- Smooth out any graininess and other artifacts of the image.

- Paint-out any defects such as dust grains.

- Crop the image to leave only the most interesting part.

- Make the image as small as visually acceptable.

- Save it as a JPEG file, applying as much compression as looks right to you.

In addition, you can, of course, have fun adding special effects, over-laying text and arrows, and so forth.

Tips for saving space (keeping image files small)

Most users still access the Web with slow analog modems, often across overloaded international links. For them, file size remains at a premium. If your images are too big, your audience will simply not load them. What can you do?

In rough order of approach, tips according to taste:

- Resize the image.

- Crop the image.

- Increase the JPEG compression.

- Simplify the background (paint it black, or smooth it, for instance).

- Use filters such as edge-enhance or erode or sharpen to make the image stronger so that it can be resized to be smaller but remain legible.

- Decrease the depth.

The GIF image format

Animated gifs
The GIF 89 image
format allows you to
add information about
an image to supplement
the image itself; the
format also allows you
to put more than one
image in a file. Netscape
have exploited these
features of GIF 89 to
make it possible to
include control
information with a
sequence of images. The
control information
allows several images to
be displayed one after
the other to produce an
animated effect.
Animated gifs have
become extremely
popluar, even displacing
Java applets written for
this purpose. Browsers
that do not understand
the code for displaying
animated gifs simply
show the first of the
sequence of images. The
color section of this
book shows two simple
examples of an
animated gif, each
constructed in a
different way.

GIF is a compact format for images or simple paintings made with computer programs. On the Web it is important to make the images as small as possible in terms of bytes so that they can be sent relatively quickly down the wire. The GIF format works by compressing areas of the same color, so a diagram such as a sales presentation flowchart squashes down to practically nothing. GIF compression is lossless, so the quality of data is preserved exactly. It can be used for photographs, but generally does a worse job than JPEG, which is generally the better format for them.

GIF comes in several flavors. You can choose between two important settings:

● Whether or not the image is to have a transparent background.

● Whether or not the image is to be interlaced.

GIF images are limited to a palette of up to 256 colors. One of these palette entries can be designated as 'transparent'. A transparent image has one color set to 'transparent' so that the background shows through. Let us suppose you decide that you have a picture of a yellow flower on a green background of leaves. If you decide to make green transparent, then any plain background on which you place the yellow flower will 'show through' to the background. You could have the yellow flower shown prettily on light blue, or grey, for example. Many graphics manipulation packages provide the facilities for making parts of pictures transparent in this way; essentially, this allows you to cut holes in a GIF image on a pixel-by-pixel basis.

Until PNG becomes widespread, GIF remains the obvious choice when you want images with transparent areas, or which are unsuitable for encoding as JPEG. One problem with GIF is that images may look significantly different from one platform to the next. This is because platforms vary in how they map red, green and blue values to the signals that are used to drive the display device. This mapping is dependent on a parameter known as the gamma value. The Macintosh partially compensates for an assumed gamma value in the image data, whereas the PC does not bother. To correct this, the browser would like to know what the gamma value is that the image file assumes. Unfortunately, this was left out of the GIF specification. C'est la vie!

How did the GIF format come about?

Graphics Interchange Format was created by CompuServe to allow users to download graphics efficiently on CompuServe's proprietary network. Later, it became the workhorse graphics format for the Web. In 1994, CompuServe announced that the LZW compression routine used in GIF infringes a Unisys patent. As a result, Unisys requires a royalty for software supporting the GIF format. This resulted in a group of graphics developers joining forces to develop a new public domain image file format. PNG or the Portable Network Graphics format will be described in a later section.

Interlaced GIFs

Interlacing may sound mysterious, but the idea is simply that rows of pixels (dots) in the image do not need to be sent to the browsers in strict sequence. Somebody had the delightfully clever idea of sending every nth row as soon as possible and then filling in the gaps. This enables images to be displayed very quickly in fuzzy form (each row is duplicated n times to fill out a rough image) and then improves as the rest of the rows arrive. If you want your audience to be able to view your images usefully while they are downloading, make sure you have the GIF's interlacing option switched on.

For faster perceived downloading, you can interlace GIF image data. This means that the image will start to appear at a low resolution and gradually get more detailed as further scan lines are received.

JPEG

JPEG (pronounced 'jay-peg') stands for the Joint Photographic Experts Group (the name of the committee that wrote the standard). JPEG is a wonderfully compact format for photographs, natural paintings and complex images to be digitized and scanned-in. It works by applying several compression recipes to squeeze images as much as you want. The miracle is achieved at the price of losing more and more of the images' original quality as you raise the compression ratio. It is worth experimenting with a high-compression ratio to see what happens: at first (at ratios of 1:15) the image seems undamaged, but as you move up past a ratio of 1:30, you start to notice a fuzziness near sharp edges, and when you reach high levels, the image deteriorates markedly.

Like GIF, JPEG comes in many flavors. The most important distinction is between good old JPG and whizzy new JPE (which is progressive JPEG). The new kind does not work on antique browsers, but may give better results on newer systems. The main thing you need to choose with JPEG is the compression ratio. A ratio of 1:30 is fine for many photographs; a ratio of 1:15 gives better quality at the price of larger files. For soft backgrounds that are meant to look a bit fuzzy, you may get away with a ratio of 1:50 or more.

JPEG has trouble with very sharp edges, which tend to come out blurred. Luckily, such edges are rare in scanned photographs. Plain black-and-white images should never be done using JPEG. GIF and PNG do much better for graphic art. JPEG simply cannot squeeze data as much for flat images with abrupt edges without introducing visible defects.

Low-cost utilities are now available for converting to the progressive format, for instance the JPEG Transmogrifier for Macintosh systems from inTouch Technologies, which is available as a standalone tool or as a PhotoShop plug-in. Another shareware tool for this is the ProJPEG PhotoShop plug-in from Aris. Free source code for JPEG is available from the Independent JPEG Group.

Portable Network Graphics format (PNG)

PNG (pronounced 'ping') is a new public domain image format created in 1995 by a group of graphics developers cooperating over the Internet. PNG is a great improvement on GIF and requires no license fees for software supporting it, unlike GIF. It is expected that GIF will fade away as more and more companies add support for PNG. As of 1996, the vast majority of new browsers will support PNG for inline images. Free source code for PNG is available from the PNG Developers Group.

PNG is a lossless compression format and faithfully preserves all pixel values, unlike JPEG. PNG has improved compression over GIF. It works much better than GIF for smoothly varying images. In addition to palette-based images, PNG supports truecolor images with up to 48 bits per pixel, and grey-scale images with up to 16 bits per pixel. This makes PNG a great choice for computer generated artwork. Unlike GIF, you can ensure your images look just as good on Windows, Macintosh systems and other platforms by including gamma values, which enable the browser to apply platform-dependent color and brightness corrections. PNG has a much faster interlacing technique, too, so users will be able to see PNG images earlier when browsing via slow connections.

Avoiding jagged edges around text and other graphics

To avoid jagged edges around text art and other graphics, designers employ a technique called anti-aliasing. This smoothes rough edges by setting boundary pixels to a mixture of the foreground and background colors. This works great just so long as someone does not change the background color. However, if the image background is transparent, then that is just what will happen. Netscape defaults to a grey background, so this is what most designers assume when they anti-alias their images. If your browser has a different background, then you will see a grey halo around the image where the boundary pixels are mixed with Netscape grey.

One solution is to set the background color using the **BGCOLOR** attribute of the BODY element. PNG offers a more effective answer, which also works correctly with background textures. For palette-based images, PNG offers the same transparency feature as GIF. You can designate one of the palette entries to make pixels with that value transparent. For true-color images, though, PNG offers a variable translucency feature. It allows you to create effects like fades, in which an image fades into the background as you move from one side of the image to the other. It works by allowing you to specify a blend factor for mixing the image with the background on a pixel-by-pixel basis. The technical guys call this an 'alpha channel'. This is highly recommended for reliable anti-aliasing as well as offering a host of new effects for soft fades and shadows.

Image conversion, color reduction and filtering, and so on

For the Macintosh: Clip2GIF is a simple shareware tool, but we like GraphicsConverter or GifConverter. DeBabelizer Lite limited edition for the Web is available free, and can be used to adjust a group of images to share a common palette, giving the browser an opportunity to show the images as the designer intended. It also allows you generate thumbnail images from full-sized images. The pay-for version handles conversion between a wide range of other formats including interlaced GIF, JPEG, progressive JPEG and PNG. The JPEG Transmogrifier is used to convert baseline JPEG images to the Progressive JPEG file format. On Windows, some useful tools are Lview Pro, PaintShopPro and HiJaak'95. UNIX users can try xv, xpaint, ImageMagik and the pbm plus collection of tools.

8.9 Thinking about the blind and visually impaired

Computers have long been able to read text files out loud, using a rather crude approach that translates groups of letters into phonemes, and then sends these as signals, via an amplifier, to a loudspeaker. This approach means that the blind or print-impaired user has little control over the document, other than to start and stop it.

HTML offers a much richer range of possibilities. Because the mark-up indicates the structure of a document, it is possible for the spoken output to indicate structures such as hyperlinks, various heading levels, list bullets, and so on.

T.V. Raman, working at Adobe Systems' Advanced Technology Group in San Jose, California, is himself blind, and has developed EMACSPEAK, a free HTML browser that exploits HTML's structure and style to generate easily understood audio cues. These cues include specially chosen audio tones and voices for different elements. For example, the listener can ask for a spoken list of headings, and at once break in and ask to hear a particular section in full. The effect is similar to what a sighted person does by skimming a table of contents and clicking on one of the items.

An EMACSPEAK session might run something like this:

Lively animated voice:	'Back, Up, Down, Next'
Deep baritone voice:	'1.1 Approach';
	'1.2 Executive Summary';
	'1.3 Acknowledgments';
	'1.4 References';
Listener:	Keystroke to interrupt and to indicate that the computer should read the section
Short tone:	'beep'
Soprano voice:	'Papers by the author'
Normal voice:	'How to Structure Documents for the Web, WWW News, pages 37–45, June 1997'
Listener:	Interrupts with a keystroke to indicate that the computer should read this bit

This very satisfactory result might seem to solve many of the problems that blind people have always faced. Unfortunately, two features of today's World Wide Web are acting to perpetuate the problems. Firstly, genuinely useful information is rather thinly spread among the sales hype and vanity publishing. This is bad enough for sighted people, and very time wasting for the blind.

Secondly, more and more pages are absolutely unusable by anyone who cannot see the attractive, colored graphics images that are comprising an increasing proportion of the Web's content. HTML offers constructs like `ALT="text"` for people who cannot view the image, but many designers simply ignore this, preferring to design entirely visual pages. Browsers such as EMACSPEAK, that depend on decoding the structure of an HTML document, will always be defeated by a tangled mix of tags for layout and tags for structure: the two should be kept separate if possible.

We have seen some absurdly complex and tricky examples of 'Web Design' including a carefully crafted simulated 'book'. We imagine that the designers of such pages would be all politeness on seeing a guide dog, and they are no doubt unaware that their behavior on the Web makes things difficult for blind readers. It is a basic point of good HTML style that all most-important pages should be accessible to all browsers.

9
INTRODUCTION TO STYLE SHEETS FOR WEB DOCUMENTS

Included in this chapter is information on:

- Associating a style sheet with a document
- Constructing a style for an HTML element using the CSS language
- Controlling the color of text and background
- Specifying the background texture for individual elements
- Altering the margins and text alignment
- Controlling white space around text and graphics in a document

Summary

At last, you can write style sheets for Web documents to control how they appear on the screen. A special style sheet language called Cascading Style Sheets (CSS) has been written for the non-programmer. With it, you can write paragraph and character styles to specify everything from font and color to margins and borders. A Web style sheet can be composed separately and then linked to documents as need be; or, you can insert the style sheet into the document head. It is also possible to write local styles using the **STYLE** attribute which, in HTML 4, is available on nearly every element.

9.1 Introduction

This chapter is an *introduction* to style sheets for Web documents using the CSS style sheet language. It tells you all about some relatively simple-to-use style sheet properties enabling you to control color and screen layout.

- If you are the sort of person who loves concise technical information, you may prefer to indulge straightaway in the *CSS Style Sheet* specification, which is freely available on the Web via www.w3.org.

- If you would like to know about some of the more tricky aspects of style sheets not covered in this chapter, there is a comprehensive book, which we recommend you purchase. This is a fairly technical description by Håkon Lie and Bert Bos, the inventors of the CSS style sheet language. Entitled *Cascading Style Sheets: Designing for the Web*, it is published by Addison-Wesley Longman Ltd, Harlow, England.

Before style sheets, an unenviable situation

Strictly speaking, HTML concentrates on the structural aspects of a document, allowing authors to mark up in a relatively simple way which parts perform which functions – whether or not they are paragraphs, headings, lists, tables, and so on. The nuances of presentation, meanwhile, are not the province of HTML and, indeed, the minutiae of layout are not supposed to be specified by using the HTML publishing language. This may come as a surprise to authors who are familiar with an **ALIGN** attribute that includes up to nine different values to specify the precise alignment of images on the page, and a **FONT** attribute to control the exact size and color of text. Know now that such features are, by and large, extras, pieces of HTML that crept in courtesy of Netscape, Microsoft and other companies that offer browsers. In 1996, we counted around 20 or so non-standard HTML elements and attributes supported by various browsers, although no single browser supported them all.

HTML style sheets to the rescue

The idea of 'cascading style sheets'
The idea is that more than one style sheet may be in operation, and 'cascade' together to give a final 'look-and-feel' to the document.

For example, the document background may be specified in one style sheet and the fonts to use specified in other, separate style sheets. There may be more than one style sheet for fonts: perhaps one for formal documents and the other for informal notices, but both would use the same standard background texture and image.

The color of text might also be specified in separate style sheets and the ultimate look of a given document would be a composite of all these mini style sheets selected on a mix-and-match basis.

Style sheets for HTML documents involve a separate and specialized language for specifying the layout of a document called *CSS*, which stands for *Cascading Style Sheet* language. The name was chosen because the inventors anticipated that more than one style sheet would 'cascade' together to give a particular layout on the screen. Potentially giving almost as much control over look-and-feel of material as would a conventional desktop publishing package, CSS style sheets relieve HTML of the burden of non-standard extensions, and free it for its proper role of structuring information.

World Wide Web Consortium members Håkon Lie and Bert Bos with contributions also from Chris Lilley, Dave Raggett and others developed CSS. Working at all hours in an office at the French government research center, INRIA (Institut National de Recherche en Informatique et en Automatique), which is pleasantly situated in Antibes in the sunny climes of the South of France, Bert and Håkon rejoiced at last in 1996 when Microsoft decided to implement CSS on their browser. Netscape soon followed suit and implemented CSS style sheets on their Netscape Communicator.

Håkon Lie

Bert Bos

Chris Lilley

Some examples of style sheets

To whet your appetite at this early stage, here are some examples of Web pages produced using CSS. Color versions of some of these examples are printed in the middle section of this book.

Keep sweet!

Do not let the milk of human kindness in your heart turn to bonny-clabber. If you do anything that is worth while, or if you are anybody, you will surely be assailed. That is your opportunity – keep sweet. If you are reviled, do not imitate your reviler and revile back; explanations never explain and vindications never vindicate. Your life must justify yourself. Keep sweet!

Everything is being attacked; and oxygen is the thing that is waging relentless war on things. Oxygen gives life, and takes it. Oxygen disintegrates all vegetation, iron, even the rocks – all excepting rock crystals. Glass and porcelain are a species of crystal, made by artificial process – time does not affect glass and porcelain – these things absorb no poisons – are antiseptic and can be easily cleaned.

Phalanstery

The word was first used by Fourier, and means literally "the home of friends". The Roycraft Phalanstery with its new addition, just completed, consists of a kitchen, scientific and modern in all of its appointments; a dining room that seats a hundred people; thirty-eight sleeping rooms; reception rooms etc., etc. That is to say that it is an INN, managed somewhat like a Swiss Monastery, simple, yet complete in all its appointments – where the traveler is made welcome. There are always a few visitors with us. Some remain simply for a meal, others stay a day, or a week, or a month. A few avail themselves of the services of our Musical Director, the Physical Instructor, or take lessons in drawing and painting.

The prices: meals, such as they are, say twenty-five cents; lodging, fifty cents. If parties of a dozen or more want accommodations, it is well to telegraph ahead to: The Bursar of The Roycrofters, East Aurora, New York.

Fancy headings can be done with style sheets

Keep sweet!

Do not let the milk of human kindness in your heart turn to bonny-clabber. If you do anything that is worth while, or if you are anybody, you will surely be assailed. That is your opportunity – keep sweet. If you are reviled, do not imitate your reviler and revile back; explanations never explain and vindications never vindicate. Your life must justify yourself. Keep sweet!

Everything is being attacked; and oxygen is the thing that is waging relentless war on things. Oxygen gives life, and takes it. Oxygen disintegrates all vegetation, iron, even the rocks – all excepting rock crystals. Glass and porcelain are a species of crystal, made by artificial process – time does not affect glass and porcelain – these things absorb no poisons – are antiseptic and can be easily cleaned.

Phalanstery

The word was first used by Fourier, and means literally "the home of friends". The Roycraft Phalanstery with its new addition, just completed, consists of a kitchen, scientific and modern in all of its appointments; a dining room that seats a hundred people; thirty-eight sleeping rooms; reception rooms etc., etc. That is to say that it is an INN, managed somewhat like a Swiss Monastery, simple, yet complete in all its appointments – where the traveler is made welcome. There are always a few visitors with us. Some remain simply for a meal, others stay a day, or a week, or a month. A few avail themselves of the services of our Musical Director, the Physical Instructor, or take lessons in drawing and painting.

Keep sweet!

Do not let the milk of human kindness in your heart turn to bonny clabber. If you do anything that is worth while, or if you are anybody, you will surely be assailed. That is your opportunity – keep sweet. If you are reviled, do not imitate your reviler and revile back; explanations never explain and vindications never vindicate. Your life must justify yourself. Keep sweet!

Everything is being attacked; and oxygen is the thing that is waging relentless war on things. Oxygen gives life, and takes it. Oxygen disintegrates all vegetation, iron, even the rocks – all excepting rock crystals. Glass and porcelain are a species of crystal, made by artificial process – time does not affect glass and porcelain – these things absorb no poisons – are antiseptic and can be easily cleaned.

Phalanstery

The word was first used by Fourier, and means literally "the home of friends". The Roycraft Phalanstery with its new addition, just completed, consists of a kitchen, scientific and modern in all of its appointments; a dining room that seats a hundred people; thirty-eight sleeping rooms; reception rooms etc., etc. That is to say that it is an INN, managed somewhat like a Swiss Monastery, simple, yet complete in all its appointments – where the traveler is made welcome. There are always a few visitors with us. Some remain simply for a meal, others stay a day, or a week, or a month. A few avail themselves of the services of our Musical Director, the Physical Instructor, or take lessons in drawing and painting.

The prices: meals, such as they are, say twenty-five cents; lodging, fifty cents. If parties of a dozen or more want accommodations, it is well to telegraph ahead to: The Bursar of The Roycrofters, East Aurora, New York.

Paragraphs can be positioned on the page with CSS

Keep sweet!

Do not let the milk of human kindness in your heart turn to bonny-clabber. If you do anything that is worth while, or if you are anybody, you will surely be assailed. That is your opportunity – keep sweet. If you are reviled, do not imitate your reviler and revile back; explanations never explain and vindications never vindicate. Your life must justify yourself. Keep sweet!

Everything is being attacked; and oxygen is the thing that is waging relentless war on things. Oxygen disintegrates all vegetation, iron, even the rocks – all excepting rock crystals. Glass and porcelain are a species of crystal, made by artificial process – time does not affect glass and porcelain – these things absorb no poisons – are antiseptic and can be easily cleaned.

Phalanstery

The word was first used by Fourier and means literally "the home of friends". The Roycraft Phalanstery with its new addition, just completed, consists of a kitchen, scientific and modern in all of its appointments; a dining room that seats a hundred people, reception rooms etc., etc. That is to say that it is an INN, managed somewhat like a Swiss Monastery, simple, yet complete in all its appointments – where the traveler is made welcome. There are always a few visitors with us. Some remain simply for a meal, others stay a day, or a week, or a month. A few avail themselves of the services of our Musical Director, the Physical Instructor, or take lessons in drawing and painting.

The prices: meals, such as they are, say twenty-five cents; lodging, fifty cents. If parties of a dozen or more want accommodations, it is well to telegraph ahead to: The Bursar of The Roycrofters, East Aurora, New York.

Color, font and text size are under style sheet control

Four layouts achieved using CSS style sheets – the text is the same in each case. The style sheet alone modifies each page.

9.2 How CSS style sheets work

If you use a computer for desktop publishing, no doubt you will be familiar with the idea of the style sheet or template. In its simplest form, a style sheet consists of a number of styles such as Normal, Indented, Heading 1, Heading 2, Heading 3, Footnote, and so on. As you type a paragraph of text, you can assign one of the available styles to it, which you select from a menu. As you assign a style to a paragraph, it takes on a number of properties that determine everything from font size to margin settings, borders and line spacing. In HTML, a similar – but not identical – idea is used.

As explained in Chapter 3, an HTML document consists of a series of paragraphs, headings, lists, tables and other elements. A style sheet used with an HTML document concentrates on these elements and, simply put, enables you to give styles to each. Thus, an element such as H1 may have a style 'Times bold, red text' or one for P 'Times 12-point, blue background and black text'. The idea is not complicated.

Typical style menu from a desktop publishing package. The CSS language allows you to devise *styles* for HTML elements.

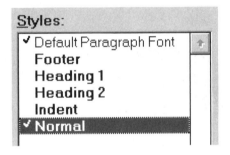

The idea of a property list to specify a style

You describe stylistic information for an HTML element by associating it with a property list. The property list as a whole describes a style for the element. It is thus similar to the familiar concept of a style as used in desktop publishing packages. Here is an example property list for an element H1.

```
H1 {font-size: 12pt; line-height: 14pt; font family: Helvetica;
font-weight: bold;}
```

You can see that the syntax is relatively straightforward. The element to which the style applies is given first and the property list follows afterwards. The property list is enclosed in curly brackets and successive properties separated by a semi-colon '; '. The properties themselves meanwhile consist of a property name and value separated by a colon ': '.

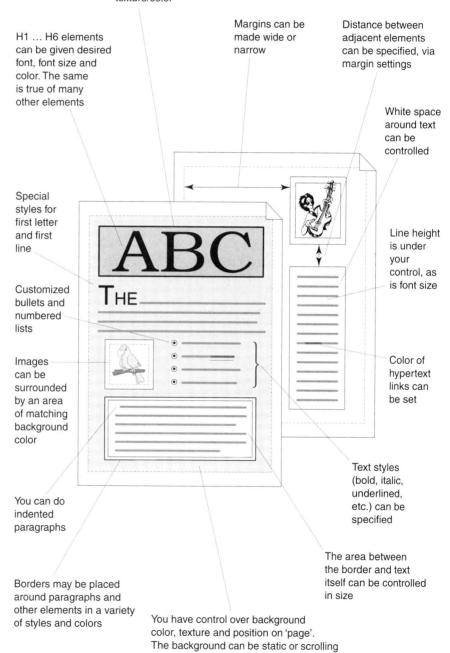

Headings, paragraphs and other elements can have own background texture/color

H1 ... H6 elements can be given desired font, font size and color. The same is true of many other elements

Margins can be made wide or narrow

Distance between adjacent elements can be specified, via margin settings

White space around text can be controlled

Special styles for first letter and first line

Line height is under your control, as is font size

Customized bullets and numbered lists

Images can be surrounded by an area of matching background color

Color of hypertext links can be set

Text styles (bold, italic, underlined, etc.) can be specified

You can do indented paragraphs

The area between the border and text itself can be controlled in size

This illustration shows you some of the aspects of layout that can be specified using CSS.

Borders may be placed around paragraphs and other elements in a variety of styles and colors

You have control over background color, texture and position on 'page'. The background can be static or scrolling

If you want to allocate a number of elements the same style, you can do so like this:

```
H1, H2, H3 { font-family: Helvetica }
```

Here all three elements are given the same property list. Commas, as you see, separate the elements to which the property list applies.

Which properties are available?

All kinds of properties are available for controlling everything from color to font, background, text position and much more (see the figure on the previous page). In this book we cover the more common and easy-to-use properties: you should consult *Cascading Style Sheets: Designing for the Web* for details of more esoteric properties and a full model of how CSS works.

9.3 Incorporating stylistic information into a document

There are four ways of incorporating stylistic information into a document:

- Placing a style sheet at the start of the HTML document

- Using a local style where necessary

- Linking a separately stored style sheet to an HTML document

- Using @import to import a style sheet

Placing a style sheet at the start of the HTML document

You can place a style sheet at the start of your HTML document by using the STYLE element (quite different from the **STYLE** *attribute*, which you will come across later). The STYLE element belongs in the document head. Easier to use than you might expect, the STYLE element is best introduced by example:

```
<TITLE>My little document with a style sheet</TITLE>
<STYLE TYPE="text/css">
P {color: black; font-family: helvetica; font-size: 12 pt}
H1 {color: green; font-family: helvetica; font-size: 20 pt}
B {color: white; font-family: helvetica; font-size" 12 pt}
</STYLE>
```

```
<BODY background=black>
<H1>Mary had a little lamb</H1>
<P>Mary had a little lamb
<P>Her fleece was <B>white</B> as snow
<P>And everywhere that Mary went the lamb was sure to go
```

You can see what happens. The browser looks at the contents of the STYLE element first and then, having digested its contents, applies stylistic rules to the document body. In our little example, H1 heading will come out in green, 20-point Helvetica type, the paragraphs of text will be green 12-point Helvetica, and the word 'white' will come out in white exactly as prescribed.

Notice that text of the document comes *after* the STYLE element. This is because the STYLE element is part of the document *head*. In general, the document head contains information *about* the document, as opposed to the text of the document itself. Note that older browsers will actually display the contents of the STYLE element – the text of the style sheet will appear on the screen 'by mistake' – but it is envisaged that gradually most browsers will hide the style sheet from view and implement its content as intended.

Implementation of CSS

You can look at the Web site http:// www.awl.com/css/ for an up-to-date list of browsers supporting CSS style sheets.

Netscape Navigator 2.0	No
Netscape Navigator 3.0	No
Netscape Communicator	No
Netscape 4.0	Implementation of core CSS 1[1]
Microsoft Internet Explorer 3.0	Partial implementation of CSS
Microsoft Internet Explorer 4.0	Full implementation of CSS 1

Spyglass has indicated that it will support CSS on its Mosaic browser, too

At the time of writing, both Netscape and Microsoft are committed to CSS.

Local styles for elements using the STYLE attribute

The section above showed you very simply how the STYLE element can be used to contain a mini style sheet for a Web document. Now we progress a bit further.

You may be familiar with the way that, in Word, Framemaker or other desktop publishing packages, the style sheet for the document may be locally overridden. Perhaps you want a particular paragraph in Helvetica 12-point type instead of the normal 10-point type, or you want to place a

---

[1] Netscape has tied its implementation strongly into its JavaScript engine. A side effect of this is that it has been hard for Netscape to implement to full CSS 1 specification.

border around a paragraph where normally none would exist. Web style sheets can also be overridden on a local basis in this manner. The trick is accomplished with the **STYLE** *attribute*.

```
<TITLE>My little document with a style sheet</TITLE>
<STYLE>
P {color: black; font-family: helvetica; font-size 12 pt}
H1 {color: green; font-family: helvetica; font-size 20 pt}
B {color: white; font-family: helvetica; font-size 12 pt}
</STYLE>
<BODY background=black>
<H1>Mary had a little lamb</H1>
<P>Mary had a little lamb
<P>Her fleece was <B>white</B> as snow
<P>And everywhere that Mary went the lamb was sure to go
<P>It followed her to school one day
<P>It made the children giggle
<P STYLE={color: red; font-size: 14pt} For every time the teacher spoke
its ears would start to <B>wiggle!</B>
```

Local style

Naming a style sheet file
A style sheet written with the CSS language should have the extension 'css'.

The **STYLE** attribute has been used here to override the normal rendering of the last paragraph. In fact, you can use the style attribute like this even if the document does not have a style sheet in the first place. Regardless of whether or not there is a STYLE element, the **STYLE** attribute can be used to allocate almost any element a style has on an ad-hoc basis, if this proves necessary. Browsers that cannot understand the **STYLE** attribute simply will render the element without the stylistic extras specified. A Netscape 2.0 browser, for example, will display the last paragraph in the usual manner without the red or the 14-point type specified.

The **STYLE** attribute is available on most elements including paragraphs, headings, tables and table cells, character mark-up, and so on.

Linking a separate external style sheet to your document

If you want to use a single style sheet for a number of documents, then why not reference it in each of the documents in question via the LINK element. An example of its use in this context might be:

A link to a style sheet

Location of style sheet

```
<LINK REL=stylesheet HREF=http://NYT.com/style TYPE="text/css"
TITLE="wonderstyle">
```

Language in which style sheet is written

LINK REL=stylesheet is a special construct used for referencing a style sheet.

The use of
REL=alternate
This allows authors to present a menu of named style sheets to readers. If the REL attribute of LINK is not used in this fashion, but a TITLE is alone supplied for a given style sheet, then that style sheet will be taken to be the default one for the document.

Use of the LINK element enables the appropriate style sheets to be retrieved in advance of, or at the same time as, the HTML document itself. Authors can use LINK elements to offer readers a choice of alternate style sheets, for example:

```
<LINK TITLE="Old" REL="alternate stylesheet" HREF="old.style"
TYPE="application/dsssl">
<LINK TITLE="New" REL="alternate stylesheet" HREF="new.style"
    TYPE="text/css">
<LINK TITLE="Wacky" REL="alternate stylesheet" HREF="wacky.style"
    TYPE="text/css">
<TITLE>Small document with style sheet</TITLE>
<H1>ACME Widgets Corp</H1>
<P>If your browser supports style sheets, try our new look in old, new
and wacky styles.
```

The HTML 4 specification of LINK includes a **TITLE** attribute, which you can see in use above. In a case in which you have a selection of different styles and each has its own URL, the **TITLE** attribute becomes very useful. What you do is make the **TITLE** a description of the style sheet ('Old style sheet', 'New style sheet', 'Wacky style sheet' and so on), with the anticipation that a menu will be drawn up by the browser for the user to choose:

| Old style sheet |
| New style sheet |
| Wacky style sheet |

The LINK element
This important part of HTML is explained fully in Chapter 12 which covers elements in the document head.

Note that the order in which alternative style sheets are listed using LINK in the mark-up does not say anything about the order of preference when it comes to their deployment.

The **TYPE** attribute can be used to specify the Internet media type and associated parameters for the linked style sheet. This enables the browser to determine if the style sheet is written in a notation that it supports. After all, although this book concentrates on CSS, other style sheet languages do exist. A whole separate brethren favor, for example, DSSSL. The **TYPE** attribute potentially lets you say, 'this style sheet is written in DSSSL,' enabling the browser to digest it accordingly.

Using @import

You can also use @import at the beginning of the document to import a style sheet from a particular location. For example:

```
@import "http://www.style.blue.css"
```

9.4 How style sheet properties interact with each other

Suppose you set the BODY of the document to 12-point, pale blue Helvetica Light on a black background. Will the entire document 'inherit' this font? The arrangement in CSS is that properties of one element are often handed down to other elements that that element contains. Thus the BODY text color and font, for example, are passed down to paragraphs. In turn, such properties will be inherited by character-level elements within those paragraphs. This means that italic and bold text will match the paragraph in which they are found.

Inheritance of properties. The diagram shows the idea of inheritance: a much-simplified explanation. Basically, style sheet properties may be inherited from one element to the next. Thus, for example, the font set for the document BODY may be passed down to its children elements and used to display these, unless, of course, they have their own overriding styles specified elsewhere.

In general, a style in the document style sheet takes precedence over a style imported from a linked style sheet. A local style overrides both.

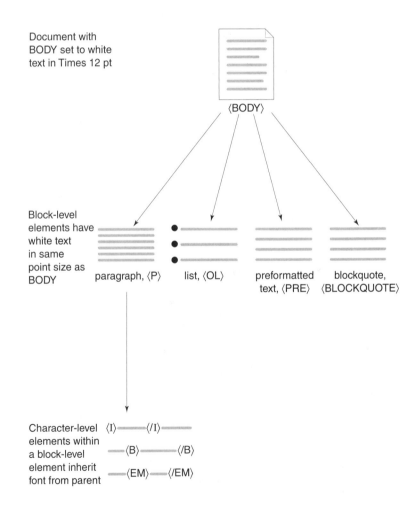

Document with BODY set to white text in Times 12 pt

⟨BODY⟩

Block-level elements have white text in same point size as BODY

paragraph, ⟨P⟩   list, ⟨OL⟩   preformatted text, ⟨PRE⟩   blockquote, ⟨BLOCKQUOTE⟩

Character-level elements within a block-level element inherit font from parent

⟨I⟩══════⟨/I⟩
══⟨B⟩══════⟨/B⟩
══⟨EM⟩══⟨/EM⟩

Expressing a property in terms of another element

CSS sometimes allows you to express the property of one element in terms of another element. For example, suppose you set the font size to 10-point type for the whole document:

```
BODY { font-size: 10pt }
```

You can then set a proportionately larger font for an individual paragraph like this:

```
P { font-size: 200% }
```

Here, line two will set the text to 20-point type, which is 200 percent of the font size of 10-point type. Were the BODY font to be set to 14-point type, this paragraph would be displayed in 28-point type. Character-level elements within a paragraph can be given a font size by the same method.

9.5   Constructing named styles for HTML elements

In previous examples, you have seen that it is possible to allocate a style to one or another HTML element. For example, you can specify that P elements should be rendered in bright purple on a green background or that H1 headings glare in 20-point type in blue Times Bold. This is all very simple, and to be frank, armed with even a relatively basic knowledge of the ideas as described so far, you should be able to produce all kinds of surprising layout effects.

That said, it is our suspicion that, once you have mastered the basics of style sheet composition, you will no doubt want to go further and graduate to the next stage. Let us then introduce you to the process of inventing your own *named styles*, a process which will bring hours of joyful fiddling to even those who are not born computer hackers.

Here are some named styles that we have invented. To use them you might insert them into a style sheet using **STYLE** as below. The names given to our styles are rendered in bold, purely for your convenience.

```
<STYLE>
.note {background:white; color:black}
.special {background:blue; color:black}
.aside {background:red; color:black}
</STYLE>
```

The three named styles are called *note*, *special* and *aside*. Note use of the dot '.' preceding each. Once included in the style sheet, styles can be applied to more or less any element you choose. You can apply a named style of this kind to almost anything, be it a paragraph, a list item, text within a table cell or any number of other elements.

Applying a named style to an element

The **CLASS** attribute is used to apply a named style to an element (the reason for this somewhat peculiar choice of attribute name will become apparent later). Here is a piece of a document to show this simple idea. The **CLASS** attribute is available on most HTML 4 elements.

Applies the named style 'special' to this paragraph

Applies the named style 'aside' to this paragraph

```
<P CLASS=special>On the subject of writing HTML, our new pony-tailed
development engineer gave us a worthy piece of advice:
<P CLASS=note>It is absolutely essential that you write HTML in a planned
and organized manner. The result should exude an elegance of design,
portray simplicity itself and should not look like a garbled piece of
computer code chewed by a stray parrot.

<P CLASS=aside>Always remember to compose Web pages so that those not
using style sheets will still see something reasonable on their
screens.
```

This produces a series of paragraphs each on a different background color:

> On the subject of writing HTML, our new pony-tailed development engineer gave us a worthy piece of advice:
> It is absolutely essential that you write HTML in a planned and organized manner. The result should exude an elegance of design, portray simplicity itself and should not look like a garbled piece of computer code chewed by a stray parrot.
> Always remember to compose Web pages so that those not using style sheets will still see something reasonable on their screens.

You can reuse these styles throughout the document as needed, applying them to all sorts of elements, and not just to paragraphs. To change the look of all the elements to which you have allocated a particular style, just alter the style definition. In a magical sweep all paragraphs with a red background can be placed on yellow – you can change the definition of the style in the style sheet and, as we say in Britain, Bob's your uncle, it's done!

Named styles for a specific type of element

In the previous section, you saw how to devise your own named styles that could be applied to a number of different HTML elements. These were in a sense *generic* styles, styles that could be applied throughout the document.

Now for a variation on this theme. Here, we demonstrate how you can invent named styles that apply to a specific type of element only. The advantage of this method is that the style sheet becomes much neater and more organized, reflecting a more structured approach to design. Supposing you contrived 20 styles for various classes of element. You would aim to make each style associated with some function of that element.

In the example below, named styles for three different kinds of paragraph have been invented. Officially, these are called *classes* of paragraph.

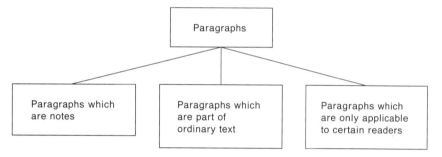

You can see that the names of each have been chosen according to their function in the mark-up, an idea that is certainly good practice. The overall effect is of a very structured style sheet that is easy to understand even if you are not the orginator of the document, and which could be modified sensibly without too much ado. The style sheets written by enthusiastic night programmers may be remarkably ingenious and conjure up layout effects well beyond the dreams of the average author. On the other hand, their code (and code it becomes!) is generally extremely hard to fathom. Go for elegance and simplicity, legibility and maintainability, if at all possible.

Here now are the classes of paragraph above written as a style sheet:

```
<HTML>
    <HEAD>
        <TITLE>Special Notice to all customers</TITLE>
        <STYLE TYPE=text/css>
            P.note { color: red }
            P.ordinary { color: green }
            P.special { color: black; font-weight: extra-bold }
        </STYLE>
    </HEAD>
<BODY>
```

How this comes out
From this HTML, an 'ordinary' paragraph in green text would first result, a 'note' in red would follow, and a 'special' paragraph in bold black would be included towards the end.

```
<P CLASS=ordinary>The first step is to heat the unit to exactly 750
degrees C. The mixture should visibly bubble and a purple vapor will
condense on the glass. Continue until the mixture has turned green
whereupon you may safely lower the heat to 500 degrees C. The condensate
should collect in the collection pod 'W' attached to the lower part of
the apparatus.
<P CLASS=note>If the condensate turns blue at any point during the
procedure, shut off heat and exit room swiftly.
<P CLASS=special>Customers who have bought the P540 model should be aware
that they will need to upgrade it to a P679 by adding a tummyometer and a
cobalt chloride fixation device. Failure to do so will result in
generation of ammonium complexes that will contaminate the mixture and
turn it yellow.
<P CLASS=ordinary>Unscrew lock 'B' and pour the condensate into a small
conical flask. Titrate against sulphuric acid to determine molarity which
should be in the region of 0.05M. Mix with 0.6M Pineapple Juice (we
recommend Safeway's) and heat gently to 40 degrees C. Continue for 6
hours. The dye will be ready for use once the mixture has cooled.
```

Applying a style to an element with a specific ID

Elements with a particular ID can be given a style in the style sheets. This is done by making the ID the target, the selector of the style:

```
#xyz CODE { font-size: xx-large }
```

An element with the ID #xyz will be allocated an extra large font size.

9.6 Built-in styles for drop-down initial characters and specially formatted first lines

Magazines such as *The Economist*, *Time* and *Newsweek* often have the first paragraph of the article with a drop-down initial character, and in some cases, the rest of the first line is in small caps – in capital letters but in a font of reduced size. CSS allows you to specify these things using the special syntax of the special built-in styles **first-letter** and **first-line**, as demonstrated below:

```
P: { color: black; font-size: 12pt }
P:first-letter { color: green; font-size: 200% }
P:first-line { color: blue; font-size: 10pt; text-transform: uppercase }
```

In this example, the styles would result in the initial letter of each P element being green with a font size of 24-point type. The rest of the first

At the time of writing we do not know how widely built-in styles will be supported by browsers.

line (as formatted on the screen) would be upper-case blue text. The rest of the paragraph would be black.

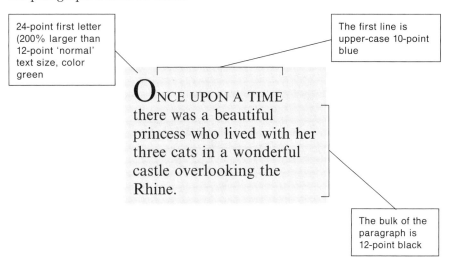

24-point first letter (200% larger than 12-point 'normal' text size, color green

The first line is upper-case 10-point blue

ONCE UPON A TIME there was a beautiful princess who lived with her three cats in a wonderful castle overlooking the Rhine.

The bulk of the paragraph is 12-point black

Here is another example of built-in styles, additionally exploiting the marvels of the SPAN element.

```
<HTML>
<HEAD>
<TITLE>The Lilac Princess</TITLE>
<STYLE TYPE=text/css>
P { font-size: 12pt; line-height=14pt }
P:first-letter { font-size: 200%; float: left }
SPAN { text-transform: uppercase }
</STYLE>
</HEAD>
<BODY>
<P><SPAN>Once upon a time</SPAN> there was a beautiful princess who
lived with her three cats in a wonderful castle overlooking the
Rhine.
</BODY>
</HTML>
```

The author has first constructed a small style sheet which includes:

- A style for paragraphs

- A style for the first letter of paragraphs

- A style for SPAN (all characters in the SPAN have been specified as upper-case). SPAN can be used to mark up a phrase or word so as to give it its own style within a block of text.

If you look in the BODY element you can see the text of the document. The **first-letter** built-in style transforms the 'O' of 'once upon a time' to make it exceptionally large and the rest of the text wraps around this. Meanwhile the SPAN element renders all the characters contained inside it into upper-case, as specified in the style sheet. This is the result:

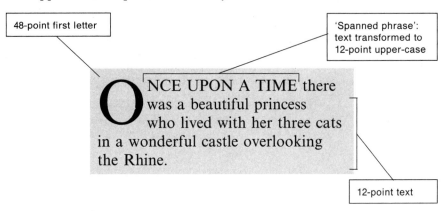

48-point first letter

'Spanned phrase': text transformed to 12-point upper-case

12-point text

The properties that apply to **first-letter** include the font properties, the color and background properties, text-decoration and text-transform, line-height and margin, padding and border properties. You could make the first letter purple in a medieval font, or black on a pink background, dark blue on a marbled texture, and so on. The possibilities are truly endless.

One thing you may have noticed from the example above is that the styles would cause *all* paragraphs to have a special initial first letter. This is perhaps not the effect that you wish.

If you want only a selection of paragraphs to come out in this special way, then there is a simple way around this problem. All you do is invent a named style with a fun initial letter and use it as required. In your style sheet you might write:

```
P.initial: first-letter {color: purple; background: yellow; font-size:
20pt; font-family: Times}
```

Then, when you want a paragraph to be portrayed resplendent on the screen with a large purple 20-point initial letter, you use the **CLASS** attribute to apply the style:

```
<P CLASS=initial>The wonders of Harrow on the Hill never cease to amaze
and the tourist will not be disappointed.
<P>Here we will find the streets avenued with trees and old-fashioned
houses.
```

The first paragraph gets the special style; the second paragraph is 'normal'.

Built-in styles for differentiating between types of hypertext link

Since Mosaic, browsers have altered the text of the link according to whether or not the link has been visited, and you can now quite easily control this at the style sheet level. What you do is make use of the built-in styles 'link', 'visited' and 'active' which are only applicable to the anchor element A. It is up to you which properties you give to each of these three built-in styles. Why not:

```
A:link { color: red }
A:visited { color: dark-red }
A:active { color: orange }
```

9.7 Worth noting: SPAN and DIV in the context of style sheets

To make it easier to apply a style to parts of a document, two new elements for use in the body of an HTML document are defined: DIV and SPAN.

DIV is used to enclose a whole chunk of the document (such as in a chapter, a section and so on), making it possible to give a whole section a distinctive style. DIV is a block-level element.

SPAN is used to give a phrase, a sentence or even a handful of characters a common style. SPAN is a character-level element.

In practice it is common to assign a named style to DIV and SPAN and then to apply the styles with **CLASS** as appropriate.

Another way of doing things is to devise a single style for DIV and SPAN that all instances of these elements in the text will then adopt:

```
DIV {font:Times; color: red; margin: 5em; padding: 10em}
SPAN {text-decoration: italic; color: black}
```

DIV and SPAN
DIV can be used to assign a common style to a number of paragraphs, headings and other elements. SPAN can be used to assign a style to a word or phrase.

Here, any series of elements will be displayed in red with the appropriate margin and padding if enclosed between <DIV> and </DIV>. Within a paragraph or other block-level element you can then use <SPAN> and </SPAN> to make the text italic and black.

9.8 Fonts for the Web

There are a number of style sheet features to allow you to control the font. The property most useful to the beginner is **font-family** with half a dozen others involved in determining whether bold or light weight, italic or normal, caps or lower case, and so on. **Font-family** lets you specify either a specific font name like 'Helvetica' or a more general font category such as 'sans serif'. The font size is specified with the **font-size** property.

You may quite reasonably wonder what happens if you specify a font which the machine displaying your document at the other end does *not* have available? Ah! This is a problem that the CSS design team has not only anticipated but also has positively racked their brains about. The solution, however, is simplicity itself: CSS allows authors to take the precaution of including a series of prioritized alternative fonts in their style sheet so that the browser on the receiving end has the benefit of choice. You might, in effect, say for example: *'If you don't have Ukrainian Lite, then use Helvetica, and if you don't have that, well, resort to any sans-serif type.'* If none of the alternatives match a font available, the browser uses its own default font instead.

The nuances of the internal procedure used by browsers for choosing the matching font are complex and clever and beyond the scope of this book. If you are interested, read Håkon Lie and Bert Bos's CSS specification (available via www.w3.org) to understand more.

Which fonts are most commonly available?

On the Macintosh, these tend to be Helvetica, Courier and Times. On the PC, you usually get Arial, Times New Roman and Courier New. Many of these are likely now to be installed on readers' machines, so you can specify them as part of your style sheet. Do, however, consider Macintosh and UNIX as well as those with PCs.

Fonts especially for computer screens

Just recently Microsoft has come up with a number of new fonts especially for computer screens. Verdana, Trebuchet and Georgia are three new fonts designed by Microsoft, explicitly for on-screen information. Comic San was the first typeface Microsoft packed with its browser and is described by Microsoft as 'a playful design reminiscent of comic-book lettering'. A bold version of the font is included with Internet Explorer. Trebuchet is described as 'full sans serif with a lot of personality, and true italics'.

The choice of font depends on font size

At 7-point type, the best choice is one of the fonts designed especially for computer screens as above. At 8-point type, the choice increases. Times New Roman, Century Schoolbook, Theatre Antoine, Old English, Nadianne, and Bookman Old Style look good, but many fonts do not work well on screen at small sizes. Fonts resembling handwriting generally work only for point sizes of 12 and above, for example, Signet Round Hand and Lucida Calligraphy. Some decorative fonts are intended for use only in larger sizes and are best kept for headings. This category includes a wide variety of styles; for example, Stencil Sans, Snowdrift, Pioneer ITC, Gallery, GlowWorm, and Braggadocio. By late 1997, we should see browsers supporting Web pages downloaded with their own fonts. This will dramatically open up the choices available to designers. Most fonts today were designed for printing and generally look poor on screen. We can look forward to a much wider availability of fonts that look good both on screen and on paper.

Fonts vary enormously in how compact they are for the same point size; for example, Trebuchet is more compact than Verdana and about the same as Comic Sans. Georgia at a point size of 8-point type appears larger than Times New Roman at a point size of 10-point type.

The point size roughly determines the height of the capital letters.

The `font-size` value can be specified in a number of units (see page 152).

Some example fonts

10-point Arial
The quick brown fox jumps over the lazy dog. 1234567890

11-point Baskerville
The quick brown fox jumps over the lazy dog. 1234567890

9-point Bembo
The quick brown fox jumps over the lazy dog. 1234567890

8-point Bodoni
The quick brown fox jumps over the lazy dog. 1234567890

10-point Bookman
The quick brown fox jumps over the lazy dog. 1234567890

14-point Brush Script

The quick brown fox jumps over the lazy dog. 1234567890

11-point Century Schoolbook Italic

The quick brown fox jumps over the lazy dog. 1234567890

9-point Courier

The quick brown fox jumps over the lazy dog. 1234567890

8-point Futura

The quick brown fox jumps over the lazy dog. 1234567890

11-point Garamond Italic

The quick brown fox jumps over the lazy dog. 1234567890

14-point Gill Sans

The quick brown fox jumps over the lazy dog. 1234567890

10-point Graphite Regular

The quick brown fox jumps over the lazy dog. 1234567890

8-point Helvetica

The quick brown fox jumps over the lazy dog. 1234567890

11-point Nimrod

The quick brown fox jumps over the lazy dog. 1234567890

14-point Old English

𝕿𝖍𝖊 𝖖𝖚𝖎𝖈𝖐 𝖇𝖗𝖔𝖜𝖓 𝖋𝖔𝖝 𝖏𝖚𝖒𝖕𝖘 𝖔𝖛𝖊𝖗 𝖙𝖍𝖊 𝖑𝖆𝖟𝖞 𝖉𝖔𝖌. 1234567890

10-point Palatino Italic

The quick brown fox jumps over the lazy dog. 1234567890

12-point Photina

The quick brown fox jumps over the lazy dog. 1234567890

10-point Rockwell Light Italic

The quick brown fox jumps over the lazy dog. 1234567890

16-point Swing Bold

The quick brown fox jumps over the lazy dog. 1234567890

10-point Tekton

The quick brown fox jumps over the lazy dog. 1234567890

8-point Times

The quick brown fox jumps over the lazy dog. 1234567890

10-point Zapf Medium

The quick brown fox jumps over the lazy dog. 1234567890

9.9 Style sheet properties for controlling font

In this section, we describe the most useful CSS properties that can be used to control the font; this also includes whether or not the text appears in italicized, boldface, or underlined type, and so on. An exhaustive list and complete description of properties can be found in the CSS specification available via www.w3.org.

Specifying the font

The kind of font you want – whether Helvetica, Times, Caesar, Chaucer or something else that strikes your fancy – is most easily done with the **font-family** property. **Font-family** takes as its value one or more *names*. These names fall into two categories. Either they consist of a *family name* or they are one of the prescribed *generic families*. Generic families should be one of:

- serif (for example Times)

- sans-serif (for example Helvetica)

- cursive (for example Zapf-Chancery)

- fantasy (like Western)

- monospace (for example Courier)

  Names for family names simply specify the font you want, for example:

- Arial

- Helvetica

- Times

- Univers

- Courier

  As you can see, the generic family is much more general than the font family. The idea of the generic family is to tell the browser the *sort* of font to use in case the font specified as the family name is not locally installed. Here are some examples of the font-family property:

```
BODY {font-family: Gill, Helvetica, sans-serif}
```

The browser will use 'Gill' by preference or 'sans serif' as third best.

```
P {font-family: Preston, Impact, Arial, Helvetica, sans-serif}
```

The browser will try the unlikely font 'Preston', then 'Impact', then 'Arial' and so on until it finds a font name that matches a locally installed font. Remember that you should use quotes for names containing white space:

```
<P STYLE= font-family: "New Century Schoolbook">
```

Setting the `font-weight` **property**

Font **Weight**

You can set the weight of the font with the **font-weight** property. This instructs the browser to use a lighter or bolder font, according to your wishes. You can specify the font-weight by using keywords or numbers. Keywords are **bold**, **bolder**, **lighter** and **normal**. For example:

```
P{font-weight: bolder}
H1{font-weight: light}
H2{font-weight: bolder}
```

You can also specify a number to indicate how dark the font should be. Choose from 100 (light) through 200, 300, 400 and so on, up to 900, which is dark.

Setting the `font-size` **property**

Font *Size*

You can control the font size with the **font-size** property. **Font-size** can be set either to an absolute value or to a relative value with respect to an existing font size.

An absolute value is specified by one of the keywords: **xx-small**, **x-small**, **small**, **medium**, **large**, **x-large** and **xx-large**. The browser will have its own idea as to what these mean in practice, and will use an internal table to map each keyword to an actual font size. In general, if a **medium** font is 10-point type, a large one is 15-point type (i.e., 10×1.5), an **x-large** one 22.5-point (15×1.5), and so on. A relative value can be specified by the keywords **smaller** and **larger**.

You can also simply specify the size of the font to be used for a particular element in terms of points (pt), inches (in), centimeters (cm) and pixels (px).

```
SPAN{font-size: smaller}
P{font-size: x-large}
```

The units used in style sheets

The following *relative* units are supported:

- em – the height of the element's font

- ex – the height of the letter 'x'

- px – pixels which are relative to the resolution of the screen – the higher resolution, the more pixels.

It is preferable to use relative units because they adjust well to the different screens that may be used to display your document.

Absolute length units that you may use are:

- in – inches

- cm – centimeters

- mm – millimeters

- pt – points (1pt = 1/72 inch)

- pc – picas (1pc = 12pt)

You can also use percentage values, which are taken relative to other values. Using these is fairly tricky and is therefore not covered in this book. You should consult more specialized literature, for example, the CSS specification itself, available via www.w3.org.

Aural style sheets
What happens if you are relying on text to speech rendering software to read Web pages? Which style sheets have already been used? Are there ways to present information aurally taking stylistic requirements into account? Indeed, there are! You can use volume, pauses, additional sounds and stereo effects. Read about this in Appendix XX.

Upper-case or lower-case?

The **text-transform** property is for controlling the case. Values allowed are one of **capitalize**, **uppercase**, **lowercase** or **none**.

- **capitalize** – this value capitalizes the first character of each word

- **uppercase** – this value places all characters in upper-case

- **lowercase** – this value places all characters in lower-case

- **none** – this is the initial value

lower-case
or
UPPER-CASE

This property applies to all elements. The transformation in each case is language-dependent, so that it will be done in different ways for each foreign language.

```
H1 {text-transform: uppercase}
```

Another related property is **font-variant**. The **font-variant** property simply allows you to choose between **normal** text and **small caps**.

```
H2 {font-variant: small caps}
```

9.10 Setting the color of the text

The **color** property sets the foreground color for a given element: it sets the color of the text. The property can be applied to almost any element so that complete documents, paragraphs or individual characters, words and phrases can be set in a different color. By associating a color with the document BODY, the whole document can be presented in the background color of your choice.

Here is how you set the text of the whole document to 'blue':

```
BODY {color=blue}
```

You can then give individual elements such as paragraphs a separate color. The result will be a series of paragraphs displayed in differently colored text to the body. For example,

```
P {color=orange}
```

sets the text for a paragraph to orange.

The same idea can be applied to all elements so that you could, for example, construct a style for bold text to be displayed purple. Just make sure that any text color looks legible on the document background. It is remarkably easy to be optimistic on this count.

How to specify color in a style sheet

The easiest way for the beginner is to specify color by using one of the standard key color names. The 16 colors are taken from the Windows VGA palette and are aqua, black, blue, fuchsia, grey, green, lime, maroon, navy, olive, purple, red, teal, silver, white, and yellow. This kind of thing is quite legitimate, for example:

```
BODY {color: black; background: white }
H1 { color: maroon }
H2 { color: olive }
```

Using numbers to specify color is certainly more difficult. A fairly common thing on the Web is a series of hexadecimal digits to specify a color. You use a '#' immediately followed by either three or six hexadecimal characters. To the uninitiated, these look pretty strange, but luckily you do not have to make up your own codes: many tools exist for the purpose of finding the correct code for the color of your fancy. See also the table of colors and codes in the color section of this book.

Appendix I gives all sorts of useful information on using color on the Web.

9.11 Specifying the background color

Background color
Background color (and texture) is not inherited as such. The reason paragraphs and other elements are usually displayed on the same color as the BODY is simply because they have, by default, a transparent background. The BODY color therefore 'shows through'. A paragraph of text will assume the background color unless given a color of its own.

The background color can be set by a property called **background-color**. This can be applied to most elements so that you can set the background color of the whole document BODY, individual paragraphs, certain characters and so on. Here is a simple example showing how to set the entire document background to a single color:

```
BODY {background-color: red}
```

In the second example, the intention is to set the paragraph background to blue, and then have white text displayed on it.

```
P {background-color: blue; font: 14 pt sans serif; color: white}
```

Giving a paragraph its
own color. The result of:

```
BODY {background-color: red}

P     {background-color: blue;
        color: white}
```

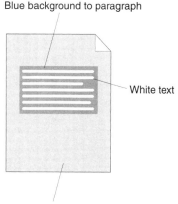

Blue background to paragraph

White text

Red background to document

9.12   Specifying a background image for an element

The **background-image** property sets the background image of an element. You specify the stored location of the image to be displayed on the background by using a URL, for example like this:

```
P {background-image: /patterns/stone.gif}
```

The **background-repeat** property controls the way that a GIF (or JPEG) image is repeated across the background to give a pattern. Possible values are **repeat** (the initial value), **repeat-x**, **repeat-y** and **no-repeat**.

 'Tile' to repeat

Effect of **repeat**,
which tiles the
whole area

repeat-x

repeat-y

top right

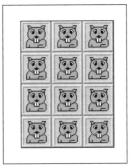

center

top left

The smaller the image, the more repeats there are. If you use **repeat-x**, you can repeat the image horizontally to give a band of images one side to the other; **repeat-y** has the effect of creating a similar band of images vertically.

The position of the background image

Related properties
CSS also has an 'umbrella' **background** property, which allows you to specify the **background-color**, **background-image**, **background-repeat**, **background-attachment** and **background-position** all in one go.

The **background-position** property specifies the position of the background image. This applies to block-level elements only and is very useful for specifying the position of a banner across the page. You can fix the banner so that it does not scroll with the rest of the document by using the **background-attachment** property.

The **background-position** property specifies the initial position of the background. A value of **right top** places the background in the top right corner of the box that surrounds the content (see diagram on page 156); **center** means the image is centered. You can also use the keywords **top left**, **top center**, **right top**, **left center**, **right center**, **bottom left**, **bottom center** and **bottom right** to position the image. For example:

```
BODY {background: url (banner.jpeg) top right}
BODY {background: url (banner.jpeg) center}
```

Do you want a scrolling image or one that remains stationary?

The property **background-attachment** determines whether or not the background image scrolls with the document.

There are two possible values: **fixed** and **scroll**. **Scroll** is the initial value.

9.13 Underlined, boxed text, blinking text and other character effects

You need the **text-decoration** property. You can choose to influence the display of a *single character* or a *whole phrase* or *paragraph*: the property can be applied to any HTML element. The values taken by **text-decoration** are:

- overline

- underline

- line-through

- blink

- box

The use of these properties is extremely simple:

```
P{text-decoration: none}
B{text-decoration: underline}
LI{text-decoration: blink}
P{text-decoration: line-through}
EM{text-decoration: box}
P{text-decoration: overline}
```

Oblique and italic text

Italic text

You use a property called **font-style** to create these effects. The values allowed are:

- `oblique`

- `italic`

- `normal`

Here is a very simple example:

```
P {font-style: italic}
```

9.14 Text spacing, indentation and alignment

Spacing of lines

The CSS

`line-height`

property cannot be applied to all elements. It specifies how far apart the

base-lines

should be.

This is done with the **line-height** property, which controls the distance between two adjacent *baselines*. These are the lines on which the text is 'set'. The browser increases the distance between baselines by adding extra *leading* (the typographical term). Here are some examples of this idea in CSS:

```
P {line-height:150%}
P {line-height:10pt}
```

In the first example, the line height is increased by 150 percent; in other words, it has been increased to one and one-half times that of the original; in the second example, the line height is simply 10-point.

The line height can be expressed in the standard CSS standard units: pt, in, cm, px and percent (%). Negative values for line height are not allowed. A value of **normal** sets the line-height to a reasonable value given the font size.

The space between words

The **word-spacing** property determines the additional amount of space that should be placed between words. The **word-spacing** property can be used with any element so that, for instance, you could arrange for a particular phrase to have increased space between words, or apply the property to a SPAN element. You specify the value for **word-spacing** as a length using one of the standard CSS units. Negative values are allowed for squashing the words closer together.

The initial value for this property is **normal**. If you want to revert to normal after spacing out words, **normal** is the keyword to choose.

```
SPAN {word-spacing: 14 cm}
P.note {word-spacing: -2 em}
```

To revert to normal:

```
P {word-spacing: normal}
```

Squashed-up or spaced-out letters

Letter-spacing determines the amount of space that should be added or subtracted between letters in a paragraph or other element.

This property works in much the same way as **word-spacing** above, and applies to any element. Negative values are allowed, enabling you to specify that text should be rendered squashed-up.

```
P {letter-spacing: -0.5 em}
P {letter-spacing: normal}
```

Indenting the first line

Negative indents
A negative indent, for example
P {text-indent: -3 em}
causes the first line to stick out beyond the limit of the paragraph.

The **text-indent** property enables you to indent the first line of a paragraph or, indeed, any other block-level element.

```
P {text-indent: 10%}
P {text-indent: 3 em}
```

Text alignment

The **text-align** property enables you to align text left, right, center and (theoretically) justified.

```
P {text-align: center}
```

9.15 Margins and white space around text and pictures

CSS makes a distinction between *content* (the text itself or the image contained within the boundary of the HTML tags), the *padding* around the content (see below), the *border* (if there is one) and the *margins*.

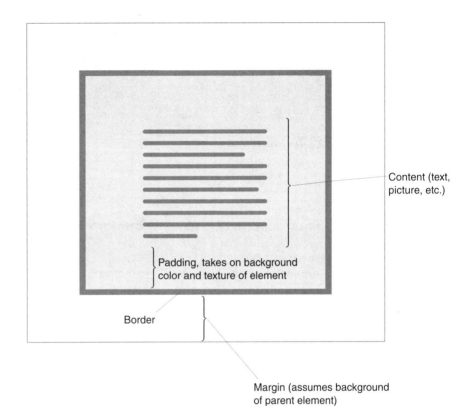

Content (text, picture, etc.)

Padding, takes on background color and texture of element

Border

Margin (assumes background of parent element)

Increasing the area around the text or graphic – control of padding

The padding is the area between the content and the border. The padding properties allow you to specify extra padding with the effect that you can increase the amount of space around a paragraph, a heading, a quotation and so on. Padding takes on the background color of the element. An element with padding will have an area around it of an identical color.

The properties involved are called **padding**, **padding-top**, **padding-right**, **padding-bottom** and **padding-left**. You can set the padding individually or with the more general **padding** property.

If there is only one padding value given, the browser supposes that this applies to all sides. If there are two or three values, those that are still missing are inferred from those given. For example, here the padding is specified for first the top and bottom and then the sides:

```
IMG {padding: 5em 7em; color: red; background: blue}
```

The top and bottom margins will be 5 em and the right and left margins 7 em. Units are as for margin settings.

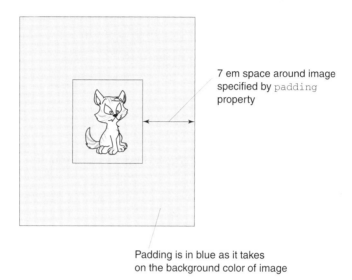

7 em space around image
specified by `padding`
property

Padding is in blue as it takes
on the background color of image

Specifying how big the margins around elements should be

The margin is the area outside the border. By adjusting the margin, you can insert space around paragraphs, single characters, IMG tags and so on. Note that the margin is 'transparent' which means that the present element's background shows through. A paragraph on a BODY with a background pattern will have a margin through which the pattern will be visible. You can specify the margin in terms of:

- points (pt)
- inches (in)
- centimeters (cm)
- pixels (px)
- percentage (%)

The properties involved are: **margin** (**margin-top**, **margin-right**, **margin-bottom** and **margin-left**). You can set the margins individually or with the single **margin** property.

The four lengths apply to top, right, bottom and left, respectively. If there is only one value, it applies to all sides; if there are two or three values, the missing values are taken from the opposite side. Horizontal margins may be negative.

Here are some examples of the margin properties in use:

```
BODY {margin: 3 em}
```

This sets all margins to 3-em units. All paragraphs and other elements in the document will start and end further from the edge of the document.

```
BODY {margin: 3 em 5 em;}
P{margin: 2 em; color: red}
```

This sets the top and bottom to 3-em units and the right and left margins to 5-em units. The paragraph has an additional margin.

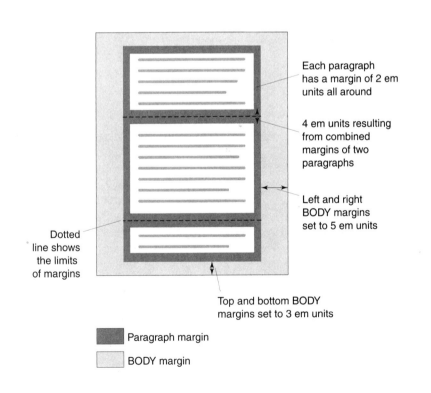

Each paragraph has a margin of 2 em units all around

4 em units resulting from combined margins of two paragraphs

Left and right BODY margins set to 5 em units

Dotted line shows the limits of margins

Top and bottom BODY margins set to 3 em units

Paragraph margin

BODY margin

9.16 Borders around elements

CSS style sheets afford unlimited play with borders around elements, allowing you to create thick, thin, dark, light and fancy borders to your heart's content. Theoretically, you can set a border for any element, but in practice things are not so simple, especially with table borders that are still in the process of being sorted out from a design point of view.

The **border** property sets all four borders in terms of width, color and style. Each side can also be set independently by using **border-top**, **border-right**, **border-bottom** and **border-left**. The **border** property has up to three values, which consist of a border-width, a border-style and a color. An element will have no border unless one is actually set.

Border-width sets the border around an element to **thin**, **medium**, **thick** or **thin**. If unspecified, the border is assumed to be **medium**. Unlike margin and padding, you cannot use this property to set different values on the four sides.

The **border-style** property sets the style of border. Values are **none**, **dotted**, **dashed**, **solid**, **double**, **groove**, **ridge**, **inset** and **outset**. You can set the horizontal borders differently from the vertical borders. The initial border style is **none**.

The properties **border-top**, **border-right**, **border-bottom**, **border-left** are used to set individual borders rather than all four at once, the latter being done with the single border property (see above).

Border-color is used to set the border color and sets the style of all four borders. For example:

```
IMG {border-color: blue; border-width: medium; border-style: ridge}
```

9.17 List style

The type of bullet is specified by the **list-style-type** property. Simple use of **list-style-type** is as follows. What you do is construct a number of styles that specify different sorts of bullets. Here we have constructed three styles called 'square', 'circle' and 'upper'. These styles can be used in the document when and where they are needed to ensure a list is displayed with the bullet of your choice. You apply the style using the CLASS element as described on page 142.

Here are the styles:

```
LI.square {list-style-type: square}
LI.circle {list-style-type: circle}
LI.upper {list-style-type: upper-alpha}
```

And here are some lines of a document that uses the styles:

```
<LI CLASS=square> This is a list item which I would like displayed with a
square bullet.
<LI CLASS=circle> And I would like this bullet item with a circle
instead.
```

Another idea is to import the bullet of your choice. A cat enthusiast might choose to import a tiny kitten as a marker for each point in her list (see below); better known choices are colored balls, arrows, or stars. Fancy bullets are done by using a property called **list-style-image**. This property takes as its value a URL. What this means is that you can specify the location of the (gif) image to use for the bullet in terms of file-name, directory, and even the machine on the Internet.

```
UL.kitten {list-style-image: url (/LI-bullets/kitten.gif)}
UL.star {list-style-image: url (/LI-bullets/star.gif)}
```

As though this were not enough, there is also a **list-style-position** property that allows you to specify where exactly you want the bullet placed. The choices are:

- **inside**, which is a bulleted list in which the text wraps around;

- **outside**, which is a bulleted list with text lined up so that all lines are evenly indented.

10
TABLES

Included in this chapter is information on:

- Constructing simple, but effective tables
- Aligning and justifying text within a cell
- Making rows of header cells act as titles for columns
- Specifying a table as a whole, and giving a caption to the table
- Making individual cells span several rows or columns
- Designing a table header and groups of rows
- Aligning text in groups of table cells
- Inheriting alignment attributes
- Drawing a border for the table using different styles
- Placing other elements, such as images, inside tables
- Speeding up table display

Backward compatibility
HTML 4 tables are
backward-compatible
with the widely
deployed Netscape table
implementation. The
ALIGN attribute is now
compatible with the
latest Netscape and
Microsoft browsers.

Summary (HTML tables)

Tables start with an optional caption followed by one or more rows. Each row is formed by one or more cells, which are differentiated into header and data cells. Cells can be merged across rows and columns, and include attributes that assist in rendering to speech and Braille, or for exporting table data into databases. The model provides limited support for control over appearance; for example, horizontal and vertical alignment of cell contents, border styles, and cell margins. You can further affect this by grouping together rows and columns. Tables can contain a wide range of content, such as headers, lists, paragraphs, forms, figures, preformatted text, and even nested tables.

The mark-up for this uses COLGROUP elements to group columns and to set default column alignment. TBODY elements are used to group rows. The **FRAME** and **RULES** attributes are used to select which borders to render.

Summary of improvements over HTML 3.2

Tables in HTML 4 are designed to work well with Web style sheets, although they do not require a style sheet, *per se*. The **STYLE** attribute soon will enable you to control properties associated with edges and interiors of groups of cells. For instance, this **STYLE** attribute provides the line style dotted, double, thin/thick; the color/pattern fill for the interior; and cell margins and font information. This will be the subject for a companion specification on style sheets.

HTML 4 tables support rendering in Braille or speech, as well as the exchange of tabular data with databases and spreadsheets. The HTML 4 table embodies certain aspects of the CALS[1] table model; for example, the ability to group table rows into three categories, each with a different kind of rendering (using the THEAD, TBODY and TFOOT elements). In line with the CALS table model, you can also specify cell alignment compactly for sets of cells according to the context.

HTML 4 includes several improvements over HTML 3.2:

- You now can align on designated characters; for example, you can align a column of numbers on the decimal point.

- You now can align cell contents that are specified on a cell-by-cell basis, or that are inherited from enclosing elements, such as row, column or the table element itself.

- You now have greater flexibility in specifying table frames and rules.

- You now have incremental display for large tables as data is received.

[1] CALS stands for Continuous Acquisition and Life-cycle Support. It is an approach to handling data used by the US Navy of the Department of Defense. A subsidiary goal has been to simplify importing tables that conform to the SGML CALS model.

- You now have a new element called `COLGROUP` that allows sets of columns to be grouped and given different width and alignment properties, as specified by one or more `COL` elements. The precise meaning of `COLGROUP` has been clarified, and `RULES=basic` has been replaced by `RULES=groups`.

- You now have support for scrollable tables with fixed headers.

- You now have improved support for breaking tables across pages for printing.

- The **FRAME** and **RULES** attributes have been modified to avoid SGML name clashes with each other, and to avoid clashes with the **ALIGN** and **VALIGN** attributes and possible future use of **FRAME** and **RULES** attributes with other table elements.

Background reading: the design of HTML tables
The HTML table model has evolved from existing SGML table models including CALS, and from the treatment of tables in common use in word processors and books.

We have attempted to put the more difficult, less essential attributes later in the chapter, so that the sections are roughly graded in the order in which you will need to study them. The impressive set of table features in HTML 4 should be good for everyone: It enables the advanced HTML user to construct tables for almost every conceivable purpose.

The good news for beginners is that you can make quite serviceable tables with just the simplest of the table elements, gradually adding others, as you become more experienced. In several cases, the more advanced features enable you to save time by working on groups of table cells, rather than on each one individually.

10.1 Introduction

HTML 4 is often used for presenting commercial, scientific and technical data, which can naturally be organized as tables. Think of railway time-tables, trigonometric tables from your schooldays, theater schedules, or even comparing the relative effectiveness of one brand of soap powder against another brand. To display such data sets effectively, you need to present them in tabular form. Unfortunately, there is no agreement as to how tables should appear. Some people like to give borders to tables, whereas others like an occasional horizontal line, and still others simply like white space. To allow for this natural variation, HTML 4 provides a basic robust mechanism for simple tables, accompanied by a set of increasingly sophisticated features for subtler formatting, when necessary.

In this chapter, we have tried to make each section build on the earlier chapters, so that you can start making simple tables right away. Since you will probably want to use several of the most attractive features such as borders, captions, and merged cells as soon as possible, we first introduce these things generally and then discuss them fully later.

10.2 Simple tables

It is much easier to use simple tables than you might expect.

A real example

The following illustration, taken straight from the World Wide Web, shows a simple, but effective use of an HTML table to list stocks and companies:

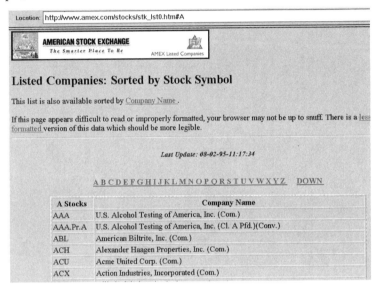

This illustration shows Netscape's basic style of table implementations. The raised/embossed appearance is consistent with the standard, although not demanded by it.

The AMEX page from which the illustration is taken (http://www.amex.com) includes the following code, which we have reformatted slightly to make it as clear as possible:

```
<TABLE BORDER=2>
  <TR><TH><B> A Stocks </B></TH><TH><B> Company Name </B></TH></TR>
  <TR><TD> AAA </TD><TD> U.S. Alcohol Testing of America, Inc. (Com.)
  <BR></TD></TR>
  <TR><TD> ABL </TD><TD> American Biltrite, Inc. (Com.)<BR></TD></TR>
  <TR><TD> ACH </TD><TD> Alexander Haagen Properties, Inc. (Com.)
  <BR></TD></TR>
  <TR><TD> ACU </TD><TD> Acme United Corp. (Com.)<BR></TD></TR>
  <TR><TD> ACX </TD><TD> Action Industries, Incorporated (Com.)
  <BR></TD></TR>
        <!-- many more lines of data ...-->
</TABLE>
```

The table is created by the `TABLE` element, qualified by the **BORDER** attribute to specify that a thick border should be drawn.

The first row of the table is specified as a table row `<TR>`, followed by two table headers `<TH>`.

AMEX has been ultra-cautious here, not a bad thing, and has ended each `<TR>` and `<TH>` with a matching `</TR>` and `</TH>`. Most probably, they generated the code with a translator from a database or word-processor file, and the translation program in best belt-and-braces style followed the simple rule, 'always put in all start and end tags'. There are, of course, cases in which an end tag is specifically not required.

The heading text has been emphasized with `<B>...</B>`. In HTML 4, this is not really necessary, as browsers and style sheets provide for special treatment to distinguish headers from table data.

After that, it is all plain sailing, as the rest of the table rows have the same structure. Like the header row, they begin with `<TR>`. Each entry is represented as a table data `<TD>` item. You can see that the browser has correctly aligned all the stocks and company names into two columns.

Writing your own tables

If you are writing HTML by hand, you always can safely omit the closing `</TR>`, `</TH>` and `</TD>` tags, because browsers immediately know from the following tags that the table row or item has come to an end. We can therefore rewrite the AMEX table of company stocks like this:

```
<TABLE FRAME=box RULES=all>             <!--new-style attributes-->
  <TR><TH> A Stocks <TH>Company Name
  <TR><TD> AAA <TD> Alcohol Testing of America, Inc. (Com.)
  <TR><TD> ABL <TD> American Biltrite, Inc. (Com.)
  <TR><TD> ACH <TD> Alexander Haagen Properties, Inc. (Com.)
  <TR><TD> ACU <TD> Acme United Corp. (Com.)
  <TR><TD> ACX <TD> Action Industries, Incorporated (Com.)
                  <!--many more lines of data...-->
</TABLE>
```

which, as you can see, is considerably shorter and simpler than AMEX's own implementation.

Even if you do not want to have headers above your table columns, all you need to create HTML tables is the following structure:

```
<TABLE FRAME=box RULES=all>
  <TR><TD>Duck   <TD>D.    <TD>1, The Pond, Florida
  <TR><TD>Mouse  <TD>M.    <TD>3, The Hole, New York
  <TR><TD>Sailor <TD>P.    <TD>of No Fixed Abode
</TABLE>
```

This gives you a result as simple as could be:

Duck	D.	1, The Pond, Florida
Mouse	M.	3, The Hole, New York
Sailor	P.	of No Fixed Abode

Floating tables

Tables are often centered on the page by default, with no text or any other HTML structure on either side of them, like the simple examples above. They are, in fact, typical block-level elements, comparable with paragraphs or lists. But if you want a table to float against the left- or right-hand margin, with text beside it, you can make it do so with the **ALIGN** attribute: you write <TABLE ALIGN=left> or =right, respectively. When a table is made to float toward the left- or right-hand margin, subsequent HTML elements, such as text and images, flow and wrap around the table if there is room. ALIGN=center does not float.

You now know everything you need to construct simple, but useful tables in your Web pages. The rest of this chapter elaborates on this knowledge, adding a wide range of elegant and powerful features.

10.3 Aligning text in individual table cells

The simplest way to control the text alignment in a TH or TD cell (header and data cells work the same way) is to set it individually. This gives you fine control over the appearance of the table, but it is repetitive, and makes your HTML bulky, and slow to display if you need to adjust every cell. We will explain better approaches later.

Aligning or justifying cell contents horizontally

HTML tables and the visually impaired
For the visually impaired, HTML offers the hope of righting the wrong those adopting windows-based graphical user interfaces caused. The HTML table model includes attributes for labeling each cell, to support high quality text to speech conversion. The same attributes also can be used to support automated import and export of table data to databases or spreadsheets.

This approach is direct. You qualify the tag of the cell in which you are interested with the **ALIGN** attribute. It can take the values `left` (the default), `center`, `right`, `justify` or `char`. For example:

```
<TABLE FRAME=box RULES=none ID=just>
<TBODY ALIGN=center>          <!--overridden by lower-level align-->
  <TR><TD ALIGN=justify>
  We would like to explain exactly why we have elected to take the
  action that we did, given that it appears that certain members feel
  that it was less than appropriate.
  <TR><TD ALIGN=right>
  In our circumstances we feel that a ragged left boundary is better
  than no boundary at all.
</TABLE>
```

Justified text (except for its last line) is made to fit both left and right boundaries of the cell. The example creates the following table:

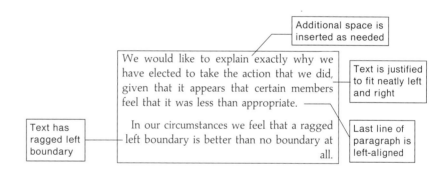

Incidentally, this example uses a frame-style border, with no lines between table cells.

Aligning cell contents vertically

Similarly, you can directly control the vertical alignment of the contents of any table cell, using **VALIGN**. It can take the values `top`, `middle` (the default), `bottom` or `baseline`. These have their common meanings, but `baseline` needs some explanation. All cells in a baseline row should have their first line of text on a common baseline; subsequent lines of text are unconstrained.

For example:

```
<TABLE FRAME=hsides>
  <TR><TD VALIGN=top>Soprano<TD>a two<BR>line cell
</TABLE>
```

arranges the 'Soprano' cell contents at the top of the cell, even though there is white space below:

Soprano	a two
	line cell

Using a horizontal-alignment character

A very useful way to organize forms (see Chapter 11 on Forms) is to align on a specific character that you arrange to occur in all lines of text (typically separated with <BR> line breaks) within a TD cell. For example, you can align on the colon (':') character so that every prompt of the form 'Wingspan:' or 'Weight:' is neatly right-aligned with the colons forming a perfect column.

Lines that do not include the alignment character are shifted by the browser to end at the alignment position.

A cell that spans several rows or columns takes its alignment from its first row or column.

The pair of HTML attributes you need for this arrangement is

```
<TD ALIGN=char CHAR=":">
```

and you can use any character you find convenient. Notice the repetition of the word 'CHAR'. You need to reserve that character for alignment purposes, so you normally cannot use a letter or digit.

Suitable characters include:

- the colon ':' which is useful for aligning text prompts

- the dot or period '.' which is ideal if you have a column of decimal numbers, as it aligns them at the decimal point

- the dash '–' if you want to line up text comments, as the dash character does not look strange either before or after a piece of text.

For example, field ornithologists might use an application containing the following table/form:

```
<TABLE>
  <TBODY>                         <!--this line is optional, actually-->
  <TR><TD ALIGN=char CHAR=":">
    <FORM>
        Wingspan : <INPUT NAME="wing" SIZE="5" ><BR>
          Weight : <INPUT NAME="mass" SIZE="5" ><BR>
        Ring No. : <INPUT NAME="rnum" SIZE="12"><BR>
        <INPUT TYPE=reset>         <INPUT TYPE=submit>
    </FORM>
</TABLE>
```

This remarkably short piece of HTML creates a neatly aligned form for the bird-ringers, like this:

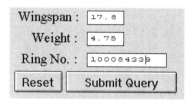

You should avoid putting further alignment attributes on the cell contents (for example, by inserting <P ALIGN=center> in a table cell) as such attributes would take priority over cell-level alignment and spoil the table's appearance. The rule is that low-level specifications take priority over high-level ones.

Setting an offset for the alignment character

If you use CHAR as described so far, browsers simply fit your text into table cells, aligning on the specified character. You can improve on this by telling the browser where, relative to the width of the table cell, you want the character to be placed.

The HTML attribute for this is

```
CHAROFF=50%
```

and you are free to enter any percentage between 0 and 100. The percent symbol is needed.

For example:

```
CHAR="-" CHAROFF=70%
```

This example aligns the cell contents so that the included '-' characters are all at 70 percent of the width of the cell, measured from the left to the right. Depending on how much text is on either side of the character, this may cause the browser to provide additional white space on one side or the other.

10.4 Table headers

The table header acts much like a header in a printed book, except that if necessary, it can be made to repeat automatically on each printed page covered by a long table, or when it is on the screen, it can remain fixed while the user scrolls the table data.

A table header consists of a single Table Head (THEAD) element, containing a group of ordinary table rows (TR), which, in turn, contain table header cells (TH). You can use the generic attributes **ID**, **LANG**, **STYLE** and **CLASS** to indicate or control the whole group. Only one header group can be specified in a table; if it occurs, it must come after the caption and column specifications (if any) and before the table body. Groups are discussed further below.

Creating table header rows

Table header rows are created by HTML code virtually identical to that for normal table rows, except that the <TH> tag replaces the <TD> tag. By default, the contents of header cells are centered, unlike data cells that are rendered flush left. Often, browsers do something to distinguish headers from data, for example, by putting headers into boldface type.

To create a header row, you write <TR> as usual, followed by <TH> tags to introduce each column with a column title:

```
<TABLE FRAME=box RULES=all>
  <THEAD>
    <TR><TH>Doric   <TH>Ionic    <TH>Corinthian
    <TBODY>
    <TR><TD>Simple><TD>Delicate<TD>Ornate
</TABLE>
```

This creates a table with six cells, three headers and three data:

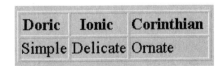

It is up to you whether or not you consider this to be made up of three columns, as the cell contents suggest, or of two rows. The HTML code, as you can see, treats rows as the major units and columns as minor or implicit.

Controlling table header cells

You can use the generic attributes **ID**, **LANG**, **STYLE** and **CLASS** in `<TH>` header cells just as in `<TD>` data cells, so you can specify their treatment in a style sheet as usual. You also can control their alignment both horizontally and vertically in exactly the same way as for `<TD>` cells. But the default usually is what you will want.

10.5 Table captions

The table caption is optional. It is usual to write normal text, but the characters you use can be marked up for emphasis, and the special character entities defined in HTML can be included. You can use the generic attributes **ID**, **LANG**, **STYLE** and **CLASS**.

More surprisingly, you can put images (`<IMG SRC=...>`) and hypertext anchors (`<A HREF=...>`) into the table caption. This enables you to directly link your tables to related material, and to incorporate icons.

By default, the table caption appears above the table. You can control this behavior with ALIGN=top, =bottom, =left or =right.

For example:

```
<TABLE FRAME=box RULES=all>
<CAPTION ALIGN=bottom>This caption goes below its table
  <TR><TD>chippendale<TD>occasional<TD>mahogany
</TABLE>
```

The above creates a table with a caption beneath it:

chippendale	occasional	mahogany

This caption goes below its table

Netscape Navigator 3.0 uses a default setting that centers the caption above its table. If it is wider than the table, it is word-wrapped over two or more lines, as necessary.

10.6 Controlling the table as a whole

Table model
A major consideration for the HTML table model is that the fonts and window sizes in use with browsers are not under the author's control. This makes it risky to rely on column widths specified in terms of absolute units or pixels. Instead, tables can be dynamically sized to match the current window size and fonts. Authors can provide guidance as to the relative widths of columns, but browsers are supposed to ensure that columns are wide enough to render the width of the largest single element of the cell's content. If the author's specification must be overridden, the idea is that the relative widths of individual columns are not drastically changed.

You can use the generic attributes **ID**, **LANG** and **CLASS** for tables, as for most other HTML elements. Tables can also be controlled by several more specific attributes, including **WIDTH** and **FLOAT**. These are discussed below.

Controlling table width

By default, tables are sized in accordance with the widths of their contents, and the available width of the screen or window into which they must fit. This is quite complicated for browsers, as there are several competing pressures to consider. You can specify the width you intend for your table (and for individual columns, as will be explained), but browsers may be unable to comply with this: if cell contents require a wider table, browsers will probably ignore your suggested width.

Widths can be supplied as screen pixels or as relative measurements using a *. Width settings can be applied equally to individual columns, groups of columns, or to whole tables. For example,

```
<TABLE WIDTH=400>
```

No space is allowed between number and unit.

The equivalent width in screen pixels depends both on screen size and on the current resolution (for example, 640×480 pixels), and cannot be predicted. Pixel measurements should therefore be avoided, if at all possible. In any case, when you are setting the widths, remember that users may not have the same font settings as you. Such matters are best left to style sheets.

Finally, you can set table width as a percentage of the space between the current left and right margins, using the % symbol. For instance:

```
<TABLE WIDTH=75%>
```

Making the table float or flow with the text

Tables are usually treated as part of the general flow of text. If you wish, you can specify that a table is to float to the left or to the right, with the rest of the text flow continuing around it. There is no default setting. For example:

```
<TABLE ALIGN=right>
```

10.7 Cells that span rows or columns

The simple approach discussed so far works very well for plain sets of data. Very often, though, you want to make the data stand out better by grouping items that apply to more than one row or column. HTML takes exactly the same approach for both <TH> and <TD> cells.

To make a cell span two or more rows, you use the **ROWSPAN** attribute, as in the following, shown below:

```
<TH ROWSPAN=2>    <--a header cell spanning 2 rows-->
```

The value, as you would expect, specifies how many <TH> or <TD> cells this particular cell is to span. Similarly, to make a cell span two or more columns, you use the **COLSPAN** attribute, as in

```
<TH COLSPAN=3>    <!--a header cell spanning 3 columns-->
<TD COLSPAN=2>    <!--a data cell spanning 2 columns  -->
```

For example:

```
<TABLE BORDER>
  <CAPTION>Table with merged cells</CAPTION>
  <TR><TH ROWSPAN=2><TH COLSPAN=3>Length/mm
  <TR><TH>body<TH>tail<TH>ears
  <TR><TH ALIGN=left>males  <TD>31.4<TD>23.7<TD>3.8
  <TR><TH ALIGN=left>females<TD>29.6<TD>20.8<TD>3.4
</TABLE>
```

This creates a table with a header that extends across the three data columns, like this:

Table with merged cells			
	Length/mm		
	body	**tail**	**ears**
males	31.4	23.7	3.8
females	29.6	20.8	3.4

There is a risk, if you apply **ROWSPAN** and **COLSPAN** attributes to different cells in a table, that those cells may overlap.

For example, here is the HTML definition of a table in which the cells called 'Sixth' and 'Seventh' overlap:

```
<TABLE BORDER>
  <CAPTION ALIGN=bottom>a BAD table with overlap</CAPTION>
  <TR><TD ROWSPAN=2>First<TD>Second<TD>Third<TD>Fourth<TD>Fifth
  <TR><TD ROWSPAN=2>Sixth              <!--bad idea!-->
  <TR><TD COLSPAN=2>Seventh<TD>Eighth    <--don't do this!-->
</TABLE>
```

The effect of this code depends on the browser. Netscape actually displays the messy consequences of the table exactly as it is specified:

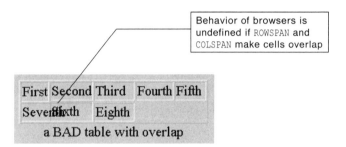

Other browsers may produce a tidier, but arguably less accurate, result by concealing the overlapped cell contents. You should clearly be careful to avoid overlaps.

10.8 Designating header, body and footer groups

In line with the US Department of Defense's CALS table model, HTML permits you to organize your table rows into header, body and footer groups, if you wish. By default, all rows are assumed to be body. You can define at most one header group and one footer group. Browsers normally display the header and footer in fixed positions at the top and bottom of the display area: if the table-body scrolls, they remain on the screen.

You can insert as many rows as you like into each group. Given the restricted number of rows of text that browsers can display, you do not need to put more than a few rows into headers or footers: some people would say that one was enough.

You can supply any of the generic attributes **ID**, **LANG**, **STYLE** and **CLASS**, or any of the alignment attributes (**ALIGN**, **CHAR**, **CHAROFF** or **VALIGN**) for any group, allowing you to control groups of rows instead of either individual rows or whole tables.

The header group

If you want a header group you put a `<THEAD>` tag at its start. There is strictly no need for a `</THEAD>` tag at the end, as the following `<TBODY>`

makes it quite clear where the group ends. But for compatibility with older browsers, it is wise to put in the closing tag.

Your header group must include at least one <TR> table row. The separate table caption also gives you an opportunity to describe the table as a whole.

The body group

Tables must have at least one body. You only need to supply TBODY group starting tags, though, if you have specified a header group, or if you want to place ruled lines between body groups (using <TABLE RULES=groups>). The tag <TBODY> then marks off the division between groups. This is useful, as it enables you to specify the alignment of the header and the body separately. For instance, you can have the header text labels centered, and the body text left-aligned. Each TBODY element must contain at least one TR (table row) element.

This ingenious model provides excellent backwards compatibility, as well as several new and useful features. For example:

```
<TABLE FRAME=box RULES=groups>
    <TR><TD>1<TD>Start of body group
    <TR><TD>2<TD>End of body group
  <TBODY>
    <TR><TD>3<TD>Another body group...
    <TR><TD>4<TD>which requires a TBODY start tag
</TABLE>
```

creates the result

This little table consists of two TBODY elements, both of which lack closing tags; the first lacks its starting tag, as well.

10.9   Organizing by columns

So far, you have seen HTML tables as collections of rows, possibly grouped. It is also possible and useful to specify table behavior by columns, for example, to make a whole column of cells a particular width, or to align the contents of such a column vertically or horizontally. Finally, you can group columns together so as to specify their behavior as a unit, in much the same way as a group of table rows.

Column widths

By default, browsers automatically adjust the widths of columns to fit both their contents and the width of the screen or window. They achieve this first by scanning all data inside the table, increasing the column width when cell contents demand more space, and then by wrapping cell contents if the available width is used up. You can simplify this process, possibly speed up table display, and gain greater control over the final appearance of the table by specifying the absolute or relative widths of the columns with the COL element. COL can only be used inside a table.

The attribute **WIDTH** allows you to set the width of the column in any of the standard-width units, such as picas, points or inches.

```
<COL WIDTH=30mm>  <--set column to 30 millimetres if possible-->
```

By default, it gives absolute width in pixels if its value is an integer without units, for example:

```
<COL WIDTH=64>  <--plain integer width means pixels-->
```

or relative width (compared to other such columns) if its value is a positive number followed by a star, like 2.5* or 6* – it does not have to be a whole number, though you may find it easier to use one. Incidentally, decimal fractions are allowed, but exponents such as 1.2^2 are not.

For example, in a seven-column table:

```
<COL WIDTH=4*  >     <!--CALS users will recognize the star * ... -->
<COL WIDTH=2.5*>     <!--It is there to simplify CALS table import-->
<COL WIDTH=1*  >
<COL WIDTH=2*  >
```

This specification lets the browser know that it is to divide the available width (already specified to be 80 percent of the window's width) into relative measures of 4, 2.5, 1, 2, 2, 2, and 2 (which add up to 15.5, in fact). The first column, for example, is therefore going to be

$4 \times 80/15.5 = 20.6\%$ (of the window's available width)

This may be beginning to give you a headache, as you remember your math teacher at school doing ratios. Luckily, such complexities are only for the browser. All you have to do is to specify the relative widths of the columns, in any units that you find convenient: HTML is your servant, not your master. You can avoid assigning fractional widths by doubling all the relative widths listed above to 8, 5, 2, and 4. The 4 is for each of the columns 4 to 7, so the ratios are now out of 31.

Notice that there is no need for a closing </COL> tag as COL does not enclose anything, but acts to modify the specification of the table as a whole.

If the browser discovers that one or more of the columns cannot be fitted into the widths you have assigned to them, it attempts to adjust the table so that everything fits. It may not succeed (especially if the window is narrow, and some columns contain long words or wide images), so your column specifications are only suggestions to the browser, although they are suggestions it always tries to obey.

Groups of columns

Columns can be grouped with the COLGROUP element. By default, there is one group. COLGROUP lets you put lines between groups of columns, for instance, or set the same properties for all cells in a group of columns. For example, a 7-column table can be organized into groups with just two extra lines of HTML:

```
<TABLE ID=spanner>
<CAPTION>Table with Grouped Columns</CAPTION>
<COLGROUP COLSPAN=5 WIDTH=1*>      <!--first 5 columns equal width-->
<COLGROUP COLSPAN=2 WIDTH=0.5*>    <!--next 2 columns half as wide-->
```

The **COLSPAN** attribute can be used in conjunction with any other attributes of COL, namely the generic **ID**, **LANG**, **STYLE** and **CLASS**; **WIDTH**, as shown here; and horizontal and vertical alignment with **HALIGN** and **VALIGN**. If you decide to specify groups of columns, you must do this after the table caption and before the table header or body groups.

Column alignment

Column alignment is specified with the same attributes used for aligning individual rows or (**THEAD** or **TBODY**) groups of rows. Note that individual TH and TD cells are aligned with **COLSPAN** and **ROWSPAN**, which are different. You can, as in those cases, choose to align the contents of all the cells in a column or group of columns either vertically, or horizontally, or both. For example:

```
<COL SPAN=3 VALIGN=top ALIGN=right>
<!--align all cells in these 3 cols-->
```

10.10 Inheritance

Structural mark-up
HTML is concerned with structural mark-up. The idea is to separate structural aspects of the document from how the document is rendered on the screen.

For tables, the alignment of text within table cells, and the borders between cells are rendering information. In practice, it is useful to group these features with the structural information, as these are highly portable between applications.

The idea is to hand over most of the rendering information to associated style sheets. The model is specifically designed to take advantage of such style sheets but not to require them.

You can specify the alignment properties of most of the table elements (COL, THEAD, TBODY, TR, TH and TD, but not of TABLE itself), as already explained in this chapter. Sometimes these properties could conflict, so you need to understand the rules that browsers use to decide which specification to use when more than one possibility exists:

- For horizontal alignment, columns have priority over rows.

- For vertical alignment, rows have priority over columns.

- Properties of cells take precedence over properties inherited from all higher structures such as rows or table bodies.

- Properties of elements contained within cells (for instance, if you have put paragraphs such as `<P ALIGN=right>...` inside cells) take precedence over cell properties.

Occasionally, you may need to know the exact precedence order for each attribute. Since language context also affects alignment (for instance, in Arabic and in other languages that read from right-to-left, horizontal alignment assumes a default of `ALIGN=right`), the **LANG** attribute is included.

Here are the rules:

```
Highest priority ------------------------------------- Lowest priority

ALIGN:  (TH|TD) > COL > TR              > (THEAD|TBODY) > default
VALIGN: (TH|TD) > TR  > (THEAD|TBODY) > COL            > default
LANG:   (TH|TD) > TR  > (THEAD|TBODY) > COL > TABLE    > default
```

For example, this shows that given `<TR ALIGN=center> <TD ALIGN=left>`, the cell contents will be left-aligned. There can be no conflict between TH and TD, as you have one or the other but not both; the same goes for THEAD, TBODY and TFOOT.

10.11 Frames, borders, rules

In place of the earlier definition of the **BORDER** attribute, which actually had several roles, HTML now uses no fewer than five **TABLE** attributes to control the ruled grid and outline:

- **BORDER** – controls frame width

- **FRAME** – controls the four lines that form the table's outer border

- **RULES** – controls the lines separating rows or columns of table cells

- **CELLPADDING** – controls the space between cell wall and cell contents

- **CELLSPACING** – controls the wall thickness, the space between individual cells

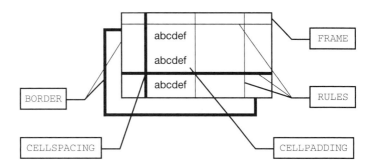

In addition, there are proposals for controlling border colors. This would be quite simple, except that for compatibility with earlier usage, **BORDER** has two meanings. We earnestly recommend that you at once switch to the new syntax, as the new picture is far less confusing than a combination of old and new.

Many existing browsers use <TABLE BORDER> to create fully bordered tables. New browsers treat this command as a synonym of FRAME=all together with RULES=all, which leads to the same fully bordered effect: such is the complexity imposed by backwards compatibility. Similar treatment will be given to BORDER=1 (or higher numbers), though BORDER=0 will sensibly be treated as a synonym of FRAME=void.

Table frames

A table frame is the box around the outside of a table. HTML provides for a range of frame attribute values. For example, if you want a full frame, you specify

```
<TABLE FRAME=box>     <!--or =BORDER-->
  ...
</TABLE>
```

The default style is to draw no frame at all. If you wish, you can also select partial frame effects with top, sides or bottom of the frame only.

Background reading: design issues associated with table rules
During the development of the HTML 4 table specification, a number of avenues were investigated for specifying the ruling patterns for tables. One issue concerns the kinds of statements that can be made. This includes support for edge subtraction as well as edge addition, leading to relatively complex algorithms. For instance, work on allowing the full set of table elements to include the **FRAME** and **RULES** attributes led to an algorithm involving some 24 steps to determine whether or not a particular edge of a cell should be ruled. Even this additional complexity does not provide enough rendering control to meet the full range of needs for tables. The current specification deliberately sticks to a simple intuitive model, sufficient for most purposes. Further experimental work is needed before a more complex approach is standardized.

The complete set of built-in **FRAME** attribute values is:

=box	all four sides of the frame
=border	same as BOX (allowed for compatibility)
=void	suppresses frame – useful with graphics or enclosed forms
=above	top side of the frame
=below	bottom side of the frame
=hsides	top and bottom sides of the frame
=vsides	left- and right-hand sides of the frame
=lhs	left-hand side of the frame
=rhs	right-hand side of the frame

Table rules

The **RULES** attribute draws the specified ruled lines between rows or columns of cells. The default is none, except that (for backwards compatibility) all is assumed if BORDER=1 or any non-zero number.

One common pattern is for horizontal rules between groups of rows. You are allowed to create several TBODY groups and the RULES=groups attribute then separates the groups with ruled lines. RULES=rows or =cols also separates the groups in this way; many browsers will use heavier lines to distinguish group separators from row and column separators.

The complete set of built-in **RULES** attribute values (shown in a table in **RULES=none** style) is:

=none	suppress rules – useful with graphics or enclosed forms
=groups	horizontal rule between groups (THEAD, TBODY, TFOOT)
=rows	as basic, plus row separators
=cols	as basic, plus column separators
=all	draw borders around all cells

Here is a simple example of **RULES=groups** used with THEAD, TBODY and TFOOT:

```
<TITLE>THEAD and TFOOT</TITLE>
<TABLE BORDER=3 RULES=groups>
  <CAPTION>Header and Footer groups</CAPTION>
  <THEAD>
    <TR><TD>Headstart
  <TBODY>
    <TR><TD>Shoulder pads increase the effect
    <TR><TD>Thorax
    <TR><TD>Abdomen
  <TFOOT>
    <TR><TD>Footprint
</TABLE>
```

The illustration shows how the rules in this case separate header, body and footer groups.

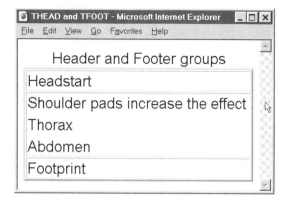

Cellpadding, cellspacing and border

Netscape 1.1 originated several attractive extensions to the rather Spartan standard set of styles in HTML 3, which can all be satisfied by drawing thin black lines where necessary. As Microsoft has taken these up, they are de facto part of standard HTML. New-style tables tend to have a characteristic appearance, as they are generally embossed and often have wider-than-usual borders.

Here is a table with the attribute **CELLPADDING** set to 10 pixels:

```
<TABLE BORDER CELLPADDING=10 CELLSPACING=0>
  <TR><TD>A<TD>Padded<TD>Cell
  <TR><TD>Can<TD>Be<TD>Cosy
</TABLE>
```

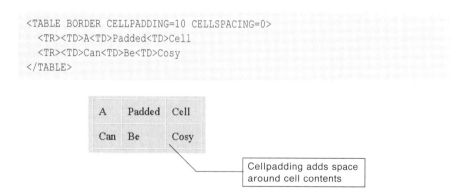

Cellpadding adds space around cell contents

One might have wanted to call this †**CELLMARGIN** or †**CELLSPACE**, since it affects the marginal space all round the cell contents, not the visible thickness of the cell walls, as one might have expected of a padded cell. **CELLPADDING** is measured in any of the standard width units (from picas to pixels). It is useful for ensuring that table contents are visually separate from each other and from cell walls.

† The dagger indicates that these attributes do not exist with this meaning.

Here, by contrast, is a table with the attribute **CELLSPACING** set to 10 pixels:

```
<TABLE FRAME=box CELLPADDING=0 CELLSPACING=10>
  <TR><TD>This<TD>Table's <TD>Cells
  <TR><TD>are <TD>Spaced  <TD>Out(man)
</TABLE>
```

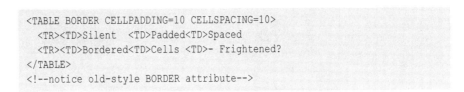

Cellspacing adds space between and around cells (in the cell walls)

This effect could well have been called †**PADDING**, with its thick solid appearance of the cell walls, but Netscape was thinking from the perspective of the cells, and this **CELLSPACING** attribute does indeed space them apart, counting in pixels.

CELLPADDING and **CELLSPACING** can be combined:

```
<TABLE BORDER CELLPADDING=10 CELLSPACING=10>
  <TR><TD>Silent   <TD>Padded<TD>Spaced
  <TR><TD>Bordered<TD>Cells <TD>- Frightened?
</TABLE>
<!--notice old-style BORDER attribute-->
```

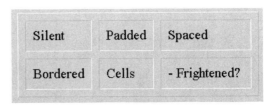

The combination of these two attributes gives a table a strong emphasis that could be useful for many display purposes. Do not overuse them.

Finally, you can also give tables a wide border (which should really have been called †**FRAMEWIDTH**), again measured in pixels. This is typically designed to give a chamfered or bevelled appearance, as if a carpenter had carefully planed off the edges to 45 degrees.

```
<TABLE BORDER=5 CELLPADDING=10 CELLSPACING=10>
  <TR><TD>Padding=10    <TD>Spacing=10
  <TR><TD>together with <TD>a thick border
</TABLE>
```

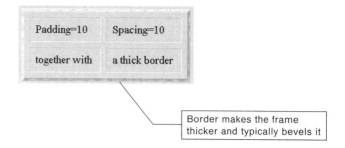

Border makes the frame
thicker and typically bevels it

Separately or together, and combined with alignment of cell contents, these attributes for table borders offer an interestingly wide range of special effects for displaying data.

You can also use character-level control of font sizes in your tables for additional emphasis, but remember that not all your readers will be able to experience the effects you are creating.

Border color

Microsoft Internet Explorer 3.0 introduced three more table attributes to control border color. They are **BORDERCOLOR**, **BORDERCOLORDARK** and **BORDERCOLORLIGHT**. All of them can be applied to TABLE, TR, TD and TH elements. The attributes all take a color name or names of RGB (hexadecimal) color value (see Appendix D). Given the increasing popularity of colorful effects on the Web, it is very possible that these will become standard features of HTML.

All three border color attributes must be used with BORDER=pixelwidth, as you will not see your pretty color unless the table has visible borders. You have two possible approaches:

- Specify a single color for the whole border with **BORDERCOLOR**, making it flat, two-dimensional.

- Specify two separate colors for light and dark parts of the border with **BORDERCOLORDARK** and **BORDERCOLORLIGHT**, making it appear three-dimensional, as long as you choose appropriately toned colors.

For example, here is a table, which has a three-dimensional yellow/green outer border, containing among other things a cell with a two-dimensional blue border:

```
<TITLE>Border Colors</TITLE>
<TABLE BORDER=10 BORDERCOLORLIGHT=yellow BORDERCOLORDARK=green
CELLSPACING=5>
  <CAPTION>Custom border colors</CAPTION>
  <TR><TD BGCOLOR=navy><FONT COLOR=white>
        Mermaids in a deep blue sea</FONT>
```

```
<TR><TD BGCOLOR=red>
        On which the Sun never Sets
<TR><TD BORDERCOLOR=blue ALIGN=center>
        Physician - heal thyself!
<TR><TD BGCOLOR=cyan ALIGN=center>
        "Nothing in Excess"
</TABLE>
```

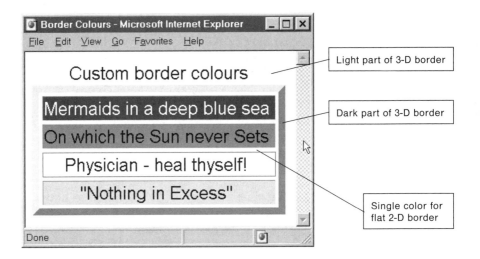

The illustration also shows a use of **CELLSPACING** to separate colored cells from the borders. Because yellow is a light color and green is dark, the table keeps its three-dimensional appearance. The effect is weakened or destroyed if inappropriate colors are chosen, for instance by reversing the green and yellow:

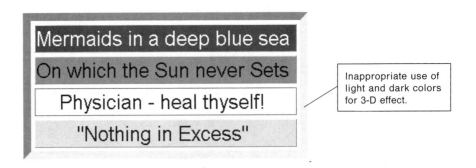

You cannot expect other browsers to observe your border color settings, but provided you are not relying on color-coding to convey meaning, there should not be any real compatibility issues.

Image backgrounds for tables

Microsoft Internet Explorer 3.0 has extended the use of the **BACKGROUND** attribute from a whole document's BODY to use within a single table or cell. This extension means you can apply **BACKGROUND** to TABLE, TD and TH elements. Given the popularity of background color, it is very possible that image backgrounds will also become standard features of HTML. Here is a simple example:

```
<TABLE BORDER RULES=groups BACKGROUND=bird.gif>
```

This tiles the table with the image, just as with <BODY BACKGROUND= your_image>:

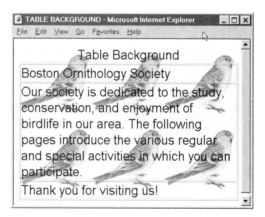

10.12 Putting other elements inside tables

There are few restrictions on what you can put inside table cells. Essentially, you can include anything that can go into normal and marked-up text, namely headers (<H3> etc.), paragraphs (<P>), lists (<UL>) and so on, form elements (see below), images, link anchors, and even arbitrarily nested tables.

Marked-up text

Text in table cells can be marked up as usual. For instance:

```
<TABLE FRAME=all>
  <TR><TD COLSPAN=3>Non-Periodic Table of Chemists
  <TR><TD>K&eacute;kul&eacute;<TD><B>Faraday</B><TD>Haber
</TABLE>
```

This is normally rendered with accents and emboldened text (if the browser can manage them) just as you would hope:

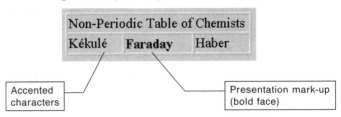

If the results of such formatting are strange, that is your problem. HTML allows you this fine degree of control over table text; it is up to you to make sensible use of it.

Forms

The chapter on forms (see Chapter 11) includes several suggestions on layout, including putting a form inside a table. It is then quite easy to achieve neat, efficient layouts that help the user fill in your forms quickly and correctly.

Here is a classic example of a form/table as viewed by Netscape:

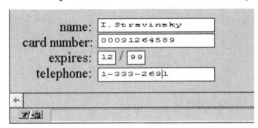

And here is the frameless table used to lay out the text labels and the form:

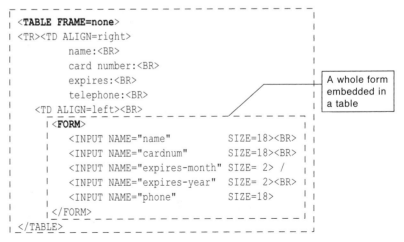

Nested tables

It is sometimes useful to be able to put tables inside table cells. You might think this would slow down the display hopelessly, but this is not so. The task force that developed HTML showed that the time taken to display big or nested tables increases only linearly with their size, so that if it is twice as big, it takes only twice as long to display – which is impressive. As for the visual appearance, you will recall that you can display tables without borders. If you make the outer table borderless, various cells can contain forms, other tables, or just text. The end result is something like a newspaper layout into rows and columns of diverse items. The layout and contents are up to you.

In other words, putting tables, and other things, inside a page-sized table is a simple and direct way of organizing an HTML page so as to make full use of the two-dimensional space available. We expect that as authors get used to the idea, the mechanism will become very popular.

Using tables for layout

Attractive examples of the use of tables for layout exist on the Web. A site we much admire, the Paleontology Museum at the University of California at Berkeley (see Chapter 18 on Designing your Web project for a discussion of the structure of their hypertext), contains both simple and more elaborate uses of tables.

The Evolutionary Thought page contains two Darwinian images framed together. This elegant appearance is created by the simple HTML table code:

```
<TABLE BORDER=5>
   <TR>
      <TD ALIGN=center>
         <IMG SRC=http://ucmp1.berkeley.edu/images/exhibit/darsmall.gif>
      <TD ALIGN=center>
         <IMG SRC=http://ucmp1.berkeley.edu/images/exhibit/darwincol.gif>
</TABLE>
```

The table has just one row, containing two cells, each with a GIF image centered within it. Notice the use of `ALIGN=center` in each row; this rather annoying repetition can be replaced by a table style, or by a single alignment applied to the whole table body.

The page has here been sized to show off the images to best advantage. The table sizes itself automatically to fit the GIF images, which in this case are much narrower than a high-resolution screen. If the page is made wide, the images remain small but more grey-space (if that is the word) appears on both sides of them, as both the table and the text are enclosed in `<CENTER>...</CENTER>` tags.

For a more elaborate example, the UCMP 'Museum' page, part of the hypertext structure discussed in our Design chapter, is dominated by a large table, and illustrated here. The page actually incorporates two other uses of tables, though these are less spectacular. It is made up of two kinds

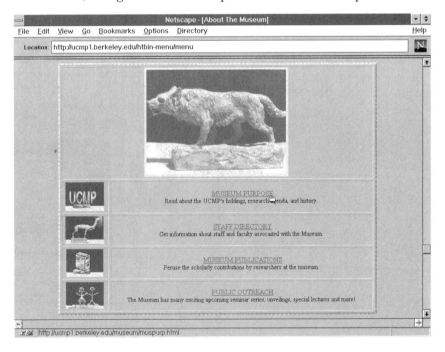

of row, the first row – containing the wolf image, centered in the table – being visibly different from the rest.

The relevant part of the page's HTML, slightly reformatted to emphasize its structure, runs as follows. We have dropped the </TD> and </TR> tags for conciseness.

First the table is declared, using a thick border and plenty of spacing and padding. The whole structure is centered on the page.

```
<TABLE WIDTH="80%" BORDER=4 CELLPADDING=1 CELLSPACING=5>
```

Then the wolf image appears, centered, in a cell spanning two columns. Without the **COLSPAN=2** attribute, the cell would appear centered in the first column. Notice that browsers assume that a cell (such as the <TD> here) must be part of a row <TR>, so the first row tag can actually be omitted, as it is here.

```
<TD ALIGN=center COLSPAN=2>
    <IMG SRC=http://ucmp1.berkeley.edu/images/direwolf5.gif>
```

Then follow four rows, identical in structure. Each contains an image, centered in column 1, and a text label centered in column 2, consisting of a hypertext anchor in a font one size larger than usual <FONT SIZE=+1>, and then on the line below (that is what the <BR> is for) a short description of the item. The second row's tags are pointed out with callout boxes.

```
<TR>
<TD ALIGN=center>
    <IMG SRC=http://ucmp1.berkeley.edu/images/muspurpico.gif>
<TD ALIGN=center><FONT SIZE="+1">
<A HREF=http://ucmp1.berkeley.edu/museum/muspurp.html>MUSEUM
    PURPOSE</A></FONT>
<BR>Read about the UCMP's holdings, research agenda, and history.<BR>
```

Begin table row

Centre contents of cell:

in this case a GIF image

```
<TR>
<TD ALIGN=center>
    <IMG SRC=http://ucmp1.berkeley.edu/images/staffdirico.gif>
<TD ALIGN=center><FONT SIZE="+1">
<A HREF=http://ucmp1.berkeley.edu/museum/staff.html>STAFF
    DIRECTORY</A></FONT><BR>
Get information about staff and faculty associated with the Museum.<BR>
```

Link anchor

Font changes continue until terminated

Line break to put label on a new line

Oversized text

The remaining lines work in exactly the same way:

```
<TR>
<TD ALIGN=center><IMG SRC=http://ucmp1.berkeley.edu/images/muspubico.gif>
<TD ALIGN=center><FONT SIZE="+1">
<A HREF=http://ucmp1.berkeley.edu/museum/muspub.html>MUSEUM
    PUBLICATIONS</A></FONT>
<BR>Peruse the scholarly contributions by researchers at the museum.<BR>
```

If HTML 4 had been available when the UCMP pages were written, the repetition in these formatting instructions could have been avoided. The museum could have chosen to use styles, or to specify column formats just once at the top of the table.

```
<TR>
<TD ALIGN=center><IMG SRC=http://ucmp1.berkeley.edu/images/puboutico.gif>
<TD ALIGN=center><FONT SIZE="+1">
<A HREF=http://ucmp1.berkeley.edu/museum/pubout.html>PUBLIC
    OUTREACH</A></FONT>
<BR>The Museum has many exciting upcoming seminar series.
```

Finally, the table is closed.

```
</TABLE>
```

The table code does not greatly increase the length of the HTML here; it enables text and images to be combined more easily than using flow commands, and it is the only sensible way to get borders. The simplicity and regularity of UCMP's code makes a striking contrast with the often-contorted HMTL that was written when graphics (GIF and JPEG images) were seen as the only way to obtain attractive effects.

10.13   **Speeding up display**

You can make the browser's life easier and keep your readers' tempers cooler, by hinting to the browser how wide the table is going to be, relative to the window in which it is to be displayed. This enables the browser to start displaying the table even before all the table data has arrived. Otherwise, the browser has to read all the data to discover the minimum widths of all the cells, and hence of all the columns, and hence of the table itself. If that is too wide, then it has to decide to clip some of the cells' contents. That could lead to an empty screen for quite a few seconds.

You can set the table's width directly, using a percentage for the **WIDTH** attribute, for example:

```
<TABLE WIDTH="80%">
```

The number of columns, specified in the **COLS** attribute, is up to you:

```
<TABLE WIDTH="80%" COLS=6>
```

but, if you allow about 5 to 10 characters per column, you cannot hope for more than about a dozen columns on screens capable of displaying 80 characters per line. (The use of Braille restricts table width even more severely.) By default, tables specified in advance in this way have columns of equal width; you can improve on this by setting individual or group column widths with COL.

Some design notes on incremental display of tables

For large tables or slow network connections, it is useful to be able to start displaying the table before all of the data has been received.

The default window width for most browsers shows about 80 characters, and the graphics for many HTML pages are designed with these defaults in mind. Authors can provide hints to browsers to activate incremental display of table contents. This feature involves the author specifying the number of columns, and includes provision for control of table-width and the widths of different columns in relative or absolute terms.

For incremental display, the browser needs the number of columns and their widths. The default width of the table is the current window size (**WIDTH="100%"**). Including a **WIDTH** attribute in the TABLE start tag can alter this. By default, all columns have the same width, but you can specify column widths with one or more COL elements before the table data starts.

The remaining issue is the number of columns. Some people have suggested waiting until the first row of the table has been received, but this could take a long time if the cells have a lot of content. On the whole it makes more sense, when incremental display is desired, to get authors to explicitly specify the number of columns in the TABLE start tag.

Authors still need a way of informing the browser whether to use incremental display or to automatically size the table to match the cell contents. For the two-pass, auto-sizing mode, the first pass determines the number of columns, whereas for the incremental mode, the number of columns needs to be stated up front. So it seems that COLS=nn would be better for this purpose than a **LAYOUT** attribute such as LAYOUT=FIXED or LAYOUT=AUTO.

These pieces of information at once save you a lot of work, and enable the browser to set up the basic structure. The browser may still not be able to comply exactly with your specification, as this depends on what you have inside the cells of the table, but it will do its best.

For example:

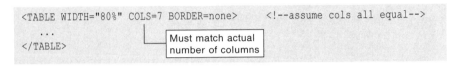

10.14 Summary

Tables provide a sophisticated, but easy-to-use mechanism for formatting data into rows and columns. The use of built-in defaults, inheritance of attributes and automatic sizing to fit table contents allows authors to construct tables with very few HTML instructions. More elaborate tables can be given captions and headers, and their contents can be aligned horizontally and vertically. It is possible to specify alignments for groups of cells, such as all header or all body cells, and to control columns of cells as if they were separate entities. Cells can also span rows or columns, and they may contain other HTML elements such as headings, paragraphs, lists, forms, images, hypertext anchors and even, nested tables.

Tables are useful for laying out forms, and for simulating frames for non-frame browsers. They are increasingly used for attractively arranging text with graphics, sometimes with contrasting color or patterned backgrounds.

11
FORMS

Included in this chapter is information on:

- Handling forms in HTML
- Using FORM elements
- Submitting forms to the server
- Designing forms, with practical tips

Summary

To remedy various shortcomings of HTML 3.2, the following new features are included in HTML 4 forms:

- The **TABINDEX** attribute is introduced to allow explicit specification of the tabbing order when traversing from one form control to another.

- The **ACCESSKEY** attribute provides for specifying direct keyboard access to form fields.

- The new attribute **DISABLED** allows you to make a form-control initially insensitive.

- The attribute **TITLE** is added to most existing elements to be a placeholder for additional information that will be rendered when the user requests help.

- The `LABEL` element associates a label with a particular form control.

- The `FIELDSET` element groups related fields together, and, in association with a `LEGEND`, can name the group.

These two new elements allow better rendering and better interactivity. Speech-based browsers can better describe the form.

- The attribute **ONCHANGE**, in association with support for scripting languages, allows form providers to include some code checking on entered data.

- The `INPUT` element has a new attribute **ACCEPT**, that allows you to specify a list of media types or type patterns for the input.

- The `FORM` element's new attribute **ACCEPT-CHARSET** is modeled on the HTTP Accept-Charset header (see Chapter 18), and can be used to specify a list of character sets acceptable to the server.

11.1 Introduction

Server-side scripts
This chapter does not cover the creation of server-side scripts to handle incoming HTML forms data, although it briefly explains their use.

A form consists of a group of fields to fill in, and these appear on the screen when a user loads the HTML document in question. Unlike other HTML elements such as headers and paragraphs, forms are designed to enable users to send information *back* to the server, rather than just retrieve information in the usual way. When you submit the contents of a form, it is sent to the server for processing by special software. If you are not a programmer, then you need to find someone who can make your forms work for you on your server. The server side of things is outside the scope of HTML, and of this book.

A paper form contains a title, some printed instructions, and various boxes for you to fill in. Sometimes you need to write your name or various numbers in these boxes; sometimes you can just insert a single letter (like 'M' for Married) in a form-field, and sometimes all you need to do is to check the box to indicate that you have selected this item. All of these mechanisms are available in HTML forms in the shape of fields, checkboxes, radio buttons, selection menus, and so on.

One advantage on-screen forms have over actual paper forms is that they are guaranteed to be legible, as all the words are keyed-in, rather than written in longhand.

Another and more significant advantage is speed: as soon as your readers have filled in their forms, they can press a button to send the form data straight to you, or at least, to your server. Everything they have inserted into the form is sent to your server for processing.

How forms are handled behind the scenes

As explained, the server has to run a specific program that can handle all incoming user information generated when the form is submitted. For example, the server might save the incoming data to a specific file or to a database. Or, if you are very ambitious, you might have an automatic reply service that enables your customers to perform certain functions such as booking a ticket for a forthcoming concert, for example. The program on your server could confirm bookings by sending your customers unique booking reference numbers, and then it would print the tickets, which would be soon mailed to you. You can see that many different levels of sophistication, and expense, are possible.

The diagram shows an example of what happens behind the scenes when a user completes a form.

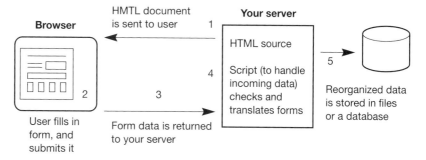

In the example, once the data has been stored, the following sequence of events usually occurs:

1. A confirmation is quickly sent back to the user and a log of changes is recorded.

2. The system reserves the seats, prints and mails the tickets, and then records the user's address for the next mail list.

As you can see from this everyday example of an interactive form, HTML on the Web, is, in fact, a mere placid surface under which there is much activity by other systems.

11.2 Why would you want information from users?

HTML forms, then, together with server scripts, render your documents truly interactive: your users can talk back. There are many possible reasons why you might want them to do this:

*   To let users give you comments and feedback on your document or the products it describes.

- To enable users to find out more about your products or services.

- To enable prospective customers to discuss technical issues with you directly.

- To allow actual customers to order products or services from you.

- To find out who is interested in your document, ideas, products or services.

- To enable users to search for and retrieve information from other search engines.

Improved information sharing

The Internet was developed for information sharing primarily for Government and Academic purposes. Many databases full of technical information exist in relatively hard-to-access formats. But HTML forms make it quite easy for organizations with such data to display Web pages; these forms can include specific and helpful explanations of what is available, as well as the easy-to-use forms themselves that let users conduct searches and then retrieve the information they need.

The process of sharing information from an existing database is similar to the common use of HTML forms. The only significant difference is that your server needs an interface to the database; although this may require some programming, usually, it is not difficult to perform.

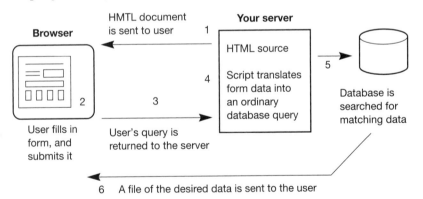

For example, several different authorities may hold data on Atlantic fish stocks. The full picture is available only by detailed study of many information sources. Suitable querying of the existing databases using HTML forms could improve understanding of the problems and help to secure international agreements on conservation of the remaining fish. Of course, the various authorities all need to provide their own forms. HTML offers a uniform and internationally agreed upon mechanism for this purpose, which should make things easier for everyone.

MAILTO: **Using HTML without forms**

The use of forms to set up a dialogue with your readers is a relatively advanced topic, and you will be able to create effective HTML documents for many purposes without ever using them. We suggest that you set up your Web pages without forms, and then carefully work out whether or not you actually need the more sophisticated interaction that forms can provide. If you only need to enable your readers to send comments, then you do not necessarily have to use forms. Instead, you can simply do the following:

- State your email address, preferably using an alias like 'Webmaster' (so that readers can write to you, or your successor in your HTML-writing job, independently), or

- Use the 'MAILTO:' keyword to connect readers' browsers to their mail tools directly.

Most browsers now handle the 'MAILTO:' mechanism, provided that their human users have remembered to fill in their email addresses and the directory paths of their mail tools. A typical use of this simple mechanism is:

```
<A HREF="MAILTO:pete@www.yourco.com">Mail to pete@www.yourco.com</A>
```

This causes a predefined mail form to appear; when filled in and submitted, an ordinary email message is sent to the address given in the HREF.

We think this is well worth knowing, as it may save you the trouble and expense of setting up the server mechanisms that you would otherwise need to handle forms. That said, email is no substitute for the power and convenience of a properly configured forms system.

11.3 Your first form

When it comes to forms handling, HTML is quite sophisticated. Luckily, you can still write a form in only a line or two. Do not worry about the details for now: the example here is just to show you that a little HTML can be very useful. The following snippet tells your server to run a script called 'savezip' when it receives the forms data, which, in this case, consists of a US postal zipcode. It might be handy for an anonymous survey, for example:

Savezip
The HTML part of this is explained in full later in this chapter. Programs on the server, such as 'savezip', are not part of HTML.

```
<FORM ACTION="savezip">
  <P>Zip or post code: <INPUT NAME="zipcode" SIZE="9">
  <P> <INPUT TYPE=submit>
</FORM>
```

This little piece of HTML displays an input field, with a standard Submit button:

Most of the other form constructs are no more complicated than this, but there are often several ways of achieving a result. For example, you can use lists to format columns of input fields, or tables, or decimal alignment: each method has its own advantages.

More sophisticated forms

Other constructs include a FILE attachment widget; images on SUBMIT and RESET buttons, and graphical SELECTion menus (using SHAPEs within OPTIONs).

It is permissible to have more than one form in a document, though this may be confusing to authors and readers. Forms may not, however, be nested, unlike tables.

This chapter introduces the various form elements one by one, with worked examples of useful types of form. Other elements (such as TABLEs and UL or DL lists), which you will often need when building forms, are incorporated in the examples, and are explained in their own chapters. Once the basic elements have been explained, the chapter concludes by showing how they can be combined in forms design to yield practical forms, ready to have scripts written for them.

11.4 HTML's form elements

Of the FORM element itself, there is little to write. You always put:

```
<FORM ACTION = "http://myserver.cobweb.com.doform">
  ... fields go here ...
  ... mixed with any body-content text and tables you like ...
  <P> <INPUT TYPE=submit> <INPUT TYPE=reset>
</FORM>
```

The form tag itself can be qualified with an HTTP **METHOD** (**=post** or **=get**) attribute, to tell the browser which HyperText Transfer Protocol method the server supports. **get** is the default. For example:

```
<FORM METHOD=post ACTION="http://www.acme.co.uk/forms/register">
```

The **ACTION** attribute, as illustrated above, tells the browser where you would like the form submitted; the default is the URL of the document itself, which usually is not what you want.

The **ENCTYPE** attribute tells the browser which MIME contents type to use when encoding form data. Its default is "`application/x-www-form-urlencoded`" which we hope you never need to change.

The **SCRIPT** attribute lets you insert a URL for a script, which the browser can fetch and interpret. Scripts are introduced in Chapter 16.

The rest of this section presents the form elements one by one.

Simple text fields

The most general form element is `INPUT`. Its simplest use is as a simple text field. Like the other form elements, it is only allowed inside `FORM` tags. As text is the default type, you need only give the field name and size. Notice the use of ordinary formatting of text:

```
<H3> Please fill in the following details for your enquiry: </H3>
<P> Surname : <INPUT NAME="surname" SIZE="20">
```

Please fill in the following details for your enquiry:

Surname : | Blenkinsop-smythes |

This shows the simplest kind of formatting, namely left-alignment hard up against the field prompt. This is less than ideal if there are several fields to consider.

When the form is submitted (the user presses the Submit button – see the section 'Submit button', below), the browser returns each field's name with its currently entered value.

An issue that you need to be aware of when designing forms is the browser window's probable width. It is nice to group related fields (for example, surname, initials, and so on), on a single line, but you have to remember that users will not necessarily see them displayed like that.

Text fields (like range and hidden fields) can be given default `VALUE`s:

```
<INPUT NAME="surname" SIZE="20" VALUE="your surname">
```

These appear in the field when first displayed, or when the Reset button is pressed – see below. Two other attributes are necessary in most uses of text and password fields:

SIZE	For fixed-pitch fonts (the default), the number of characters to display.
	For variable-pitch fonts, the number of en units (defined as half the width of the widest character in the font) visible in the field.

MAXLENGTH The maximum number of text/password characters allowed.

Generic attributes of FORM elements

You can qualify any INPUT element, including TEXT, with several generic attributes. We will list them just once, here:

ID Identifier unique in this document. Allows hypertext links to point to this field by referencing the identifier (this is described in Chapter 7, 'Hypertext links')

LANG Language identifier

CLASS To attach a style to this element

TYPE TEXT (the default); other types include RADIO, CHECKBOX, PASSWORD and so on

NAME Field name, returned with the field value data when submitted

VALUE Initial value for the field

Multi-line text fields

Multi-line text was formerly handled with TEXT, but this unintentionally limited input to 1024 characters. Using TEXTAREA helps you over that hurdle, so that you can make multi-line fields as large as you need. Of course, if your server is bombarded with replies, this means you will need megabytes of free storage. The syntax is pleasantly straightforward:

```
<TEXTAREA NAME="request" ROWS=2 COLS=64>
    Please overtype this with your request.
</TEXTAREA>
```

The HTML can be read as saying:

'create a free-format input textarea called "request" with a viewport of two rows of 64 characters displayed on the browser screen. Prefill the text area with the words "Please overtype this with your request".'

It is important to understand from the above example that the input text is not limited to 2×64 characters. As the user continues typing, the text scrolls away. The specified rows and columns define what used to be called a viewport onto the text area: you are, in effect, looking through a small window into a much larger room, which can hold as much text as you please.

The result is a free-format input field like this:

```
        Please overtype this with your request.
```

You can see that the text between the TEXTAREA tags is used to initialize the field (compare this with the **VALUE** attribute for INPUT TYPE=TEXT). The scrollbars make it clear that the text is allowed to extend beyond the narrow limits of the visible text area.

A fixed-pitch font such as Courier is normally used in input areas for simplicity, but browsers can actually use proportional fonts like Times or Arial as long as they wrap text properly. Of course, width in characters does not have a definite meaning with proportional fonts.

The meaning of the size declared with 'COLS=64' therefore depends on the type of font in use:

- **fixed-pitch font:**

    declared number of columns = **width in characters**

- **proportional font:**

    declared number of columns = **width in en units**

Horizontal and vertical scrollbars, as shown in the example above, are typically provided on computers with windowed environments. Text-only browsers may allow scrolling by means of the cursor keys on the keyboard.

You should always include a NAME, as with the INPUT types. Generic attributes have their usual effects.

Here is an example from the Web of a form that consists principally of a multi-line text area:

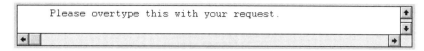

Location: http://rs6.loc.gov/mail.html

Send Your Comments to the Library of Congress

We would be interested in hearing your comments on our server. Mail can be sent directly to the Library by filling out the greater, or a browser that supports forms (including Mosaic's hidden fields). Please be sure to fill in your name and email forwarded to the Library through the UIUC Mail Gateway.

Although the message box has an indefinite horizontal scroll capacity, please use carriage returns to ensure that long line.

Please enter your name here: `Harpo Marx`
Please enter your email address here: `harpo@funny.com`
Enter the subject of the message here: `LC WWW Server`
Type your message below and click on the **Send Mail** button.

```
Hi, I wanted to tell you about|
```

Send mail!

The structure is simple enough for you to guess, so we will not list the HTML. Notice that no attempt has been made to align the fields, and that the prompts for the fields and the instructions for the text area flow into each other visually instead of seeming to be distinct items. Also, placing the Submit button, also called the 'Send Mail' button, on the right is unusual, and the Reset button (which you press if you decide you do not want to send a message) has been omitted altogether. See below for a discussion of how to lay out forms effectively.

Radio buttons

You obtain radio buttons in HTML by specifying an INPUT field with TYPE=RADIO. Both NAME and VALUE are mandatory.

Radio buttons are the exception to the rule that input fields must have unique names to identify their contents, as the way that you tell the browser that these radio buttons go together is to give them the same name. Their behavior is like a set of old-fashioned mechanical push-buttons on a radio set: when you press one, the previously pressed one pops out again. So, a set of radio buttons in a form returns just one, which is the one selected by the user. You will be relieved to hear that only the selected one's data is returned to the server.

The syntax is simple and regular. You give each button a name and supply some text for the user to read beside the button.

You **must** mark **exactly one** button as 'checked'. This button will be shown in the 'yes' state when the form is first displayed (and when the form is reset). If you mark more than one button as checked or none at all, it is an error. The browser's behavior is not defined, and it may do something unpredictable such as checking only the first button – or only the last one.

To help you avoid missing anything, it is best to arrange your radio button declarations in a column (this example, like the others, must be included within <FORM>...</FORM> tags, and with SUBMIT and RESET buttons too):

```
<P><B>Which is your favorite bean:</B><P>
<INPUT TYPE=radio NAME=coffee VALUE="Java">Old Brown Java
<INPUT TYPE=radio NAME=coffee VALUE="Sumatra">Sumatra Blue Lingtong
<INPUT TYPE=radio NAME=coffee VALUE="Mocha" CHECKED>Mocha
<INPUT TYPE=radio NAME=coffee VALUE="Jamaica">Jamaica Mountain
<INPUT TYPE=radio NAME=coffee VALUE="Kenya">Kenya Peaberry<P>
```

This setup creates a beautiful row of radio buttons like this:

Notice that the **CHECKED** attribute is set for our favorite Mocha coffee: we supply it by default, which means initially, and when the RESET button is pressed. To repeat, you must make exactly one button the checked default.

Checkboxes

Checkboxes are more versatile than radio buttons, as you can have as many of them selected as you like. So if it makes sense to check two or more items, you use checkboxes, not radio buttons. Alternatively, you can use a multiple-choice SELECT menu. Each checkbox has just two states – checked or not checked. Most browsers use an X to indicate that a checkbox is checked.

Separate-item checkboxes

The syntax is virtually identical to that for radio buttons:

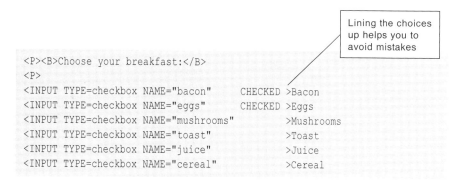

```
<P><B>Choose your breakfast:</B>
<P>
<INPUT TYPE=checkbox NAME="bacon"       CHECKED >Bacon
<INPUT TYPE=checkbox NAME="eggs"        CHECKED >Eggs
<INPUT TYPE=checkbox NAME="mushrooms"           >Mushrooms
<INPUT TYPE=checkbox NAME="toast"               >Toast
<INPUT TYPE=checkbox NAME="juice"               >Juice
<INPUT TYPE=checkbox NAME="cereal"              >Cereal
```

Your browser will initially display the above as something like this:

Choose your breakfast:

☒Bacon ☒Eggs ☐Mushrooms ☐Toast ☐Juice ☐Cereal

The user is then free to check or uncheck any or all of the boxes.

One important difference between radio buttons and checkboxes can be seen when you look carefully at the examples. With checkboxes, you can check off as many checkboxes as you please. In this case, we have assumed that everyone will want bacon and eggs for breakfast. With radio buttons, we have offered users to choose a variety of coffee via a radio button. Only one choice is possible.

Checkboxes for variations on a theme

In this example, all the checkboxes have unique names, so the breakfast menu consists of separate items. Another use of checkboxes is for variations on a single theme. For instance, you could offer your customers a range of ice-cream, rather than just one. People could have one scoop of each kind.

Your ice-cream checkboxes would be declared like this:

```
<FORM>
<H4>Please check each box for a scoop of that freshly-made
ice-cream:</H4>
  <INPUT TYPE=checkbox NAME="ice" CHECKED>Vanilla
  <INPUT TYPE=checkbox NAME="ice" CHECKED>Strawberry
  <INPUT TYPE=checkbox NAME="ice">Pistachio
  <INPUT TYPE=checkbox NAME="ice">Walnut
  <INPUT TYPE=checkbox NAME="ice" CHECKED>Rum'n'Raisin
  <P><INPUT TYPE=submit>  <INPUT TYPE=reset>
</FORM>
```

The effect is like this:

Please check each box for a scoop of that freshly-made ice-cream:

☒ Vanilla ☒ Strawberry ☐ Pistachio ☐ Walnut ☒ Rum'n'Raisin

[**Submit Query**] [**Reset**]

You can see that three scoops are pre-selected to encourage your customers to buy. They can uncheck them and choose just one scoop if they prefer.

The Submit button sends only the checked boxes' names and values to the server (as for radio buttons), whereas, just as you would expect, the Reset button puts the checkboxes back to their initial states – in this case, as shown in the figure.

The ice-cream submission includes the input field name ('ice') together with the name of each flavor of ice-cream checked at the time the Submit button is pressed. The data sent back therefore says, for example:

```
"ice=Vanilla+ice=Strawberry+ice=Rum'n'Raisin".
```

A program on the server unpacks all this again into its component parts, so that the consumer's order can be processed.

Menus (single- and multiple-choice)

Menus provide a preferred alternative to input fields when potential choices are known in advance. They use up less screen space than radio buttons (for single selections) or checkboxes (for multiple selections), so they are especially useful in instances in which numerous data must be gathered on a form.

Textual menus

The basic syntax is a SELECT element that contains several OPTION elements:

```
<P><B>Select the kinds of music you like:</B><P>
<SELECT MULTIPLE NAME="music">
  <OPTION SELECTED>Jazz
  <OPTION>Rock
  <OPTION>Blues
  <OPTION>Folk
  <OPTION>Gamelan
</SELECT>
```

The example shows three options that the user has selected at one time. If MULTIPLE is omitted from SELECT, then only one option can be selected; that is, the menu simulates radio behavior. Individual options can be marked SELECTED. Obviously, you can only mark one option as SELECTED if you have specified a single-choice menu.

When the Submit button is pressed, the name ('music') is sent back with *each* of the selected options.

File attachments

The file attachment mechanism lets the user attach files to be submitted with the form. For instance:

```
<INPUT TYPE=file>
```

Graphic browsers normally use a field, accompanied by a button that calls up a file dialog box, to allow users to browse through their directories:

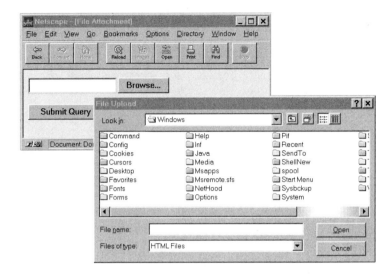

To use the file attachment, you must also put the **ENCTYPE** attribute in the FORM tag:

```
<FORM ENCTYPE="multipart/form-data"...>
```

This tells the browser to be ready to submit data as files as well as files in the usual encoding.

The Submit button

The Submit button's basic structure is

```
<INPUT TYPE=submit>
```

The default button label depends on the browser. Netscape's is quite typical:

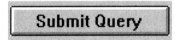

Ways you can ring the changes are:

- **VALUE** to change the default label

```
<INPUT VALUE="Submit Query Now" TYPE=submit>
```

Occasionally, this may be useful, but more likely, it can lead to confusion.

- **NAME** to distinguish which Submit button was pressed

```
<INPUT NAME="casual" VALUE="Casual Inquiry" TYPE=submit>
<INPUT NAME="urgent" VALUE="Purchase Order" TYPE=submit>
```

This makes the zipcode example look like this:

The example suggests a context in which you *might* want to provide more than one Submit button. In general, there should be exactly one – the user submits the data or not, and the server-side scripts (to handle the returned data) are as simple as possible. Prioritizing is notoriously tricky, but at least in instances in which people need to decide whether or not to spend money, they can usually get their act together and press the right button.

It is up to the server to do something sensible with the returned name and value of the Submit button.

- **SRC** to put an image on a Submit button

```
<INPUT SRC="launch.gif" ALIGN=left TYPE=submit>
```

The specified image is fetched and used instead of the default text. **ALIGN** has its usual behavior, as with IMG and TABLE; with ALIGN=left, for instance, the image floats down to the left margin, and allows text to wrap to its right.

If you are going to use an image Submit button, choose something visual; for example, christening an ocean liner by breaking a champagne bottle across its bows, launching a US space shuttle, or an Olympic sprinter at the starting blocks waiting for the gun.

- TYPE=image and SRC=image_url to return a location on a Submitted image

    This slightly bizarre hangover from HTML 2.0 consists of an image that behaves like a Submit button, though its type is not Submit. The x and y coordinates of the click, measured from the top-left corner of the image, are returned to the server. The **NAME** attribute as usual identifies the field responsible for the input. A **VALUE** attribute can be provided (compare ALT for IMG elements) for text-only browsers: it is ignored in graphics. Netscape uses the **NAME** attribute for this purpose. An **ALIGN** attribute works exactly as for TYPE=submit buttons. For example:

```
<INPUT TYPE=image NAME="b" SRC="bird.gif" VALUE="clickable image">
```

The effect is to display the image as a clickable button, typically with a colored border. When the user clicks on it, x and y position data are returned URL-encoded as shown in the illustration below, in the form:

```
?name.x=xvalue&name.y=yvalue
```

For example:

```
?b.x=23&b.y=114
```

The server can use the data to determine that, in this example, the tail of the bird was clicked on, and can provide information accordingly.

form.html?b.x=23&b.y=114

- TYPE=button
  Finally, a BUTTON type is provided for use with scripts such as Java. Programmers can make scripts respond to clicks using the onClick intrinsic event, for example to run consistency checks or to fill in derived fields (Gender must be male if Title=Mr, for instance).

The Reset button

The Reset button's basic structure is

```
<INPUT TYPE=reset>
```

The button's action is to reset all fields in the form to their initial values, which may be blank.

It has exactly the same **VALUE** and **SRC** variations as the Submit button. There is surely no reason to display more than one Reset button on any form. We do not suggest modifying the Reset button's default appearance unless you have very good reason to do so. An inherent advantage for the default Submit and Reset buttons is that they require no image traffic between server and client. They are also highly recognizable in their standard form.

Hidden fields

If you need to preserve some status information, such as a transaction identifier, with the form data, then a hidden field is the way to do it. HTTP servers do not usually remember such information, as it would require a lot of processing and could slow down the server's response to users.

The user sees nothing special, but the contents of any hidden fields are sent with the rest of the form data. It is up to your server to do something sensible with the information; and, indeed, to ensure that something sensible was put in the field to start with. You need to discuss this with your server provider if you have any special requirements.

```
<INPUT TYPE=hidden NAME=transact VALUE=T501">
```

Password fields

You can ask users to supply a password in a form:

```
<P>Your Password : <INPUT TYPE=password NAME=pwd>
```

This creates an input field like this:

Your Password : ` * * * * * * * `

The password type is exactly like single-line text input, except that a star or space is echoed to the screen in place of each character of the actual password text typed in by the user. Existing HTTP sends the data in plaintext, so your users' passwords are in no way secure against sniffer programs. Secure HTTP, for example, will improve on this.

11.5 Submitting forms

The user fills in your elegant masterpiece and presses the Submit button. This sends the complete set of inputs to the URL specified by the **ACTION** attribute; it uses the method specified in the **METHOD** attribute. The two possible methods are **get** and **post**. **get** appends the returned data to the URL, whereas **post** sends the data separately.

```
<!--call a user-written program-->
<FORM ACTION="http://www.mammon.com/programs/savezip" METHOD=post>
```

This says that the savezip handler program on your server is to process the encoded form data, which is posted separately. For this, you have to use HTTP.

If you do not specify a recipient with **ACTION=...** HTML simply sends the data to the document URL, which usually will not be what you want. You need to sort out with your server provider (preferably before you start designing your forms) how to deal with returned data: it is likely they have some standard software for the job. The obvious thing to do is to stick it in a file, which you fetch with FTP or which they mail to you every so often.

It is outside the scope of this book to describe how to set up a server complete with form handlers. A recent book with good, intelligible coverage of all this is *Spinning the Web: How to Provide Information on the Internet*, by Andrew Ford, International Thomson Publishing, 1996. Ford's account of how to handle data returned from forms is necessarily a bit more technical than most of our descriptions, and demands some familiarity both with programming and with the UNIX operating system.

11.6 Form design

Design principles

A great deal has been written about form design, not only for user interfaces, especially with databases, but also in bureaucracies around the world. We would not want to add to the mountains of paper on the subject. Some useful principles to bear in mind are:

- Regularly laid-out forms are easier to understand and are more likely to be completed.

- Formatting in a single column is easy and effective.

- It is simple to align prompts (using decimals) if they all end in ':' or another shared character.

- Related fields (title, forename and surname) should be together, e.g., on a line.

- Dividing lines (<HR>, table borders) and background color can visually group related fields.

Freedom of layout

HTML gives you a free choice of form layout, allowing you to use any of the mark-up elements discussed in this book. This section discusses how you can use lists and tables to organize your forms. You could take other routes: for example, forms within <PRE>...</PRE> tags can be laid out very simply with spaces and line breaks. The price you pay is that forms in PRE come out in fixed-pitch text, in place of the more usual, and more attractive, proportional fonts.

Platform independence

Typically, other forms languages give you a particular language intended for use on one computer platform that also comes with one, and only one, software tool, such as a database. In contrast, HTML is platform independent; it is completely portable, its browsers and servers are available on numerous machines and operating systems, and it can readily interface to nearly any database or software tool.

This 'platform independence' is a very desirable property. If you develop your forms for a Microsoft Windows NT server running on a personal computer and you find it is unable to handle all the business it generates, you can move to a fast UNIX box without changing your HTML at all. Of course, you will have to modify any scripts that depend on the operating system.

Similarly, your users can look at your forms with browsers running on UNIX workstations, Apple Macintoshes, Personal Computers, or even traditional ASCII text-only terminals. Provided their browsers correctly interpret the HTML, the exact appearance on their screens is not important. They can fill in your forms and submit them as if they were all using identical machines.

Single-column forms

Many simple form applications can be handled quite adequately using a single column of input elements, such as text fields, radio buttons, and so on. At least three ways to achieve respectable-looking, single-column forms exist:

- Using lists

- With a table using right-alignment for prompt labels and left-alignment for fields

- With a single table cell, using decimal-alignment to center the prompt characters

We will demonstrate each approach in turn.

Lists

Both plain lists (`<UL PLAIN>`) and definition lists (`<DL>`) offer possibilities for arranging input fields. Here is a simple example using definition lists:

```
<FORM>
   <DL>
      <DT>Initials:<DD><INPUT NAME="initials" SIZE="5" >
      <DT>Surname: <DD><INPUT NAME="surname"  SIZE="20">
      <DT>Zipcode: <DD><INPUT NAME="zipcode"  SIZE="9" >
   </DL>
      <INPUT TYPE=reset> <INPUT TYPE=submit>
</FORM>
```

In a typical browser, the result (Reset and Submit buttons not shown) is like this:

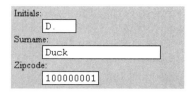

The effect is not unpleasant, but it takes up more screen space than it should, and you have no control over the positioning of the fields: in this browser, the indentation is arguably too small for our purpose. You may be able to use a style sheet to organize things better for you.

Right- and left-aligned table data cells

A more powerful, but messier approach is to use a table with two data cells (`<TD>`) for each row: the one on the left is to contain right-aligned text prompts; the one on the right, left-aligned fields.

```
<FORM>
   <TABLE>
      <TR> <TD ALIGN=right>Initials:
              <TD ALIGN=left ><INPUT NAME="initials" SIZE="5" >
      <TR> <TD ALIGN=right>Surname :
              <TD ALIGN=left ><INPUT NAME="surname"  SIZE="20">
      <TR> <TD ALIGN=right>Zipcode :
              <TD ALIGN=left ><INPUT NAME="zipcode"  SIZE="9" >
   </TABLE>
   <INPUT TYPE=reset> <INPUT TYPE=submit>
</FORM>
```

The effect is something like this:

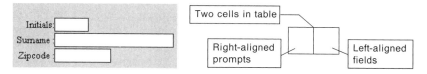

This is much more like what most database people expect from a form.

A single decimally-aligned table data cell

A more compact and arguably more elegant way to achieve the same result is to align all the fields vertically within a single table cell, by specifying a convenient character to which to align. This mechanism is designed for lining up decimal points with digits both sides, but is equally fine for aligning colon prompts with text one side and fields the other – it is a neat example of the generality of HTML. You specify 'ALIGN=char' and state that the alignment character is to be a colon (CHAR=":"). Remember to put in line breaks (<BR>) to force browsers to format the fields in a column.

For example:

```
<FORM>
    <TABLE><TR ALIGN=char CHAR=":">
      <TD>
          Initials:<INPUT NAME="initials" SIZE="5" ><BR>
          Surname :<INPUT NAME="surname"  SIZE="20"><BR>
          Zipcode :<INPUT NAME="zipcode"  SIZE="9" ><BR>
    </TABLE>
      <INPUT TYPE=reset> <INPUT TYPE=submit>
</FORM>
```

The effect is the same.

Multi-column forms

The general case is naturally a form that is too complex to fit into the single-column mould, even if that is distorted to allow 'twin' fields (such as month and year) to share a line. The main problem is to align fields that have the appearance of regularity, although they are different sizes. Some assumption has to be made about the likely space available on the typical browser's window.

The table is the only construct in HTML that permits the required degree of precision in aligning and positioning. Many cells and rows may be needed, and with careful design, to achieve a visually satisfying result.

You can nest tables, so you can set up a large table that contains, in one or more of its data cells, a column-of-fields table, as described above. You can then save screen space by placing two or more columns beside each other. Remember, though, that this could force some users to scroll sideways to see some of the fields. It is wise to remember that many users will have screens capable of displaying lines of no more than 80 characters.

11.7 HTML 4 extensions to forms

In this section of proposed improvements for HTML 4:

- Why more powerful forms are needed
- Providing access keys
- Enabling tabbing
- Adding tooltip/balloon help information
- Adding clickable labels to controls
- Grouping fields into accessible sets

Why more powerful forms are needed

Earlier versions of HTML provided simple forms, which lacked several features that users are coming to expect. For example:

- The tabbing order for moving between fields or hypertext links was undefined.

- There was no provision for keyboard shortcuts for particular actions, nor for access keys to drive menus.

- The label text for radio buttons and checkboxes was not active; that is, clicking on label text did not push the neighboring button.

- There was no means of marking up groups of related form fields to support speech-based browsers for the print-impaired.

- There was no provision for checking values as they were entered into form fields. All checking was done at the server, when the form's contents had been submitted.

- The range of form-field types was limited in comparison with modern user interfaces. For instance, there were no data entry grids or number entry sliders, while forms themselves were restricted to single pages.

- Servers could not update individual fields in submitted forms; instead, they had to send complete HTML documents back to clients, causing screens to flicker as browsers hurried to redraw entire displays.

It is proposed to introduce several elements and attributes into HTML 4 to remedy some of these problems. They should make forms easier and quicker to use. The newcomers are:

- **ACCESSKEY**=letter

- **TABINDEX**=number *and* **NOTABSTOP**

- **TITLE**="little bit of help that pops up"

- <LABEL>

- <FIELDSET> *and* CAPTION="name of fieldset"

- Support for using OBJECTs as form fields

Some of these are comfortably backward-compatible with HTML 3; others cannot be, either because they need scripts or because old browsers are unable to display them sensibly. Further extensions are anticipated, for instance: better control types, enhanced menus, multiple-page layouts and server-driven updates. These exciting possibilities are not discussed further here.

Providing access keys

ACCESSKEY is proposed to be a single-character attribute on LABEL, CAPTION and A (anchor) tags. Its purpose is to make forms accessible to systems without a mouse, especially those designed for people with disabilities. It also offers quick performance for advanced users.

ACCESSKEY provides a case-insensitive keyboard shortcut for clicking on a label or anchor. So when the access key is 'U', for example, it does not matter whether the user types 'u' in upper- or lower-case characters. On Windows, the first instance of the access key character in the label or anchor is Underlined. Any single-character key can be used for access. Special keys like Enter and Control cannot be used, and it is unwise to select keys such as £ or Ü, which do not occur on all keyboards. Each key can be used only once in any HTML page. The keyboard combination for selecting the access key is ALT (held down) and the desired character. For example:

```
<LABEL ACCESSKEY>="U">User Name
  <INPUT TYPE="input" NAME="username">
</LABEL>
```

To complete this example: when the Windows user types ALT-U (prompted by the U in the field label), the input box called 'username' is given the focus, just as if the user had pointed the mouse at the field and clicked on it. (The photograph shows an English keyboard.) The presence of the focus in a text field is indicated by a vertical bar, which acts as a text cursor:

ACCESSKEY works in much the same way for hypertext anchors:

```
<A HREF="toc.html" ACCESSKEY="T">Table of Contents</A>
```

which can be rendered as shown and selected with ALT-T:

Table of Contents

Users who want to make use of access keying to activate links need to configure their browsers to highlight anchors in color, rather than by underlining.

Finally we should warn that not all legal characters are genuinely free for you to use, at least at the top level. Windows browsers typically allocate ALT-F for the File menu, ALT-E for the Edit menu, ALT-V for the View menu, and ALT-H for the Help menu, among others. You may find less room to maneuver than you expect.

Enabling tabbing

If you have several windows open on your screen, and you press the 'A' key, you might be selecting 'Acquire' if a graphics editor has the focus of attention, but the same keystroke might select 'Annotate' or 'Add' in other tools. The effect of a command depends on the current focus.

Similarly, within a document the focus can be at any of several places. It can be moved either by the mouse, or by cursor control commands (usually Tab and Reverse-Tab) from the keyboard. The 'keyboard focus' determines which object in an HTML document gets keyboard events of this sort.

Until now, most browsers have required use of the mouse to move the focus, and have ignored the keyboard altogether. This made life more difficult than it needed to be for people with disabilities. Other browsers have allowed tabbing, based on the order in which form elements, such as INPUT, appear in the HTML. The proposed HTML 4 attributes **TABINDEX** and **NOTABSTOP** identify elements, which the user can reach with the tab key.

Both **TABINDEX** and **NOTABSTOP** can be supplied with any element that can accept the keyboard focus, including form fields, hypertext links, embedded objects and client-side image maps.

The TABINDEX attribute

The **TABINDEX** attribute specifies an integer value for a particular tag, forming part of the order in which the tab key traverses the document, for example:

```
<A HREF=home.html TABINDEX=4>Home Page</A>
```

If the focus was with **TABINDEX=3**, then pressing the tab key puts the focus on the Home link anchor; similarly, if the tag with **TABINDEX=5** had the focus, then a reverse tab (SHIFT-Tab) would move the focus back to our Home link again. (The photograph shows an English keyboard.)

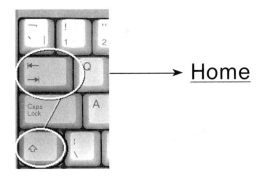

Home

Note that tabbing to a tag does *not* activate it. Once the user has reached the desired object (giving it the focus), whether by tabbing or pointing, it can be activated with the Enter key. If it is a hypertext link, activation means traversing the link; if it is a radio button in a form field, it means selecting that option (and deselecting the other options); if it is a checkbox it means checking or not checking that option; and so on.

The tabbing order is usually the order in which items appear in the document, unless overridden by **TABINDEX** or **NOTABSTOP**. The situation is more complicated when you have embedded objects in your HTML. Embedded objects (and objects that they contain) can form parts of the tabbing sequence. Client-side image maps can be defined to let users tab through their hotzones, for instance. Because of this complexity, there is no reason why pressing tab should work properly until the whole of a form is loaded. It may be worth putting in a note at the top of any complicated forms, to tell your users to be patient.

Each successive tab keystroke takes the cursor to the input element with the next tab index value. After visiting the element with the highest tab index, the next tab keystroke returns the focus to the initial element. Pressing SHIFT-Tab moves the focus in reverse tabbing order.

TABINDEX values do not have to be consecutive, and they do not have to begin at 1, but they must all be different. So, a set of tab indices running 2, 4, 6, 8 is fine, as is 8, 4, 6, 2; but 2, 2, 3, 4 is forbidden as the first tab position is ambiguous.

For example:

```
<INPUT TYPE=text   NAME=a TABINDEX=1>
<INPUT TYPE=button NAME=skipme NOTABSTOP>    <!--Cannot tab here-->
<INPUT TYPE=text   NAME=b>                   <!--Implicit tab stop!-->
<INPUT TYPE=text   NAME=c TABINDEX=2>        <!--THIRD tab stop-->
```

The NOTABSTOP **attribute**

NOTABSTOP simply causes elements that have it to be left out of the tab order, for instance:

```
<INPUT TYPE=text NAME=skipthisone NOTABSTOP>
```

Providing tooltip/balloon help with TITLE

Users of personal computers and Macintoshes are familiar with the little bits of text that float near the cursor when it hovers over a control: tooltips and balloon help. The tips make the systems easier to use, but do not interfere with normal operations in any way. It is proposed that HTML 4 should allow you to provide the same kind of assistance to your users. For example, if you create a set of index buttons in the form of images inside link anchors, you can add a tip to each button to make it clear what each one is supposed to do.

Tips are provided with the **TITLE** attribute. (Do not confuse this with the TITLE element, which gives a title to the whole document.) You can attach tips to anchors, links, images, controls, objects, applets, areas, and the new FIELDSET element, which is also described in this chapter. Different browsers display tips in different ways: tooltips and balloon helps are obvious possibilities, but other operating systems may display tip text in a status bar.

For example:

```
<IMG SRC=main.gif TITLE="Click where you want to go today">
<A HREF=details.html TITLE="More details of HTML 4">Details</A>
```

On Windows, tooltips are rendered with a floating yellow box, as illustrated below. Other systems use different renderings.

Adding clickable labels to controls

Labels for radio buttons and checkboxes were missing from earlier versions of HTML. You could put bits of text next to your form fields, but when your users clicked on the label text, nothing happened. This was a minor nuisance for most people, but a critical failing for the print-impaired. Speech-based browsers were forced into relying on **NAME** and **VALUE** attributes to access form fields.

LABEL associates a textual description with an input control, and makes it clickable. In the special case of an option button or a checkbox, a click on the text label changes the stored value (on or off). Labels can be associated either implicitly or explicitly.

Implicit labeling

Implicit labeling means wrapping the **LABEL** tag around a control such as a form field: the implication is that whatever is inside the tag is meant to be associated with the label's text. Implicit labels can contain only one object or control. The label's text may appear before or after the control. Labels cannot be nested. The diagram illustrates the mechanism.

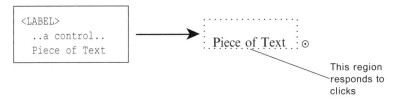

For example:

```
<LABEL ACCESSKEY=U>User Name
<INPUT TYPE="text" NAME=username ID=username>
</LABEL>
```

Explicit labeling

Sometimes, you may want to position your labels independently of their controls. Explicit labeling makes this possible. For example, you might want to have the labels in the first column of a table, and the controls in a second column. To do this, you explicitly associate each label with its control, using the **FOR** attribute. The **FOR** attribute references the control's **ID**; the control must be on the same HTML page. You can provide more than one label for a control by creating several **FOR**-marked references. The diagram illustrates the mechanism: the effect for the user is much the same as for implicit labeling.

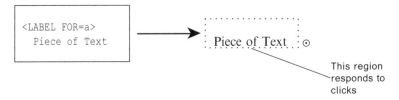

For example:

```
<TABLE><TR>
  <TD><LABEL FOR=username ACCESSKEY=U>User Name</LABEL>
  <TD><INPUT TYPE=text NAME=username ID=username>
</TABLE>
```

Grouping fields into accessible sets

FIELDSET and **LEGEND** are meant to improve the accessibility of HTML's forms for people with disabilities. For example, in a speech-synthesized browser, they allow the blind user to move from group to group by spoken command.

FIELDSET is a nestable container (of fields and field sets). It can optionally contain a single **LEGEND** which assigns a caption to a **FIELDSET**.

LEGEND simply names the contained set of fields. If supplied, it must immediately follow the **FIELDSET** tag.

A box is drawn around each **FIELDSET** group. The group's caption can be **ALIGN**ed to the **TOP** or **BOTTOM** of its fieldset if desired: the default is **TOP**. The contained fields can be organized with <P> or <BR> into a column, or with a <TABLE> to achieve more elaborate effects. Such tables should be drawn without borders to avoid confusion with fieldset boxes.

The following example shows a form consisting of two banks of radio buttons. Each is constructed as a fieldset inside a table cell, complete with caption, access key, and tab index. Each individual radio button has its own access key, to be pressed once its fieldset has the focus. The HTML looks a little complicated, but once you have seen that each item is done the same way, it is quite easy to write.

```
<FORM>
<TABLE><TR>

<TD><FIELDSET>
<LEGEND ACCESSKEY=V TABINDEX=1>Vehicle</LEGEND>
<P><LABEL ACCESSKEY=S>
<INPUT TYPE=radio NAME=Vehicle VALUE=Saloon>Saloon Car</LABEL>
<P><LABEL ACCESSKEY=E>
<INPUT TYPE=radio NAME=Vehicle VALUE=Estate>Estate Car</LABEL>
<P><LABEL ACCESSKEY=P>
<INPUT TYPE=radio NAME=Vehicle VALUE=Pickup>Pickup Truck</LABEL>
<P><LABEL ACCESSKEY=J>
<INPUT TYPE=radio NAME=Vehicle VALUE=Jeep >Jeep</LABEL>
</FIELDSET>
```

```
<TD><FIELDSET>
<LEGEND ACCESSKEY=E TABINDEX=2>Engine Capacity</LEGEND>
<P><LABEL ACCESSKEY=C>
<INPUT TYPE=radio NAME=Engine VALUE=S>Compact: &lt; 1000cc</LABEL>
<P><LABEL ACCESSKEY=M>
<INPUT TYPE=radio NAME=Engine VALUE=M>Medium:  1000-1999cc</LABEL>
<P><LABEL ACCESSKEY=L>
<INPUT TYPE=radio NAME=Engine VALUE=L>Large:   2000-2999cc</LABEL>
<P><LABEL ACCESSKEY=X>
<INPUT TYPE=radio NAME=Engine VALUE=X>eXtra:   &gt; 3000cc</LABEL>
</FIELDSET>

</TABLE>
<P><LABEL TABINDEX=3><INPUT TYPE=submit></LABEL>
<LABEL TABINDEX=4><INPUT TYPE=reset></LABEL>
</FORM>
```

Here is how the example fieldset form could appear on an HTML 4 browser:

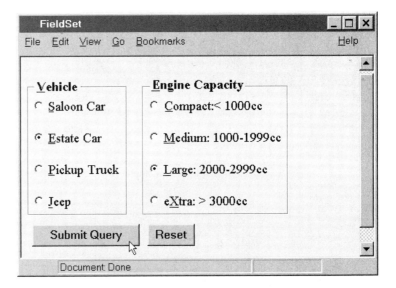

In this example, when the form is first displayed, the Vehicle fieldset has the focus, because it has the lowest tab index (1 in this case). The user can specify an Estate Car immediately by pressing ALT-E (meaning Vehicle, Estate). Speech or other special means may activate the keys.

The Engine Capacity fieldset can then be reached by pressing the tab key. Notice that the form's Submit and Reset buttons should also be made accessible to keyboard entry: the example code provides tab indices for them. The effect of repeated tabbing in the form is therefore to rotate (forwards or backwards) around the predefined tab sequence:

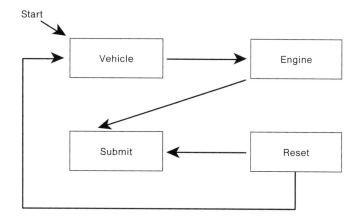

In practice, we expect that the combination of HTML elements and attributes used in this example – form, table, fieldsets and captions, access keys, and tab indices – will become the normal way that forms are represented in HTML. Tools will generate all these constructs by default.

Speech-based browsers allow fieldsets to be selected directly: the user just speaks the name of the desired fieldset, as given in its caption. (Field values such as 'Engine' were already available to speech-based browsers in HTML 3.) For example, the user could say 'Engine' and then 'Medium' to locate the fieldset and push the required radio button.

11.8 Summary

This chapter illustrated the use of forms and the HTML constructs available for on-screen dialogues. These included input elements, both textual and graphical, and standard buttons to submit the form or to reset it.

Forms are not themselves difficult to write, though good visual design is a skilled art. HTML forms (running on browsers) require the support of scripts that are specifically written for the server. For more information on scripting, see Chapter 16.

HTML allows an unlimited range of sophisticated forms to be created and operated, thus – with suitable scripts and secure networks – opening up the World Wide Web (and the Internet) to business interaction and commercial traffic.

12
THE
DOCUMENT
HEAD

Included in this chapter is information on:

- Giving a title which the browser can use to bookmark your document
- Preparing your document for indexing by search engines
- Linking your document to others to facilitate such things as printing a collection of documents and devising toolbars to navigate through a series of documents
- Linking your document to a style sheet: the STYLE element
- Using the SCRIPT element
- Using the BASE element
- Using NEXTID

Summary

This chapter covers a number of elements:

- TITLE – which defines the document title, and is always needed.

- ISINDEX – which is for simple keyword searches. The **PROMPT** attribute is included in the standard.

- BASE – which defines a base URL for resolving relative URLs. It has the attributes **HREF** and **TARGET**.

- STYLE – which is used for inserting style sheet information into a document. STYLE has the attributes **TYPE**, **MEDIA** and **TITLE**.

- SCRIPT – which is used for scripting HTML documents and is described in Chapter 16.

- META – which is used to supply information about the document: the language in which the document is written, information for indexing robots to use, and so on. Attributes are **LANG**, **SCHEME** and **HTTP-EQUIV**.

- LINK – which is used to define typed relationships with other documents. LINK is useful in printing collections of documents from the Web, for devising toolbars, for linking style sheets, and so on. Attributes are **HREF**, **REL**, **REV**, **TYPE** and **MEDIA**.

TITLE, SCRIPT and STYLE are containers, and they require both start and end tags. The other elements are not containers, and end tags are forbidden. Note that browsers should not render the contents of the SCRIPT and STYLE elements.

12.1 Introduction

When you get a memo or an email, it is normally accompanied by information other than the text of the memo itself: who the author is, what the content is about, who is to get a copy, the date of issue, and so on. Software engineers sometimes call this *meta information*.

Position of the HEAD element and associated elements
The elements of the document head cannot appear in the middle of the document: you should always insert them at the beginning. The order of elements within the head is, however, not significant.

The head of an HTML document contains meta information of this sort. There are a number of elements involved, namely LINK, TITLE, META, SCRIPT STYLE, ISINDEX and BASE. Strictly speaking, these should be inserted into the document head which is delineated by the <HEAD> and </HEAD> tags. In practice, however, the HEAD element does not need to be explicitly included by the author, for the browser is clever and will guess its intended location. Indeed, the first element to appear in most documents is the TITLE element. The browser will realize that by including the TITLE element, and by your placing it correctly at the beginning of the document, a HEAD element is implied, even if it is not actually included.

Having explained the basic concept of the document head, we will now introduce the elements of the document head one by one. We also will explain what they do and how to use them.

12.2 The TITLE element

The minimal document
The TITLE element is always required. In fact, the minimal HTML document consists of the TITLE element alone.

The TITLE element is very simple, but mandatory for every document: every HTML document must contain a TITLE element. The title should identify the contents of the document as unambiguously as possible, and may be used in a history list (a list of which Web sites you have visited), and as a label for the window that displays the document.

The TITLE element may not contain anchors, paragraph tags, or other elements. It should consist of text together with character entities, if needed for accented letters and symbols.

The length of titles is unlimited; however, long titles may be truncated in some applications. To minimize this possibility, keep titles to fewer than 64 characters. Also keep in mind that a short title, such as Introduction, may be meaningless out of context. An example of a meaningful title might be:

```
<TITLE>The Wembley Botanical Garden </TITLE>
```

12.3 The ISINDEX element

ISINDEX
This element has now been deprecated.

This element tells the browser that the current document is an index which users may search. The ISINDEX merely informs the browser of this fact: the ISINDEX element does not magically make the document searchable.

The ISINDEX mechanism predates forms. In those days, the idea was that, if the ISINDEX were present, users could type a line of text as a query, which was then sent back to the same URL from which the document was retrieved. The query consisted of a simple character string that performed a keyword search. This string was constructed by adding a question mark (?) to the end of the document URL, followed by a list of keywords that were separated by plus (+) signs. Initially, this mechanism was used to allow people to use the Web to look up telephone numbers in a CERN telephone directory.

Although ISINDEX is supposed to occur in the document head, many browsers allow it to be placed anywhere in the document.

During the early days of the Web, ISINDEX was not adequate for the needs of the Web, and people wanted to supplement it with a more powerful language, so that authors could provide a range of form elements. These additional form elements could be such things as radio buttons, checkboxes, menus and input fields. The NCSA Mosaic team liked this idea and did all the hard work to implement forms.

The PROMPT attribute

Netscape's extensions to HTML 2.0 included the PROMPT attribute for ISINDEX. This attribute now is included in HTML 4. You can use the **PROMPT** attribute to change the default prompt supplied by the browser, for example:

```
<ISINDEX HREF="phone.db" PROMPT="Enter Surname:">
```

12.4 The LINK element

You will have seen in previous chapters how the anchor element A marks up hypertext links between information held on the Web. You click on the label of the hypertext link and new material is downloaded and then displayed on the screen. The LINK element is also concerned with links between information, but these links are of quite a different kind. Rather than defining jumps from one document to another, LINK serves to simply bind a given document to various other items associated with it. Classic examples are a style sheet to be linked to the document; a linked color palette to display a document; a table of contents for the text, and an online glossary of terms. All of these can be linked to a document via LINK.

The REV and REL attributes

LINK has a number of attributes and these include **REL** and **REV**. Using the **REL** and/or **REV** attributes, you can specify the nature of the link established by a LINK element. The **REL** attribute describes a forward relationship; the **REV** attribute is used to define the reverse relationship. This is explained more clearly below.

Suppose you have an online book, which is long and divided into chapters. The chapters themselves are divided into sections, each of which is an HTML document. **REL** and **REV** can be used to tie the pieces of the book together.

The **REL** attribute enables you to specify, for example, 'this document belongs to that chapter' or 'this chapter belongs to that book'. When you come to print a chapter, or to display a chapter on the screen, the browser can, by using these relationships, decide which section or chapter should be dealt with next.

Here is the kind of structure that you might represent with LINK. In this diagram, you can see that doc1.html, doc2.html and so on, are related to chap2.html by the relationship *section-of*. The index is related to chap2.html by the relationship *index-of*, and the contents are the *contents-of* chap2.html. Relationship names can include hyphens, dots, letters, and the numbers 0 to 9.

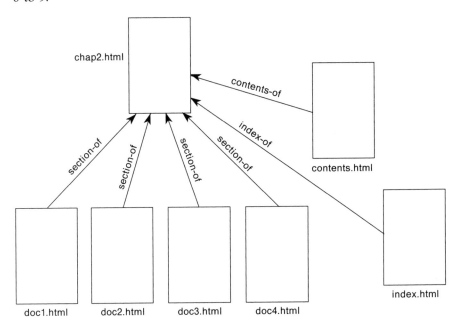

How are LINK **REL** statements expressed in HTML? The document head for doc1.html might contain:

```
<HEAD>
<TITLE> Document 1</TITLE>
<LINK REL=section-of HREF="chapter2.html">
</HEAD>
```

Here you can see the use of the **HREF** attribute to tell you the name of the file that **REL** points to. LINK can take the **HREF** attribute to specify a URL just as the anchor element can.

Reverse links

The idea of the **REV** attribute is perhaps harder to understand. **REV** stands for 'reverse'. Look at the following which you might insert in contents.html:

```
<LINK REV=contents-of HREF=book.html>
```

What does this mean? Diagrammatically, this is what you are saying:

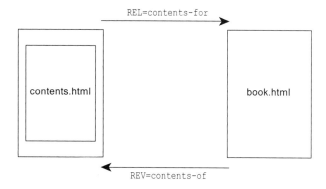

Summary of REV and REL for the technical
A link from document A to document B with REV=relation expresses the same relationship as a link from B to A with REL=relation. Note that relationship names are case insensitive. See also the A (anchor) element which also uses the **REV** and **REL** attributes.
  Following the precedent set by HTML 2.0, **REL** and **REV** can take a space-separated list of relationship values. Relationship values can be defined in *profiles*. See page 235.

In ordinary English, this approximates to:

- contents.html is the table of contents of book.html

- book.html has a table of contents contents.html

The **REV** attribute gives the relationship from the book to the table of contents. The **REL** attribute gives the relation from the table of contents to the book.

A browser can exploit the idea of REV=contents by seeing it as an indcation that a contents file exists for Chapter 2, and consequently fetching it across the Internet and placing it in a separate frame on the screen.

Support for REV and REL

Although HTML 4 certainly includes the use of LINK **REV** and **REL** in this kind of fashion, browser support is still minimal.

It has been a chicken-and-egg situation. Since there has been little software to exploit typed links, users have seen little motivation for creating them. But things may be changing quickly, as we will explain in a moment.

The author already exploits LINK **REL** and **REV** when printing the HTML 4 specification, which, of course, is done as a series of HTML documents. To make the specification easy to work with, each individual file is kept nice and small. LINK is then used to define the relationships among the parts, in the sort of way described above. A piece of custom software then effectively follows the links and places the files into a linear sequence, ready to be printed in order.

Suggested relationship names for LINK
The following are just some suggested names for `LINK REL`:
  `REL=next`
  `REL=previous`
  `REL=contents`
  `REL=index`
  `REL=navigate`
  `REL=collection`
`REL=navigate` is used to target a document containing a navigational aid such as a map of the Web site. `REL=collection` is used to target an entity like a 'book' or a 'report' composed of a collection of smaller documents.

The light on the horizon appears to be that Microsoft, in its quest to unify its Desktop Explorer with Internet Explorer, is looking at ways of viewing Web sites as a tree of files on the screen, and this may lean forward in the direction we would like. Each node in the hierarchy of Web files would be an icon on the screen that could be expanded to reveal descendants, or collapsed to hide the descendants. You might, for example, click on a book to see its descendent chapters, and on a chapter to see its component HTML files.

As a result of its intent, Microsoft is putting significant resources into technology for representing collections of HTML documents this way, and given Microsoft's vast resources, this will inevitably lead to new tools that exploit the relationships that exist between files. At last, it will become worthwhile for authors to express relationships between documents using `LINK` **REL** and **REV** and similar ideas.

This whole business might have been solved a long time ago if the early browser vendors had acknowledged lessons learnt from centuries of experience with written material, that authors go to great pains to construct an effective way of reading material in sequence. Then, they might have given authors the means to string different Web documents together in linear sequence, even if those documents also were linked in other ways. In real hypertext systems, you often come across the idea of a set sequence through a 'web' of text, known as a guided tour, or path. This idea is lacking from the Web as we use it today. Other computerized hypertext systems have at least offered a 'previous' and 'next' button for users who are following just such a path through linked information.

`LINK` and toolbars for a document

So far we have shown relationship names for `LINK` **REL** and **REV** such as 'index', 'contents', and so on. Other names may of course be used. Obvious choices are `LINK REL=next` and `LINK REL=previous`. These would be exploited by software that generates on-screen buttons in a toolbar:

If you were using a file called doc32, for example, you might see the buttons labeled 'previous' and 'next' permanently displayed. Clicking on these would move you between documents, as need be. Behind the scenes the 'previous' and 'next' buttons would be marked up like this:

```
<LINK REL=Previous HREF=doc31.html>
<LINK REL=Next    HREF=doc33.html>
```

The idea of profiles to house standard names for LINK attributes REL and REV

Document hierarchies
In a hierarchical arrangement of documents the following LINK REL/REV names have been suggested:
   REL/REV=child
   REL/REV=parent
   REL/REV=top
   REL/REV=sibling

You may be wondering by now who has control over the names of relationships established with LINK. It is obvious that 'index', 'previous', 'next' are useful, but why not 'prev-version', 'copyright-notice' and any number of others? In fact, **REV** and **REL** names can be potentially anything you want. After all, their meaning is significant only if there is software to process them.

Since it seems unlikely to HTML 4 designers that a central repository of **REV** and **REL** names will ever exist, a new idea is born.

The HTML 4 design team imagines that different sub-sets of **REV** and **REL** names are likely to exist for different applications and documents. Now, if each list of these names can be given its own unique URL, authors can make reference to the list of their choice in the document head. The browser will then know where to look so that it can see what the relationship names used by the author mean, and respond accordingly. Originally given the name of *lexicon*, such a list for interpreting **REL** and **REV** names is now to be called a *profile*.

The PROFILE attribute

With this idea of profiles in mind, the HEAD element has, in HTML 4, a new **PROFILE** attribute. This provides a unique URL which points to definitions for link relationship names (for LINK and A), for property names (for META) and for class values (for the **CLASS** attribute). The **PROFILE** attribute might indicate as follows:

```
PROFILE="http://www.acme.com/profiles/core">
```

Sequences of documents
In a sequence of documents the following LINK REL/REV names have been suggested:
   REL/REV=begin
      (or first)
   REL/REV=end
      (or last)
   REL/REV=next
   REL/REV=previous
      (or prev)

The profile might be a human-readable list or go further and provide machine-readable definitions.

The format of the profile file

The exact format that the profile file format has not yet been decided. The **PROFILE** attribute is nonetheless in place for developments as soon as they come.

An existing example of a profile is the Dublin Core. This is still at prototype stage at the moment, and the exact syntax is in transition. The idea is that LINK **REL** can have a number of values that are linked to the way that books are classified in libraries, for example the Dewey system, and the system of classification used by the Library of Congress.

To allow the possibility of extending the **PROFILE** attribute to provide a list of profiles, browsers should consider the value as a white-space separated list of URLs. For the moment, only the first item is significant.

LINK and style sheets

As explained in Chapter 9, LINK can be used to specify linked style sheets; HTML 4 includes the ability to specify alternative style sheets and also a cascade of links to other style sheets. HTML 4 also allows you to specify that a style sheet is only appropriate to certain media.

In the example below, three different style sheets are included. Note the use of REL=stylesheet in each to indicate a forward link, and also the **MEDIA** attribute to specify whether or not the style sheet is for use with screen display or for printing on paper.

```
<LINK REL=stylesheet MEDIA=print HREF="corporate-print.css">
<LINK REL=stylesheet MEDIA=screen HREF="corporate-screen.css">
<LINK REL=stylesheet HREF="techreport.css">
<STYLE TYPE="text/css"> p.special {color: red; font-size 12 pt}
</STYLE>
```

The MEDIA attribute

The **MEDIA** attribute is used to indicate that the resource pointed to by a LINK element (the resource is usually a style sheet) is designed for a particular medium. The **TYPE** attribute can be used to specify the Internet media type and associated parameters for the linked resource. This allows the browser to disregard linked style sheets in notations that it cannot understand without having to waste time contacting the server.

Specifying alternative versions of the document for printing

You can also use the LINK element to specify alternative versions of the current document for use when printing, for example:

```
<LINK REL=alternate MEDIA=print
   HREF="mydoc.ps"
   TYPE=application/postscript>
```

Specifying language variants of this document

If you have prepared translations of this document into other languages, you should use the LINK element to reference these. This allows an indexing engine to offer users search results in the users' preferred language, regardless of how the query was written.

```
<LINK REL=alternate HREF=mydoc-fr.html
   LANG=fr TITLE="A la lune">
<LINK REL=alternate HREF=mydoc-de.html
   LANG=de TITLE="An der Mond">
```

Linking related documents
The following are suggested LINK REL/REV names for related documents:
  REL/REV=citation
  REL/REV=definition
  REL/REV=footnote
  REL/REV=glossary

LINK and collections of Web pages

When word-processing documents or presentations are automatically converted into HTML, this generally results in a collection of HTML pages. It is helpful for search results to reference the beginning of the collection in addition to the page hit by the search. Use the LINK element with REL=begin along with a TITLE, as in:

```
<LINK REL=begin HREF=page1.html TITLE="General Theory of Relativity">
```

12.5 The META element

The META element can be used to include name-value pairs describing properties of the document, such as author, expiry date, a list of keywords and so on. For the less technical, this idea is best explained by example:

```
<META NAME="Author" CONTENT="Dave Raggett">
```

Here, the **NAME** attribute specifies the property name, the *author*, in this case, whereas the **CONTENT** attribute gives the author a value (Dave Raggett). Here is a similar example:

```
<META NAME="Audience" CONTENT="all">
```

Here, the property name is *audience* and the value is *all*. In the following case, the author has included a number of META statements with the aim of indexing the document according to keywords, and also including information on copyright, date of publishing and author, as well:

```
<META NAME="author" CONTENT="John Doe">
```

```
<META NAME="copyright" CONTENT="&copy; 1997 Prize Breeds Ltd.">
<META NAME="keywords"  CONTENT="piglet,guinea,breeding">
<META NAME="date"      CONTENT="23 Jan 1997 16:05:31 GMT">
```

The META **NAME**s that you can use – just like the names for **REL** and **REV** – are unlimited. But, although you can use any **NAME** you please, consider that names are of no significance until a program processes them in some way and attaches meaning to them.

Although it has been suggested that a certain few names should be standard by default, people will probably want to invent their own special list together with processing information. Such information could be stored as a *profile* together with names for **REL** and **REV**, as explained in the previous section on LINK. The **PROFILE** attribute on HEAD should be used to indicate the URL of the profile applicable.

The `HTTP-EQUIV` **attribute to create a header in the HTTP response**

Should I use HTTP-EQUIV?
It all depends on how your server is configured. You need to talk to your Web site designer/administrator before using this feature. The administrator should have a definite strategy for the use of META in documents as a means to provide search engines with information.

The **HTTP-EQUIV** attribute can be used in place of **NAME** and has a special significance when documents are retrieved via HTTP. Servers may use the property name specified by the **HTTP-EQUIV** attribute to create a header in the HTTP response sent back to the browser. For example:

```
<META HTTP-EQUIV="Expires" CONTENT="Tue, 20 Aug 1996 14:25:27 GMT">
```

will result in the HTTP header being sent down the wire with the file:

```
Expires: Tue, 20 Aug 1996 14:25:27 GMT
```

This kind of information can be used by the browser cache to determine when to fetch a fresh copy of the associated document.

```
<META HTTP-EQUIV="Keywords" CONTENT="Nanotechnology, Biochemistry">
<META HTTP-EQUIV="Reply-to" CONTENT="dsr@w3.org (Dave Raggett)">
```

would generate:

```
Keywords: Nanotechnology, Biochemistry
Reply-to: dsr@w3.org (Dave Raggett)
```

When the **HTTP-EQUIV** attribute is absent, the server does not generate an HTTP response header for this meta-information, for example:

```
<META NAME="IndexType" CONTENT="Service">
```

Do not use the `META` element to define information that should be associated with an existing HTML element, for example like this:

```
<META NAME="Title" CONTENT="The Etymology of Dunsel">
```

META **to supply search engines with data**

A common use of `META` is to specify a list of keywords that can be exploited by search engines. The items in the list are separated by commas:

```
<META NAME="keywords" CONTENT="vacation,Greece,sunshine">
```

See the inset on page 241 for more information on this subject.

META **to instruct the browser to display a sequence of pages in succession**

Browsers widely support the use of `META` to refresh the current page after a few seconds, perhaps replacing it with another page.

```
<META NAME="refresh" CONTENT="3,http://www.acme.com/intro.html">
```

The content is a number that specifies the delay in seconds, followed by the URL to load when the time is up. This mechanism is generally used to show people a fleeting Greetings page. You can think of it as someone ushering you through a door into a room.

META **and the Platform for Internet Contents Selection (PICS)**

The Platform for Internet Content Selection (PICS) is an infrastructure for associating labels (metadata) with Internet content. Originally, it was designed to help parents and teachers control what children are allowed to access on the Internet; however, it also facilitates other uses for labels, including code signing, privacy, and intellectual property rights management. The following shows how you can use `META` to include a PICS label:

```
<HEAD>
<META http-equiv="PICS-Label"
   CONTENT='(PICS-1.1 "http://www.gcf.org/v2.5"
      labels on "1994.11.05T08:15-0500"
      until "1995.12.31T23:59-0000"
      for "http://w3.org/PICS/Overview.html"
      ratings (suds 0.5 density 0 color/hue 1))'>
   <TITLE>..title goes here..</TITLE>
</HEAD>
...contents of document here...
```

The use of META to specify default scripting and style sheet languages

META can be used to specify the default scripting and style sheet languages. You can also use it to set the default style when you have provided a range of alternative styles using LINK and STYLE elements. The use of the **HTTP-EQUIV** attribute allows these properties to be set by HTTP headers, making it easy for site managers to impose a standard style.

The LANG attribute to specify the language of the META CONTENT

The **LANG** attribute can be used with META to specify the language for the value of the **CONTENT** attribute, for example:

```
<META NAME=author LANG=fr CONTENT="Arnaud Le Hors">
```

This helps speech synthesizers to pronounce the text of the document properly, with the right accent!

Using the SCHEME attribute to help qualify NAME

The **NAME** attribute specifies property name and the **CONTENT** attribute gives this property a value. Is it possible to say more about how this value should be interpreted? Under what scheme should it be processed? When a value ascribed to the **NAME** attribute may be interpreted in more than one way, you can use the **SCHEME** attribute. An example is the use of a scheme value with NAME=description to indicate the **CONTENT** is a Library of Congress classification number, a Dewey Decimal System number, a Medical Subject heading, or Art and Architecture Thesaurus descriptor.

Style sheets

The screens on this and the following pages show you how the same content can be presented in different ways. The BODY of each HTML page is exactly the same; only the STYLE element changes each time. They are designed by Simon Daniels of Microsoft. You can see them on www.microsoft.com/truetype/css/gallery.

heading 1 ——

class = opening ——

heading 2 ——

class = section 2 ——

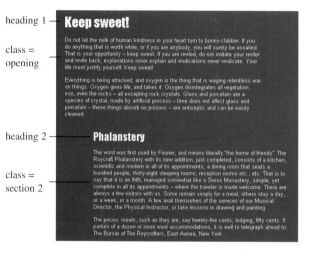

Points to note are as follows:

(1) The use of the <STYLE>....</STYLE> tags to delineate the style sheet.

(2) The use of named styles such as `.credit`, `.opening` and `.section3`. These can be applied to a variety of elements once defined.

(3) The use of built-in styles for specifying the color and weight for hypertext links.

(4) Use of % to specify relative size of text and also of margins.

(5) The use of five alternatives for font-family including the general description 'sans serif'.

```
<STYLE  TYPE="text/css">
<!--
BODY { background: black;
    color: white }
.contrast { background: darkblue }
P    { color: white;
    font-size: 100%;
    margin-left: 20%;
    margin-right: 20%;
    font-family: Arial, Helvetica, helv,
sans-serif }
.credit   { margin-left: 10% }
.opening { margin-left: 10% }
.section3 { margin-left: 10% }
.section2 { margin-right: 10% }
H1, H3 { font-size: 120%;
    margin-left: 10%;
    margin-right: 20%;
    font-weight: medium;
    color: white;
    font-family: Impact, Arial,
Helvetica, helv, sans-serif }
H2 { font-size: 120%;
    margin-left: 20%;
    margin-right: 20%;
    font-weight: medium;
    color: white;
    font-family: Impact, Arial,
Helvetica, helv, sans-serif }
A:link   { color: coral;
    font-weight: bold;
    text-decoration: none; }
A:visited  { color: purple;
    font-weight: bold;
    text-decoration: none; }
.descript { color: silver;
    font-size: 80%;
    margin-left: 10%;
    margin-right: 20%;
    font-family: Verdana, Arial,
Helvetica, helv, sans-serif }
.topline {color: silver;
    margin-left: 10%;
    margin-right: 10%;
    font-size: 80%;
    font-family: Verdana, Arial,
Helvetica, helv, sans-serif }
-->
</STYLE>
```

heading 1

class = opening

heading 2

class = section 2

This screen is taken from the same sequence as the previous one. Note use of Microsoft's new font Verdana, designed especially for screen display. Arial is specified in the style sheet for the benefit of browsers without Verdana installed.

- 'coral', 'silver', and 'cornsilk' are color names not necessarily supported by all browsers: it is best to specify colors by numeric values.

- Comic Sans MS is another font designed by Microsoft for on-line information. Notice the inclusion of alternative fonts for browsers without this font.

- Notice the use of TYPE="text/css" to tell the browser that the style sheet is written in CSS.

```
<STYLE  TYPE="text/css">
<!--
BODY { background: black;
    color: white;
    font-size: 80%; }
.contrast { background: cornsilk }
P    { color: black;
    font-size: 80%;
    margin-left: 15%;
    margin-right: 20%;
    font-family: Verdana, Arial,
Helvetica, helv, sans-serif }
H1, H2, H3 { font-size: 180%;
    margin-left: 10%;
    margin-right: 20%;
    font-weight: medium;
    color: coral;
    font-family: Comic Sans MS, Arial,
Helvetica, helv, sans-serif }
.descript { color: silver;
    margin-left: 10%;
    margin-right: 10%;
    font-family: Verdana, Arial,
Helvetica, helv, sans-serif }
A:link   { color: coral;
    font-weight: bold;
    text-decoration: none; }
A:visited  { color: purple;
    font-weight: bold;
    text-decoration: none; }
.topline {color: silver;
    margin-left: 10%;
    margin-right: 10%;
    font-size: 80%;
    font-family: Verdana, Arial,
Helvetica, helv, sans-serif }


-->
</STYLE>
```

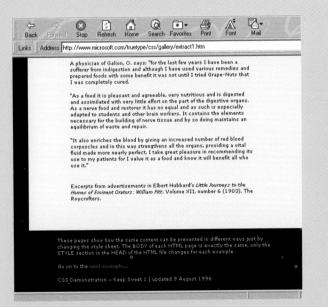

This second screen is the continuation of the first. The purple text at the bottom is a visited hypertext link – you can see from the style sheet that links not yet visited are orange – (A:link {color: coral;), and that those visited are purple.

Keep sweet!

Do not let the milk of human kindness in your heart turn to bonny-clabber. If you do anything that is worth while, or if you are anybody, you will surely be assailed. That is your opportunity – keep sweet. If you are reviled, do not imitate your reviler and revile back; explanations never explain and vindications never vindicate. Your life must justify yourself. Keep sweet!

Everything is being attacked; and oxygen is the thing that is waging relentless war on things. Oxygen gives life, and takes it. Oxygen disintegrates all vegetation, iron, even the rocks – all excepting rock crystals. Glass and porcelain are a species of crystal, made by artificial process – time does not affect glass and porcelain – these things absorb no poisons – are antiseptic and can be easily cleaned.

Phalanstery

The word was first used by Fourier, and means literally "the home of friends". The Roycraft Phalanstery with its new addition, just completed, consists of a kitchen, scientific and modern in all of its appointments; a dining room that seats a hundred people; thirty-eight sleeping rooms; reception rooms etc., etc. That is to say that it is an INN, managed somewhat like a Swiss Monastery, simple, yet complete in all its appointments – where the traveler is made welcome. There are always a few visitors with us. Some remain simply for a meal, others stay a day, or a week, or a month. A few avail themselves of the services of our Musical Director, the Physical Instructor, or take lessons in drawing and painting.

Keep sweet!

Do not let the milk of human kindness in your heart turn to bonny-clabber. If you do anything that is worth while, or if you are anybody, you will surely be assailed. That is your opportunity – keep sweet. If you are reviled, do not imitate your reviler and revile back; explanations never explain and vindications never vindicate. Your life must justify yourself. Keep sweet!

Everything is being attacked; and oxygen is the thing that is waging relentless war on things. Oxygen gives life, and takes it. Oxygen disintegrates all vegetation, iron, even the rocks – all excepting rock crystals. Glass and porcelain are a species of crystal, made by artificial process – time does not affect glass and porcelain – these things absorb no poisons – are antiseptic and can be easily cleaned.

Phalanstery

Three more layouts achieved with the aid of CSS. The use of a style sheet means that even large headings are loaded quickly by the browser. The current fashion for using an image for headings in unusual fonts and large sizes has meant that Web pages often take a long time to load. With style sheets, pages should materialize faster, simply because less bytes of information need travel across the Internet.

HTML editors

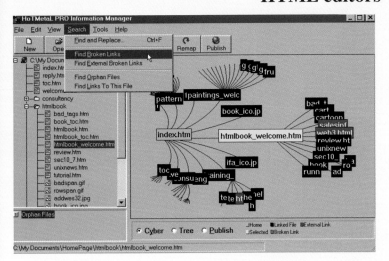

HoTMetaL PRO is one of the many HTML editing tools now on the market, available from SoftQuad (http://www.softquad.com). HoTMetaL PRO allows you to see how all your Web pages are linked together, and enables you to locate and fix any broken links or orphaned pages.

HTML frames

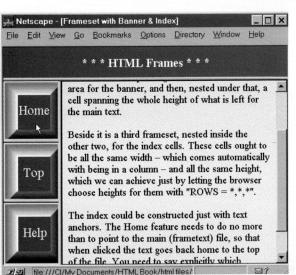

A frame design with index buttons

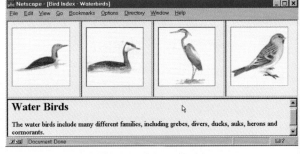

Frames are ideal for graphical layouts

Frames enable you to leave parts of your display in place while the user scrolls through or replaces other parts interactively. The frames chapter (pages 246–80) explains how to incorporate text and graphics, as in the images above, and how to avoid some of the pitfalls, like the dreaded hall-of-mirrors effect, right.

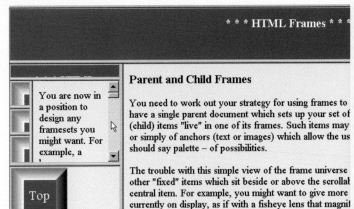

The hall-of-mirrors effect

Animations by GIFs and by JavaScript

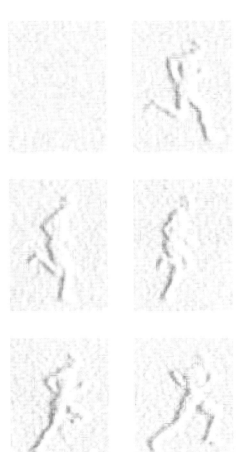

Running Man Animation Using GIF 89a Construction Set

The animation is a composite GIF with the following structure:

```
Header GIF89a Screen (80 x 104)
Loop (100 iterations)
    Control (delay 5/100ths of a second)
    Image running1.gif
    Control
    Image running2.gif
    Control
    Image running3.gif
    Control
    Image running4.gif
    Control
    Image running5.gif
```

The final image is made of the 5 separate images. The GIF construction set, from Alchemy Mindworks inc, does all the hard work for you, and you only have to manage one image file (and presumably one HTML page) on your web site, instead of 5 (or 6) images, a framing document and a couple of frames.

The loop parameter is only understood by Netscape Navigator 3 and Internet Explorer. The control blocks are all identical in this case, with a simple delay specified. It is also possible to indicate a transparent color, a wait for user input, and an action to be performed when removing the image (you can use the previous image, or the background, or leave it as it is).

> GIF Construction Set is shareware from
> Alchemy Mindworks Inc
> PO BOX 500
> Beeton, Ontario
> Canada L0G 1A0
> 1-800-263-1138 or 1-905-936-9500
> http://www.mindworkshop.com

Running an Animation using JavaScript

The JavaScript interpreter is built into most modern browsers, very little code needs to be downloaded by your readers – what you can see by viewing the source of this file is all there is.

```javascript
<script language="javascript">
function runner(){
   var run = new Array();

     // populate the array to go round and round
   run[0]="running0.jpg";
   run[1]="running1.jpg";
   run[2]="running2.jpg";
   run[3]="running3.jpg";
   run[4]="running4.jpg";
   run[5]="running5.jpg";

       // and run the animation
   for(j=0; j<25; j++)
     for(i=0; i < 6; i++){
        document.images[0].src = run[i];
        for(k=0; k<500; k++) 1=1;
     }
}
</script>
```

Examples of dynamically-generated Web pages

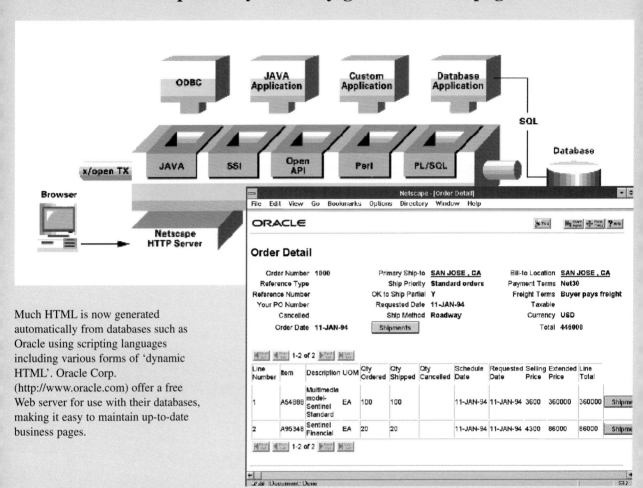

Much HTML is now generated automatically from databases such as Oracle using scripting languages including various forms of 'dynamic HTML'. Oracle Corp. (http://www.oracle.com) offer a free Web server for use with their databases, making it easy to maintain up-to-date business pages.

Quite a different use of interaction is illustrated by this colorful page. The child visiting the site colors in Mr. Stripey's jumper by clicking on the menu-palette and on areas of the image.

Contents ◀◀ *Painting Book* ◀◀ *Picture & Palette*

Finding out more about HTML and style sheets

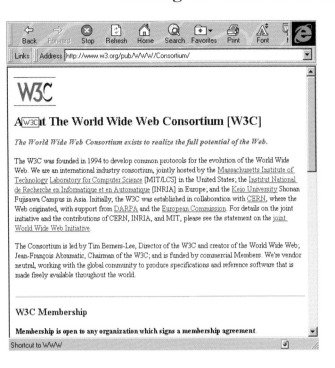

The next pages are taken from the World Wide Web Consortium's site, available on www.w3.com. All kinds of information on HTML, HTTP, style sheets, internationalization of the Web, security on the Internet and much more, is posted on the W3C pages.

Leading the Evolution of the Web...

W3C Launches the International Web Accessibility Initiative

"Given the explosive growth in the use of the World Wide Web for publishing, electronic commerce, lifelong learning and the delivery of government services, it is vital that the Web be accessible to everyone. The Web Accessibility Initiative will develop the tools, technology, and guidelines to make it possible to display information in ways that are available to all users."
-- President William Jefferson Clinton

· *Tired of Waiting?* HTTP 1.1, CSS1 and PNG Can Make the Web As Much As 2-8 Times Faster

· **Public Release of** Jigsaw 1.0 Alpha 5 -- **the** HTTP 1.1 **Compliant Server**

· Employment Opportunities within W3C

User Interface

HTML
Style Sheets
Document Object
Model
Math
Graphics and 3D
Internationalization
Fonts
Amaya
Arena

Technology and Society

Accessibility
Digital Signature
Initiative
Electronic
Commerce
PICS
Intellectual Property
Rights

The HTML 4 specification is available online if you click here.

HTML Math is an up-and-coming area. You can find out the latest here.

Style sheets are covered extensively: you can depart from here on a tour of both the technicalities of style sheets and their implementation.

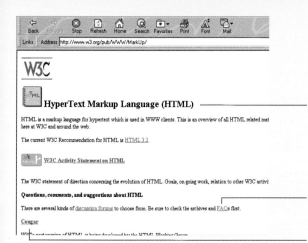

New developments in HTML are covered by the W3C Web pages. Technically-minded readers can delight in the on-line HTML 4 specification and ponder the DTD.

Questions on HTML answered.

HTML 4 was originally code-named 'Cougar'.

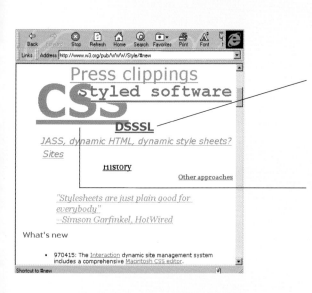

DSSSL is an alternative style sheet language to CSS but is not yet widely supported. You can find out about it here.

You can find a selection of examples of style sheets here, and also of sites using them.

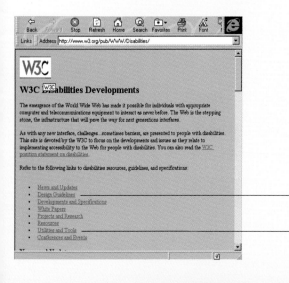

Find out how to design your Web pages so that people with disabilities are able to use the information.

Look at the tools currently available for doing this.

Color on the Web

The Safe Palette for Browsers, explained in Appendix I. This appendix explains all about reliable choice of palettes for color on the Web.

256 color adaptive palette without diffusion

Browser-safe palette with diffusion

Browser-safe palette without diffusion

256 color adaptive palette with diffusion (24k)

Browser-safe palette without diffusion (16k)

64 color adaptive palette with diffusion (16k)

256 color adaptive palette with diffusion (32k)

Browser-safe palette with diffusion (18k)

64 color adaptive palette with diffusion (22k)

Browser-safe palette and no diffusion

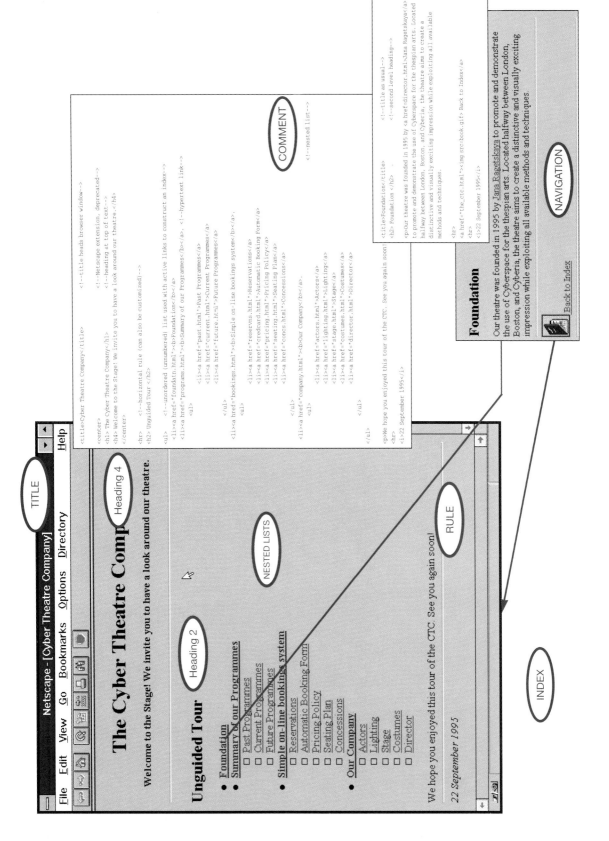

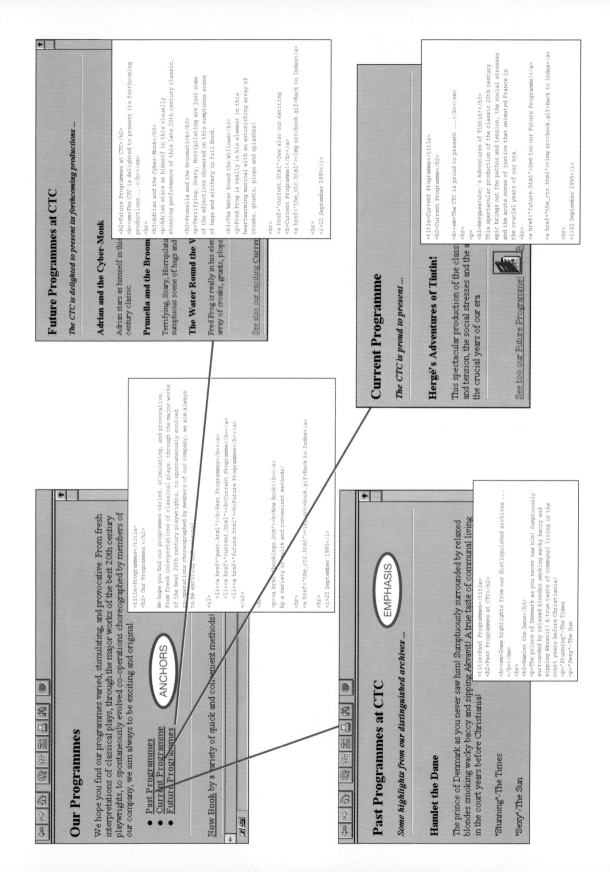

Future Programmes at CTC

The CTC is delighted to present its forthcoming productions ...

Adrian and the Cyber-Monk

Adrian stars as himself in thi[s]
century classic

Prunella and the Broom[stick]

Terrifying, Scary, Horripilati[ng]
sumptuous scene of hags, plops

The Water Round the W[illows]

Fred Frog is really in his elem[ent]
array of croaks, grunts, plops

See also our exciting Curr[ent]

HTML source (Future Programmes):

```
<h2>Future Programmes at CTC</h2>
<b><em>The CTC is delighted to present its forthcoming
productions ...</b></em>
<hr>
<h3>Adrian and the Cyber-Monk</h3>
<p>Adrian stars as himself in this visually
stunning performance of this late 20th century classic.
<h3>Prunella and the Broomstick</h3>
<p>Terrifying, Scary, Horripilating are just some
of the adjectives showered on this sumptuous scene
of hags and witchery in full flood.
<h3>The Water Round the Willows</h3>
<p>Fred Frog is really in his element in this
heartwarming musical with an astonishing array of
croaks, grunts, plops and splashes!
<hr>
<a href="current.html">See also our exciting
<b>Current Programme!</b></a>
<a href="the_ctc.html"><img src=book.gif>Back to Index</a>
<hr>
<i>22 September 1995</i>
```

Current Programme

The CTC is proud to present ...

Hergé's Adventures of Tintin!

This spectacular production of the class[ic]
and tension, the social stresses and the a[cute]
the crucial years of our era

See too our Future Programme!

HTML source (Current Programme):

```
<title>Current Programme</title>
<b><em>The CTC is proud to present. ...</b></em>
<h2>Current Programme</h2>
<hr>
<p>
<h3>Herg&eacute;:'s Adventures of Tintin!</h3>
This spectacular production of the classic 20th century
epic brings out the pathos and tension, the social stresses
and the acute sense of justice that animated France in
the crucial years of our era.
<hr>
<a href="future.html">See too our Future Programme!</a>
<a href="the_ctc.html"><img src=book.gif>Back to Index</a>
<hr>
<i>22 September 1995</i>
```

Our Programmes

We hope you find our programmes varied, stimulating, and provocative. From fresh
interpretations of classical plays, through the major works of the best 20th century
playwrights, to spontaneously evolved co-operations choreographed by members of
our company, we aim always to be exciting and original

- Past Programmes
- Current Programme
- Future Programmes

Now Book by a variety of quick and convenient methods!

HTML source (Our Programmes):

```
<title>Programmes</title>
<h2> Our Programmes </h2>

We hope you find our programmes varied, stimulating, and provocative.
From fresh interpretations of classical plays, through the major works
of the best 20th century playwrights, to spontaneously evolved
co-operations choreographed by members of our company, we aim always
to be exciting and original

<ul>
<li><a href="past.html"><b>Past Programmes</b></a>
<li><a href="current.html"><b>Current Programme</b></a>
<li><a href="future.html"><b>Future Programmes</b></a>
</ul>

<hr>
<p><a href="bookings.htm"><b>Now Book</b></a>
by a variety of quick and convenient methods!
<hr>
<a href="the_ctc.html"><img src=book.gif>Back to Index</a>
<hr>
<i>22 September 1995</i>
```

ANCHORS

Past Programmes at CTC

Some highlights from our distinguished archives ...

Hamlet the Dane

The prince of Denmark as you never saw him! Sumptuously surrounded by relaxed
blondes smoking wacky baccy and sipping Akvavit! A true taste of communal living
in the court years before Christiania!

"Stunning"-The Times

"Sexy"-The Sun

EMPHASIS

HTML source (Past Programmes):

```
<title>Past Programmes</title>
<h2>Past Programmes at CTC</h2>
<b><em>Some highlights from our distinguished archives ...
</b></em>
<hr>
<h3>Hamlet the Dane</h3>
<p>The prince of Denmark as you never saw him! Sumptuously
surrounded by relaxed blondes smoking wacky baccy and
sipping Akvavit! A true taste of communal living in the
court years before Christiania!
<p>"Stunning"-The Times
<p>"Sexy"-The Sun
```

Bookings

<u>Reservations</u> can be made by telephone, personal visit, or by credit card over the Internet.

Here is a table of our <u>Pricing</u> policy, with seating plan and concessions.

We look forward to seeing you in our audience, and to meeting you after the performance in the theatre bar.

 <u>Back to Index</u>

Netscape - [Automatic Reservation]

File   Edit   View   Go   Bookmarks   Options   Directory   Help

Automatic Reservation

You can use this form to book over the Internet.

Enter the following details:

Name: _____

Credit Card Number: _____

Credit Card Expiry Date: _____

Number of Seats wanted: ___

Seating Area: ● Front Stalls ○ Rear Stalls ○ Circle
○ Box

Phone number: _____

[Submit Query]   [Reset]

(FORM)

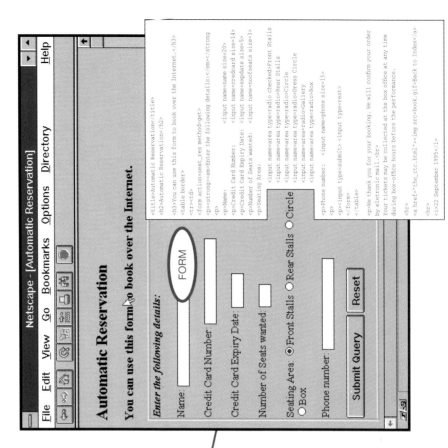

```
<title>Automatic Reservation</title>
<h2>Automatic Reservation</h2>
<h3>You can use this form to book over the Internet.</h3>
<form action=seat_res method=get>
<p><strong><em>Enter the following details:</em></strong>
<p>
<table border>
<tr><td>
<p>Name:              <input name=name size=20>
<p>Credit Card Number:    <input name=credcard size=14>
<p>Credit Card Expiry Date:   <input name=expdate size=5>
<p>Number of Seats wanted:   <input name=noofseats size=3>
<p>Seating Area:
           <input name=area type=radio checked>Front Stalls
           <input name=area type=radio>Rear Stalls
           <input name=area type=radio>Circle
           <input name=area type=radio>Dress Circle
           <input name=area type=radio>Gallery
           <input name=area type=radio>Box
<p>Phone number:    <input name=phone size=15>
<p>
<p><input type=submit> <input type=reset>
</form>
</table>
<p>We thank you for your booking. We will confirm your order
by eletronic mail.<br>
Your tickets may be collected at the box office at any time
during box-office hours before the performance.
<hr>
<a href="the_ctc.html"><img src=book.gif>Back to Index</a>
<hr>
<i>22 September 1995</i>
```

Reservations

There are 3 ways of reserving seats at CTC:

1. Personal Visit
2. Telephone
3. <u>Credit Card over the Internet</u>

If you choose to visit us personally, you may be assured of a warm welcome. You can enjoy a coffee while you peruse our latest programme. Our specially-trained staff will be happy to assist you

You may telephone us on the day and collect your tickets up to 30 minutes before the performance. Just call

0123 456 - 7890 and ask for Cynthia.

Or you can decide which performance you wish to see by looking through our on-line <u>Programmes</u>, and then book immediately by <u>Credit Card</u>

(PARA)

HTML codes omitted for clarity.

Our Pricing Policy

We want our productions to be enjoyed by all. Accordingly we offer a range of prices to suit all pockets, with generous concessions for those in need. Our Seating Plan shows the layout of the theatre, with our standard prices.

Special Concessions are available to the disadvantaged, to groups, and to individuals booking matinees in advance.

You can book by a variety of quick and con... details.

ANCHOR

```
<title>Pricing</title>
<h2>Our Pricing Policy</h2>

We want our productions to be enjoyed by all. Accordingly
we offer a range of prices to suit all pockets, with
generous concessions for those in need.

Our <a href="seating.html">
<b>Seating Plan</b></a> shows the layout of the theatre,
with our standard prices.

<p>
Special <a href="concs.html">
<b>Concessions</b></a> are available to the disadvantaged,
to groups, and to individuals booking matinees in advance.
<hr>
```

Our Concessions

We offer generous concessions for those in need

1. **Unwaged, Disabled, Pensioners, Students**

   35% of standard rates on production of ID, either booked at least 24 hours in advance, or standby. Available for all performances Monday - Thursday and all matinees.

2. **Groups**

   75% of standard rates for groups of 8 - 20 people, booked at least 1 week in advance.

   60% of standard rates for groups of more than 21 people, booked at least 2 weeks in advance.

3. **Advance Matinee Bookings**

   60% of standard rates, book...

```
<title>Concessions</title>
<h2>Our Concessions</h2>

We offer generous concessions for those in need.
<p>
<OL>
<LI> <b>Unwaged, Disabled, Pensioners, Students</b><p>
     35% of standard rates on production of ID,
     either booked at least 24 hours in advance,
     or standby. Available
     for all performances Monday - Thursday
     and all matinees.<p>

<LI> <b>Groups</b><p>
     75% of standard rates for groups of 8 - 20 people,
     booked at least 1 week in advance.<p>
     60% of standard rates for groups of more than 21
     people, booked at least 2 weeks in advance.<p>

<LI> <b>Advance Matinee Bookings</b><p>
     60% of standard rates, booked at least 1 week
     in advance.<p>

</OL>
```

Seating Plan & Prices

Our seating is among the most modern and comfortable in the world. All seats have an unsurpassed view and acoustic whether the theatre is full or not. Our choice of materials and our wide gangways make for total convenience and safety.

Click for seat prices & availability

IMAGE MAP

Our Pricing Scheme

Our standard prices cover the full range from elegant boxes for that special party to simple but good seats in the balcony. Group discounts and Concessions are available for all performances. We hope everyone will enjoy themselves at CTC.

- Box £100
- Back Stalls £50
- Front Stalls, Dress Circle £25
- Circle £10
- Balcony £5

LIST

```
<title>Seating Plan</title>
<h2>Seating Plan & Prices</h2>

Our seating is among the most modern and comfortable in
the world. All seats have an unsurpassed view and acoustic
whether the theatre is full or not. Our choice of materials
and our wide gangways make for total convenience and safety.
<hr>

<table>      <!--table used to lay out the document-->

<td><H3>Click for seat prices & availability</H3>
<A HREF="noseat.html">
<IMG SRC="seatplan.gif"
         ALT="a clickable seatplan goes here"
         width=300
         height=200
         units=pixel
         ISMAP>
</A>

<td><p><h3>Our Pricing Scheme</h3>
Our standard prices cover the full range from elegant
boxes for that special party to simple but good seats
in the balcony. Group discounts and <a href=concs.html>
Concessions</a> are available for all performances.
We hope everyone will enjoy themselves at CTC.
<ul>
<li>Box £100
<li>Back Stalls £50
<li>Front Stalls, Dress Circle £25
<li>Circle £10
<li>Balcony £5
</ul>

</table>
```

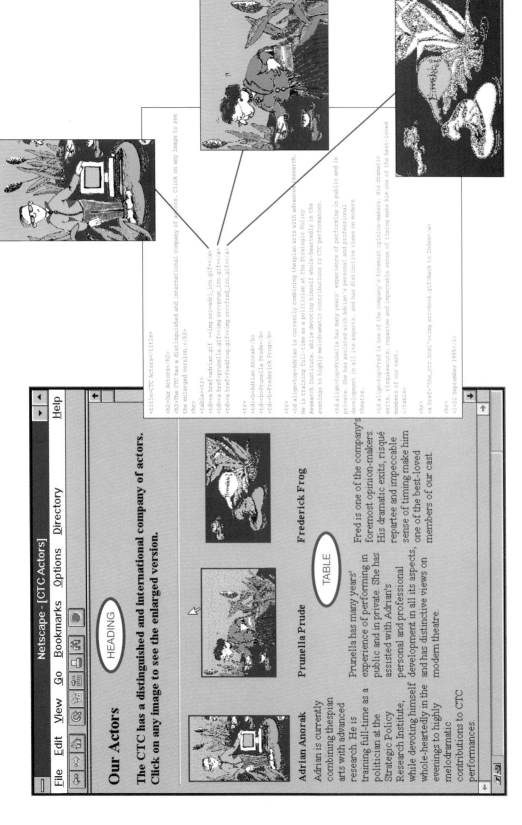

Our Company

The CTC company is completely democratic. Equal weight is given to the stage lighting technicians as to the direction or cast. Since roles are, in any case, shared evenly between members of the company, traditional distinctions are completely broken down in a direct demonstration of the CTC's free and open spirit.

Our Actors are involved in design and scripting as well as performance.

Our Lighting & Sound are vital and creative elements in all our productions.

Our revolutionary Stage Management is world-famous.

Jana's Costumes, Hats, Shoes, & Properties are as functional as they are visually distinctive.

Our Director is taking us to a new tomorrow.

Back to Index

Lighting & Sound

The CTC is justly famous for Dave Ragetsko's innovative approach to stage lighting and sound effects. Every aspect of modern technology is dramatically exploited to make our theatre one of the most sought-after places for stage technicians.

Stage Management

Set Design has always been kept to a minimum at CTC. While not espousing outdated Method-Acting Minimalism, Jana believes that backdrops ought never to upstage the action on set.

Famous sets have included Ragetsko's black stage, lit with the latest black floodlights while the auditorium was brilliantly illuminated. Critics marvelled while Ragetsko was heard to mutter

"Get th...

Costumes

Costumes for all CTC productions are designed and handmade by Jana herself, assisted by Prunella. Jana is an expert needlewoman and likes nothing better than a weekend by the fireside running up a complete set of costumes for a traditionally Tudor rendering of Shakespeare's Plantagenet plays

Direction

The CTC is directed by its founder Jana Ragetskaya

Jana eschewed training at traditional theatrical centres like RADA and the RSC, preferring instead to develop her own methods by *dynamical interaction* with the theatre company, allowing the ferment of ideas, movements, and emotions to determine the form of any particular piece.

This revolutionary approach has been the dynamo which has driven the CTC ever onward, with many exciting new companies following in its wake.

Jana has led many workshops and seminars on her methods, and is well-known in drama circles for her trenchant criticism of method acting and blind pursuit of technique.

IMAGE

Back to Index

```
<title>Our Company</title>
<h2>Our Company</h2>

<h3>The CTC company is completely democratic. Equal weight is given
to the stage lighting technicians as to the direction or cast.
Since roles are, in any case, shared evenly between members
of the company, traditional distinctions are completely broken
down in a direct demonstration of the CTC's free and open
spirit.</h3>

<hr>

<p>Our <a href="actors.html">
<b>Actors</b></a> are involved in design and scripting as well as
performance.

<p>Our <a href="lighting.html">
<b>Lighting & Sound</b></a> are vital and creative elements in
all our productions.

<p>Our revolutionary <a href="stage.html">
<b>Stage Management</b></a> is world-famous.

<p>Jana's <a href="costumes.html">
<b>Costumes, Hats, Shoes, & Properties</b></a> are as functional
as they are visually distinctive.

<p>Our <a href="director.html">
<b>Director</b></a> is taking us to a new tomorrow.

<hr>

<a href="the_ctc.html"><img src=book.gif> Back to Index</a>

<hr>

<i>22 September 1995</i>
```

```
<title>CTC Director</title>
<h2>Direction</h2>
The CTC is directed by its founder Jana Ragetskaya.
<hr>

<table>
<td><IMG SRC="director.gif">
<td>Jana eschewed training at traditional theatrical centres like RADA
and the RSC, preferring instead to develop her own methods by
<em>dynamical interaction</em> with the theatre company, allowing the
ferment of ideas, movements, and emotions to determine the form of any
particular piece.
<p>
This revolutionary approach has been the dynamo which has driven the
CTC ever onward, with many exciting new companies following in its wake.
<p>
Jana has led many workshops and seminars on her methods, and is
well-known in drama circles for her trenchant criticism of method
acting and blind pursuit of technique.
</table>

<hr>

<a href="the_ctc.html"><img src=book.gif>Back to Index</a>

<hr>

<i>22 September 1995</i>
```

As an example, here is a Dewey Decimal System subject (dds):

```
<META NAME=description SCHEME=dds
   CONTENT="04.251 Supercomputers systems design">
```

Another example, this time for an identifier property using the ISBN scheme:

```
<META NAME=identifier SCHEME=ISBN CONTENT="0-8230-2355-9">
```

The permitted values and their interpretation for each property name are defined by the profile, as explained in the section on LINK.

How indexing engines use META information

Some indexing engines look for META elements that define a comma-separated list of keywords/phrases, or which give a short description. At the very least, these can be used when presenting the search results to help users pick the most promising match.

```
<META NAME=keywords    CONTENT="vacation,Greece,sunshine">
<META NAME=description CONTENT="Idyllic European vacations">
```

How to make your Web pages properly indexed

Sometimes people find their sites have been indexed by an indexing robot, or, that a resource discovery robot has visited part of a site that for some reason should not be visited by robots. In recognition of this problem, many Web robots offer facilities for Web site administrators and content providers to limit what the robot does. This is achieved via two mechanisms: a 'robots.txt' file and the use of META tags in specific Web pages.

In a nutshell, when a robot visits a Web site, say 'http://www.foobar.com/', it first checks for 'http://www.foobar.com/robots.txt'. If it can find this document, it will analyze its contents to see if it is allowed to retrieve the document. You can customize the 'robots.txt' file so that it will apply only to specific robots, and to disallow access to specific directories or files.

Here is a sample 'robots.txt' file that excludes all robots from the entire site:

```
browser: *    # applies to all robots
Disallow: /   # disallow indexing of all pages
```

Where to create the 'robots.txt' file

The robot will simply look for a '/robots.txt' URL on your site, where a site is defined as an HTTP server running on a particular host and port number. For example:

Site URL	URL for robots.txt
http://www.w3.org/	http://www.w3.org/robots.txt
http://www.w3.org:80/	http://www.w3.org:80/robots.txt
http://www.w3.org:1234/	http://www.w3.org:1234/robots.txt
http://w3.org/	http://w3.org/robots.txt

There can only be a single '/robots.txt' on a site. Specifically, you should not put 'robots.txt' files in user directories, because a robot will never look at them. If you want your users to be able to create their own 'robots.txt', you will need to merge them all into a single '/robots.txt'. If you do not want to do this, your users might want to use the Robots META Tag instead.

Some tips:

- URLs are case sensitive, and the '/robots.txt' string must be all lower-case.

- Blank lines are not permitted.

There must be exactly one browser field. The robot should be liberal in interpreting this field. A case-insensitive substring match of the name without version information is recommended.

If the value is '*', the record describes the default access policy for any robot that has not matched any of the other records. It is not allowed to have multiple such records in the '/robots.txt' file.

The Disallow field specifies a partial URL that is not to be visited. This can be a full path, or a partial path; any URL that starts with this value will not be retrieved. For example,

```
Disallow: /help
```

disallows both /help.html and /help/index.html, whereas

```
Disallow: /help/
```

would disallow /help/index.html but allow /help.html.

An empty value for Disallow indicates that all URLs can be retrieved. At least one Disallow field must be present in the 'robots.txt' file.

The Robots META tag

The Robots META tag allows HTML authors to indicate to visiting robots whether a document may be indexed, or used to harvest more links. No server administrator action is required. In the following example, a robot should neither index this document, nor analyze it for links.

```
<META NAME="robots" CONTENT="noindex, nofollow">
```

The list of terms in the content is ALL, INDEX, NOFOLLOW and NOINDEX. The name and the content attribute values are case insensitive.

Note: In early 1997, only a few robots implement this, but this is expected to change as more public attention is given to controlling indexing robots.

12.6 The BASE element

The BASE element allows you to include the URL from which all relative links in the document are taken in the document head. In HTML 2.0 and HTML 3, the BASE element must include an **HREF** attribute whose value is the URL in question.

The BASE element is used, for example, when the document is on two servers or can be reached by two different paths.

Suppose 'http://www.nano.dr.org' is the URL you use to access a document. If someone places a hypertext link in that document using a relative URL, that URL will be resolved to that location from which the document was downloaded. Now, if 'http://www.nano.dr.org' is not the original location for that document, the relative URL will be wrongly resolved. By using the BASE element, you can specify the correct and original URL for that document and all relative URLs will be resolved using this definitive URL accordingly. For example:

```
<BASE HREF="http://www.tricks.nano.com">
```

All relative URLs will be resolved using this rather than simply the URL from where the document was retrieved.

The TARGET attribute

The **TARGET** attribute can be used to name a frame or to use a new window. You can set a default for all hypertext links in the document with the **TARGET** attribute on the BASE element.

12.7 The NEXTID element

The NEXTID element is a parameter read and generated by text editing software to generate unique identifiers. This tag takes a single attribute, which is the next document-wide alphanumeric identifier to be allocated of the form z123.

When modifying a document, existing anchor identifiers should not be reused, as these identifiers may be referenced by other documents. Human writers of HTML usually use mnemonic alphabetical identifiers.
Example:

```
<NEXTID N=Z27>
```

Browsers may ignore the NEXTID element. Support for NEXTID does not impact browsers in any way.

12.8 The SCRIPT element

The SCRIPT element allows you to include scripts in languages such as JavaScript or Visual Basic Script. Scripts allow you to change the default behavior of an HTML document, and are particularly useful for fill-out forms. You can ensure that form fields match appropriate constraints, and provide derived fields (whose values are computed from other fields). See Chapter 16.

12.9 The STYLE element

The STYLE element may be used to contain stylistic information, as explained in Chapter 9 on Style Sheets. One or more STYLE elements may be included in the document HEAD as need be. The STYLE element requires a start and an end tag as shown below.

The STYLE contents – that is, the mark-up within the STYLE element, should not be displayed to the browsers as such, but used merely to apply styles to other elements and to alter the color, background and other stylistic aspects of layout. Here is an example of the STYLE element:

```
<HEAD>
<TITLE>Title</TITLE>
<STYLE TYPE="text/css">
   H1 { font: sans serif }
   P  { color: red }
</STYLE>
</HEAD>
```

The STYLE element has a number of attributes:

- **TYPE**   Internet media type for style
- **TITLE**   Advisory title for this style
- **MEDIA**   Whether for paper, screen output, and so on

The `TYPE` attribute

The **TYPE** attribute can be used to specify the Internet media type and associated parameters for a linked style sheet. This allows the browser to disregard style sheets written in formats that it cannot understand.

The `TITLE` attribute

The **TITLE** attribute is used to group `LINK` and `STYLE` elements that together define a named style. All members of the same style must have exactly the same value for **TITLE**, but elements without the **TITLE** attribute are always applied (unless they are inappropriate to the current media).

The `MEDIA` attribute

This is used to indicate that stylistic information specified has been designed with a particular medium in mind – output on paper, for example, rather than output on the screen. Values are as per the **MEDIA** attribute of `LINK`.

13
FRAMES

Included in this chapter is information on:

- What frames are
- Creating basic frames
- Using frames elegantly

Summary

Frames divide a browser window into two or more document windows, with each displaying a different document, or a different part of the same document. Frames in an HTML or SGML document can cause a Web page to appear to be divided into multiple, scrollable regions.

For each frame you can assign such things as name, source document locator, dimensions, border alignment and decorations, scroll and resize behavior, file and topic maps, style sheets, and so on.

- **Names** – You can place an anchor in any frame, link to any addressable object, and then place that object into any named frame.

- **Source document locator** – You can use whatever addressing scheme your user agent supports, including URLs and filenames.

- **Dimensions** – You can rigidly or flexibly lay out a two-dimensional grid of rectangular blocks.

- **Border alignment and decoration** – You can adjust the position of the left- and right-hand margin; the top and bottom margin; and the alignment of the frame. You can also render the borders of a frame any color you like, or you can make them appear to be invisible.

- **Scrolling** – Frame scrollbars can be set manually, or you can let the browser turn on scrollbars if the document is larger than the current horizontal or vertical size of the frame.

- **Resizable** – Frames are normally resizable in the browser, but that feature can be disabled so the frame may not be resized.

- **File and topic maps** – You can place a file or a topic navigator into a frame. For example, the navigator could be a collapsible listing of any of the following: a file system, a listing of document headings, thumbnail sketches of document images, or an index of any element type.

Frame design is not difficult, but you need to understand how to go about it before you attempt some of the more subtle approaches. Sneak a preview of the end of the chapter if you like, but then turn back and read through the basics. Your patience will be rewarded.

13.1 What frames are

A set of frames divides the browser's display window into any reasonable number of rectangular areas. Each frame displays a linked HTML file, so that it gives you a neat way to organize your pages. Unlike tables, whose contents are fixed, frames can contain scrollable text, and their contents can be updated or replaced in response to user input or to programmed actions.

Here is an example of a commercial Web site made with a set of frames, from Easynet, an Internet Service Provider:

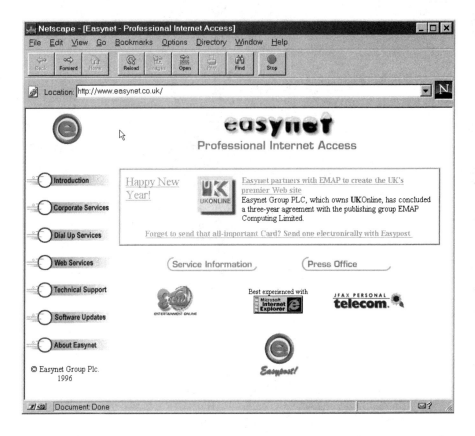

And here is the delightfully short piece of HTML which sets up the Easynet frames:

```
<TITLE> Easynet - Professional Internet Access </TITLE>
<FRAMESET FRAMEBORDER="0" FRAMESPACING="0" BORDER=0 COLS="169,*">
  <FRAME SRC="/easynet/menu-net.html" NAME="menu"
      MARGINWIDTH=0 MARGINHEIGHT=0>

  <FRAMESET FRAMEBORDER="0" FRAMESPACING="0" BORDER=0 ROWS="*">
    <FRAME SRC="/easynet/main.html" NAME="main" MARGINHEIGHT=0>
  </FRAMESET>

  <NOFRAMES>
    <BODY BGCOLOR="#ffffff" TEXT="#000000" LINK="#ff8000"
        VLINK="#07A35F">
    <TABLE> ...material for older browsers was here... </TABLE>
    </BODY>
  </NOFRAMES>

</FRAMESET>
```

We have left out most of the NOFRAMES content as it is not relevant here.

When you click on an item in the index, such as Software Updates, the display in the frame called 'main' changes, but the index stays where it is:

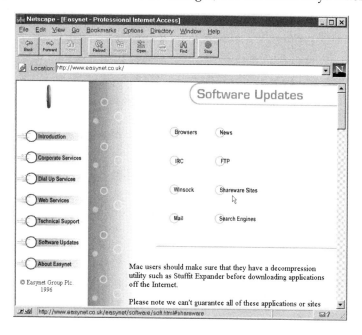

As you can see, the text in the frame continues off the bottom of the window. You can just scroll down to the rest of it:

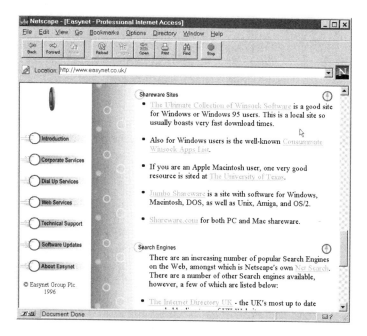

The headings, text, links and other body content elements within the frame work just as they do in an ordinary HTML page. The rest of this chapter shows how you can make frames as beautiful and clear as these professional examples.

A frame can contain pretty much anything you can do in HTML (just like a window for a Macintosh or Windows program). You can fix the things which you would like to stay on screen in their own static frames. These can include buttons that change the whole display, if necessary, by setting up whole new sets of frames. Other buttons can replace the contents of any single frame. The user scrolls through varying bits of information, typically in a large frame containing mostly text. A popular idea is to have an index frame on the left-hand side: each index entry is a permanently available hypertext link.

Some browsers, including older versions such as Netscape 1.0 and text-only models such as Lynx, cannot display frames. You can provide for them by including a document body with text and graphics, either simply explaining that a frame-capable browser is needed, or offering a frame-free version of your pages.

New browsers, including both Microsoft Internet Explorer 3.0 and Netscape Navigator 3.0 (and later versions), provide full support for HTML frames.

Use of frames

The effect of using frames is to simplify your HTML pages. This is because the approach separates the description of **how** you want your Web site displayed, from **what** it contains. A 'framing document' describes the arrangement of frames in the browser; each frame contains a link to a document which is to appear in it or in another frame.

The pages with the actual content are freed from having to contain tables to arrange the text and images in complicated arrangements. You are also freed from having to duplicate indexes and cross-reference links, because you can leave them on display in fixed frames.

The convenience and power of frames unfortunately does not mean that all applications are instantly improved by waving the frame fairy's magic wand over them. Far from it – there are some scandalously bad and unnecessary uses, apparently purely to be on the latest bandwagon. We would not like to name names, but some multinational companies that should know better are clear examples.

Frames are a hindrance if they merely add decorative frills, introduce needless complexity (and possibly bugs) or slow down the proceedings. They benefit your application if they make a visit to your site easier, more understandable, simpler, and perhaps more fun. They can do this in several ways:

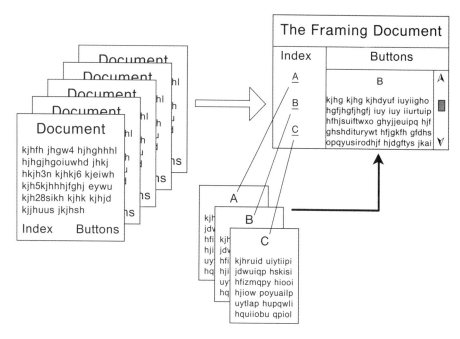

Before: Every page had its own buttons, links, index, graphics, title, background, data, and so on. Updating meant changing them all.

After: The framing document sets everything up, just once, and the other documents are simple. The index and other buttons load the documents into frames using targeted links.

- by providing index and navigation controls only once

- by keeping fixed locations for help, information, navigation, index to make things easier to find

- by offering context-sensitive navigation and references

- by using familiar left-to-right and top-to-bottom layouts to indicate sequences of activities

- by grouping related items together visually

You can probably think of other ways to use frames effectively.

How frames work

The attractive and convenient results of using frames have the price of a certain amount of indirectness. Instead of just shoving your entire HTML into one document, you usually need at least **three** files: a framing document, one or more indexing documents, and some content (normal HTML pages). The set-up is shown in the diagram below.

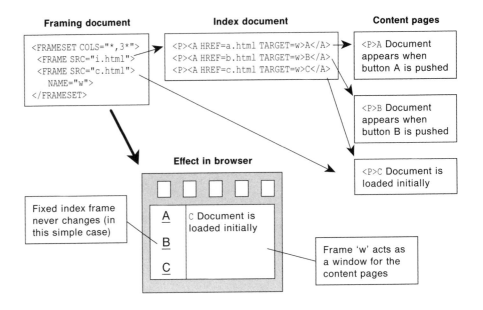

The framing document itself defines the initial appearance of your Web site, using links to start-up documents. To make anything else happen, you need to create further links, from those start-up pages, to the rest of your content pages (text, graphics, and so on). Those links can be simple text anchors, or can be graphical buttons, image maps and so on. They direct the browser to load your content pages into whichever frame you want. The diagram shows just one such document frame in use, next to an index frame.

Where the idea for frames came from

HTML pages have become more sophisticated with each generation of browsers. To understand what the shouting is all about, consider the tale of how computer displays have improved in the past thirty years or so.

In the beginning you fed a batch of key-punched computer cards into the computer and eventually got a printout. If anyone had a screen at all, it was for the operator, and he or she had a little monitor with bright green text on it, which scrolled off the screen just as the paper scrolled out of the line printer. The old HTML elements like <TT> and <PRE> are pretty much like that. Your text is formatted just as it used to be, in a simple typeface, and it starts at the top of the screen and pours down the page with lines of text. The only difference is that you have to use the scroll bar.

Then, people noticed that the operator's keyboard and screen were a lot more convenient than punched cards and green printouts, and so, inter-active computing was born. You had a screen which could be scrolled, but

IBM 650 mainframe
computer

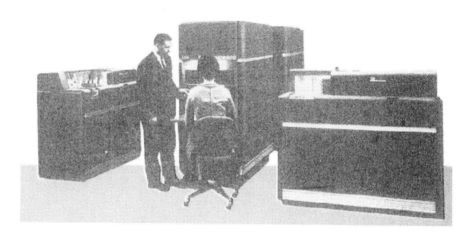

quite often you moved a cursor up and down and you could press different buttons to execute commands. The simple HTML arrangement of headings such as <H3> and text <P> and horizontal rules <HR>, together with anchors <A HREF=...> resembles this sort of interface. The emphasis is still on top-to-bottom text, but various structures have been added.

Finally, Xerox and MIT Media Lab researchers developed the idea of a graphical user interface, and allowed people to have different bits of information in different windows on the screen: these might individually scroll, or not, but the windows stayed where they were. Apple took the idea over and the rest is history. This is where HTML frames come in: they are the 'windows' into your documents and graphics.

Notice that this simple idea has a major impact on page design. Before frames came along, you showed page A, the user clicked on an anchor on page A and the browser showed page B instead. The whole browser display area was used to show the new page. But with frames, a click on an anchor replaces just one frame, probably. Naturally, it must still be possible to clear away all the frames and start again, as when the user surfs to another Web site. But as long as a visitor remains within your site, you can leave your frames in place.

This concept opens the way for displays resembling advertising banners to promote your goods and services. It also permits you to construct index buttons and suchlike that always stay in place ready for use. Incidentally, frames actually allow you to simplify 'text only' pages, as you no longer need make the effort to put in headers and indexes and cross-references, similar in style or even identical on each page. You put the headers and indexes and whatnot in their own frames, just once – and they stay there.

Once you understand these reasons behind the idea of frames, the rest – we promise – is easy.

13.2 Basic frames

Designing your frame layout

Your preliminary task is to sketch your set of frames on a piece of paper, so you know what you are trying to achieve. It is best to think which frames should be 'read' first, and to put them at the top or on the left. You should also decide which frames need to have a fixed size, and which should take up all available space.

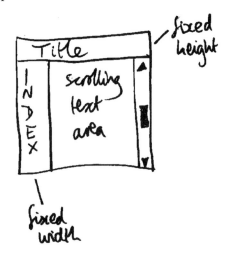

Even a rough, simple sketch, like the one shown above, is often enough to save time on a design which does not meet your needs – the picture makes clear whether or not you have forgotten something. You may also like to draw in the links to other files, as in the diagram in the section above.

Frame document structure

Frames are created and controlled through three elements: FRAMESET, FRAME and NOFRAMES.

A Web page containing frames is created by a main or 'framing' document. This document defines the frame regions on the browser, and identifies the HTML document that is initially to appear in each frame. A hypertext anchor in one of those documents can target any frame, so that (for example) a click on an image in your index frame can update any other frame's display. The special feature of framing documents is that they have a FRAMESET instead of a BODY. The FRAMESET element describes the frames that make up the page, and the FRAME elements specify the sub-documents that appear initially within it.

The frameset may only contain frames, nested framesets (for more complicated layouts with subframes), and a NOFRAMES element. The NOFRAMES element provides an alternative display for browsers that do not support frames, in much the same way that the **ALT** attribute of IMG lets you provide a textual description of an image for non-graphical browsers.

Since there is no point using frames unless there are at least two of them, your simplest framing documents have the structure:

```
TITLE
FRAMESET
    FRAME
    FRAME
    NOFRAMES
        BODY
```

If you go back and examine the Easynet example at the start of this chapter, you will find that it has this straightforward structure.

To complete the frameset, you need to specify how many rows and columns of frames you want, and what each frame is to contain. These tasks require you to supply attributes of FRAMESET and FRAME, as explained below.

Framesets

A frameset divides the browser window into rectangular regions. Each such region can be either a frame or a subsidiary frameset. The FRAMESET tag defines the actual size and layout of the frames, using the **ROWS** and **COLS** attributes described below.

A framing document has no BODY because it simply contains a set of frames, each of which probably does use the BODY element in its own HTML document. FRAMESET requires an end tag. You **must not** put any normal HTML elements (like H1 or P or IMG) that occur in the document body before the first FRAMESET tag, or the frames will all be ignored by the browser.

A TITLE is the only thing you should normally put before your first FRAMESET: it is allowed because it is part of the document head, not the body.

Sharing the space into rows and columns

The **COLS** and **ROWS** attributes of FRAMESET determine how many frames there are in the set, and how they share the available space. Both take the same kinds of value, so we will describe them together.

Both attributes take a list of values (such as percentages or actual pixels), separated by commas or spaces. If you define only the **ROWS**, you get one column taking up the entire available space:

```
<FRAMESET ROWS="20%,30%,50%"> <!-- percentages -->
   <!-- only 1 column -->
   ...
</FRAMESET>
```

Similarly, if you define only the **COLS**, you get one row:

```
<FRAMESET COLS="200,500,100"> <!-- pixels -->
   <!-- only 1 row -->
   ...
</FRAMESET>
```

Finally, a full FRAMESET specification defines both **ROWS** and **COLS**:

```
<FRAMESET ROWS="50%,50%" COLS="20%,70%,10%">
   <!-- two rows, three columns -->
   ...
</FRAMESET>
```

You have to supply either a **ROWS** or a **COLS** attribute. As you have guessed, each value determines the width (for columns) and height (for rows) of the framed regions; the number of width and height values supplied determines how many rows and columns you get. So, if you specify:

```
<TITLE>Frame with Three Columns</TITLE>
<FRAMESET COLS="20%,30%,50%">
  <FRAME SRC="cell1.html">
  <FRAME SRC="cell2.html">
  <FRAME SRC="cell3.html">
</FRAMESET>
```

with no **ROWS** value, the frameset is divided vertically into three column-like regions: the first one's width is 20 percent of the current frameset (or browser window if we are at the top level as shown in the illustration), the second region's width is 30 percent, and the third region's width is 50 percent.

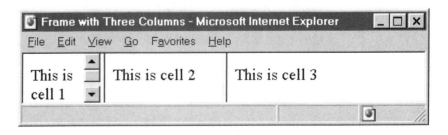

Similarly, if there is a **ROWS** value but no **COLS** value, the frameset is divided horizontally into row-like regions.

```
<TITLE>Frame with Three Rows</TITLE>
<FRAMESET ROWS="33%,33%,33%">
  <FRAME SRC="cell1.html">
  <FRAME SRC="cell2.html">
  <FRAME SRC="cell3.html">
</FRAMESET>
```

HTML documents to appear in frames can control their own background, colors, and typography. They do this in the usual way, with a BODY element and normal body content (such as headings and paragraphs). For example, cell1.html could specify colors like this:

```
<TITLE>Cell 1</TITLE>
<BODY BGCOLOR=green TEXT=yellow>
  <P>This is cell 1
</BODY>
```

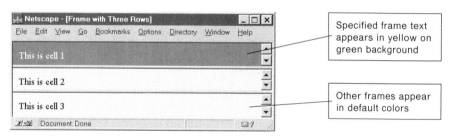

Specified frame text appears in yellow on green background

Other frames appear in default colors

When you supply values for both **ROWS** and **COLS**, the frameset is divided into a grid of rows and columns. This simple mechanism allows you to accommodate a large number of frames in an area, provided that you are happy with a regular grid. (You can achieve more complicated effects such as a row of cells along the top and down one side, around a single large area, by nesting framesets.)

Here is a simple grid:

```
<TITLE>Frameset of 2 Rows x 3 Columns</TITLE>
<FRAMESET ROWS="50%,50%" COLS="20%,*,30%">
  <!-- two rows, three columns -->
  <FRAME SRC=cell1.html>
  <FRAME SRC=cell2.html>
  <FRAME SRC=cell3.html>
  <FRAME SRC=cell4.html>
  <FRAME SRC=cell5.html>
  <FRAME SRC=cell6.html>
</FRAMESET>
```

Frameset of 2 Rows x 3 Columns - Microsoft Internet Explorer			_ □ ×
File Edit View Go Favorites Help			
This is cell 1	This is cell 2		This is cell 3
This is cell 4	This is cell 5		This is cell 6
Done			

Sharing the space between frames

To share the available height and width among your frames, you need to specify a list of **ROWS** or **COLS** values in each frameset. The **ROWS** and **COLS** attributes both take comma-separated lists of values. These can be:

- fixed sizes in pixels
- percentages (between 1 and 100) or
- relative scaling values

Fixed size in pixels

A simple numeric value means a fixed size in pixels. For instance:

```
<FRAMESET ROWS="100,500,200">
```

Together with the relative size values (written with a *) described below, fixed values are useful for making a graphic, such as an image map or button, fill an entire frame. For instance, to fit a button image into a frame of height 100, you could write (in the HTML file loaded into that frame):

```
<IMG SRC="backbutton.gif" HEIGHT=100>
```

to match the FRAMESET **ROWS** value. You should ensure that the frame is big enough to display the entire image, remembering that the margins also take up space. At least one of the other frame rows should be specified with *, a relative value, if at all possible. Exactly the same applies to columns.

The total height of all the rows must equal the height of the window. The browser may therefore normalize row heights. For instance, if in the last example you had accidentally written

```
<FRAMESET ROWS="10%,10%" COLS="20%,*,30%">
```

instead of ROWS="50%,50%"..., the visible effect would have been the same, at least in a well-behaved browser. Much the same applies to column widths. Since browsers can override specified pixel values in this way, the best you can do to get predictable results is to include at least one relative value (*) to occupy the unknown surplus of space.

A problem with fixed sizes in pixels is that what users see depends on the resolution of their screens. A viewer with a 640 × 480 screen is guaranteed not to like an HTML framing document which assumes that a width of 1000 pixels is available: half the columns will be literally off the screen, together with any link anchors they may contain. Generally it is best to use fixed sizes only for things that cannot be resized.

Percentage (%)

You write percentages as values between 1 and 100, with the usual % sign. These ought, naturally, to add up to 100. For instance, to specify three rows, the first and the last being smaller than the center row:

```
<FRAMESET ROWS="20%,60%,20%">
```

If you get it wrong and make the total greater than 100, it often does not matter, as all the contributing percentages are scaled down.

If the total is less than 100, and relative-sized frames exist, extra space is given to them. When there are no relative-sized frames, all the percentages are scaled up to make a total of 100 percent.

For example, suppose you accidentally specify

```
ROWS="50%,50%,50%"
```

Each entry is one-third of the sum of all the entries (150 percent), so the browser shares out the space evenly, giving each frame one-third of the height.

Relative value (*)

You write relative values with a star or asterisk '*'. By itself, '*' means 'give this row or column all the remaining space'. This is useful with either fixed pixel count or percentages, as it saves you from having to guess how large the user's display is. You simply specify widths or heights where you have definite requirements, and leave the rest to the browser.

A list of several relative values tells the browser to divide the remaining space evenly among them. For example:

```
<FRAMESET ROWS="*,*,*">
```

creates three rows of (approximately) equal height.

If there is a value in front of a '*', that row or column gets that much more relative space. For example, "2*,*" gives two-thirds of the space to the first frame, and one-third to the second.

Mixing values of different types

You can mix absolute pixel counts with percentages or relative values to specify frame widths and heights more freely. This is usually the most convenient approach.

For example, here is a frameset with four columns, the rightmost being of fixed width (100 pixels), and the other three sharing the rest of the space in the ratio 1:1:2:

```
<FRAMESET COLS="*,*,2*,100">
```

Here is a frameset with three rows, the first and the last being of fixed height, and the middle row taking up the remaining space:

```
<FRAMESET ROWS="100,*,100">
```

Finally, here is a frameset with four rows, the first a fixed percentage of the total height, the second a fixed height in pixels, and the third and fourth sized relatively:

```
<FRAMESET ROWS="30%,400,*,2*">
  <FRAME ... > <FRAME ... > <FRAME ... > <FRAME ... >
</FRAMESET>
```

Suppose the browser window is currently 1000 pixels high. The first frame row gets 30 percent of the total height, that is, 300 pixels; the second row gets 400 pixels, since an absolute amount was specified. This leaves 300 pixels to be divided between the other two frames. The fourth row's height is specified as '2*', so it will be twice as high as the third, whose height is only '*' (1*). Therefore the third row gets 100 and the fourth 200 pixels of height.

If the user resizes the window to 800 pixels high, the rows become 240, 400, 107 and 53 pixels high: notice the change in proportions. For instance, the fourth row changes from occupying 20 percent to only 6.6 percent of the available height.

As a general guide, it is best to make large frames relative, and to specify relationships relatively except where you have graphics or other items which demand a fixed size.

Frames

Each FRAME element defines a single frame in a frameset. The FRAME tag stands by itself: the element has no contents and no end tag. The correct idiom is therefore

```
<FRAMESET ... > <FRAME ... > <FRAME ... > <FRAME ... > </FRAMESET>
```

Controlling the behavior of individual frames

FRAME has the following attributes:

- SRC   specifies the frame's default document
- NAME   identifies a possible link target
- BORDER   emphasizes or hides borders
- BORDERCOLOR   selects color for the borders
- FRAMEBORDER   suppresses drawing of borders
- FRAMESPACING   sets extra space around frames
- MARGINWIDTH   sets widths of left and right margins
- MARGINHEIGHT   sets heights of top and bottom margins
- NORESIZE   locks out resizing by user
- SCROLLING   controls presence of scrollbars

Of these the most important is SRC, as it puts a document in the frame when first drawn. Anchors in that document, or in other frames, can then change the frame's contents dynamically.

The attributes, their allowed values, and their uses are explained below.

Specifying the frame's source document

The SRC attribute of a frame gives the address of the document to be displayed in it. A frame without a SRC is displayed as a blank space the size the frame would have been; it may be filled dynamically when the user clicks on a link anchor in another frame, or by the activity of a script. Here are some examples:

```
<FRAME SRC="woodwork.html" SCROLLING=yes>

<FRAME SRC="http://www.carpentry.com/">

<FRAME>   <!-- an empty frame; can be filled later -->
```

Identifying the frame for use as a target

The **NAME** attribute gives a name to a frame so it can be TARGETed by links in other documents. Such links usually derive from other frames in the same document. The **NAME** attribute is optional; by default all windows are unnamed. Names must begin with an alphabetic character (so names like '1stFrame' starting with a digit are not allowed).

For example:

```
<!-- in the framing document -->
<FRAME NAME="maintext">

<!-- in a document for another frame -->
<A HREF="text5.html" TARGET="maintext"> 5 </A>
```

Controlling the border

The **BORDER** attribute determines whether or not a border is visible and its relative thickness. If present, borders are drawn around the frame. If absent, there are no borders, but by default space is left for them, so the same frame with and without **BORDER** has the same width. For example:

```
<FRAME SRC="frontiers.html" BORDER=4>
```

You have two possible reasons for giving **BORDER** a value:

First, you can emphasize some frames at the expense of others. For example, a frame with a border of 4, containing a sub-frame with a border of 1, looks more attractive than if they both share the same default border width:

Here is a	subframe	with
thin	frame	borders

Second, by explicitly setting **BORDER** to zero, you can reclaim the space originally reserved for borders between cells, if you need a particularly compact grid-like layout. If you want to do this, you probably need to set **MARGINHEIGHT** and **MARGINWIDTH** to small values, as well.

Setting the border color

BORDERCOLOR sets the color of a frame's visible borders. You can use any of the pre-defined HTML color names, or name any color with an RRGGBB hexadecimal triplet. You ought to have a **BORDER** attribute in the main FRAME element to guarantee that your borders are visible in all their finery: but many browsers default to displaying borders in a tasteful shade of grey, so you may get away without one.

For example:

```
<FRAME SRC=psychedelic.html BORDERCOLOR="fuchsia">

<FRAME SRC=math.html BORDERCOLOR="#FF00AA">
```

Watch out for what happens if you put different colors in one frameset. Since cells share borders with their neighbors, if you set the one on the left, the one(s) to its right get their left border colored for them. Most browsers work left-to-right and top-to-bottom, incidentally, giving each border the first color that could apply to it.

For instance, we could apply **BORDERCOLOR** to the first and the third cells in a row:

BORDERCOLOR= "fuchsia"	← this border is fuchsia this border is pink →	BORDERCOLOR= "FF00AA"
↑ this border is fuchsia	the borders of this cell in Netscape Navigator 3.0 are fuchsia, fuchsia, and pink, whereas you might expect grey	

You can see that by setting **BORDERCOLOR** for just two cells out of six, many or all of the cells have their border color affected in some way. Incidentally, Microsoft's Internet Explorer 3.0 does not display border color.

One stylistic point about the choice of border color: many browsers now attempt a three-dimensional appearance, so that each border is bright on its top/left, and dark on its bottom/right. You will get best results if you choose colors of medium brightness, like fuchsia and pink and red, rather than extremes such as charcoal grey or light yellow.

Suppressing borders

FRAMEBORDER controls the frame border display. At the time of writing, agreement has not been reached on the syntax for frame border values.

Set to 'no' (Netscape) or '0' (Microsoft), no frame borders are drawn.

Set to 'yes' (Netscape) or '1' (Microsoft), the borders for the frame are drawn (the default behavior). The attribute might be useful if you want to suppress borders temporarily to see how the document would look without them.

Adding space around a frame

FRAMESPACING allows the setting of extra space around frames, to give the appearance of inline frames. The 'value' should be the distance required all around the frame in pixels. For example:

```
<FRAME SRC="wide.html" FRAMESPACING=10>
```

Adjusting a frame's margins

MARGINWIDTH gives you some control of the left- and right-hand margins for a specific frame. Its value is in pixels. Margins cannot be less than one; this ensures that frame objects cannot touch frame edges, and always leave some space for document contents. If you do not specify a margin width, the browser chooses a default value. For example:

```
<FRAME SRC=marginal.html MARGINWIDTH=50>
```

MARGINHEIGHT works just like **MARGINWIDTH**, except that it controls the upper and lower margins. For example:

```
<FRAME SRC=marginal.html MARGINHEIGHT=25>
```

Preventing resizing

NORESIZE does not take a value. It is simply a flag to forbid frame resizing by the user. For example:

```
<FRAME SRC=fixed.html NORESIZE>
```

Users typically resize frames by dragging a frame edge to a new position. Note that if any frame adjacent to an edge is not resizable, that entire edge is restricted from moving, affecting the resizability of other frames in different ways, as indicated in the diagram below.

	← this edge cannot be moved
`<FRAME SRC=fixed.html NORESIZE>` This frame has a fixed height and width.	. . . so this frame cannot be resized
↑ this edge can be moved up at the expense of the top row!	. . . and this one has fixed width.

By default, all frames are resizable.

Controlling scrollbars

SCROLLING indicates whether or not the frame is to have scrollbars.

- 'yes' makes scrollbars always visible on that frame.

- 'no' results in scrollbars never being visible.

- 'auto' instructs the browser to decide whether scrollbars are needed, and to place them where necessary. That is, with 'auto', the frame has scrollbars only if the document is larger than the current size of the frame.

The **SCROLLING** attribute is optional; the default value is 'auto'. If scrollbars are switched off, users can see the full contents of a frame only when it is large enough to display them all. This is just what you need for graphics.

Naming and targeting frames

Targeting gives you a degree of control over which frame a document or object appears in, when a user clicks on an anchor or otherwise traverses a link in a frame document. Targeting can be employed by itself for a document space that is best viewed with multiple top-level windows (e.g., a list of subjects window, and a window displaying the current subject), but it is most useful in conjunction with frames.

Previously when a user clicked on an anchor, the inbound document either appeared in the window the user had clicked in, or alternately (and under the user's control) appeared in a completely new window. Targeting windows for delivery allows you to name specific windows, and target certain documents to always appear in the window bearing the matching name.

Windows can be named in three ways:

- in the FRAME element

```
<FRAME NAME="window_name">
```

The name is specified as an attribute of the frame itself.

- in a link anchor

```
<A HREF="url.html" TARGET="window_name">
```

This is a targeted link, in this case, using an ordinary link anchor; though you can also use LINK, BASE, AREA and FORM for various special purposes. Whichever you choose, HTML assigns a target window_name to a link. The document loaded from that link behaves exactly as if it had a window_name set in its FRAME.

- in an HTTP window-target

```
window-target: window_name
```

The document is sent with the optional HTTP window-target header. This forces the document to load in the window named window_name, or if such a window does not exist, one is created and the document is loaded in it. This mechanism is, of course, outside HTML.

Using TARGET

TARGET specifies the frame where a document is to appear. This can be added to various HTML anchor elements (such as A and LINK) to target specific frames for their links. TARGET has only one form, which is:

```
TARGET="window_name"
```

By default, an anchor actually in a frame loads its document right there.

NAME is an attribute of the FRAME element. By naming a frame, its contents can be changed with the use of a **TARGET** attribute in your anchor elements, or in the BASE element of a document referred to in an anchor. By referring to a particular frame with the TARGET element, you control which frame will display the document.

The rules for TARGET priorities

The rules for targeting are not really complicated, but you should know that there are different ways of achieving particular results.

- The TARGET value of an anchor overrides all others.

- If an anchor does not contain a TARGET, it uses the TARGET specified in the document's BASE.

- If the BASE element does not contain a TARGET, the document loads into the frame that the anchor is in.

- If the anchor or BASE elements contain a TARGET whose value is not an existing frame's NAME, the document creates a new instance of the browser, and that instance behaves like an individually named FRAME. Be careful not to use the same name in different framesets: if you defined a name in a frameset which is no longer on display, then any document targeted on that name is treated as frameless and popped into a new browser – not at all what you might have wanted.

Note: A right-click (or click-and-hold) on an anchor in the browser pops up a menu. When 'Open This' is selected, it overrides the TARGET attributes and loads into that same frame.

– on A or LINK

The anchor tag normally specifies a document to be loaded when the link is traversed; adding the **TARGET** attribute to these elements forces the document to be loaded into the targeted window. The A and LINK anchor elements can specify that a linked document should be displayed in a named frame. Therefore you must NAME any frame which is to be a delivery target, and use this name in the A or LINK anchor.

Here is an example of targeting specific frames using an A element.

```
<FRAMESET ROWS="45%,10%,45%">
  <FRAME NAME="upper">
  <FRAME NAME="middle" SRC="sources.html">
  <FRAME NAME="lower">
</FRAMESET>

<!-- In "sources.html" -->
<UL>
  <LI><A TARGET="upper" HREF="uppr.html">Top Page</A>
  <LI><A TARGET="lower" HREF="lowr.html">Bottom Page</A>
</UL>
```

Clicking on the first anchor displays the document 'uppr.html' in the frame called 'upper'; clicking on the second displays 'lowr.html' in 'lower'.

– on BASE

Targeting BASE causes all otherwise untargeted links in a document to be targeted to the same window. A BASE TARGET establishes a default window_name for all links in a document. This default is overridden by any specific TARGETs in individual anchor elements. For example:

```
<BASE TARGET="main_window">

<A HREF="subsidiary_text.html" TARGET="small_window">
```

– on AREA

Just as you can make a frame the target of a link anchor in your HTML text, you can make a frame the target of an AREA in an image map. (The AREA element describes a shaped area in a client-side image map.) This arrangement specifies a link to traverse when the user clicks within the defined area of the image map. The **TARGET** attribute to AREA then specifies that the browser must load the linked document in the targeted window. For example:

```
<AREA SHAPE="shape" COORDS="x,y,..." HREF="url.html" TARGET="window">
```

– on FORM

A FORM normally displays its results in the same window where the user submitted it. If you add a **TARGET** attribute to the FORM, the results are loaded into the targeted window, just as you would expect. For example:

```
<FORM ACTION="url" TARGET="window_name">
```

Built-in TARGET behaviors

Normal window names for the **TARGET** attribute begin with an alphabetic character (such as 'w'). But there are some special targets, all of which begin with the underscore character (_), providing some very useful built-in behaviors. These special targets are explained in the table.

TARGET	Effect on the linked document
_blank	The document is opened in a new, unnamed, blank window.
_self	The document is opened in the same frame that was clicked in (i.e. same frame as the anchor). This can override a globally assigned BASE target.
_parent	The linked document is loaded into the immediate FRAMESET parent of this document, or like **_self** if the document has no parent.
_top	The 'parent' frameset of the current frame collapses to a single frame, and the document is displayed there in the full browser window. This defaults to acting like **_self** if the document is already at the top. It is useful for breaking out of an arbitrarily deep FRAME nesting.

Support for non-frame browsers

To cater to text-only, Braille and speaking browsers which do not know about frames, you should add some NOFRAMES information. Frame-capable browsers ignore all tags and data between starting and ending NOFRAMES tags, so you can write a traditional HTML document body (with headings, paragraphs and so on) to substitute for the frames.

The best way to do this is to insert the NOFRAMES element just before the outermost </FRAMESET> end-tag, and then to put a BODY inside it. You can then safely create the alternate document inside the BODY:

```
<FRAMESET>
  <FRAME ... >
  <FRAME ... >    <!-- frames as before -->
  <FRAME ... >
  <NOFRAMES>
    <BODY>
      <H1>This browser does not display Frames</H1>
      <P>This document is designed for use with a frame-capable browser
         such as Netscape Navigator 3.0 or Microsoft Internet Explorer
         3.0. The description below is a short summary of what the frames
         display...
    </BODY>
  </NOFRAMES>
</FRAMESET>
```

The effect of this, in a browser that cannot handle frames, is to display or otherwise process the body as shown below. In a frame-capable browser, NOFRAMES has no effect at all.

This browser does not display Frames

This document is designed for use with a frame-capable browser such as Netscape Navigator 3.0 or Microsoft Internet Explorer 3.0. The description below is a short summary of what the frames display

You may want to simulate your frame layout within NOFRAMES using HTML tables, taking advantage of the **ROWSPAN** attribute to make the cells share the height as desired. You insert the simulated frame contents directly in the table cells. For instance:

```
<TABLE BORDER>
   <TR><TD ROWSPAN=1>This is cell 1
      <TD ROWSPAN=2>This is cell 2
   <TR><TD ROWSPAN=2>This is cell 3
   <TR><TD ROWSPAN=2>This is cell 4
   <TR><TD ROWSPAN=2>This is cell 5
</TABLE>
```

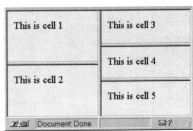

Layout using tables can become quite complicated, because it is not intuitively obvious how cells spanning rows and columns will nest together (notice the tricky order in which the cells appear in the table). Also, unless you are generating your content dynamically from a database, the whole layout is fixed when you design it.

Floating frames

Microsoft Internet Explorer 3.0 introduces floating frames with a special IFRAME element. As the name suggests, these behave like floating images (IMG) or tables (TABLE) with the same **ALIGN** attribute: when aligned left or right, the surrounding text flows around the frame.

Unlike FRAME, which is only allowed in the context of a framing document's FRAMESET, IFRAME stands alone in a normal document's body. All the usual frame attributes can, however, be applied to it, so we will not go over them again. Here is a simple example:

```
<IFRAME FRAMEBORDER=3 SCROLLING=no ALIGN=right SRC="banner.html">
</IFRAME>
```

This produces the 'floating' effect shown in the illustration at the top of the next page.

Note the curious syntax: the closing tag is required. The apparent intention is to enable authors to insert ordinary frames within IFRAME to provide an alternative for other browsers. Unfortunately, it is not easy

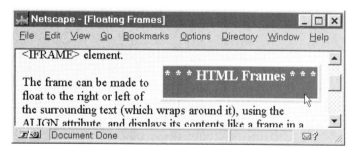

to do this. If you put your frame specification in the middle of some text, browsers ignore it, while if it goes at the top of the document, the text is ignored. You can pair your IFRAME with a floating table:

```
<IFRAME FRAMEBORDER=3 SCROLLING=no ALIGN=right SRC="banner.html">
   <!-- contents for non-IFRAME browsers -->
  <TABLE ALIGN=right BORDER=3 BGCOLOR=blue>
    <TR><TD><FONT COLOR=white>
      <H3>* * * HTML Frames * * *</H3>
  </TABLE>
</IFRAME>
```

This quite closely matches the floating frame effect, as the Netscape illustration shows, but compatibility is an issue. In any case, if you have to insert a floating table, why use IFRAME as well?

13.3 Using frames elegantly

Designing frame layouts

The task of achieving more complex layouts is easier and more direct with frames than with tables (see Chapter 11), as they are designed to nest neatly to subdivide areas as desired. What is more, you have a free choice of giving rows priority over columns, or vice versa (since the outermost frameset gets priority); whereas tables always give priority to the rows.

You are now in a position to design any framesets you might want. For example, a typical commercial home page consists of a banner across the top, with a column of cells down the side of a main area. This can readily be set up using nested framesets. Our basic design concept is like this:

banner area (fixed)	
index 1	the main text area (scrolling)
index 2	
index n	

We need a cell spanning the whole width of the area for the banner. It can contain text, graphics, or an animation powered by a script. We will put in a simple, colored text banner:

```
    <!-- banner.html -->
<TITLE>Star-Spangled Banner</TITLE>
<BODY BGCOLOR=blue TEXT=white>
<CENTER>
    <H3>* * * HTML Frames * * *</H3>
</CENTER>
</BODY>
```

When we want something more sophisticated, we can replace the banner file without affecting the frame design at all.

Then, nested under the banner, we want a cell spanning the whole height of what is left for the main text. It is for an HTML file containing some of the text of this chapter. The index buttons will have to refer to this window (to change the text that appears in it) so it has to have a name:

```
<FRAME SRC="frametext.html" NAME="frametext">
```

Beside it is a third frameset, nested inside the other two, for the index cells. These cells ought to be all the same width – which comes automatically with being in a column – and all the same height, which we can achieve just by letting the browser choose heights for them with `ROWS="*,*,*"`, putting in an asterisk for each cell.

The index could be constructed just with text anchors. The 'Home' feature needs to do no more than to point to the main (frametext) file, so that when clicked the text goes back home to the top of the file. You need to say explicitly which window you want the text to appear in, as otherwise it replaces the 'Home' anchor itself. So the HTML is:

```
    <!-- home.html, text version -->
<A HREF=frametext.html TARGET=frametext>Home</A>
```

Nowadays, though, most HTML sites seem to have buttons to push, so what we will do is to make some GIF images of buttons, and use them as anchors:

```
    <!-- home.html, graphics version -->
<A HREF=frametext.html TARGET=frametext>
<IMG SRC=home.gif ALT=Home></A>
```

The other buttons are constructed in just the same way.

One more refinement is to eliminate the rather wide margins that browsers thoughtfully place around the contents of your frames: these are fine for text, but a nuisance for images like buttons. So we will set both **MARGINWIDTH** and **MARGINHEIGHT** to their minimum value, 1. It may be wise to set the button frames to NORESIZE if you think the user should not disturb your arrangement.

The framing document's HTML therefore contains three nested framesets:

```
<TITLE>Frameset with Banner & Index</TITLE>
<FRAMESET ROWS = "15%,85%">
  <FRAME SRC="banner.html" SCROLLING=no>
  <FRAMESET COLS="100,*">
    <FRAMESET ROWS="*,*,*">
      <FRAME SRC=home.html SCROLLING=no MARGINWIDTH=1 MARGINHEIGHT=1>
      <FRAME SRC=top.html  SCROLLING=no MARGINWIDTH=1 MARGINHEIGHT=1>
      <FRAME SRC=help.html SCROLLING=no MARGINWIDTH=1 MARGINHEIGHT=1>
    </FRAMESET>
    <FRAME SRC="frametext.html" NAME="frametext">
  </FRAMESET>
</FRAMESET>
```

The illustration shows how the layout appears in a browser.

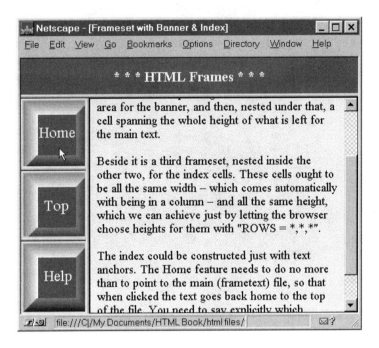

We have put in only three index buttons, but the basic frame design is quite suitable for several more.

Parent and child frames

You need to work out your strategy for using frames to suit your purpose. The simplest approach is to have a single parent document which sets up your set of frames (like the example above). All your other (child) items 'live' in one of its frames. Such items may consist of text, images, video, scripted animations, or simply of anchors (text or images) which allow the user to select from your menu – or perhaps we should say palette – of possibilities.

The trouble with this simple view of the frame universe is that you probably want the index and other 'fixed' items which sit beside or above the scrollable text to change depending on the scrollable central item. For example, you might want to give more detail of the parts of the index related to the item currently on display, as if with a fisheye lens that magnifies the nearest objects but shrinks all the others. This approach fits neatly with the general Hypertext idea of putting in cross-references to related items. For instance, if we are displaying images of waterfowl, then Divers, Grebes and Herons should all be readily accessible, whereas more distant relatives such as Hoopoes and Woodpeckers can all be grouped under a few blanket headings such as Other Birds without inconveniencing the user. We could organize the screen as shown in the illustration.

If the user clicks on one of the water birds, the main text area fills with a description of that family. But if the user clicks on the image of the small bird on the right, representing Other Birds, the row of bird-icons is replaced, along with the text:

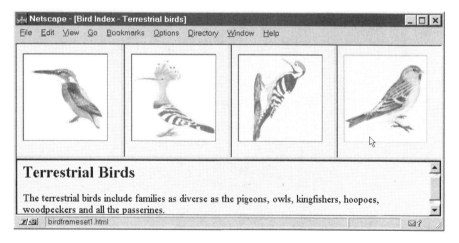

If you have followed this reasoning, then you can see that the simple approach does not quite give you what you want. Instead, what you need to do is to replace not only the central item (the current subject matter), but also some or all of the other frames, keeping the style and appearance of the whole frameset but changing subtly the contents. In general, the safest approach is to provide a different parent for each child. This is quite feasible if you are generating your HTML from a database, but a bit tedious if you are writing the HTML manually.

Here is what we might want from the example frameset from the previous section. We replace the main text, and at the same time replace the first index button, changing it from 'Home' to 'Back':

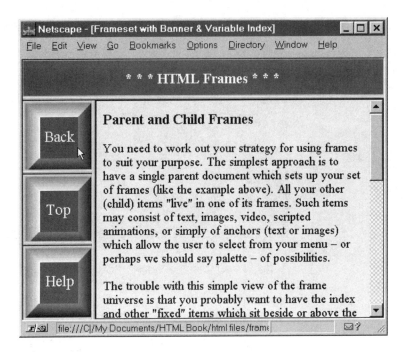

This frameset is, naturally, virtually identical to that for the 'Home' frameset. Only the sources for the 'Back' icon and the main frame text are changed:

```
<TITLE>Frameset with Banner & Variable Index</TITLE>
<FRAMESET ROWS="15%,85%">
  <FRAME SRC="banner.html" SCROLLING=no>
  <FRAMESET COLS="20%,80%">
    <FRAMESET ROWS="*,*,*">
      <FRAME SRC=back.html SCROLLING=no MARGINWIDTH=1 MARGINHEIGHT=1>
      <FRAME SRC=top.html  SCROLLING=no MARGINWIDTH=1 MARGINHEIGHT=1>
      <FRAME SRC=help.html SCROLLING=no MARGINWIDTH=1 MARGINHEIGHT=1>
    </FRAMESET>
    <FRAME SRC="frametext2.html" NAME="frametext">
  </FRAMESET>
</FRAMESET>
```

But how do we call up and display this frameset? If we simply put:

```
    <!-- home.html, bad version -->
<A HREF="frameset2.html">              Wrong!
<IMG SRC=home.gif ALT=Home></A>
```

then we get the dreaded hall-of-mirrors effect:

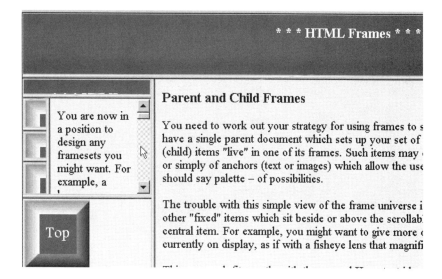

What we actually want is to tell the browser that the new frameset is to *replace* the existing one, not to nest within it. The trick is just to target the link to the top level, so that the frameset displays in the whole browser, not in the little frame meant for the icon. The top-level frame target is called simply '_top':

```
    <!-- home.html, good version -->
<A HREF="frameset2.html" TARGET="_top">
<IMG SRC=home.gif ALT=Home></A>
```

The effect is to make the browser redraw its whole display area.

Where the desired new layout is in fact the same as before, and only one frame has different contents, we could instead target it directly. The simplest way is naturally just to put an anchor in the main window; when clicked, it updates that window, just as in pre-frame HTML a click on a link always redrew the whole browser window.

Obviously if the number of frames (e.g., for different configurations of index buttons) or their layout has changed, we have no choice but to redraw the lot.

To get back to the first frameset we need another two-line HTML file in the same style:

```
    <!-- back.html -->
<A HREF="frameset1.html" TARGET="_top">
<IMG SRC=back.gif ALT=Back></A>
```

The Ornithology example works in exactly the same way, except that we chose a bird-icon row in place of a button-icon column. The first frameset is simply:

```
<TITLE>Bird Index -- Waterbirds</TITLE>
<FRAMESET ROWS="200,*" >
  <FRAMESET COLS="*,*,*,*">
    <FRAME SRC=diver.html>
    <FRAME SRC=grebe.html>
    <FRAME SRC=heron.html>
    <FRAME SRC=landbirds.html>
  </FRAMESET>
  <FRAME SRC=waterbirdstext.html NAME="birdtext">
</FRAMESET>
```

and the HTML files it calls up are equally small and plain.

The files associated with the Other Birds icons, for example, are structured like this, with a **TARGET="_top"** attribute to restart with the specified new frameset:

```
   <!-- landbirds.html -->
<A HREF=birdframeset2.html TARGET="_top">
  <IMG SRC=bird.gif ALT=Bird></A>
```

The files associated with the icons for the individual water birds are all structured like diver.html, with a **TARGET="birdtext"** attribute to leave the frame structure alone, but to replace the text in the main frame:

```
   <!-- diver.html -->
<A HREF=divertext.html TARGET="birdtext">
  <IMG SRC=diver.gif ALT=Diver></A>
```

This delightfully compact file instructs the browser to display the Diver-icon shown at the top left of the illustration below. If the icon is clicked on, the targeted link anchor makes the browser display whatever text is in 'divertext.html' in the main frame, as shown at the bottom of the illustration opposite.

Not all index buttons need to change framesets. Things like 'Help' may need to, if they are context-sensitive; things like 'Search' probably do not; again, unless you want to use the context in some way to guide the search operation.

Whether or not you choose to use just one frameset or many framesets, we hope that we have inspired you to start creating some beautiful and informative frame pages.

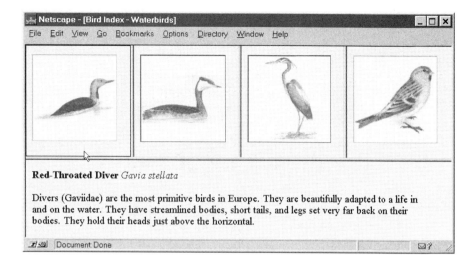

Applications of frames

Frames are so useful that soon you will certainly be thinking up your own applications for them. Here are some off-the-peg ideas to get you started.

Static frames for tools and notices

You can put elements that a user should always see, such as:

- button bars
- logos
- copyright notices and
- title graphics

in individual frames locked into place on the browser window.

Live frames for fun and information

HTML aficionados call frames 'live' if they scroll or contain things that move or jiggle about in a more-or-less lively way: either when clicked on, or all by themselves. Fashionable designers and web-weavers have swiftly seized upon the possibilities of frames for brightening up Web sites. You may like to use live frames for

- documents
- icons
- interactive forms

- videos

- multimedia

- topic maps

and anything else that can react to user input or programmed activity. Your users can navigate your site in live frames, clicking on easy-to-find icons in nearby static frames.

Functional tables of contents

A frame can contain interactive tables of contents with links that, when clicked, display results in an adjoining frame. Such tables of contents can be static or interactive with:

- collapsible lists

- graphical maps of document structure (giving a fisheye lens view), or

- displays of file and link architectures

Frames make it easier than ever before to present information clearly and concisely, and allow readers to navigate with certainty through large collections of documents. Hypertexts, including the Web, used to be heavily criticized for losing the reader in Hyperspace after a few clicks. Now everyone can build a navigate-in-your-sleep site without programming.

Single-page, query-and-answer displays

Frames designed side-by-side permit queries to be posed and answered on the same page, with a static frame holding the query form, and the other presenting the results live in a scrollable frame. In a left-to-right language like English, it is natural to have the query on the left and the results on the right.

Summary

Frames make possible virtually any two-dimensional arrangement of static and interactive frames that you might want. You can place information in any one rectangular block independently of the overall page or of other frames on the page. This dramatic simplification (you do not have to remember what you did in any other document) makes possible a quantum jump in sophistication. Web designers have taken to frames like ducks to water. Try them for yourself.

14
IMAGE MAPS

Included in this chapter is information on:

- Creating image maps and navigation
- Creating server-side image maps
- Creating client-side image maps

Summary

HTML 4 supports the idea of *client-side image maps* that allow hypertext links to be associated with shaped regions of an image. The client-side processing mechanism extends the anchor element and provides backward compatibility with all existing browsers. It removes the need to duplicate image maps with textual hypertext menus for non-graphical browsers.

Server-side image maps using `ISMAP` are still supported.

14.1 Introduction

Image maps have been popular on the Web since the arrival of the `IMG` element in HTML that is used to insert graphics into Web pages. Essentially, an image map is a picture with hotzones. Each hotzone is associated with a different hypertext link: clicking in a hotzone results in specific information being sent across the Internet for display as that link is triggered.

Image maps may be handled either by the server or by the browser. These two alternatives are known as server-side and client-side image maps, respectively. These two alternative systems are now explained.

14.2 Server-side image maps

In server-side processing, when the user clicks on an image, the location of the click, in terms of its x and y coordinates, is passed by the browser to the server. The server, on receiving information about the location of the click, employs a *map* file which says that, for such and such an (x, y) location, this or that information should be sent down the wire back to the browser.

Take for example, a map of the United States. If the user clicks anywhere in the area of 'Nevada', for example, the browser will then send those particular coordinates to the server. The server will then look up those coordinates and discover that it should respond by sending a file called 'nevada.htm' across the Internet and back for display on the screen.

The HTML to specify a server-side image map

Here is an example of some HTML used to describe a server-side image map:

```
<A HREF="http://myserver.myplace.com/~user/logo.map">
<IMG SRC="http://myserver.myplace.com/~user/images/logo.gif" ISMAP></A>
```

Here you can see two files are involved. The file referenced by the **HREF** attribute is the map file, here called 'logo.map'. This is the file held on the server that maps the coordinates of clicks to their corresponding URLs that point to information which it will send back to the browser.

The second file is the graphic to be presented to the user, which, in this case, is the file 'logo.gif'. The addition to the IMG element is the **ISMAP** attribute, that the browser uses to indicate that the image is part of an image map. **ISMAP** will turn the area clicked by the user into coordinates.

Another example of server-side processing

Look at the following image map. This is taken from the home page of AccessHP (http://www.hp.com):

This is represented in HTML as:

```
<P><A HREF="/cgi-bin/imagemap/ahp/ahpHome-B.map">
<IMG ALT="Navigation Bar" SRC=/ahp/Bottom.gif
  WIDTH=504 HEIGHT=29 ISMAP></A>
```

This is a paragraph with a hypertext link containing an IMG element. Absolutely critical is the inclusion of an **ISMAP** attribute within the IMG element, as this has the effect of making the browser send the clicked location to the server. Note that the click event is sent to the URL given by the **HREF** attribute of the enclosing hypertext link, and not the **SRC** attribute of the IMG element. The other attributes are icing on the cake.

The **ALT** attribute gives a text string for browsers that cannot display images, and which can be shown in place of the image. In other words, on a text-only browser such as Lynx, you would see a hypertext link with the label 'Navigation Bar'.

The **WIDTH** and **HEIGHT** attributes speed up the initial display of the document, allowing the browser to continue formatting the rest of the document without having to wait for the image data to specify the image size.

Such a server-side image map is processed as follows:

(1) When the user clicks on the image, the browser sends a request for the URL of the document associated with the clicked area.

(2) The server examines the image map file, and sends back the appropriate URL.

(3) The browser then sends the server the request for the corresponding document.

If the browser does not support graphics, the server has no way of knowing which choice was selected. As a result, many Web pages offer a conventional hypertext menu that uses text-based labels in addition to the graphical menu.

The map file

The map file is a text file that may reside anywhere on the Web server. Usually the file is suffixed with '.map', but how you name it is irrelevant, so long as you reference it correctly in the HTML. It consists of three elements: the shape of the area to be clicked, the URL that is 'mapped' to the clicked area and the x- and y-point coordinates that comprise the shape of the clicked area. For the above example, the map file would look like this:

```
rect http://myserver.myplace.com/~user/main.html 8,5 81,34
circ http://myserver.myplace.com/~user/news.html 117,11 154,50
poly http://myserver.myplace.com/~user/info.html 209,45 248,45 282,45
    209,45
default http://myserver.myplace.com/~user/goback.html
```

In this file, three shapes are defined, these being the most common. The first, a rectangle, is specified by 'rect'. The coordinates measure from the top left-hand corner to the bottom right-hand corner. The second shape, 'circ', is a circle measured by the left-hand, top, right-hand and bottom coordinates. The final shape named 'poly' is a polygon measured by the x- and y-points of its vertices.

Defined as 'default', the final entry in the map file specifies the URL for the rest of the image. If the user clicks on an area other than the rectangle, circle or polygon, the file 'goback.html' returns to the browser. 'Default' need not be specified, but it should be included so the user is not left clicking relentlessly on an area that is not mapped.

At first, constructing such a file may seem complicated, but many programs exist that eliminate the need to sit with an imaging program and calculate the coordinates of the area you wish to be clickable. For example, Macintosh practitioners have WebMap, whereas Windows users have a program called Map This. UNIX gurus may implement Mapedit to create the map file.

The server process

How Web servers handle image maps depends on the type of server used. Initially, servers used CGI scripts to interpret clicks and return URLs, and some still do. It is becoming more common for servers to have internal code that allows them to interpret image maps. The HTML and map file above work on such a server, NCSA's server, httpd version 1.5. If your server is not equipped with such code, the URL you use in your HTML may look like this:

```
<A HREF="http://myserver.myplace.com/cgi-bin/imagemap/~user/logo.map">
<IMG SRC="http://myserver.myplace.com/~user/images/logo.gif" ISMAP></A>
```

In this case, the **A HREF** attribute points to the cgi-bin, where the image map script is located. The information following '/cgi-bin/imagemap/' tells the process where your map file is located. Since the majority of Web servers have some sort of image map handler, it is merely a matter of finding out how your server deals with image maps.

14.3 Client-side image maps

A new player in the arena of image maps is the client-side image map. Because the image map resides solely on the browser, the overhead of the two-step process of server-side image mapping is eliminated. Using client-side image maps also eliminates the need for doubling up on image maps with text menus, since this technique is backward compatible. Two different techniques exist for client-side image maps: using the OBJECT element specification (fully described in Chapter 15) and the MAP element.

Using OBJECT

When used for a client-side image map, the OBJECT element encompasses everything you need to complete the effect. The following HTML:

Commas are optional in the COORDS lists.

```
<OBJECT DATA="menu.gif" SHAPES>
<A HREF="answer.html" SHAPE="rect" COORDS="11,0,80,55">
    the answer page</A> |
<A HREF="link.html" SHAPE="rect" COORDS="83,7,217,40">link-o-rama</A> |
<A HREF="home.html" SHAPE="rect" COORDS="224,27,302,61">home</A>
</OBJECT>
```

will appear like this in a browser that supports client-side image maps:

The image map, graphically.

But in a browser that does not support the OBJECT specification, or even images, the user will see:

the answer page | link-o-rama | home

The key to using client-side image maps with the OBJECT element is in the **SHAPES** attribute.

SHAPES **in image maps**

When the browser encounters an OBJECT tag with an accompanying **SHAPES** attribute, it knows to look for anchor elements within. The traditional anchor elements (<A HREF=...> and </A>) have been extended to include the **SHAPE** and **COORDS** attributes, allowing an association between a hypertext link and an area of the image that is within the OBJECT element. An added benefit of using this method for text representation is the ability to use any legal HTML mark-up, so if you want the text to be of <H1> size, it is well within the realm of possibilities.

The **SHAPE** and **COORDS** attributes of the anchor tag can be of one of these types:

- **SHAPE="default"**
- **SHAPE="rect" COORDS=**"left x, top y, right x, bottom y"
- **SHAPE="circle" COORDS=**"center x, center y, radius"
- **SHAPE="poly" COORDS=**"x1, y1, x2, y2, x3, y"

In these instances, the x- and y-point coordinates are measured from the top and left of the image, in pixels. They also may be represented with percent symbols, in which case the coordinates would represent percentages of the height and width of the image. **SHAPE="default"** simply means that the clickable area is that of the entire image.

The visually impaired community has strongly argued in favor of the shaped-anchor mechanism, as it forces authors to provide a way for readers to follow the links regardless of which browser they are using.

Overlapping images

If the image you want to use for a client-side image map has two areas that overlap, take care to specify which region points where. However, in those instances in which two or more areas do overlap, the preferred method is first in, first out. This simply means that the first area defined for the image map takes precedence over later area definitions.

Good old `ISMAP`

You can still use the **ISMAP** attribute if you want to enable image maps that contact the server. In fact, you can use **ISMAP** in conjunction with **SHAPE** and **COORDS** if you want the target of a clicked region to remain unknown to the user. This could come in especially handy for designing games on the Web.

When you use the **ISMAP** attribute, the browser will append the coordinates of the click to the URL as query data – that is to say, with a question mark followed by the coordinates. For instance, if the user clicks an image at location (6, 61) on an image in which the backing link is 'http://www.spleen.com/main.html', the URL sent will be 'http://www.spleen.com/main.html?6,61'.

The `MAP` element

Spyglass, Inc. designed the `MAP` element as another method for implementing client-side image maps. For the most part, the `MAP` element mimics server-based image maps; but in this case, the map 'file' is part of the HTML document itself.

```
<OBJECT DATA="menu.gif" USEMAP="#menumap"></OBJECT>
<MAP NAME="menumap">
  <AREA HREF="answer.html" ALT="the answer page"
        SHAPE="rect" COORDS="11,0,80,55">
  <AREA HREF="link.html" ALT="link-o-rama"
        SHAPE="rect" COORDS="83,7,217,40">
  <AREA HREF="home.html" ALT="home" SHAPE="rect" COORDS="224,27,302,61">
</MAP>
```

As in the **SHAPES** example, the **SHAPE** and **COORDS** attributes play an important role in passing the user action. They behave in very much the same way. Note the use of the **ALT** attribute, as well. Text can be added here for browsers that do not support images, but no HTML mark-up is possible. Another important factor with the `MAP` element is that it is incompatible with HTML 2.0-level browsers.

14.4 Summary

Image maps provide an artistic method of navigation. When they are used in conjunction with the traditional system of hypertext links, image maps can create an inventive way for users to negotiate your information. Whether you choose to implement client- or server-side techniques in creating image maps, you will find that image maps enhance both the look and functionality of your site.

15
THE OBJECT ELEMENT

Included in this chapter is information on:

- Incorporating general information about simple use of the OBJECT element as an alternative to IMG
- Using OBJECT to insert Java applets and other plug-ins into your document
- Using the PARAM element

Summary

The `OBJECT` element extends HTML to support a general mechanism for the insertion of multimedia objects, including Java applets, Microsoft's Component Object Model (COM) objects (for example, ActiveX Controls) and ActiveX Document embedding, as well as a wide range of other media plug-ins. This approach allows objects to be specified in a general manner and also provides the ability to override the default implementation of objects.

15.1 Introduction

In its prototype days, the Web could only display information as textual mark-up, with limited or no visual mark-up. Although this limited, text-only mark-up was fine for essays that discussed Elvis Presley movies, it was difficult to display representations of original works of art, such as those on display at MoMA, the Museum of Modern Art, in New York. Then, a group of developers at NCSA thought it a good idea to be able to show images, and, from this effort, arose the `IMG` element.

With time, developers added more functionality to the Web. HTML elements for mark-up other than text began to appear, with the `APP` and `APPLET` elements coming from Sun Microsystems; the `DYNSRC` attribute from Microsoft, and the `EMBED` element from Netscape. The World Wide Web Consortium saw all this, and decided to create one element to control the entire body of non-text elements in HTML. Initially, the W3C called this new element `INSERT`, but it has been changed in favor of the `OBJECT` element.

In a nutshell, the `OBJECT` element controls all the items that enabled the Web to become the phenomenal success it has. The manipulation of pictures, movies, sounds and even small applications all come under the auspices of the `OBJECT` element. Coincidentally, the functionality of these items also boldly contributes to the fun of the Web, as well. This is not to say that an original, 300-page, all-text thesis that examines allegory and subtext in Elvis Presley's *Viva Las Vegas* is not a good bedtime read, but a picture really is worth one thousand words.

The `OBJECT` element comes with many attributes, as well as an accompanying element, `PARAM`, which we will explain later in this chapter.

The `OBJECT` element supersedes the `IMG` tag, and allows for backward compatibility for use with older browsers. This means that in instances in which you would normally use an `IMG` element, you may now use `OBJECT`. A key element of the `OBJECT` specification is its ability to use many different parameters and properties for the objects inserted into the document. The `OBJECT` element also allows for some direct manipulation of those objects, as explained below. The `OBJECT` element is designed so that, depending on the browser and the speed of the connection, if it will take a long time to download the actual object itself, then the `OBJECT` tag itself will be downloaded and displayed, thereby letting the user know that the requested object will be coming shortly, thus enticing the user to stick around.

A simple example

The easiest way to explain how the `OBJECT` element works is to show it in action:

```
<OBJECT DATA="trampoline.mov" TYPE="application/quicktime">
<IMG SRC="me_jumping.jpg" ALT="I like to jump.">
</OBJECT>
```

In this example, the browser can choose one of two methods to judge whether or not it should display the inline graphics image 'trampoline.mov' as part of the document. On the one hand, the **TYPE** attribute is a fast way for the browser to determine if it can actually play the movie without bothering to download the entire file. On the other hand, the browser may be so old that it has no knowledge of the `OBJECT` element, and it displays a JPG image, instead. But this is only the tip of the `OBJECT` element iceberg.

The `DATA` attribute for the URL

The **DATA** attribute contains the URL of whatever data the object needs in the document. For instance, if the object you wish to manipulate is a Java applet, using the **DATA** attribute, you would point your browser to the compiled Java files on your server. The browser knows what type of information is contained in the **DATA** attribute. The browser knows this because searching for the **CLASSID** attribute is one of the first searches the browser performs; if the browser does not find the **CLASSID** attribute, it then searches for the **TYPE** attribute. For example:

```
<OBJECT DATA="nietzsche.gif">
<OBJECT DATA="/users/~sartre/sounds/nausea.au"></OBJECT>
<OBJECT DATA="http://www.either.org/java/kierkegaard.class"></OBJECT>
```

The `CLASSID` attribute for the URL that identifies implementation of the object

This element contains a URL that identifies the implementation of the object. For example:

```
<OBJECT CLASSID="java:Notice"></OBJECT>
    <!-- uses the 'java:' URL scheme -->
<OBJECT CLASSID="/stuff/phosphates.tcl"></OBJECT>
```

The **CLASSID** attribute tells the browser what to expect from the object. In some object systems, **CLASSID** acts as an identifier for the type of object. Since this is the case in Java, unlike the APPLET element, you may not suffix your program with the default '.class'. In this instance, the named Java object will use its 'main' method to start running. The **CLASSID** attribute can be left out of the OBJECT element. In that case, the browser uses the **TYPE** attribute for the Internet media type, described below.

The TYPE attribute for the Internet media type

The **TYPE** attribute contains the Internet media type, which is, in other words, the information that tells the browser how to interpret the object you wish to display. This is how it works: You specify the object with the **DATA** attribute. The browser then retrieves the **TYPE** attribute before it downloads anything else, so that it is then able to disregard objects it does not support. For example:

```
<OBJECT DATA="apple.jpg" TYPE="image/jpg"></OBJECT>
<OBJECT DATA="/movies/comic/keaton.avi" TYPE="application/avi"></OBJECT>
```

The CODEBASE attribute

The **CODEBASE** attribute is an additional URL that holds the implementation for the object in question. This is necessary if the **CLASSID** attribute, which describes the implementation of an object, needs another URL. If no **CODEBASE** attribute is specified, the base URL for the object is used. For example:

```
<OBJECT CLASSID="Bicycle" CODEBASE="/applets/motion/"></OBJECT>
```

In this case, the implementation for the applet 'Bicycle' is kept in the '/applets/motion' series of subdirectories located below the current working directory.

Note on the CLASSID, TYPE and CODEBASE attributes

In the event that the browser cannot represent these three attributes, the actual contents of the OBJECT element will be displayed. This ensures backward compatibility and also allows you to nest OBJECT elements of different types to please everyone. To expand on the example at the beginning of the chapter:

```
<OBJECT CLASSID="java:bouncing" CODEBASE="http://school.edu/users/frog/">
<OBJECT DATA="trampoline.mov" TYPE="application/quicktime">
<OBJECT DATA="me_jumping.jpg" TYPE="image/jpg">
</OBJECT>
</OBJECT>
</OBJECT>
```

Here, the browser first tries to start the Java applet named 'bouncing'. If the browser does not support Java, it then attempts to play the QuickTime movie 'trampoline.mov'. In the event that this movie does not run, the browser then will display 'me_jumping.jpg'. Is it not nice making everyone happy?

The CODETYPE attribute to specify an Internet media type

The **CODETYPE** attribute specifies the Internet media type of the object's **CLASSID** attribute. This information is received before the contents of the **CLASSID** attribute. The browser can then use this information in order to decide whether or not the **CODETYPE** attribute is supported, and then to download the object based on this decision. For example:

```
<OBJECT CLASSID="Mendelssohn" CODEBASE="/composers/"
    CODETYPE="application/java-vm">
</OBJECT>
```

Use of the ID attribute as a unique document-wide identifier

The **ID** attribute is used as a unique document-wide identifier for the object. You could use the **ID** attribute to name an object so that other objects could reference it. It also comes in handy if you want the object to be the destination of a hypertext link. The **ID** attribute takes the form of any upper- or lower-case letters, not including characters that contain either diacritical marks, numerals or '-' and '.' characters. For example:

```
<OBJECT ID="bird" DATA="/images/bald_eagle.gif" TYPE="image/gif">
</OBJECT>

<OBJECT ID="first" CLASSID="step_one.tcl" CODEBASE="/examples">
</OBJECT>
```

Use of the `DECLARE` attribute to declare but not instantiate the object

You may use the **DECLARE** attribute to declare, but not instantiate, the object. This means you have 'marked a place' for the object, without bringing it to life. The **DECLARE** attribute also allows you to enable a PARAM element for one object to be a separate object. We will discuss more about the PARAM element later in this chapter.

The **DECLARE** attribute creates a condition of late binding for the object. This means that the object will not be instantiated until it is called – either by another object or when the user clicks on the link, as shown in the following example.

```
<OBJECT ID="bigfoot" DECLARE CLASSID="MonsterTruck"
    CODEBASE="/pages/java/">
</OBJECT>
I spend a good deal of time at <A HREF="#bigfoot">the races</A>.
```

Depending on the type of object, the **DECLARE** attribute may create a wholly separate and independent copy of the object. In the above example, when the user selected the link, the OBJECT specified as **DECLARE** was hit, and replaced the current page with the object, an instance of the MonsterTruck applet.

The `STANDBY` attribute for a standby text message

The **STANDBY** attribute provides a text message to the user who is waiting for an object to download. It can contain any legal HTML characters, including character entities for special letters. For example:

```
<OBJECT CLASSID="BigHonkinApp" CODETYPE="application/java-vm"
    STANDBY="You should stick around for this one...">
</OBJECT>
```

The `ALIGN` attribute to position the object

The **ALIGN** attribute tells the browser where to position the object. This positioning can be either in relation to the text of a document, or independent of the text. There are eight different specifications for the **ALIGN** attribute.

- `texttop`

- `textbottom`

- `middle`
- `left`
- `textmiddle`
- `right`
- `baseline`
- `center`

The **ALIGN=texttop** specification puts the top of the object in line with the top of the text line where the object appears.

The **ALIGN=middle** specification aligns the middle of the object with the baseline of the text. The baseline is the line on which all text rests – not the bottom of the text. This means that the middle of the object is not aligned with the descenders of certain characters, so it would be wise to mind your 'p's and 'q's.

The **ALIGN=textmiddle** specification aligns the middle of the object between the baseline and the x-height of the current font. The x-height is considered the height of a lower-case x in alphabets that use the Latin-1 alphabet. If only upper-case letters are used, then x-height is the height of an upper-case X. For alphabets other than those that read from left-to-right with the Latin-1 alphabet, **textmiddle** is considered to be the middle of the height of the text.

Using **ALIGN=baseline**, the object's bottom is aligned with the baseline of the current text.

ALIGN=textbottom puts the bottom of the object in line with the bottom of the text, rather than the baseline.

ALIGN=left makes the object float down and to the left-hand margin of the document. Any text after the object flows past the right-hand side of the object.

ALIGN=right does almost the exact same thing as **ALIGN=left**, except in the other direction. In this case, the object floats down and to the right, making any subsequent text wrap on the left.

ALIGN=center moves the object to the end of the current line of text, then positions it between the left and right margins. Any following text starts at the beginning of the next line.

The NAME attribute to allow an object contained in a form to become part of the submission

The **NAME** attribute allows an object contained in a FORM element to become part of the submission. If there is no accompanying **DECLARE** attribute for the object, then the browser will send the contents of the **NAME** attribute along with any data from the object. How the object actually gets the data is dependent on the object system. For example:

```
<FORM METHOD="post" ACTION="/cgi-bin/interpret_object.cgi>
<OBJECT NAME="formControl1" CLASSID="clsid:1377FFC-26AF-44308034"
    CODETYPE="application/x-oleobject"></OBJECT>
</FORM>
```

Here, the ActiveX control would receive data from the user by whatever means the programmer deemed.

Units of measurement used in `OBJECT`

The `OBJECT` element uses what are called 'standard units' in the corresponding attributes that control the measurement of objects. The default value for these units is an integer that signifies the number of pixels on screen.

```
<OBJECT HSPACE=20 VSPACE=40></OBJECT>
```

Another method is the use of a screen percentage, as below. For **WIDTH** attributes, the percentage is the space between the left and right margins. For **HEIGHT**, it is the percentage of the height of the current window.

```
<OBJECT HEIGHT=20% WIDTH=33%></OBJECT>
```

One may also use fixed units of measurement by means of an abbreviation of the type of unit following a floating-point number. For instance, a specification of '0.75in' would denote a three-quarters' inch length. The allowed unit specifications are 'pt' for points, 'pi' for picas, 'in' for inches and 'cm' for centimeters.

```
<OBJECT BORDER=14pt></OBJECT>
```

Although using points and picas for measurement will certainly please the graphic designers, we must note that very few browsers actually support the use of those measurement units.

The `WIDTH` attribute to specify the width of the visible area of an object

The **WIDTH** attribute specifies the width of a box that surrounds the visible area of an object. The **WIDTH** attribute uses standard units to judge this. The browser may use this attribute to scale an object to the width given.

The HEIGHT attribute to specify the height of the visible area of an object

The **HEIGHT** attribute specifies the height of the box enclosing the visible area of the object. The browser may use the **HEIGHT** attribute to scale an object to the measurement given in standard units.

The BORDER attribute to specify the border

The **BORDER** attribute specifies the displayed border around an object if that object is part of a hypertext link. The standard unit measurement specified here will gauge the width of the line that comprises the border. If you do not want the object to display a border, use **BORDER=0**.

The HSPACE attribute

The **HSPACE** attribute tells the browser the width of the space to the left and right of the box surrounding the object. The **HSPACE** attribute is used to separate an object from the text that comes before and follows the object.

The VSPACE attribute

The **VSPACE** attribute indicates the height of the space to the top and bottom of the box around the object.

15.2 The PARAM element to provide parameters for the object

As stated earlier, the OBJECT element has a colleague element, PARAM. The PARAM element works in conjunction with OBJECT to provide more property values (parameters) for the object, enabling more functionality from it. A PARAM element can be used to initialize an object or to add more data to the object.

Another use of the PARAM element can be found when you use OBJECT **DECLARE** to late-bind objects in your document. Take for instance, this very fictional example:

```
<OBJECT DECLARE ID="otis" TYPE="application/x-enunciator"
    DATA="Otis.vox"></OBJECT>
<OBJECT ID="vplayer" CLASSID="VoicePlayer.prg"
    CODEBASE="http://host.somewhere.net/makebelieve/"
    DATA="bad_poetry.txt">
<PARAM NAME="voice" OBJECT VALUE="#otis"></OBJECT>
```

In this case, the VoicePlayer program will read bad poetry using the voice of Otis. The PARAM element references an object from within another object using the traditional anchoring method with the # symbol. There are several attributes used by the PARAM element to pass information along to its object.

- **NAME**
- **VALUE**
- **VALUETYPE**

The NAME attribute

Of all the attributes of PARAM, the **NAME** attribute is the only required one. As one might surmise, the **NAME** attribute indicates the name of the property one wishes to pass to the object. Using upper- or lower-case characters in naming the property is up to the object system used.

The VALUE attribute

The **VALUE** attribute contains the PARAM element's value. To the browser, this is nothing more than a regular string of text that needs to follow the normal rules of character entities ('<' and '>' for '<' and '>' and so on). However, the real significance of the **VALUE** attribute comes from the object and how the object interprets that string. The object will first find the **NAME** attribute, then use the **VALUE** attribute attached to the **NAME** attribute for its intended purpose.

In conjunction, the **NAME** attribute and the **VALUE** attribute look like this:

```
<OBJECT...>
<PARAM NAME="rain_color" VALUE="purple">
</OBJECT>
```

The VALUETYPE attribute

The **VALUETYPE** attribute lets the object know what type of **VALUE** is passed. It may be one of three unique types:

- **REF**
- **OBJECT**
- **DATA**

The REF attribute

The **REF** attribute tells the object that the type of value passed is a URL. For instance,

```
<PARAM NAME="laughter" REF VALUE="/pages/sounds/maniacal.au">
```

would pass the URL '/pages/sounds/maniacal.au' to the 'laughter' property of the object using the PARAM element.

The OBJECT attribute

The **OBJECT** attribute assigns another object to the property. This referenced object must exist within the same document as the PARAM. **VALUETYPE OBJECT** is primarily used to point to other objects that have been declared but not instantiated by means of the **DECLARE** attribute.

```
<OBJECT ID="nightmares" CLASSID="DreamScape"
    CODEBASE="/pages/java/" CODETYPE="application/java-vm">
<PARAM NAME="evil" OBJECT VALUE="#clown">
</OBJECT>
    <!-- The following is passed through the PARAM above -->
<OBJECT ID="clown" CLASSID="Bobo"
    CODEBASE="/pages/java/" CODETYPE="application/java-vm">
</OBJECT>
```

The DATA attribute

The **DATA** attribute will pass the value to the object as a string for interpretation. This is the default behavior for **VALUETYPE**. This string must obey all the laws of HTML when it comes to character entities.

```
<PARAM NAME="message" DATA VALUE="What are you looking at?">
```

Here the 'message' name is associated with the brusque value, then handed off to the object, for what one hopes is a lesson in manners.

15.3 Summary

The OBJECT specification is one of the more complex in HTML 4.0, but this complexity serves a higher purpose, uniting the previously warring factions of non-text HTML elements. Now there is a way to put everything from embarrassing photos of your loved ones to a financial calculator into the same document, by use of the same mark-up. With rapid advancements in technology, more types of Web-based objects are created on a seemingly daily basis. By using the `OBJECT` element, you can take advantage of all the multimedia that makes the Web a highly evolved content delivery platform.

16
CLIENT-SIDE SCRIPTING

Included in this chapter is information on:

- Using client-side scripting
- Using SCRIPT
- Using event handling
- Examples of script macros

Summary

HTML 4 extends HTML to support client-side scripting of HTML documents and objects embedded within HTML documents. Scripts can be supplied in separate files or embedded directly within HTML documents in a manner independent of the scripting language. Scripts allow HTML forms to process input as it is entered: to ensure that values conform to specified patterns, to check consistency between fields and to compute derived fields.

Scripts can also be used to simplify authoring of active documents. The behavior of objects inserted into HTML documents can be tailored with scripts that respond to events generated by such objects. This enables authors to create compelling and powerful Web content.

16.1 Introduction

When the World Wide Web began, its intention was to enable people to publish and share information in a fairly simple fashion. As time has gone on, however, the Web has become more interactive with a media-rich format, in which users are often required to respond to and to be entertained by the information on their screens.

At first, multimedia on the Web was handled at the server end. Servers handled forms – they responded to the actions of users, they distributed content, and they even affected the way documents looked on the screen. The server required a certain amount of memory, and relied on a reasonable bandwidth connection between it and the client. This sending of data back and forth between client and server meant an increase in latency time – the amount of time that was spent waiting for things to happen.

With the advent of client-side scripting, the responsibility for many tasks falls to the browser rather than the server. Now that the browser plays a more important role, the Web designers have room to think about producing interesting and informative content rather than worrying whether or not the server has enough RAM. Used either in tandem with the OBJECT specification, or on its own, client-side scripting allows more flexibility and interactivity on the Web than previously available. With the HTML 4.0 specification, greater provisions exist for widespread proliferation of client-side scripting.

Scripting languages themselves are not covered in this book The HTML 4.0 client-side scripting specification was merely designed to unify the set of tags used in scripting. With this in mind, this chapter concentrates on the usage of the tags and the surrounding specification, rather than the details of any particular scripting language – a subject beyond the scope of this chapter.

16.2 The SCRIPT element

At the base of all client-side scripting is the SCRIPT element. You may use the SCRIPT element – and its mate, </SCRIPT> – anywhere within the HTML document as many times as necessary; although, as we will see later, sometimes its placement is important to how it functions. The accepted practice is to place any and all scripting within the document's `<HEAD>` and `</HEAD>` tags. This way, the browser has a chance to interpret the script, if necessary, before the rest of the document loads.

16.3 The SRC attribute to reference a URL for an externally loaded script

One of the attributes of the `SCRIPT` element is **SRC**, which you can use to reference a URL for an externally located script, although making the browser fetch another document from the server appears to defeat the purpose of client-side scripting. If your `SCRIPT` tag uses the **SRC** attribute, any information contained within the `SCRIPT` tag is ignored in deference to the URL.

16.4 LANGUAGE to specify scripting language

The **LANGUAGE** attribute was initially used to specify which scripting language you used. Here, you would include information to assist the browser in its interpretation of the script using specifications such as the following:

```
<SCRIPT LANGUAGE="JavaScript"></SCRIPT>
<SCRIPT LANGUAGE="VBScript"></SCRIPT>
```

However, this should be avoided in favor of the other attribute, the **TYPE** attribute.

16.5 TYPE to specify scripting language as Internet media type

The **TYPE** attribute performs very much the same task as the **LANGUAGE** attribute, but it does so by specifying the language as an Internet media type. The Internet media type tells the browser how to interpret the information, in the same way the browser knows how to interpret a file labeled 'text/html' or 'image/gif'.

```
<SCRIPT TYPE="text/javascript"></SCRIPT>
<SCRIPT TYPE="text/vbscript"></SCRIPT>
```

Default scripting languages: Use of <META> with <SCRIPT>

Default scripting languages
The default is JavaScript if **LANGUAGE**, **TYPE** and META give no clues. In the event that no **TYPE** or **LANGUAGE** attribute has been set, the browser will look for a META tag or an HTTP response header to set the default scripting language of the document. If there is no **TYPE**, **LANGUAGE** or META element and no HTTP response header has been set, HTML 4.0 assumes the script language type to be JavaScript.

If there is no **TYPE** or **LANGUAGE** attribute specified in each SCRIPT tag, you can use a META tag within the HEAD elements to declare which language to use. Again, this uses the Internet media type for the scripts. For example:

```
<META HTTP-EQUIV="Content-Script-Type" Content="text/vbscript">
```

Default scripting languages: Use of HTTP headers with <SCRIPT>

If there is no META tag, a default scripting language can also be specified by an HTTP header that comes in a response from the server. It looks like this:

```
Content-Script-Type: text/tcl
```

This approach only works if you have the ability to set such headers on the server that holds your documents.

In both of the above cases, if there are several META tags or HTTP headers, the last one specified is the one that is applied to the document. For instance, if the document contains both:

```
<META HTTP-EQUIV="Content-Script-Type" Content="text/vbscript">
<META HTTP-EQUIV="Content-Script-Type" Content="text/tcl">
```

the browser will assume the default scripting language is tcl.

Backward compatibility and SCRIPT

On occasion, an older browser will access your document and it may not be able to interpret scripts at all. If this is the case, you need to make sure your script can handle such eventualities and provide alternative content with NOSCRIPT or 'hide' your script with HTML comments.

16.6   The NOSCRIPT element

The SCRIPT element has a counterpart in the NOSCRIPT element, which is included for browsers that cannot support client-side scripting. If this is the case, all content placed between the NOSCRIPT elements is displayed to the user. The most common use of the NOSCRIPT element is to goad users into downloading the latest version of a Web browser.

```
<NOSCRIPT>
<P ALIGN=CENTER>
If you were using a more recent script-compatible browser, you would see
some cool stuff here.
</NOSCRIPT>
```

As you can see, NOSCRIPT may contain the entire proper HTML mark-up you wish to add.

16.7 Using HTML comments

Another method that is used to hide the actual script contents from older browsers is to use the HTML comment syntax. Browsers will ignore everything between the <!-- and --> elements, so most scripters will put their work between these tags. Of course, it is important to remember to put the <SCRIPT> and </SCRIPT> elements outside the comment elements; otherwise, the browser will ignore everything, leaving you scratching your head, wondering why nothing works.

16.8 Example of simple <SCRIPT>

The following example shows all the above elements working together within the context of an HTML document and uses the obligatory 'Hello World' example:

```
<HTML><HEAD><TITLE>The Document</TITLE>
<SCRIPT TYPE="text/javascript">
<!-- Comment to hide the script content from older browsers
    document.write("<H1>Hello World!<\/H1>");
// End hiding -->
</SCRIPT>
<NOSCRIPT>
Normally, I would say hello, but not until you get a better browser.
</NOSCRIPT>
</HEAD><BODY></BODY></HTML>
```

There are a few things to notice with the above script. The first is that it illustrates a feature of some scripting languages, namely dynamic updating of a document. That means that as the document is loaded by the browser, the script is interpreted and then is displayed on screen. In the above example, document.write( ) has the same effect as if you created an HTML document like this shown below:

```
<HTML><HEAD><TITLE>The Document</TITLE>
</HEAD><BODY>
<P><H1>Hello World!</H1>
</BODY></HTML>
```

The benefit of dynamic content comes in handy when performing functions such as the following: returning content based on which browser has accessed the document or putting the current local time on the document, as with this example:

```
<HTML><HEAD><TITLE>A Simple Clock</TITLE>
<SCRIPT TYPE="text/javascript">
<!-- Hide from older browsers
function tickTick()
{
    var today = new Date();

    var display = today.getHours() + ":" +
    ((today.getMinutes() < 10) ? "0" : "") +
    today.getMinutes() + ":" +
    ((today.getSeconds() < 10) ? "0" : "") +
    today.getSeconds();

    document.clockform.clock.value = display;
    setTimeout("tickTick()",1000);
}
// --> End hiding
</SCRIPT></HEAD>
<BODY onLoad="tickTick()">
<FORM METHOD=post ACTION="#" NAME="clockform">
<INPUT TYPE=TEXT NAME="clock" SIZE=10>
</FORM>
</BODY></HTML>
```

Time marches on.

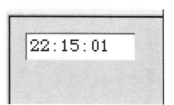

Character escape sequences

Also note the backslash ' \ ' in the end tag for the header in the script:

```
document.write("<H1>Hello World!<\/H1>");
```

This is in place as an escape character to allow the script interpreter to view the tag as data from the script rather than as an element of the mark-up. This comes from conforming HTML parsers that view the SCRIPT element as an end tag open element. This means that for each <SCRIPT>, the parser expects a complementary </SCRIPT>, or closing tag. For example if you did not use the preceding slash you would see the following:

```
document.write("<H1>Hello World!</H1>")
```

Your script might cause an error, with the browser claiming that you closed an element that had no opening; or, the browser might even close another element that was opened earlier in the document. Even if the browser you use causes no such fuss, it is better to use the escape character and be safe.

Scripting languages use varying methods for escape sequences. For example, JavaScript and tcl use the backslash ' \ ' in VBScript, but one may use the Chr() function to produce the same character:

```
document.write("<H1>Hello World!<" &Chr(47) + "H1>")
```

Comments within the SCRIPT

The last thing to notice is the use of comments within the script. In the above JavaScript example, a C++ style comment marker is used:

```
// End hiding -->
```

This is used to hide the HTML comment marker from the JavaScript interpreter, which would give you the business when it came across the -->. Other languages have their own comment syntax. For example, VBScript uses a single quote:

```
' End hiding -->
```

and tcl uses:

```
# End hiding -->
```

16.9 Event handling

A major plus of client-side scripting comes in event handling. As the name would suggest, this is when some event initiated by the user gets handled by a script. In many instances, these events use intrinsic (built-in) events to trigger the script response. These event handlers may be tied to specific objects within an HTML document, or a script that only targets particular elements may handle the entire document.

The underlying script engine is responsible for binding different objects in an HTML document to their associated event handlers. If the script engine supports many languages, then it is possible to bind an object in one language while at the same time performing event handling in another language. The idea behind this is to overcome potential shortcomings that may arise in any given scripting language.

Binding HTML objects to scripts

The main method used to bind objects and events comes from the document mark-up of the HTML. For example, **ID** attributes identify objects that occur anywhere in an HTML document, whereas the **NAME** attribute identifies objects that reside within the scope of an enclosing FORM element. Some languages may even support scripting for objects using the OBJECT or IMG tags. These attributes bind to event handling scripts through the runtime implementation of the scripting language. By using these attributes, one can control child documents through event-handling scripts in a parent document (or FRAME), or even control non-document objects, such as the browser itself.

```
<HTML><HEAD>
<TITLE>Browser Checking</TITLE>
<SCRIPT TYPE="text/javascript">
<!--
function checkType()
{
    var returnString = "<H2>I see you are using ";
    returnString += navigator.appName;
    returnString += ", version ";
    returnString += navigator.appVersion;
    returnString += ".<\/H2><HR WIDTH=300 ALIGN=left>
        A good choice, if I do say so myself.";

    document.write(returnString);
    document.close();
}
// -->
</SCRIPT>
</HEAD>
<BODY onLoad="checkType()">
<NOSCRIPT>
Scripts? You can't handle the scripts!
</NOSCRIPT>
</BODY></HTML>
```

Catering to all your users.

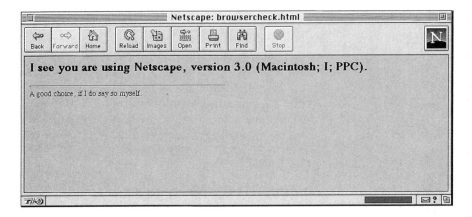

How exactly scripts reference objects is under the control of the scripting language. In JavaScript, specific names such as 'document. form.element[0].value' will return the value of the first element of a form, assuming that value is not null or undefined. Another method of referencing objects depends on the context of the script. If the script appears in a FORM, then objects bearing the **NAME** attribute will take priority over ID-labeled objects.

The latter reference method may cause problems in some scripting languages. In VBScript, for example, the scope of object references is limited to given modules, but the language has no strong way of determining where the module begins and ends. In these languages, you are probably better off by closely associating the handler to the object it references with a specific name.

Event handling and scripts

Possibly the best example of event handling is forms handling. When forms are submitted, you may need to check to see whether or not a value has been input, or if that value is of the correct data type. This is an ideal time to use event handling on the form elements, rather than depending on the server to check the contents.

One important thing to remember when dealing with submitting forms is that if you want INPUT, TEXTAREA or SELECT elements to be recognized as part of the form you are submitting, they must have a **NAME** attribute and be contained within the FORM elements. If either condition is not met, the element is not considered to be part of the form. This practice may sound odd, but it allows for more flexibility in building a user interface by using these elements in conjunction with scripting while they exist outside the scope of the FORM.

For example, the script that allows the user to see what something submitted might look like before actually sending it to the server is shown below:

```
<HTML><TITLE>Message Board</TITLE><HEAD>
<SCRIPT TYPE="text/javascript">
function preview( form, img)
{
    var headline = form.elements.HEADLINE.value;
    var message = form.elements.MESSAGE.value;
    var preview = window.open("","preview","scrollbars=1,
                        width=500,height=500");
    if ( preview.opener == null )
        preview.opener = self;

    preview.document.open();
    preview.document.write("<HTML><HEAD><TITLE>Preview</TITLE></HEAD>
                        <BODY BGCOLOR='#ffffff'><IMG SRC=")
    preview.document.write( img );
    preview.document.write("ALIGN=center><FORM METHOD=post><BR><BR>
                        <FONT FACE=arial SIZE=3><B>")
    preview.document.write( headline );
    preview.document.write("</B></FONT><HR>
                        <PRE><FONT FACE=arial SIZE=3>")
    preview.document.write( message );
    preview.document.write("</FONT></PRE><CENTER>");
    preview.document.write("<HR ALIGN=center WIDTH=80%>
                        <HR ALIGN=center WIDTH=60%>
                        <HR ALIGN=center WIDTH=40%>");
    preview.document.write("<P><INPUT TYPE=BUTTON
                        VALUE='Finished With Preview'
                        onClick='self.close()'></CENTER><BR>
                        </FORM></BODY></HTML>")

    preview.document.close();
}
</SCRIPT>
</HEAD><BODY BGCOLOR='#ffffff'><FORM ACTION="/Something" METHOD=post>
<TABLE><TR>
  <TD><IMG SRC="pages.gif"></TD>
  <TD><H2>The Message Board</H2></TD>
</TR></TABLE>
<HR><UL>
  <LI>Please enter a Message for the Message Board.
  <LI>Click on "Preview!" to see what it will look like.
  <LI>You may use any HTML mark-up you wish.
  <LI>When finished previewing, click "Submit Message" to send your
      message in.
</UL><P><HR>
<P><B>Headline</B><BR>
<INPUT TYPE="text" NAME="HEADLINE" SIZE="65" MAXLENGTH="65">
<P><B>Message</B><BR>
<TEXTAREA NAME="MESSAGE" ROWS="17" COLS="67" WRAP=physical></TEXTAREA>
<HR><INPUT TYPE=SUBMIT VALUE="Submit Message">
</FORM>
```

```
<FORM METHOD=post>
<INPUT TYPE=BUTTON VALUE="Preview!"
onClick="preview(document.forms[0],'pages.gif' )">
</FORM>
</BODY></HTML>
```

The Preview script in action.

In this script, the 'Preview' button is contained in a separate form. The button is the only element in the form, and it is not part of the information sent when the user clicks the 'Submit Message' button. In this way, you can create elaborate interfaces that can handle all kinds of input.

Form event handling with tcl

```
<INPUT TYPE=TEXT NAME="employee_name" SIZE=15>
<SCRIPT TYPE="text/tcl">
proc check_name{}
{
    if { [employee_name value] == johnbigboote }
        myButton enable 1
    else
        myButton enable 0
}
employee_name onChange check_name
</SCRIPT>
```

In the case of this TEXT element, myButton is enabled if the user enters johnbigboote in the employee_name field. This, of course, is no substitute for proper Web server security, since the user can simply view the document source to see what the proper value for employee_name should be, but it illustrates the concept of event handling. When the employee_name field changes the check_name{} script is notified with the intrinsic onChange event, thus performing the correct action.

Form event handling with JavaScript

```
<HTML><HEAD><TITLE>A Form Handler</TITLE>
<SCRIPT TYPE="text/javascript">
<!-- Hide the script content
function form_checker( form )
{
    var numElements = form.elements.length;
    var submitFlag = true;
    for ( var i = 0; i < numElements; i++ )
    {
        if ( ( form.elements[i].value== "" ) ||
            ( form.elements[i].value == null ) )
        {
            if ( ( form.elements[i].name != "SUBMIT" ) &&
                ( form.elements[i].name != "CLEAR" ) )
                alert( "You forgot to fill in the " +
                form.elements[i].name + " value. Please try again." );

            submitFlag = false;
            break;
        }
    }
    if ( submitFlag )
        form.submit();
}
// End hiding -->
</SCRIPT>
</HEAD><BODY>
<H2>Please answer all the questions.</H2>
<FORM ACTION="/URLHandler" METHOD=post>
What is your name?<BR>
<INPUT TYPE=TEXT NAME="FullName" SIZE=30><P>
What is your quest?<BR>
<INPUT TYPE=TEXT NAME="Quest" SIZE=25><P>
What is your favorite color?<BR>
<INPUT TYPE=TEXT NAME="Color" SIZE=15><P>
<INPUT TYPE=BUTTON NAME=SUBMIT VALUE=" Submit Now!"
onClick="form_checker( this.form )">
<INPUT TYPE=RESET NAME=CLEAR VALUE="Clear The Form">
</FORM></BODY></HTML>
```

In this case, the entire form is handled by the script, passed as a parameter to the `form_checker()` script. The script loops through all the form elements, checking for a blank field, avoiding the BUTTON elements, since we are not concerned with their values. Again, this all takes place thanks to an intrinsic event; this time, the `onClick()` that is bound to the BUTTON object. This generic script simply ensures that all form fields were completed. If this is the case, `submitFlag` tells the form that it can be submitted to whatever server-side process is specified.

16.10 Going further with forms

You could perform more specific data-type checking, such as the person who actually entered a number rather than another character. For instance, if the above script needed to know the airspeed velocity of an unladen swallow and if the user did not specify African or European in the answer, the script could prompt for such information.

A script can even respond to certain values that the user enters, such as this navigation controller:

```
<HTML><HEAD><TITLE>URLSelector</TITLE>
<SCRIPT TYPE="text/javascript">
<!-- Hide the script content
var menuWin = null;
function URLSelector()
{
    menuWin = window.open("","URLSelector","toolbar=no,
                        location=no,status,directories=no,
                        resizeable=no,width=300,height=150");

    if ( menuWin != null )
    {
        if ( menuWin.opener == null )
            menuWin.opener = self;

        menuWin.document.open();
        menuWin.document.write("<HTML><HEAD><TITLE>URLSelector</TITLE>" );
        menuWin.document.write("<SCRIPT TYPE=\"text/javascript\">" );
        menuWin.document.write( "function chooseOne(form){" );
        menuWin.document.write( "var choice = form.SELECTOR;" );
        menuWin.document.write( "var i = choice.options.selectedIndex;" );
        menuWin.document.write( "opener.location.href =
                        choice.options[i].value;}" )
        menuWin.document.write( "</SCRIPT></HEAD><BODY>" );
        menuWin.document.write( "Selecting from the Locations below will
            take you there.<HR><FORM METHOD=post>" );
        menuWin.document.write( "Locations:
            <SELECT NAME=\"SELECTOR\" onChange=\"chooseOne(this.form)\">" );
```

```
        menuWin.document.write( "<OPTION SELECTED
            VALUE=\"http://www.w3.org/\">
            World Wide Web Consortium</OPTION>" );
        menuWin.document.write( "<OPTION SELECTED
            VALUE=\"http://home.netscape.com/\">
            Netscape</OPTION>" );
        menuWin.document.write( "<OPTION SELECTED
            VALUE=\"http://www.microsoft.com/\">
            Microsoft</OPTION>" );
        menuWin.document.write( "</SELECT><P><INPUT TYPE=BUTTON
            VALUE=\"Close the URLSelector\" onClick=\"self.close()\">" );
        menuWin.document.write( "</FORM></BODY></HTML>" );
        menuWin.document.close();
    }
}
// -->
</SCRIPT></HEAD><BODY>
<H2>This will launch the URLSelector</H2>
<P><HR WIDTH=300 ALIGN=left><P>
<FORM METHOD=post>
<INPUT TYPE=BUTTON VALUE="Launch the URLSelector"
onClick="URLSelector()">
</FORM></BODY></HTML>
```

The URLSelector
window.

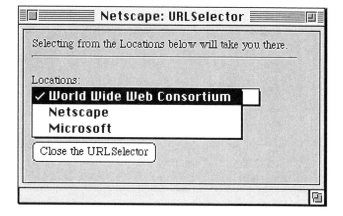

Intrinsic events

The term 'intrinsic events' refers to events that are built into the HTML
specification. The listing of these is as follows:

- `onLoad`

- `onFocus`

- `onUnload`

- onBlur
- onClick
- onSubmit
- onMouseOver
- onSelect
- onMouseOut
- onChange

These event names are case insensitive, and they deal with many common events and attributes. The language used to handle intrinsic events is determined by the scripting language used.

A small precaution

Because of the 'inline' nature of the intrinsic event handlers, the reserved HTML characters '&' and '"' should instead be written as '&' (or '&#38') and '"' (or '&#34'), respectively. Also, any intrinsic event handlers should be enclosed in either single or double quotes. For instance:

```
<INPUT TYPE=TEXT NAME="luka" VALUE="upstairs" onChange="if
(upstairs(this.value, second floor)) { seenMeBefore() }">
```

onLoad

The load event occurs when a browser has finished loading a document or all the FRAMEs within a FRAMESET. The event handler activates the script when the load event occurs. This event may only occur with BODY or FRAMESET elements.

```
<BODY onLoad="alert( &quot;Love That Load!&quot; )">
```

onUnload

Oddly enough, the unload event occurs upon exiting a document. Again, this can only be used with BODY or FRAMESET elements. This also comes in very handy when you cannot stand saying goodbye.

```
<BODY onUnload="alert( &quot;So Long, Farewell, Auf Wiedersehen,
Goodbye.&quot; )">
```

onClick

Click events occur when a FORM element or an anchor is clicked with the mouse. Buttons, checkboxes, radio buttons, submit and reset buttons are all FORM elements that generate click events. OnClick() is useful in forms to check data before the form is ever submitted. Hypertext links also generate click events, so as to launch child windows and the like, as is the case with the URLSelector above. This event may only occur with INPUT and ANCHOR elements.

```
<INPUT TYPE=RADIO NAME="name" VALUE="sartre"
onClick="existenceOrEssence( this.value )">
```

onMouseOver

This event is triggered by the mouse cursor moving over either an anchor or an AREA element. It can only be used with these elements.

```
<A HREF="super.html" onMouseOver="window.status=&quot;A Super Link&quot;;
return true;">Here is a Super Link</A>.
```

The changing status of the window, courtesy of onMouseOver.

onMouseOut

This event is triggered by the mouse cursor leaving an anchor or AREA element. Again, it can only be used with these elements.

```
<A HREF="verycool.html" onMouseOut="window.status=&quot;Boy, did you miss
out.&quot;; return true;">This is Very Cool</A>
```

onFocus

When a field receives the input focus, either through the mouse or the tab key, the focus event is triggered. It could be used in lieu of context-sensitive help or balloon help. This is different from selecting an item in a field that generates a select event. OnFocus may only be used with SELECT, INPUT and TEXTAREA elements.

```
<INPUT TYPE=TEXT NAME="amount" onFocus="alert(&quot;Please enter how much
money you wish to send me.&quot;)">
```

Although the above example is a reasonable usage of the onFocus event, the authors make no guarantee that anyone will actually send you money if you try it.

onSelect

The select event occurs when either a single- or multi-line section of text is highlighted within a text field. It only works with INPUT or TEXTAREA fields.

```
<TEXTAREA NAME="story" ROWS=10 COLS=10
onSelect="toPumpkin(this.value)">Once upon a time...</TEXTAREA>
```

onBlur

onBlur
onBlur was a humorous idea by Netscape programmers.

Blur events happen when a field loses input focus. Think of it as the opposite of onFocus, which is exactly what it is. You can use this method to check individual elements in the form as the user moves through and enters information. Blur events only work with SELECT, INPUT and TEXTAREA elements.

```
<HTML><HEAD>
<TITLE>Math Made Easy!</TITLE>
<SCRIPT TYPE="text/vbscript">
<!--
Sub Number_onBlur()
    inNumber = document.inForm.number.value
    outNumber = inNumber * inNumber
    message = inNumber & " squared becomes " & outNumber
    MsgBox message, 0, "Easy Math"
End Sub
// -->
</SCRIPT></HEAD>
<BODY>
<H2>Math Made Easy!</H2><HR>
<P>Slept through most of high school?
<BR>Can't square numbers to save your life?
<BR>Go ahead, try this:
<P>
<FORM NAME=inForm METHOD=post>
Enter a number then click outside of the box to have it magically
squared:
<INPUT TYPE=TEXT NAME=Number SIZE=3 MAXLENGTH=3>
</FORM></BODY></HTML>
```

onChange

The change event executes its handler when a form field loses input focus and the value has changed. This is another good place to check data integrity before submitting the form. It only works with SELECT, INPUT and TEXTAREA elements.

```
<INPUT TYPE=TEXT NAME="number" onChange="if (!checkNumeric(this.value))
{ alert(&quot;Please enter a Number. Or else.&quot;)}">
```

onSubmit

The submit event occurs when the user submits a form. It can only be used with a FORM element, and depending on the script language, it may control whether or not the form's contents are actually sent to the server.

```
<FORM METHOD=post ACTION="/DoSomething" onSubmit="checkAllData(this)">
```

Script macros

Client-side scripting can also be used to include macros to set HTML attributes. These attributes can depend on objects that have already been specified in the document. The macro can be made of one or more statements in the default scripting language. The macro is evaluated when a document is loaded (or reloaded) but not if the window is resized or redrawn.

The syntax of the macro requires you precede the macro with an ampersand ('&'), enclose it in braces ('{}') and follow it with a semicolon (';'). If you leave off the semicolon, the trailing brace is treated as part of the macro body. Finally, quotations are always needed around the attribute if it holds a macro.

The macro will first be processed by the SGML parser which looks for any special character entities, such as ". Then the script engine parses the macro contents for evaluation. Any string that results from the evaluation then gets passed to the browser.

A few examples of scripting macros

If you want to confuse your users on a pseudo-random basis, although we do not advise it, look at the example below:

```
<BODY BGCOLOR='&{ randomColor() };' TEXT='&{ randomColor() };'
LINK='&{ randomColor() };' >
```

If you wish to change the contents of a document 'after hours':

```
<IMG SRC='&{(Date.getHours > 23)?&quot;naughty.jpg&quot;:
&quot;nice.jpg&quot;};'>
```

Or if you want to size an image based on another object in your document:

```
<IMG SRC="arrow.gif" HEIGHT="100" WIDTH=&{'document.banner.width/2'};'>
```

16.11 Summary

The breadth and depth of client-side scripting is something best explored by delving into the different languages themselves. Look at them all, find the one you like best, and experiment. The only limit to scripting is your own ingenuity. Others have designed entire sites using client-side scripting that produce everything from stud poker games to <http://www.rhodes.com/stud> through neural network simulations <http://www.ozemail.com.au/~infoxs/programs/nn/neural.htm>. With the unlimited possibilities of scripting, it is time for you to give it a try.

17
INTERNATIONALIZATION OF THE WEB

Included in this chapter is information on:

- Unicode and its importance in the internationalization of the Web
- Specifying the language associated with a given HTML document or an individual HTML element
- Specifying the direction in which text is read: left-to-right or right-to-left
- The HTML elements designed to facilitate the internationalization of the Web

Summary

To facilitate a truly international Web, the HTML 4 specification includes several new features and recommends that Unicode be adopted as the document character set. Numeric character references are to be interpreted using this character set, which includes Latin-1 as the first 256 character values. Other points to note from the HTML 4 specification with respect to internationalization are as follows:

- A set of named character entities is provided for assisting rendering text with mixed left-to-right and right-to-left character sequences.

- The `DIR` attribute can be used to indicate the base directionality for the contents of a given element. This affects the way the browser renders the text on the screen.

- The `BDO` element can be used to override the directionality, if appropriate.

- The `Q` element provides language-dependent quotation marks and allows search engines to identify quotations embedded within surrounding text.

- The `LANG` attribute can be used on many elements to affect the rendering of contents.

- In many languages, text justification may assume a different default value than in Western languages. The `ALIGN` attribute, admitting values of `left`, `right`, `center` and `justify`, is added to a selection of elements. This can default to `right`, if appropriate to the language in question.

- The `LINK` and `META` elements are involved in specifying the language of the current document and in informing the browser of language variants.

17.1 Introduction

This discussion is a brief look at a large subject. It concentrates on the new HTML tags included in HTML 4 for the purpose of publishing documents in languages other than Western European languages (especially English), which at the moment certainly dominate the World Wide Web.

The computer industry now is making an energetic effort to make sure that the Web truly is used worldwide. Apple and Microsoft both have had to come to terms with operating system support for the subtle mechanisms needed for displaying all kinds of scripts. Now it is the Web's turn to be truly international and to live up to its name.

Be warned that internationalizing a Web site is not a simple matter of replacing Latin characters with, say, Arabic ones. Even if you could do that directly, you would probably find that your forms were all wrong: for example, you would have the labels on the wrong side of the user-input fields. You would want right-justification in all the places where you had used left-justification in the English version. And all your neat calculations about the relative widths of images and texts would likely be wrong, as well. If the problems of internationalizing seemed like news from a far country, perhaps they now sound a little closer to home.

Who is active in this field?

It was in late 1994 that the HTML working group began to think about the Web and that it could publish in a larger number of languages and scripts than it had been. Particularly active in this field today are Gavin Nicol of Electronic Book Technologies, Glenn Adams of Spyglass, and Martin Dürst of the University of Zurich.

The adoption of Unicode

One of the most important arguments of the Internationalization enthusiasts is that Unicode should replace the present Latin-1 character set for encoding text sent over the Web in HTML, a move that is regarded as one that would overcome the serious limitations of Latin-1.

Given that the world's scripts together use thousands of symbols – Arabic, Japanese and Chinese, Devanagari and Malayan, to name but a few – how can these scripts possibly be sent down the wire in a form that all computers on the receiving end will understand? The solution is to use a universally understood system of computer codes.

Each different symbol, be it a Latin 'A', a Greek Alpha, or a Hebrew Aleph, has its own standard, coded form within Unicode. In fact, there are several different 'A's, as well: Unicode usually provides a different code for each combination of a letter with an accent or diacritical mark – those little squiggles or other symbols that appear above or below letters in many languages.

i18n explained
You often see literature on the Internationalization of the Web written simply 'i18n'. If you look there are 18 characters between the 'I' and 'n' of *Internationalization.*

Unicode is already in the process of being adopted by the Web. It is a recognized approach to the encoding of international characters, enshrined in an international standard (ISO 10646).

Latin-1 is an 8-bit encoding language. Because the codes for each character are only 8 bits long, they can only cater for 2 to the power of 8 characters in all. This amounts to 256 different possibilities, by no means enough to cover the thousands of symbols in scripts used worldwide.

Unicode is, however, a 16-bit encoding language. The number of codes that it can cater for is 2 to the power of 16, which works out to more than 65,000 possibilities. This is more like it: so far, 40,000 of the possible 16-bit numbers have been used up, in characters and languages such as written

Chinese characters, Thai, Bopomofo, Bengali, Tamil, Tibetan and many other scripts. Unicode also makes provision for a certain number of user-defined characters, just in case some have been missed out somewhere.

The difference between characters and glyphs

Unicode distinguishes between characters and glyphs. Roughly speaking, a glyph is the visual depiction of a character: it is how the character appears on screen or on paper.

According to the view adopted by Unicode, a font contains glyphs, and not characters. In practice, the distinction between these two concepts is often difficult to maintain, partly because such a distinction has rarely been made in the past. The result of this historical confusion between the two concepts is that many existing character sets encode 'glyphs', and, for reasons of backward compatibility, these 'glyphs' now appear in Unicode as 'characters'. Examples of glyphs that are not characters are the Roman ligatures 'ff' and 'fi' – each of which is comprised of two genuine characters.

Can today's browsers understand Unicode?

Can today's browsers understand Unicode? Unfortunately, not. The day when all browsers can display all of Unicode still is some way off. Eventually, we hope to see a universal browser able to understand Unicode and able to select the right font (if it is installed) to display the corresponding glyphs. A second-best choice is an adaptable browser, one that could be upgraded on the fly upon encountering text in a new script.

Glyph servers

One current makeshift solution to the problem is the use of glyph servers. The idea is that browser requests are redirected to these computers when an unsupported script is required to display an HTML document. The glyph server proxy retrieves the document on behalf of the client, but instead of transmitting it transparently, looks at the HTML text and then replaces each data character that the client cannot display with an `<IMG>` element pointing to a server-generated image of the correct glyph. The client then receives the modified HTML, retrieves the numerous images, and generates a fairly correct display, at the expense of tremendously increased network bandwidth, the impossibility of adjusting font size and style and of further text processing (such as simply searching for a word). The whole process is very slow, of course, but such servers do, indeed, exist.

Specifying the language in HTTP

Currently, the server sends very little information about the language in which a document is written, although the Web's protocol (HTTP) does already allow you to include information of sorts. A future version of HTTP, 1.1, is expected to include a mandatory parameter called *charset*, which will change all this.

The charset parameter is already provided by MIME and is attached to the type in the content-type header line. It is a pity that the charset parameter is almost never used in practice; some browsers even declare unrecognized media type when they see it!

There is also the suggestion that the anchor element, A, and also the LINK element should have an attribute **CHARSET** whose value hints to the browser the character encoding used by the resource to which it points. This should be the appropriate value of the MIME character set for that resource.

Content negotiation

Content negotiation is where the server and client are negotiating a mutually agreed-upon character set and document. This is something that certainly should take place in the future. Also consider what happens when a browser submits a form to a server. Any text sent should be correctly tagged to ensure proper interpretation by the server, and submitted in a character encoding that the server will understand.

HTML tags associated with internationalization of the Web

Having covered very briefly some of the ideas and concerns of those who are trying to make the Web a more international place, we go on to the features of HTML 4, which facilitate writing documents in different languages. These are as follows:

- The **LANG** attribute for setting the language for the content of HTML elements, be it the content of the BODY, a single paragraph, a list item or other element. **LANG** is one of the standard HTML 4 attributes.

- The **DIR** attribute for setting the local directionality of text.

- The BDO element for BiDirectional Override.

- The Q element for inline quotations.

- The LINK and META elements in the context of the international Web.

17.2 The LANG attribute to specify the language for an element

The LANG attribute
LANG can be used on most elements, including empty elements such as LINK, META and IMG.

An HTML element generally has a *content* – literally the text, image or other item(s) it contains. The **LANG** attribute specifies the language of the content: whether it is in German, French, Japanese, Russian and so on. Available for nearly all elements, the **LANG** attribute can be used to specify the language of the whole document, individual paragraphs, list items, headings, and so on. Needless to say, the contents of such elements are not actually *translated* into the language specified, but the way that they are rendered on the screen is affected.

Here is an example of LANG at work, influencing the way in which the document is rendered on the screen:

```
<P LANG=fr>
```

This tells the browser that the whole paragraph P should be rendered in the correct way for documents written in French.

Defining the language for the entire document

How do you specify the language for the document? There are various ways of doing this:

- Configuring your Web server to send the Content-Language header with all documents, for example, for English:

  ```
  Content-Language: en
  ```

  This is the recommended method at the time of writing although the matter is still up for debate.

- Stating similar information in the META element:

  ```
  <META HTTP-EQUIV=Content-Language CONTENT=en>
  ```

  Note, however, putting a lot of META elements in the document slows down the appearance of the document.

- Using the **LANG** attribute on the BODY element, as explained in this section.

There are two main ways in which the **LANG** attribute influences the display of text on the screen.

- First of all, it deals with character disambiguation, in cases in which the character encoding is not sufficient to resolve to a specific glyph.

Country codes
For more information
on this subject see the
list provided in
Appendix F and also on
page 326.

- Second, it makes sure that quotation marks, hyphenation, ligatures and spacing are correct for the language in question.

The **LANG** attribute also helps speech rendering software to pronounce things using the correct accent.

The **LANG** attribute takes a value equal to a natural language code, for example en-cockney, fr, de, da, el, it and so on. A natural language is regarded as one that is spoken, written or otherwise conveyed for the purpose of communicating between people. Computer languages are excluded from this definition of natural language.

In the example below, the author has specified that the browser should treat the document as though it was written in French – at least to start with – but then, he specifies a section to be written in German. All the **LANG** attribute does is render punctuation and certain aspects of layout *in the manner expected for the specified language*. This might involve getting the hyphenation, ligatures and spacing correct.

```
<BODY LANG=fr>
... en français ...
<SPAN LANG=de>...auf deutsch...</SPAN>
... en français ...
</BODY>
```

In this example you can see the use of the SPAN element to indicate smaller parts of the text that are in German. By using the **LANG** attribute in conjunction with the SPAN element, you have the opportunity to specify a new language literally halfway through a paragraph. The SPAN element is very useful for this purpose.

The LANG **attribute with the** META **and** LINK **elements**

With the META element, the language refers to the language used within the **CONTENT** attribute (see Chapter 12). For the LINK element, the language refers to the resource specified by the **HREF** attribute, and to the language used by any **TITLE** attribute (see Chapter 12).

Language variants of the same document

If you want to tell the browser that there are different versions of the document in different languages, HTML 4 anticipates that you will use the LINK element to generate a small menu on the screen. The items in the menu will be the values for the **TITLE** attributes so that:

Some language codes

de	German
it	Italian
nl	Dutch
gr	Greek
es	Spanish
pt	Portuguese
ar	Arabic
ru	Russian
ch	Chinese
ja	Japanese
hi	Hindi
ur	Urdu
sa	Sanskrit
en	English

```
<LINK REL=alternate HREF=mydoc-fr.html
    LANG=fr TITLE="A la lune (French translation)">
<LINK REL=alternate HREF=mydoc-de.html
    LANG=de TITLE="An der Mond (German original)">
<LINK REL=alternate HREF=mydoc-en.html
    LANG=en TITLE="To the moon (English translation)">
```

might generate a small menu consisting of:

A la lune (French translation)

An der Mond (German original)

To the moon (English translation)

The DIR attribute to set the direction of text

A lot of languages read from right-to-left. As yet, however, the Web has catered to those languages that read from left-to-right.

The DIR (DIRection) attribute tells the browser which way text should be displayed. The DIR attribute takes one of two values:

- ltr ('left-to-right')

- rtl ('right-to-left')

If omitted, the direction is inherited from the parent element. For example, if you have used the LANG attribute on the document BODY to indicate that text is in a language which is written from right-to-left, then paragraphs, lists, and other items in the document will indeed be written with that directionality. The DIR attribute can, however, be used to over-write a specific phrase with its own directionality of text.

The SPAN element in conjunction with the DIR attribute

You can change the directionality of a phrase by using the SPAN element, in conjunction with the DIR attribute. This idea can be used to demonstrate how DIR works.

Here is an elaborate example to show that you can nest directions as deeply as you please. Once you realize that each <SPAN DIR=...> tag goes on applying until its </SPAN> end tag is reached, but that any text inside another SPAN element, inside the first one, is controlled by the latest SPAN direction specified, then you should not find the results too difficult to understand. In a word, SPAN DIR constructs can be nested, rather like parts of the previous sentence.

Here goes:

```
<SPAN DIR=ltr>
green
<SPAN DIR=rtl>
blue
<SPAN DIR=ltr>
red
</SPAN>
pink
</SPAN>
purple
</SPAN>
```

This extraordinary example comes out as:

green knip red eulb purple

Honest. The word 'green' naturally appears on the left, as the first SPAN element says normal left-to-right.

Then follows a *right-to-left* sequence of pink, red, and blue. The 'red' is inside this again, in left-to-right order, so it appears as usual, but the words 'pink' and 'blue' are actually reversed.

Finally, purple follows at the end of the SPAN which began with 'green'.

If you look at how we have printed the nesting of the SPANs, you can see that careful layout makes SPANning look quite logical. If you just sprinkle SPAN elements about your text, the results are just plain confusing.

The **DIR** attribute can in fact be used on most elements and not just with SPAN. The only elements with which it cannot be combined are BR, HR, NEXTID, META and BASE. None of these elements is allowed to include the **DIR** attribute; however, every other HTML 4 element is.

The BDO element

BDO attributes
BDO has a **DIR** attribute to specify directionality. This can take values of **ltr** and **rtl** as previously described. It also takes the **LANG** attribute.

The BDO element stands for 'bi-directional override' and is a special element for those cases in which the directionality of text cannot be resolved unambiguously from context. Suppose you are reading an Arabic document from right-to-left. Certain phrases, particularly part numbers, formulas and telephone numbers, may need to be read from left-to-right. The BDO element specifies a directional override for such cases with the **DIR** attribute actually specifying whether or not the override is left-to-right or right-to-left.

The Q element for inline quotations

The Q element can, in HTML 4, specify a language-dependent rendering of short quotations, depending on the language and platform capability. What this means, is that quotations marked-up with Q should, if the browser knows that the language of the document is, say, German, be rendered as quote marks for a Q element using German convention. So, the browser should correctly display:

„Komm, das Essen ist fertig"

The French use their own flavor of quote marks:

«Viens voir le lapin.»

Q elements can be nested so that you can even specify different styles for single and double quotes[1]. Here we use different styles for single and double quotes to demonstrate how this might work:

Sarah was quite sure that the fluffy black-and-white guinea pig was a baby skunk. "I assure you it is a guinea pig," said the pet shop owner. "It just looks like a skunk because its hair is so long." Suddenly, there was a gasp from Peter who had been watching the animal intently. "Look," he cried, "The 'skunk' has had babies!"

The word *skunk* is nested inside another quote and so is surrounded by single quotes.

The ALIGN attribute in the context of scripts reading from right-to-left

In Arabic, Hebrew and in other languages that read from right-to-left, the default text alignment on the screen is right, instead of the default left-text alignment, as it is for Western European languages. The elements P, HR, H1– H6, OL, UL, BLOCKQUOTE and ADDRESS need to be aligned differently for different languages, which the browser must take into account. The **ALIGN** attribute associated with these elements must have **ALIGN=right** as the default.

---

[1] The authors do apologize for yet another example to do with guinea pigs, but with so many in residence, examples involving these most endearing animals spring so easily to mind.

18
DESIGNING YOUR
WEB PROJECT

Included in this chapter is information on the following:

- Specifying the design of your pages
- Structuring hypertext
- Making sure people can find your Web pages
- Writing HTML
- Choosing the right tools, text editors and how to debug

Summary

Web pages are systems made of HTML. Web designers face similar tasks to designers of any other systems. This chapter introduces concepts and techniques for:

- Web specification (writing down the requirements)

- Web design, by thinking through the structures you need

- writing the HTML, possibly with tools or export filters

- testing and debugging, to track down common problems

- rollout and maintenance, to keep your users happy.

Most authors will want to use tools rather than write all their HTML by hand. New tools are appearing all the time. This chapter introduces examples of some of the main kinds of tools available.

Special design issues covered include how to make your site easy to navigate, and how to help new users find it.

18.1 Introduction

Every journey begins with a single step, runs the proverb. When you look at some of the dazzling and complicated documents now on the Web, you may feel the task is impossible – or, conversely, that you must rush out and make your own at once. Both attitudes limit your ability to create. The truth is that you can make beautiful HTML documents, and that they can become complicated. You can succeed if you organize the task into sensible steps.

18.2 Specifying what you want

The vital first phase of any project consists of deciding what it is you want to build. It may seem obvious, but you can't have it until you say what it is. Many systems of all sizes have failed simply because they were designed without clear requirements. When we talk about requirements, our friends say, 'But, that's just common sense.' So it is, but, perhaps, common sense is rarer than many people imagine.

Good hypertext matches the way its users approach it. You can only achieve such a structure by designing it according to its requirements. These may include, for example:

- structure and content of information to be presented (the message)

- intended readership (kinds of people, types of visit)

- information to be returned (in forms or email)

- data to be collected automatically (logs, usage statistics, sales figures)

- marketing and public relations aspects (desired impression and image to be conveyed)

- privacy and payments (who can access what, freely or on what conditions)

- security (defense against unwanted intrusion).

Specification does not have to entail a lot of fuss: small HTML systems will be fine if specified as a one-page document (possibly pointing to sources of text and graphics). Larger commercial systems may be best specified using a requirements or design tool, with the advantage that HTML can be automatically generated with the correct link and `ID` structures. You then have a much-simplified job when building and testing.

18.3 Hypertext design

Our friends who saw this chapter at once told us 'But no-one designs their hypertext.' Well, that is why so much of the Web is such a mess, and why it can be so frustrating when you want to find something. You will not get your design right first time, so aim to throw one away.

Design principles

This section gives a few general principles for designing hypertext (not necessarily in HTML).

Draw a diagram of the desired structure

Since HTML naturally forms a network of documents, it is sensible to draw a diagram (or a set of nested diagrams) illustrating how you want the network to behave. Do you need reverse links? What sort of index or table of contents do you want? Now is the time to decide.

Discuss the design

Small HTML systems can easily be designed by hand. It is helpful to have a supply of large plain drawing paper. A self-printing whiteboard (an expensive device, basically a rotating screen with a built-in photocopier) is a great convenience for the design of business systems: you discuss the design with your colleagues, sketch what you want on the board, and press the button for copies. Rich industrialists can achieve the same effect using a videoconferencing system, which allows them to share a drawing on their screens while working at separate locations.

Good questions to ask when discussing a design are:

- Is the design consistent?

- Does it cover what you want?

- Should any items be dropped?

- Are the topics presented in the right order and prominence?

Use a tool for large Web sites

Large HTML systems may be designed using a Computer-Aided Software Engineering (CASE) tool. CASE tools let you put together a family of diagrams, which can be checked automatically for internal consistency. This is nice when you have lots of pages with dozens of links between them. The diagrams are best printed out in landscape format; you can then work directly from the printout to your HTML tags, ticking off each link anchor on the diagram as you insert it into the HTML. Authoring tools can check whether links are well formed, but it is up to you to make sure you put them in!

Structuring hypertext

This section looks at some ways of organizing information into manageable structures that your readers can understand, illustrating the approaches with examples from the Web.

Trees

The basic pattern for hypertexts is the tree. The top page gives a quick summary and introduction, and contains links (<A HREF=...> anchors) to pages covering the main topics. These in turn link to more detailed pages, so the structure branches into a tree. Tree-structure is the best way to manage complexity, but it results in slow navigation between branches. Navigation aids such as indexes are therefore vital.

Tree.

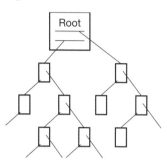

- Good for explanations, magazines
- Quick overview, more detail at lower levels
- Navigation aids useful (top, index buttons)
- Allows DIY story – reader chooses own path
- Allows teach yourself, multi-choice answers

We have already referred to the glorious pages of the University of California at Berkeley's Museum of Paleontology (http://ucmp1.berkeley.edu). These pages are an informative delight, and it would take many hours to study all of them. The layout of the UCMP pages, using Tables, is discussed in Chapter 11. Here, we will focus on the hypertext design, in other words the relationship of the pages to each other.

The UCMP Welcome page.

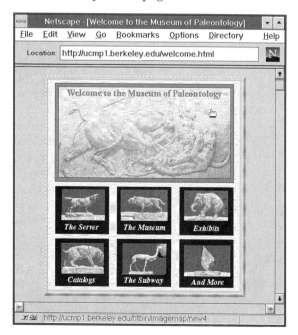

The Welcome page branches out to seven main topics, ranging from the vigorous sculptures used as icons, through the details of the Web server, a puff for the Museum itself (see illustration in Chapter 11, Tables), and only then to the Exhibits (see illustration below), which is, presumably, what everyone came to see. The principle is well known to supermarkets – you put the most desirable goods at the back, so that visitors have plenty of time to notice the other goods on the way there.

The Catalogs are more serious navigation tools. Then comes the subway (see below) and the 'And More' section, a bit of a ragbag of miscellaneous topics. Each of these half-dozen sub-trees itself branches into a further half-dozen paths for the museum visitor to explore: the structure is a richly branched tree.

The UCMP Exhibits page.

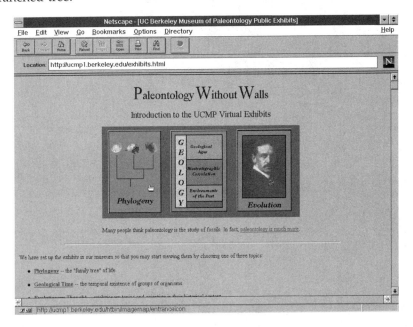

The Exhibits page leads to[1] phylogeny, the study of the origins and connections of species, to a wonderfully rich display on the subject of Geological Time, the 'UCMP Time Machine' (see p. 336) and to an interesting exhibit on Evolutionary Thought.

The Subway (see illustration) consists of a large image map to appeal to visitors old and young, in the form of a paleontological subway route-map. You just click on the 'station' you want to go to, and there you are: paleontology is much more than dinosaur fossils, is the lesson. The Museum has managed to be both adventurous and cautious in its hypertext design: the subway is accompanied by a simple list of link anchors (blue underlined text under the map) for text-only visitors.

[1] Notice that links are provided both graphically and textually to give all users access to the exhibits, though it would be a shame to visit UCMP without a graphics browser.

The UCMP Subway page.

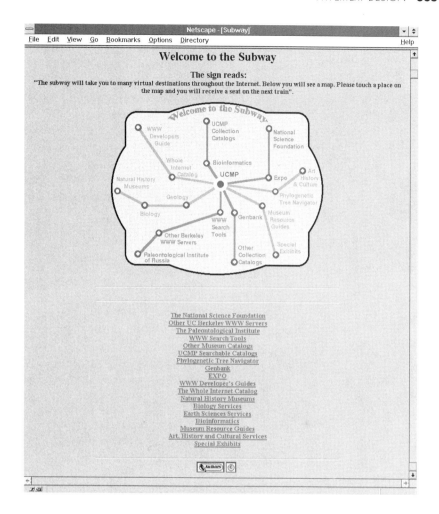

Similarly, despite the attractive subway-map concept, the plan of the hypertext is just a hierarchy with rather few cross-links. This simplicity of design is well worth imitating.

With the 'Geological Time Machine', UCMP has had the conceit of representing the fossil record very naturally as a sequence of time stages, and the visitor as a time traveller in a Tardis (see illustration). A scrolling list in an HTML <FORM> lets the visitor set the time controls, and the Submit button, wittily renamed 'Ride the Web Geological Time Machine...' starts the time travel.

The page gives access to several dozen topics. In general we would advise against such a large choice, but here it seems quite natural. An alternative would have been to set the coarse time control (Precambrian, Paleozoic, Mesozoic, Cenozoic) and then the fine, but the Museum reckoned, probably correctly, that direct access was more exciting. This kind of decision is the stuff of hypertext design.

The UCMP Time
Machine page.

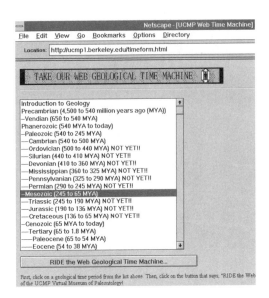

At the bottom of the main Exhibits page, which as we have seen leads to
a wealth of material, is a Navigation Toolbar. This provides three kinds of
index, which the museum calls 'lifts' (i.e. time- and space-travel elevators)
enabling the visitor to search for any taxon (classification), any geological
period, or any topic described in the museum's pages.

As these 'Lifts' are similar in design, we will illustrate just one of them.
The Taxon lift is a hierarchically indented list, again implemented using
an HTML <FORM>, with a renamed Submit button. Since this is provided as

The UCMP 'Web
Lift'.

a shortcut for quick navigation, some knowledge on the part of the visitor can reasonably be assumed. The use of a Latin hierarchy, in which *Aves (Birds)* are seen to be *Theropods*, which are *Vertebrates* which are *Chordates*, is thus appropriate here, whereas it would be quite unreasonable as the primary means of access to these exhibits. Of course, the hierarchy also has some didactic value on its own as a guide to evolutionary history.

By these means, the Museum's enormous range of material is made readily accessible: indeed, it is now open to all Web users, not just people who live near Berkeley, so the pages must be reckoned to have greatly increased the Museum's outreach.

We cannot resist giving a glimpse of the UCMP time machine itself, a set of pages which one might be proud of, even without the rest of the Museum's hypertext. Apart from the actual geological periods, there is a beautiful introduction to stratigraphy at the 'entrance' to the Museum:

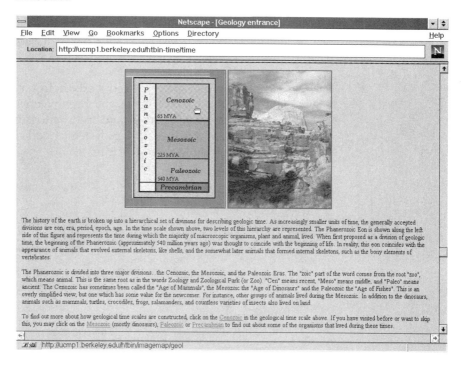

Doors naturally lead from there to the various geological ages, or you can simply click on the age in which you are interested (the cursor shows a pointing hand ☞ in Netscape when over something clickable). For instance, dinosaur-lovers will at once travel to the Mesozoic age.

The Mesozoic summary page gives access, with a search field, to suitably exciting Mesozoic animals, and via the buttons to detailed exhibits on Stratigraphy, Fossils of this time, and to Fossil Localities. There is also another chance to ride the time machine.

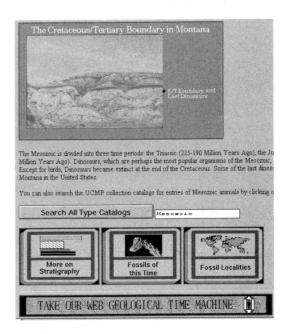

The Mesozoic is divided into three time periods: the Triassic (225-190 Million Years Ago), the Ju... Million Years Ago). Dinosaurs, which are perhaps the most popular organisms of the Mesozoic, Except for birds, Dinosaurs became extinct at the end of the Cretaceous. Some of the last dinos... Montana in the United States.

You can also search the UCMP collection catalogs for entries of Mesozoic animals by clicking o...

The UCMP pages repay detailed study both for the intrinsic interest of the material, and for their elegant and highly accessible structure. It is not easy to construct such a useful and informative hypertext. The diagram below summarizes this tour of http://ucmp1.berkeley.edu/, UCMP's Web site, showing its simple Tree structure.

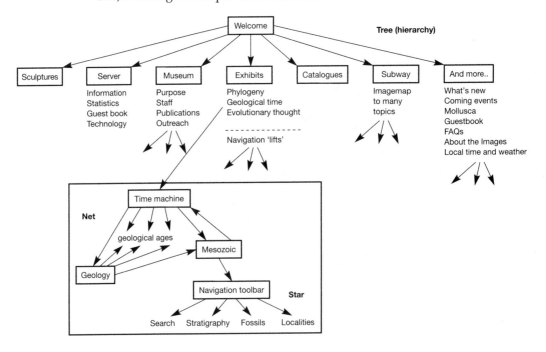

Nets

Richer patterns of interconnection turn naturally into networks: no-one sets out to design a Net in the way that they may decide to build a tree, say. Networks allow unlimited freedom, with which comes, inevitably, the possibility of getting lost or going wrong. A partial cure is to provide a default (List-like) path through the net with Next and Back buttons; another approach is to put a little map on screen showing where the current page fits into the broader picture.

Network.

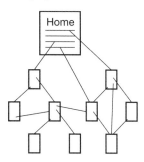

- Good for encyclopaedias, museums, science
- Easy to browse to related topics
- Navigation aids essential
- Rich cross-linking teaches relationships

The Web has come in for a lot of criticism because of the number of unstructured sites and the confusing connections between them. Help to defeat the critics by making your pages orderly and satisfying to read. If you draw a diagram like the figure to show how your pages fit together, you will probably spot several immediate structural improvements that you could make with little effort.

The ultra-hip magazine *Wired* has its own decidedly wacky Web pages on http://www.hotwired.com/ (see illustration).

Once you have recovered from the shock of the imagery, though, you can see that the page is mostly a list of links to other pages, so the structure is probably tree-like.

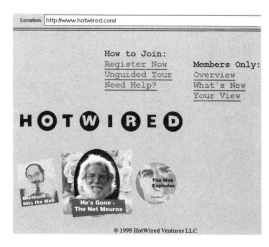

The authors, fearless explorers of the Web, strapped on their Solar Topis, spread on their mosquito repellent, and unsheathed their machetes, to discover just how the HotWired pages are organized.

The Overview looked a promising place to start (see illustration). The whizzy iconography and clashing colors (purple/yellow harmonies, primary blue, red, ...) disguise the rather conventional tree structure. Each of the main items – Signal, World Beat, Piazza, Renaissance 2.0, Coin, and Wired, gives access to a colorful list of topics and articles. These may be unintelligible to the squarer reader, but the structure is as straight and true-blue as Big Blue.

The second item under Signal is called Fetish. Spraying on a little more jungle juice, and sharpening our machetes to a dangerous degree, we ventured in.

Fetish seemed, at the time of visiting, indeed to contain items of apparel and things to buy, but nothing that would shock your maiden aunt. (Only the colors...)

At the foot of the page was a conventional Navigation Toolbar (yes, you can imagine its appearance) with buttons labelled Search, Help, and Threads (of discussion by readers). These are in fact provided on all or most of the HotWired pages. In addition, links give immediate return access to the Overview, What's New, and Your View pages, turning this into a network structure.

The Unguided Tour (from the home page) offers a description of each of the regular features (Signal, etc.) which HotWired calls channels, by analogy with radio (see illustration). Each of these contains a link to the Register Now page, so once again this is a simple network.

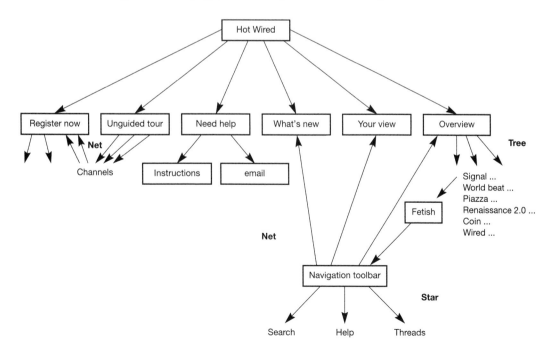

If you want to create unconventional and exciting pages, then, the lesson from HotWired is to select strange and novel material, draw interesting graphics, and use a very plain tree structure with cross-references for easy navigation. Your readers may be disoriented by your subject matter, but there is no excuse for losing them in a jungle of hypertext.

HotWired have also used exemplary Navigation Toolbars, showing that even these can be made interesting to look at. The presence of the Unguided Tour, Need Help, and Instructions pages makes it quite clear that they have taken the need for comprehensible navigation very seriously, however wild and woolly their surface image.

The structure of the HotWired hypertext is summarized in the diagram at the bottom of p. 341.

As usual, it is largely a **Tree** (hierarchy), but with **Star**-like Navigation tool links and regularly laid out jumps to other interesting places in the **Network**.

Stars

A Star gives direct access from one page to a whole lot of others directly. Every Index, Navigation Toolbar, or top-level Contents page forms a star.

Star.

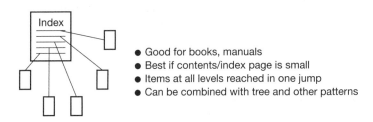

- Good for books, manuals
- Best if contents/index page is small
- Items at all levels reached in one jump
- Can be combined with tree and other patterns

An attractive example of the Star can be found on the Mystic Fire pages (http://mosaic.echonyc.com/mysticfire/) where various philosophers are presented, with forms, which you can use to order books and cassettes for further study. For instance, Alan Watts, a philosopher of the 1960s, has his own home page, shown below. He liked the East enough to want to show that you could tell stories using ideograms, long before everyone started to use icons for everything:

'This simple tale hardly needs translation:' from *TAO, The Watercourse Way*, Alan Watts, 1975.

Each Mystic Fire page contains a short biography, a photo or two, and links to snippets of the philosopher's work to illustrate the main themes. This star-shaped plan is quite general in application.

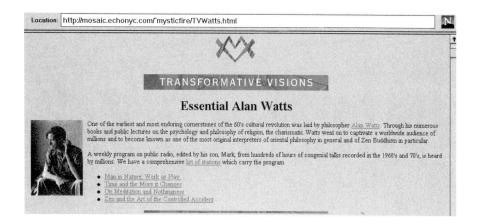

This page can be seen to branch star-wise to four sections of Watts' work, which are actually sections of the same HTML file as the page shown. The anchor 'Alan Watts' paradoxically branches back to the main Mystic Fire index of philosophers, which is itself a star with a ray leading to each person's home page.

A third (and typical) star-pattern occurs in the navigation tool at the bottom of each home page, including Watts':

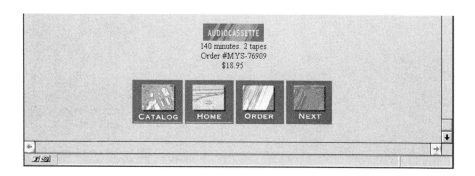

The Next button subverts the structure into a List (see below) by stepping to the next philosopher in line. Here is the structure of the Watts pages:

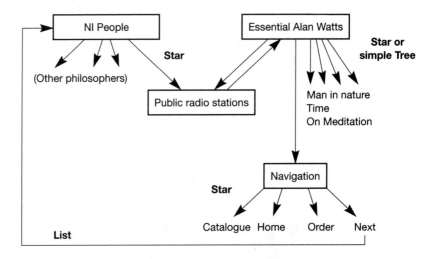

Lists

Lastly, we must mention the oldest structure of them all, the list. It has its uses, such as for scanned-in books, or for guided tours through your Web site. You can of course make the list branch just a little bit by putting in some links to images.

A list structure is illustrated on the Alan Watts diagram above, where the Next button at the end of each philosopher's page steps to the next philosopher. Of course, if you are interested in the Tao and Confucianism, the fact that the Next Philosopher in alphabetic order is a Vienna Positivist may not help you much. Since books are to a large extent sequential lists (of pages, of chapters,...), the list structure is quite familiar, but this example makes clear its inherent limitations.

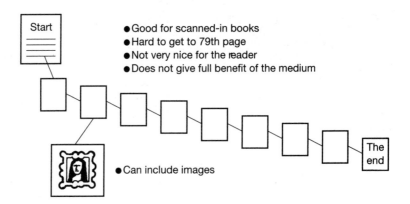

Designing to be found

From a lofty visionary perspective, such as that of the inventor of hypertext, Ted Nelson, the whole of the World Wide Web is a single enormous hypertext! He kindly volunteered the following lines for this book:

'At last the world has populist, anarchic electronic publishing on networks.
World Wide Web is like karaoke: anyone can do it, with no training, and that's great.'

Ted Nelson (Inventor of hypertext)

Nelson has for long made clear in his writings that the global, permanent, electronic medium he envisages should encompass all forms of knowledge, and be thoroughly indexed and referenced with reusable components. The Web, simple-minded as it is, is certainly far from these goals of universal knowledge-sharing, so he is being polite when he praises it in the words quoted above. We agree with the sentiment 'anyone can do it', though perhaps we know enough to take issue with the phrase 'with no training'.

At least the Web is starting to be indexed reasonably efficiently, if not to the degree envisiged by Ted Nelson. Popular search sites, such as Webcrawler (http://www.webcrawler.com), Lycos (http://www.lycos.com) and Yahoo (http://www.yahoo.com), provide both keyword search and hierarchical classifications of URLs. The color section illustrates the use of search engines. Indexing is also improving as commercial publishers 'add value' by selling organized views of the Web for particular subject areas, professions, and activities.

The value of your site depends on whether the right people visit it: this may be just a few dozen colleagues if you are running a club or a research site, or millions of punters if you are marketing a beer or a movie. In a small group, you can simply tell your friends your site's URL; for a public site, you need to consider how people are going to hear about it.

If you are not in a hurry, you can just wait a few weeks for the search engines' spiders to find you. The spiders are simply programs that retrieve HTML pages, scan them for links, and retrieve all the linked pages, indexing them as they go. There are several kinds of search engine, and they behave differently.

The classifying engines attempt, often with human help, to assign sites to pre-defined categories: this is problematic, as you discover when your smart new object-oriented design tool is rudely shoved into 'Databases' where nobody will ever think of looking for it. A few sites let you suggest categories.

The keyword engines send out spiders which work mainly on <TITLE> contents, with some input from <H1> and likely-sounding <A> links. You may therefore be able to help people find you by putting several keywords into your page titles. Some crafty marketing men have wised up to this mechanism, and have tried to subvert the indexes by flooding their pages and titles with repeated keywords. The inevitable Darwinian response (as the antelopes get faster, so do the cheetahs) is for the search engines to penalize repetition.

The indexing engines blindly race around the Web (cave spiders, perhaps?) constructing free-text indexes of everything they find (though they all seem to ignore images). Users can search either on lists of keywords, which only have to be on the same page, or on particular phrases. The engines return a percentage score which gives users a very rough idea of how good the match is. You can help such people find you by choosing less common keywords or phrases. Words like 'computer' and 'network' are not going to help much, as they occur in millions of pages; specific phrases like 'spatial autocorrelation' or 'cosmic background micro-wave radiation' will narrow down the odds considerably. Rare individual words automatically get a high score, so if you can sensibly include a Zymurgy or a *Zyzzogeton* in your pages, people interested in fermentation chemistry or South American leafhoppers will find you at once!

You can increase the effectiveness of your site by submitting a description of it to the main search sites. Organizations are even springing up just to help you do this! One that offers a free service is Submit-it at http://www.submit-it.com; others charge stiff fees. Businesses may well consider paying for submission services as well as advertising.

Finally, you can get people to your site by making it useful: both through the quality of information you provide, and the links to related sites. If your links are helpful enough, people will keep a bookmark to your links page. And, of course, you can negotiate mutual links with your colleagues, friends, clients and suppliers – you point to them if they point to you.

Page design

Corporate Web users generally want to impose their own style on their Web pages. They may employ graphic artists to design icons and logos, menu-bars, and diagrams. Professional page designers may be involved in document layout. Where the HTML is to be prepared by people with other backgrounds, the design department typically produces a booklet of guidelines for authors, telling them not to use too many different typefaces, and laying down rules about diagram and image design. They are aware of the power of images in influencing people, and may specify color schemes and use of the logo. If they are wise, they also produce examples of their schemes online in HTML, with simple templates to fill in or copy.

As it is costly and inflexible to have every page professionally designed, a sensible compromise is to have the welcome splash and the top-level pages made to look good. The lower-level details (written by the technical people) can then be formatted simply, and perhaps converted automatically from documents or databases.

The *Byte* magazine site (http://www.byte.com) is a good example of a large body of information which is formatted almost entirely automatically: it is attractive, helpful, and easy to search. The site has a regular, hierarchical structure which reflects its business: a magazine comes out each month; there are product reviews and feature articles in each issue; each article contains text and graphics, and each image appears with a caption, and so on. The HTML is generated in a way which exploits these regular patterns. You need to understand the requirements of your site in the same way, so that you can structure your information appropriately.

18.4 Writing the HTML

With a solid set of requirements behind you and a decently worked-out design, you can safely go ahead 'with soldering iron and wire-wrap gun' (Fred P. Brooks). This section looks at how to work systematically, and then at the choice of authoring tools.

Working systematically

It helps if you have text and graphics ready-named as a complete set of (non-marked-up) files before you start on the HTML. Other people like the feeling of composing at the organ, and insist on writing text while editing graphics while inserting tags while creating URLs (...while playing the drums, tuba, and cymbals between their knees). Scripts (Chapter 16) and programming can follow later.

We commend to you the dentist's maxim:

'Stay with each tool as long as possible'.

It is far more satisfactory to create all the images, then to insert all the tags, and then to test them all, than to switch continually from one tool to another. If you do all the images together, they will probably harmonize in style as your mind will be focused on the visual task.

You should at least choose your own style consciously, and find your own way of being systematic. We find a checklist on a piece of paper very helpful. The figure shows a simple hand-written example of a kind that we find helpful, for the Theatre example (see the Color Section). Ruled columns are useful because they make it obvious when an item has been missed out. If you start by simply listing the pages and add comments as you go along then there is really no extra work involved in making a list – on the contrary, the list will save you effort time and again.

A hand-written checklist is helpful when constructing hypertext pages.

	Layout	Links	Text	Problems
Theatre	ok	ok	ok	
Programme	sort out priority	ok		typefaces too complicated
Current		ok		
Future				images? provisional dates?
Bookings		ok	ok	firm vs enquiries
Reservations		ok		
Pricing				
Company		ok		
Actors				

Choosing your tools

New tools, which purport to make designing and maintaining Web pages easier than being cheated by a team of used-car salesmen, are appearing all the time. It is therefore impossible to say anything comprehensive about the tools on offer. What we can do is to say what kinds of tools there are, with examples, and give you some clues as to which kind might suit you.

The main kinds of tools on offer at the moment are:

- export filters from data stores such as spreadsheets and databases
- HTML script editors
- what-you-see-is-what-you-get (WYSIWYG) HTML page editors
- HTML tag editors

You will also probably want to use some graphics tools (see Chapter 9) to prepare suitable images.

Export filters

One increasingly popular approach to creating HTML is not to write it at all – directly. Instead, you use your normal tools and then export HTML when you want to share data on the Internet or your Intranet.

Many spreadsheets, databases and other more specialized software tools can export HTML. They typically include a filter somewhere among their menu options to convert their own patent data structure to one or several HTML pages. HTML is a general way to represent information, so there is no one 'right' way to translate from, say, a database to a sequence of Web pages.

The ideal export filter would efficiently translate a mixture of headings, text and graphics into a neatly linked set of pages, with HTML headings, paragraphs (or tables) and GIF or JPEG images standing in for the original data. Unfortunately tools are rarely so highly optimized. Obviously it is handy to get something at the touch of a button, but you may get better results by doing the job yourself.

For example, Microsoft provides filters called Internet Assistant for Word documents and PowerPoint presentations, in the form of free add-on macros. You can download the latest versions from ftp.microsoft.com. The filter for PowerPoint slide-shows, for instance, takes the text and graphics of each slide and makes all of it into a largish GIF image, soaking up your Web site's storage and your users' bandwidth. The images sit in a dull background with standardized forward and back buttons. The Word filter does not export images, which makes life awkward.

If your favorite tool does not already export HTML in the form you would like, it may be feasible to write a macro or script to create HTML

Hypertext can be generated automatically from sources such as databases.

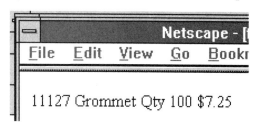

files from the tool's data. For example, if you want some special layout from a database written in Microsoft Access, you could write a program in Visual Basic to retrieve records from your tables, and structure HTML tables to suit your needs. The HTML may correspond not to the original tables as such, but to database joins or views which may be easier for readers to interpret. Ever after, when you need to update your hypertext – each week or month – you just run your macros and the job is done. Of course you still have to enter the data into the database and verify it. You can make finishing touches by hand, if you want.

HTML script editors

The simplest approach (for the toolmaker) is to offer you something which writes HTML for you as a good old-fashioned script, letting you press a button to see the effect in a browser. A typical editor of this kind is WebEdit, which looks like this:

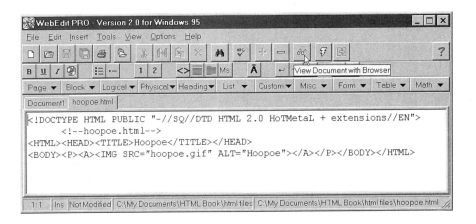

As you can see, you get a Chinese-typewriter-sized array of buttons to push, and a raft of drop-down menus for everything from Page commands to the HTML 3.2 math proposal tags. When you are ready to see the fruits of your labor in your favorite browser, you push the pair-of-spectacles button and up the browser pops with your new page.

This approach certainly makes it quicker to construct HTML, and greatly reduces the chances of mistakes. It does not do much to help with layout: you need as clear an idea of the desired page design as when you are using a simple text editor together with a browser for development. The button-pushing model also fails if there is not a button for some just-released tag or attribute. The version illustrated lacks any Frames features, for instance. When tools do not do what you want, you soon end up using a simple text editor out of sheer frustration.

WYSIWYG page editors

Most of the tools on offer attempt some kind of WYSIWYG editing. An example of this kind of tool is WebExpress. Just as in a word processor, you press buttons or make menu selections to get various tools, which do familiar jobs like inserting images or creating tables. Also as in a word processor, you need never see what dark tricks the tool gets up to behind the scenes (what do you suppose Word does when you insert an image, for instance?). Here is WebExpress in action:

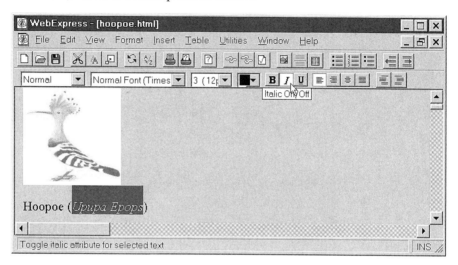

This is starting to look distinctly easy, as well as broadly familiar to users of Word for Windows. Operations like applying a style or italicizing a phrase look and are similar to Word's, so you may well find this class of tool intuitively obvious to use.

Tag editors

SoftQuad's HoTMetaL editor is unique among the editors we have seen in trying to create a complete visual idiom for HTML other than simply the obvious one (WYSIWYG). The point of view is of an author who is interested in and familiar with tags, in much the same way that a programmer might be used to (and want to see) programming language constructs such as IF and WHILE. You just press a button or choose an option from a menu, and HoTMetaL does the rest, enabling you to create HTML without actually typing out all the tags yourself. A specimen is shown on the next page.

As you can see, the image automatically displays itself (if you so choose). HoTMetaL very sensibly comes with a separate rules file, so updates can be issued just by replacing the parsing rules.

More examples of HoTMetaL at work can be found in the color section.

18.5 Testing and debugging

Once your *Chef d'oeuvre* is declared complete, you absolutely **must** check it out.

'Life is one darn thing after another.'

President Calvin Coolidge

The *ONLY* way to be sure your HTML is correct is to go through all of it, and to check that everything works as intended. Even if you checked it already.

– Aw, mom, we did that yesterday! –
– Adapt, Wilbur. –

You need to start at the beginning, without any preconceived notions of what has and has not been done: by definition, you do not know what you have forgotten! This is so difficult to do on a large system, that conventional wisdom deploys an independent team to do the testing. You will be fine checking your own HTML as long as you maintain a sort of detached concern, like a traditional hospital doctor on the ward round: 'oh, that's an interesting problem . . .'

Testing approaches

Any approach that checks everything is fine. You may like to do something like this:

- Make a list of all your HTML documents. Rule a dozen columns.

- Spell-check them all. Tick them off as you go.

- View the documents in your browser. Check that all the text is visible and paragraphed.

- Check that header levels and character-level mark-up look appropriate.

- Check that figures, forms, tables, and anchors are correctly formatted and fit their context. Extra space or breaks, or conversely more careful flow of text, can make a big difference.

- Fill in all form fields and submit them. Check that the right messages are sent.

- Follow every link. Check that all of them go where they should.

- Try out every hotzone on clickable images. Check the links work as intended.

- Look at the system again from the beginning, as a reader. Are more links needed to make the system usable or comprehensible? Are navigation aids needed?

- Finally, look at each document in the system, as a designer. Does it look worthy of your efforts? Could the graphic design or page layout benefit from a little more effort?

- View your hypertext with a different browser. Sometimes pages which look great in one browser are horrible in another.

Once you have cleared your HTML through this process, it may not be perfect, but it will be tough and usable.

Some common mistakes

HTML is not a devious and tricky language like C or APL ('x/+^%='), nor does it growl at you with incomprehensible messages, as a C programming language compiler does:

```
syntax error at line 658: unknown identifier
```

HTML's very friendliness, though, can give you trouble: the browser silently goes crazy, offering you no obvious clue as to what was wrong. Maybe the noisily raving C compiler is, after all, preferable. There are several tools now available (look on the Web with Yahoo (http://www.yahoo.com) or W3 (http://www.w3.org) for the latest details) which can check your HTML in the same way that a compiler checks a computer program. HAL offer an HTML validation service which does the same thing. They will undoubtedly pick up some mistakes that you did not notice. These may include:

● invisible text

● case sensitivity

● unclosed tags

● swapped filenames

● omitted quotation marks

● squashed text

● PC/UNIX incompatibilities.

Here are some hints to help you spot these sorts of problem.

Invisible text

The famous invisible text is easily created: just put it inside a tag. For instance:

```
<H3 I wanted this to be my title></H3> <!-- no good -->
```

In fact, the line should have read

```
<H3> I wanted this to be my title</H3>
```

Case sensitivity

Text in URLs is often case sensitive, so that

```
<A HREF="fred.html#f1"> <!-- no good -->
```

is not at all the same thing as

```
<A HREF="fred.html#F1">
```

and indeed the links don't work if the labels are in the wrong case. Your browser very probably has different tricks up its sleeve. Sensitivity to case, to white space (present or absent), to supposedly optional tags, or to recent features of HTML, are all likely candidates for small bugs. Note that UNIX **is** case sensitive.

Unclosed tags

What is wrong with

```
<H2>Another Section<H2> <!-- no good -->
```

You spotted it at once? You need a closing `</H2>` tag with a '/'. It is also quite easy to end up (after a little manual editing and re-arrangement) with HTML such as

```
<H2>Another Level 2 Section</H3> <!-- no good either! -->
```

which is unlikely to work: most browsers do not assume that a wrong-level closing tag should close a heading. Look through your text with a browser (or better, two different browsers) for suspicious signs, such as whole sections in bold face.

People often forget the whole closing tag, too. For instance, if most of a document appears in *italics, you need to put in an* `</EM>` *or* `</I>` *somewhere close to where the italicizing started!*

Swapped filenames

Everyone has written

```
<LINK HREF="topform.html"> <!-- no good -->
```

when they meant

```
<LINK HREF="formtop.html">
```

and then wondered what was going wrong. If you keep a **printed listing** of your files this should not happen often.

Obsolete absolute addresses

Similar chaos readily breaks out when moving files to new directories or servers, unless you are very careful to use purely relative addressing and a fixed structure. For example, perhaps your home page used to be in 'systems/web/homepage/' but you moved it to 'public/website/' and suddenly all your links are broken. This was because your links contained absolute addresses such as

```
<A HREF="http://acme.com/systems/web/homepage/index.html">
```

This naturally does not work when that file is no longer in that directory. The safe way to refer to a file in the same directory as the current page is simply to name it, for example

```
<A HREF="index.html">
```

This address is *relative* to the current directory.

To go up the directory structure, use '`../`'. For instance, you could write

```
<A HREF="../index.html">
```

for the index file which is in the parent of the current directory. Again, the address makes sense because it is relative to the current location. Notice that HTML uses the forward slash (/) to mark a directory (as in UNIX), rather than a PC-style backslash character (\).

To go down to a child directory, just name it, with a forward slash after the directory name. For example,

```
<A HREF="products/index.html">
```

links to the index file in the products subdirectory of the current one.

Finally, to go across to a sister directory, you have to go up to your parent and down again, as in

```
<A HREF="../images/image3.jpg">
```

Some HTML editors now come with a supposedly convenient feature for publishing your pages: they convert references to your local directories into absolute references to directories on your Web site. We think this is a terrible idea! With relative addressing, you can leave your HTML unaltered when you publish it. This style brings a big advantage: if readers download several of your pages and copy (part of) your directory structure, the links between the files will work: readers can study your pages conveniently and cheaply off-line.

Incidentally, if you are working on a PC, you can still use UNIX-style relative addresses complete with forward slashes: all browsers understand these. So use relative addresses.

Omitted quotation marks

Different browsers have varying reactions to missed quotation marks.

```
<A HREF=myfile.htm>
```

or

```
<A HREF="myfile.htm>
```

may or may not work. Browsers are becoming stricter with this kind of mistake. Quotes are necessary in multi-word identifiers, and you certainly cannot expect your browser to cope with:

```
<H3 ID="multi-word identifier >MWI</H3> <!-- no good -->
```

Squashed text

It is really very easy to forget some <P> or <BR> tags. Your browser blithely ignores your 'unwritten mark-up' in the form of carriage returns in your documents! For instance:

```
<P>
I wanted this to be line 1. <!-- no good -->
And this to be line 2.
I hoped this would be line 3.
```

Unfortunately, this is shown on screen as:

I wanted this to be line 1. And this to be line 2. I hoped this would be line 3.

It worked on my PC

PCs running DOS/Windows are insensitive to case, allow the use of underscores in filenames, and still generally use three-character file extensions. So

```
<A HREF="DOS_file.htm">Some DOS text</A> <!-- no good -->
```

is quite legal on a PC, and when you test your HTML, your DOS/Windows browser will succeed in finding the right file. But when you install it on a UNIX server, the link may fail, for several reasons. You need to put

```
<A HREF="portable.html">Some portable text</A>
```

You should write file names in URLs:

- in lower case,

- with no underscores, and

- with the four-character extension '.html' (depending on your server).

Some PC browsers are too relaxed about directory references also. You should not put a slash (/) before the name of a child of the current directory if you are using relative addressing. So

```
<A HREF="/subdirectory/index.html"> <!-- no good -->
```

is wrong: you need to say

```
<A HREF="subdirectory/index.html">
```

instead.

It worked in UNIX

UNIX allows you to use long file names, as do other operating systems like Apple's and new versions of Windows. While DOS/Windows browsers remain in wide use, it is best to use short file roots (up to 8 characters) so that there is no risk of ambiguity. For instance:

```
<A HREF="thisfileisverylongindeed.html">
```

and

```
<A HREF="thisfileisshort.html">
```

both appear to DOS when used locally on a DOS/Windows browser as if they were

```
<A HREF="THISFILE.HTM">
```

Since not many people develop on a UNIX workstation and publish on a PC, this is not generally a serious problem, but it is annoying to people who want to navigate off-line through your hypertext, using their PC.

18.6 Rollout and maintenance

Rollout is the start of a maintenance process, not the end of the cycle. You will always need to make updates in style and content. If you tested carefully, you will not need many changes in mechanism.

It is sensible to include a form for recording mistakes or suggestions, or at least a 'mailto:' URL with your return address:

```
<A HREF="mailto:author@feedback.acoustic.com">Send Feedback to Author</A>
```

This calls up a mail tool using the configuration you set up in your browser, from a normal-looking hypertext link anchor:

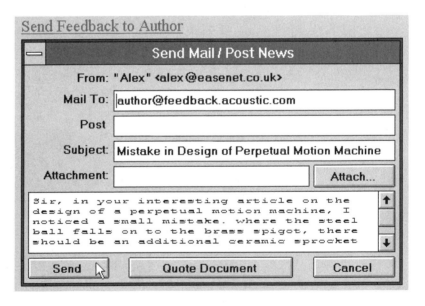

This enables your readers to give you their feedback. It is the most important part of the whole process! Do not treat comments as a nuisance; responding to comments with further development is the only way that you can hope to give your readers what they want. If you get a heap of comments, this means that plenty of people are reading your hypertext!

Incidentally, the use of a mail alias, like the 'author' of the example, or the widely used 'Webmaster' is advisable, as these names can stay constant whereas people change jobs. Aliases also make it easy when you need to filter your mail: you can separate out all Web mail from your personal letters, for instance.

POSTSCRIPT

The story of the World Wide Web with apologies to Alan Watts

Appendix A
EXAMPLES OF TAGS

This appendix is a pure list of examples. Its function is to remind the reader of the syntax of particular tags where the general idea is remembered but some help with the details is needed. The examples do not do anything at all sensible, but we hope they are (individually) constructed correctly and will prove useful as an *aide mémoire*.

If you want to try the tags out in your browser, please insert a line or paragraph break (
 or <P>) before each example. Such separators have been omitted here for clarity. It has occurred to the authors that this appendix forms an interesting testbed for browsers which claim to be HTML 4.0-compliant. We are happy for it to be copied and used in this way provided that the authors' names and the publisher are acknowledged.

Finally, this list of examples cannot be comprehensive, but we have tried to include specimens of almost every HTML element and many useful combinations of their attributes, using a wide range of HTML idioms. The obsolete <MENU> and <DIR> elements have been omitted on purpose. Appendix B is believed to be a complete list of *standard* HTML 4.0 tags and attributes.

HTML document

```
<HTML>                                                 <!--formally contains whole document-->
```

Comments

```
<!--remarks like this are ignored by the HTML 4.0 parser-->
```

Head

```
<HEAD>                                                 <!--often omitted-->
<BASE HREF="http://my.dir/docs/thisdoc.html">          <!--URL of document itself is mandatory-->
<ISINDEX prompt="Enter keywords separated by commas">  <!--document already has a searchable index-->
<LINK REL=ToC HREF="thistoc.html">                     <!--table of contents-->
<LINK REL=stylesheet HREF="ourstyle.dsssl">            <!--associated style sheet-->
<TITLE>Examples of HTML 4.0 tags</TITLE>               <!--the only mandatory element in HTML 4.0-->
<META NAME="generator" content="Ian's HTML formatter">
<STYLE>                                                <!--local style-sheet-->
    P        {color: green; font-style: italic; text-indent: 200}
    P.simple {color: black; font-style: bold}
    H1       {text-indent: 30}
    H2       {text-indent: 60}
    H3       {text-indent: 90}
</STYLE>
</HEAD>
```

Frameset

```
<!--divide up display area into rectangular containers--><!--must be directly after head-->
<FRAMESET ROWS="10%, 80%, 10%">                        <!--give first frame 10% of available height-->
   <FRAME SRC="ourlogo.html" SCROLLING="no">
   <FRAME SRC="maintext.html" NAME="main">
   <FRAMESET COLS="100, *">                            <!--nested frameset-->
     <FRAME SRC="top.html" NORESIZE>                   <!--exactly 100 pixels wide, not resizeable-->
     <FRAME SRC="menubar.html">                        <!--relative-sized, occupies rest of the width-->
   <FRAMESET>
<NOFRAMES>This web site is best seen with a frames-capable browser.</NOFRAMES>
</FRAMESET>
```

Body

```
<!--main part of HTML document-->                      <!--see Appendix D for colours-->
<BODY ID="wasp" BGCOLOR="#FCFCB0" TEXT=navy>           <!--dark blue text, pale yellow background-->
```

Divisions

```
<DIV CLASS=abstract ALIGN=center>This appendix is an aide memoire for HTML 4.0.</DIV>
```

Headings

```
<H1>GENERAL HEADING</H1>                  <!--most browsers use large fonts-->
<H2>MAJOR HEADING</H2>                     <!--to distinguish the heading levels-->
<H3>Lieutenant Heading</H3>
<H4>Sergeant Heading</H4>
<H5>Corporal Heading</H5>                  <!--some browsers may allow more levels...-->
<H6 CLASS="soldier">Private Heading</H6>   <!--but 6 is the lowest defined in the standard-->
```

Paragraph

```
<P ALIGN=center>This paragraph is centered.
<P CLASS=simple>This paragraph uses the 'simple' style.
<CENTER>Centered<BR>Text</CENTER>
```

Line break

```
line 1<BR>                                <!--unlike <P>, doesn't insert white space-->
line 2<BR CLEAR=left>                      <!--go down until left margin is free of floating images-->
```

Hypertext link

- To an index of documents on the Web:
  ```
  <A HREF="http://www.w3.org/"> Home of Short Acronyms </A>
  ```

- To a target section in same document, with inline graphic button:
  ```
  <A HREF="#anchorage">
     <IMG SRC="alaska.gif">
     Jump to Anchorage Section
  </A>
  ```

- Link target (somewhere in the document) for the above:
  ```
  <A NAME="anchorage">
  <DIV CLASS=section ID="anchorage">...</DIV>
  ```

- To a target section in a related document:
  ```
  <A HREF="hardware.html#req36">Requirement 36: Fail-Safe Data Storage</A>
  ```

- Link target in "hardware.html" for the above:
  ```
  <H3 ID="req36">Fail-Safe Data Storage</H3>
  <P>The system <B>shall</B> preserve all data in the event of failure.</P>
  ```

- Link to bitmap image file:
  ```
  <!--it is polite to warn users of large files-->
  <A HREF="flowers.gif"> Basket of Flowers <I>(184 kBytes)</I> </A>
  ```

- To bitmap image file with matching inline graphic icon used as button:
  ```
  <A HREF="kk.gif">
     <IMG SRC="kk_icon.gif">
     KaraKoram Sunset
     <I>(171 kBytes)</I>
  </A>
  ```

- To files identified by clicking on areas of a mapped image:

```
<MAP NAME="hotspots">
   <IMG SRC="diagrams/navigation.gif" USEMAP="#hotspots" ALT="Navigation Chart">
      <AREA SHAPE=rect COORDS="344 31 524 71" HREF=index.htm TITLE="Index">
      <AREA SHAPE=rect COORDS=" 96 84 276 124" HREF=roadmap.htm TITLE="Help">
      <AREA SHAPE=rect COORDS="608 80 788 120" HREF=latest.htm TITLE="News">
</MAP>
<NEXTID>                                          <!--next item on pre-planned path-->
```

Informational mark-up

```
<ABBR TITLE="WC">Fo</ABBR> (short for Foricas)        <!--abbreviation-->
<ANYM TITLE="European Member">MEP</ANYM>              <!--acronym (first letters of other words)-->
<EM>emphasized words</EM>                             <!--usually italicized-->
<CITE>Hamlet, act 3, scene 1, line 12</CITE>         <!--typically italicized too-->
<CITE>Sophie, for exceptional bravery in venturing unarmed   <!--no formal structure-->
   into a multi-user dungeon to rescue her son</CITE>
<STRONG>highlighted text</STRONG>                     <!--usually emboldened-->
<CODE>while not valid(input) do<BR>                   <!--usually fixed pitch-->
   getuser(input) </CODE>                             <!--but meaning is not same as PRE or TT-->
<VAR>starship_velocity</VAR>                          <!--computer program variable-->
<KBD>MYFILE.GIF ENTER</KBD>                           <!--to be typed in by user-->
<INS>Text Just Inserted</INS>
<DEL>Deleted Text</DEL>                               <!--useful in legal documents-->
<DFN>grok</DFN>, to get a mental grip on a concept   <!--defining instance of a term-->
<Q>Then he said                                       <!--language-sensitive quotation marks-->
   <Q>I do, I do</Q>                                  <!--alternating if nested,
and fainted.</Q>                                           e.g. "...'xxx'..." in UK-->
<SAMP CLASS="rawtext">##########</SAMP>              <!--literal sequence of characters-->
<SPAN STYLE=simple>This sentence is in the 'simple' style.</SPAN> This sentence is not.
```

Presentation mark-up

```
<B>Bold Face</B>
<I>Italics</I>
<STRIKE>Struck Through</STRIKE>
<U>Underline</U>
<TT>TeleType Font</TT>
<BIG>BIG LETTERS</BIG>
<SMALL>The Fine Print</SMALL>
<SUB>subscripted</SUB> below normal
<SUP>superscripted</SUP>above normal
<BDO DIR=rtl></BDO>                                   <!--override default direction of text-->

<FONT SIZE=2 COLOR="navy">size 2 typeface in Navy Blue</FONT>
<BASEFONT SIZE=4>basefont size set to 4, which is two sizes smaller than usual
<FONT SIZE=-1 FACE="Arial">one size smaller than current basefont,
   i.e. size 3, Arial if available</FONT>
```

Image

```
<!--see also HYPERTEXT LINK for more examples-->
<IMG SRC="whale.gif" HEIGHT=100 ALT="Whale" ISMAP>
<IMG SRC="banana.gif" ALIGN=right WIDTH=200 BORDER=3 VSPACE=10 HSPACE=10>
```

Unordered list

```
<UL TITLE="Reminders">
   <LI>Walk Dog
   <LI>Buy Milk
   <LI>Sew on Button
</UL>
<UL TYPE=square>                              <!--also=disc, =circle-->
   <LI>Conservative
   <LI>Traditionalist
   <LI TYPE=disc>Hippie
</UL>
```

Ordered list

```
<OL><B>Opening Decent Claret</B>
   <LI>Pull out the cork
   <LI>Let it breathe for an hour
   <LI>Pour gently.
</OL>
<OL TYPE=i START=5>                           <!--Roman numerals-->
   <LI>Centurion                             <!--TYPE=A for capitals, =a for lower case-->
   <LI>Legate                                <!--TYPE=i for small Roman, =I for large-->
   <LI>Gladiator
   <LI>Legionary
   <LI TYPE=I VALUE=10>Procurator
</OL>
```

Definition list

```
<DL STYLE="Dialogue"><B>Quite a Question</B>
   <DT>The Goddess Parvati
      <DD>Initiate me into the knowledge of the Guru.
   <DT>The God Shiva
      <DD>The Guru is not different from the conscious Self.
</DL>
```

Table

```
<TABLE BORDER=1 ID=scores WIDTH=25%>          <!--table width resizes with window-->
   <TR><TH>Name    <TH>Runs<TH>Wickets
   <TR><TD>Botham <TD>199 <TD>5              <!--table data cells-->
   <TR><TD>Gower  <TD>3    <TD>1
   <TR><TD>Gatting<TD>101 <TD>2
</TABLE>
```

```
<TABLE BORDER=5 CELLSPACING=5 CELLPADDING=25>    <!--thick frame, space between cells-->
   <TR>                                           <!--can also specify COL, COLGROUP-->
      <TD><IMG SRC="tony.gif">
      <TD><IMG SRC="paddy.gif">
      <TD><IMG SRC="john.gif">
   <TR>
      <TD BGCOLOR=red>Tony                         <!--table cells with own backgrounds-->
      <TD BGCOLOR=orange>Paddy
      <TD BGCOLOR=blue>John
   <TFOOT>
      <TR><TD COLSPAN=3 ALIGN=right
              NOWRAP>Legal, decent, honest, and truthful
</TABLE>
```

Horizontal rule

```
<HR>                   <!--default is a solid bar across full page-->
<HR CLASS=section>     <!--style sheet defines handling of this rule-->
<HR SIZE=3>            <!--line thickness-->
<HR WIDTH=300>         <!--width across page in pixels; also %-->
<HR ALIGN=center>      <!--also =left, =right-->
<HR NOSHADE>           <!--force solid bar-->
```

Preformatted text

```
<PRE ID="Georgia" style="Songsheet">
   "Sherman's dashing Yankee boys will never reach the coast"
      -- So the saucy rebels said, and 'twas a handsome boast.
   But they had forgot, alas, to reckon with the host.
      (refrain) As we were Marching Through Georgia.
</PRE>
```

Block quote

```
<BLOCKQUOTE ID="Panegyric" style="Prose">
Some of the evil of my tale may have been inherent in our circumstances.
For years we lived anyhow with one another in the naked desert, under the
indifferent heaven. By day the hot sun fermented us; and we were dizzied by
the beating wind. At night we were stained by dew, and shamed into pettiness
by the innumerable silences of stars. We were a self-centred army without
parade or gesture, devoted to freedom, the second of man's creeds, a purpose
so ravenous that it devoured all our strength, a hope so transcendent that
our earlier ambitions faded in its glare.<BR>
   <CITE TITLE=Lawrence><I>Introduction "Foundations of Revolt",<BR>
   from: The Seven Pillars of Wisdom, T.E.Lawrence, 1926</I>
   </CITE>
</BLOCKQUOTE>
```

Address

```
<ADDRESS ID="King Hal">
   Henry Tudor<BR>
   The White Tower<BR>
   London<BR>
   England<BR>
</ADDRESS>
```

Form

```
<!--obtain inputs from users-->
<FORM METHOD=post ACTION="http://www.hospital.gov/patients">
<P>Patient Number:                                    <!--text field-->
   <INPUT NAME="pid" SIZE=20>                          <!--visible size of field-->
<FIELDSET TITLE="Details">                             <!--draw box around related fields-->
   <CAPTION>Patient Details</CAPTION>                  <!--caption for fieldset box-->
   <P>Blood Group:                                     <!--radio buttons-->
      <INPUT NAME="bgp" TYPE=radio CHECKED>A           <!--default choice-->
      <INPUT NAME="bgp" TYPE=radio>B
      <INPUT NAME="bgp" TYPE=radio>AB
      <INPUT NAME="bgp" TYPE=radio>O
   <P>Allergies:                                       <!--checkboxes-->
      <INPUT TYPE=checkbox NAME="alg">pollen
      <INPUT TYPE=checkbox NAME="alg">house dust
      <INPUT TYPE=checkbox NAME="alg">tartrazine
   <P>Diet:                                            <!--select menu-->
      <SELECT NAME="foo">
         <OPTION SELECTED>omnivore                     <!--the default-->
         <OPTION>vegetarian
         <OPTION>kosher
         <OPTION>vegan
         <OPTION>no salt
      </SELECT>
</FIELDSET>
<P><TEXTAREA NAME="notes" ROWS=6 COLS=64>              <!--multi-line text area-->
   Please overtype this with any special notes.       <!--initial text in area-->
</TEXTAREA>                                            <!--end tag mandatory-->
<P>Existing Patient Record File (optional):           <!--file attachment-->
<INPUT NAME=rec TYPE=file ACCEPT="rec/*">             <!--accept only record files-->
<LABEL ACCESSKEY="U">User name to authorize access
   <INPUT NAME="username">
</LABEL>
<INPUT NAME=hhh TYPE=hidden> transaction prec 2       <!--hidden field for state info-->
<INPUT VALUE="Submit Patient Record" TYPE=submit>     <!--submit button-->
<INPUT TYPE=reset>                                     <!--reset button-->
</FORM>
```

Applet

```
<!--small Java Application Program to be loaded with Web Page-->
<APPLET CODEBASE="java/applets/" CODE="jigglytext" HEIGHT=200 WIDTH=300>
   <PARAM NAME="direction" VALUE="diagonal">          <!--parameters are arbitrary name/value pairs-->
   <PARAM NAME="speed" VALUE="3">
   <P>Your browser is not displaying the <B>Java</B> applet on this page.         <!--non-Java text-->
</APPLET>
```

Object

```
<!--multimedia object - image, sound, movie clip-->
<OBJECT DATA="objects/sounds/Kronos_Quartet.wav" ALT="The magical sound of Kronos">
   <PARAM NAME="tone" VALUE="normal">
   <P>Kronos demonstrate that serious modern music can be fun, and that rock can be serious.
   Have you ever heard Jimi Hendrix' <I>Purple Haze</I> set for Violins, Viola, and Cello?
</OBJECT>
```

Script

```
<HEAD><SCRIPT LANGUAGE="javascript">              <!--scripts can be in various languages-->
function runner() {                               <!--functions are defined in document head-->
   var run=new Array();
   run[0]="running0.jpg";      // populate array to create animation data
   run[1]="running1.jpg";
   run[2]="running2.jpg";
   run[3]="running3.jpg";
   run[4]="running4.jpg";
   run[5]="running5.jpg";

   for (j=0; j<25; j++)        // and run the animation
      for (i=0; i < 6; i++) {
         document.images[0].src=run[i];
         for (k=0; k<500; k++) l=1;
      }
}
<NOSCRIPT><p>Your browser is not displaying a Javascript in this page.</NOSCRIPT>
</SCRIPT></HEAD>
<IMG SRC=running5.jpg>         <!--resources such as images must be loaded: the script cannot load them-->
<FORM>
   <TD><INPUT TYPE=button VALUE="Run" onClick="runner()"> <!--button is a simple way to run script-->
</FORM>

<SCRIPT LANGUAGE="VBScript">                        <!--only works on Microsoft platforms-->
   <!--
   Today=inputbox("Enter today's date")
   Today=cdate(Today)
   Tomorrow=Today+1
   document.write(Tomorrow)
   //-->
</SCRIPT>
```

End of document

```
</BODY></HTML>                              <!--formal end of HTML doc-->
```

Appendix B
ALPHABETICAL LIST OF HTML 4 TAGS

This is a list of elements in HTML 4 along with attributes. It is written in a concise manner so that you can read it quickly. Cross-references to other glossary entries are printed in **boldface** type. References in angle brackets <...> are HTML tags.

Appendix A gives examples of the tags in this list. Each entry states:

What the element does – its function in the document

The attributes for that element. We generally give a hint as to possible attribute values, for example, SRC=URL meaning that the **SRC** attribute takes as its value a URL. Alternative attribute values are listed with a vertical bar, e.g., left|right. The HTML 4 standard attributes are **ID**, **CLASS**, **STYLE**, **LANG**, and **DIR**.

What it can contain:

- **Contains text** – the element has a start and end tag. Between the two you can write any text string or text-level element such as: <B>this is bold</B>.

- **Contains blocks** – you can include any text, structured with any elements that break the text into blocks: <P>, <PRE>, <DIV>, <CENTER>, <BLOCKQUOTE>, <HR>, lists, forms, fieldsets, tables.

- **Contains bodytext** – you can include text, blocks, headings such as <H2>, and <ADDRESS>.

- **Empty** – the element has no end tag and cannot contain other mark-up in the form of HTML elements. It appears as a start tag only, possibly with attributes, e.g., <HR WIDTH=75%>.

- **Special cases** are listed explicitly, e.g., <FRAMESET> can optionally contain <NOFRAMES>.

<!-- -->

Comment, e.g. `<!-- an HTML comment -->`.
Comments can be seen in the HTML source
which users can view if they wish, but not
when pages are displayed normally by
browsers. Empty. No attributes.

<A>

Hypertext link anchor: start has `HREF=URL`,
end may have `NAME=ID` for names link end.
Contains text. Attributes are:
`NAME=ANCHORNAME`, `HREF=URL`, `REL` and `REV` (for
forward and reverse links), `TITLE` (for an
advisory title string), `ACCESSKEY` (a short-cut
key), `SHAPE`, `COORDS` (for use with `OBJECT`
shapes), `TABINDEX` (position in tabbing order),
`NOTAB` (exclusion from tabbing order),
`onClick`, `onMouseOver`, `onMouseOut` (all for
scripting). Also has standard HTML 4
attributes.

<ADDRESS>

Authorship and contact details for the current
document. Contains text or `<P>` elements. Has
standard HTML 4 attributes, but not `TITLE`.

<ACRONYM>

Acronym, word made up of initial letters of
other words. Contains text. Has standard
HTML 4 attributes, plus `TITLE`.

<APPLET>

This tag is supported by all Java-enabled
browsers. Applet resources (including their
classes) are normally loaded relative to the
document URL or `<BASE>` element if it is
defined. The `CODEBASE` attribute is used to
change this default behavior. If the `CODEBASE`
attribute is defined, then it specifies a
different location to find applet resources.
The value can be an absolute URL or a
relative URL. The absolute URL is used as is
without modification and is not affected by
the document's `<BASE>` element. When the
`CODEBASE` attribute is relative, then it is

relative to the document URL or `<BASE>` tag
if defined. `<TEXTFLOW>` avoids the problems
with SGML mixed content. It can always be
omitted *except* when the `APPLET` element does
not have any content. White space, comments
and `PARAM` elements do not count as content
for this purpose. `TEXTFLOW` was introduced
into the DTD to satisfy SGML parsers, but it
is ignored by current Web browsers.

Attributes include the standard HTML 4
attributes including `TITLE`. Also:
`CODEBASE=URL` (the code base),
`CODE=CLASS_FILE` (required),
`NAME=APPLET_NAME` (name of applet),
`ALT=TEXT_ALTERNATIVE` (for display in place
of applet), `ALIGN` (vertical or horizontal
alignment), `HEIGHT=PIXELS`, `WIDTH=PIXELS`
(suggested height and width in pixels),
`HSPACE=PIXELS`, `VSPACE=PIXELS`
(horizontal and vertical gutters),
`DOWNLOAD=IMAGE_SEQ_ NUMBER` (image
download order).

<AREA>

Shaped areas within mapped images (`<MAP>`)
acting as hypertext links. Empty. Attributes
are `SHAPE` (the shape of the region), `COORDS`
(always needed except for `SHAPE=DEFAULT`),
`HREF` (region acting as hypertext link), `NOHREF`
(a region that has no action), `TITLE` (advisory
title string for balloon help), `ALT` (description
for text-only browsers), `TABINDEX` (position in
tabbing order), `NOTAB` (exclude from tabbing
order), `onClick`, `onMouseOver`, `onMouseOut`.
Has standard HTML 4 attributes, plus
`TITLE`.

<B>

Bold face. Contains text. Has standard HTML
4 attributes, plus `TITLE`.

<BASE>

In document head, the URL of the HTML
document itself to form the basis of other
URLs relative to it. Empty. Has `HREF` attribute
which is mandatory.

<BASEFONT> (This tag is now deprecated)

Sets reference size of font for normal text. Offsets can be set with <FONT>. Empty. Required attribute SIZE=BASEFONTSIZE.

<BDO>

Bi-directional override for use with left-to-right and right-to-left marks. Contains text. Attributes: LANG=LANG_NAME and DIR=LTR|RTL.

<BIG>

Larger font than usual. Contains text. Has standard HTML 4 attributes, plus TITLE.

<BODY>

The whole body of an HTML document, i.e., everything except the <HEAD>. Can be given attributes for BACKGROUND (tiled) image, BGCOLOR as well as LINK, VLINK, ALINK and TEXT colors e.g., TEXT=NAVY. Contains bodytext (headings, text, blocks, and <ADDRESS>). Has standard HTML 4 attributes, but not TITLE.

Further attributes are onLoad and onUnload which are involved in scripting.

<BLOCKQUOTE>

Block quote, for sizeable chunks of quoted text. Contains bodytext. Has standard HTML 4 attributes, plus TITLE.

**
**

Forced line break within a paragraph (*see also* <P>). Empty. Can specify textflow with CLEAR=LEFT, RIGHT, ALL. Has standard HTML 4 attributes, but not TITLE.

<CENTER> (This tag is now deprecated)

Centers everything inside it between left and right margins. Short for <DIV ALIGN=CENTER>. Contains bodytext.

<CITE>

Citation such as a reference to a scientific paper. Contains text. Has standard HTML 4 attributes, plus TITLE.

<CODE>

Specimen of computer program code (*see also* <VAR>). Contains text. Has standard HTML 4 attributes, plus TITLE.

<COL>

Column specification, for use within a <TABLE> element only. Empty. Attributes: can align as for <TD>; WIDTH=PIXELS or WIDTH=0.5* (etc.), for relative widths of columns; SPAN= NO_OF_COLS.

<COLGROUP>

Column group, for use within a <TABLE> element only. Contains <COL> elements. Attributes as for <COL>.

<DD>

Definition of a <DT> item within a <DL> list. Contains text or blocks. Has standard HTML 4 attributes, but not TITLE.

<DEL>

Deleted characters, usually struck through with a horizontal line. Contains text. Has standard HTML 4 attributes, plus TITLE.

<DFN>

Definition. Contains text. Has standard HTML 4 attributes, plus TITLE.

<DIR> (This tag is now obsolete)

Directory list. Included in standard for historical reasons and not in widespread use.

<DIV>

HTML division to show document structure. Notice that headings such as <H3> do not automatically create divisions. Contains bodytext. Can justify contents e.g., ALIGN=CENTER. Has standard HTML 4 attributes, plus TITLE.

`<DL>`

Definition list. Contains `<DT>` terms and `<DD>` definitions, normally paired. Attributes include `<COMPACT>`. Has standard HTML 4 attributes, but not `TITLE`.

`<DT>`

Term to be defined by a `<DD>` item within a `<DL>` list. Contains text. Has standard HTML 4 attributes, plus `TITLE`.

`<EM>`

Emphasized characters, usually italicized. Contains text. Has standard HTML 4 attributes, plus `TITLE`.

`<FIELDSET>`

Contains (and draws a border around) a set of `<FORM>` fields related in meaning, optionally with a `<CAPTION>`. Attributes are `TITLE= NAME_OF_FIELDSET` and the standard HTML 4 attributes.

`<FONT>` (This tag is now deprecated)

Font size, either absolute or relative to `<BASEFONT>`. Preferred way of specifying fonts is with class attribute and a style sheet. Contains text. Attributes are `SIZE=+NUMBER| -NUMBER`, `COLOR=COLORNAME|#RRGGBB`.

`<FORM>`

Form to be completed by the user. Various kinds of form-input fields are defined with the `INPUT`, `TEXTAREA`, `SELECT`, and `OPTION` elements. Contains bodytext (form fields with surrounding labels, often structured with `TABLE` or `LIST` elements). Required attribute `ACTION=URL`. Other attributes are: `METHOD` (`get|post`) see HTTP specification; `ENCTYPE` (Content-Type) 'application/x-www-form-urlencoded', `onSubmit` (associated with scripting), `TARGET` (where to render result), `ACCEPT-CHARSET` (list of supported charsets). Also the standard HTML 4 attributes, plus `TITLE`.

`<FRAME>`

Frame to occupy a rectangular part of the browser's viewing area, resizing dynamically, and containing the document referenced in a URL. Use of `NAME` attribute permits documents in other frames to target linked documents to the named frame. Empty. Attributes include: `NAME` (name of frame for targeting), `SRC` (source of frame content), `FRAMEBORDER` (request frame separators), `MARGINWIDTH` (margin width in pixels), `MARGINHEIGHT` (margin height in pixels), and `NORESIZE` (allows users to resize frames).

`<FRAMESET>`

HTML structure appearing immediately after the document head in place of the document `<BODY>` and containing one or more `<FRAME>` elements, creating a display as a set of rectangular panels in place of a single viewing area. Framesets may be nested. Can also contain a `<NOFRAMES>` element. Attributes indicate how to share the available space into rows and/or columns, e.g., `ROWS="10%,80%,10%"`, `COLS="*,3*,2*"`. Also has `onLoad` and `onUnload` (associated with scripting).

`<HEAD>`

HTML document header material. Must include `<TITLE>`; can also contain the elements `<ISINDEX>`, `<BASE>`, `<SCRIPT>`, `<STYLE>`, `<META>`, `<LINK>`. Has a single attribute, `PROFILE` for specifying a URL pointing to a list for interpreting meaning of `LINK` and `META` names.

`<H1>...<H6>`

HTML heading. Levels 1 through 6 are defined (e.g. `<H6>`); some browsers permit lower levels (7, 8, 9, and so on) also. Contains text. Has standard HTML 4 attributes, plus `TITLE`.

`<HR>`

Horizontal rule. Empty. Has the following attributes: `ALIGN` (`left`|`right`|`center`), `NOSHADE`, `SIZE` (in pixels to specify the width of the rule), `WIDTH` (to specify width across the page), as well as `CLASS` and `STYLE`.

`<HTML>`

Records version of HTML expected for a document. Formally contains the entire document, consisting of the `<HEAD>` followed by the `<BODY>`. Start and end tags optional.

`<I>`

Italics. Contains text. Has standard HTML 4 attributes, plus `TITLE`.

`<IMG>`

Image; must be qualified by 'SRC=...' to indicate the file containing the (GIF, JPEG, and so on) image to display. Empty. Attributes are `SRC=URL` (required), `ALT=TEXT_ALTERNATIVE`, `ALIGN=TOP`|`MIDDLE`|`BOTTOM`|`LEFT`|`RIGHT` (left and right cause float to margin and text wrapping), `HEIGHT=PIXELS`, `WIDTH=PIXELS`, `BORDER=PIXELS`, `HSPACE=PIXELS`, `VSPACE=PIXELS`, `USEMAP` (use `<MAP>`), `ISMAP` (use map on server), `TITLE`. Also has the standard attributes `ID`, `CLASS` and `LANG`.

`<INPUT>`

Field such as input text, radio button or checkbox for use within `<FORM>`. Effect is to return a name, value pair e.g., 'HEIGHT=TALL'. Empty. Attributes include: the standard HTML 4 attributes, plus `TITLE`, `TYPE=TEXT`|`PASSWORD`|`CHECKBOX`|`RADIO`|`SUBMIT`|`RESET`|`FILE`|`HIDDEN`|`IMAGE`|`BUTTON` (type of widget), `NAME=NAME_TO_BE_RETURNED_WITH_VALUE`, `TITLE=NAME_OF_FIELD`, `CHECKED` (pre-selected item for radio or checkbox), `SIZE=FIELDSIZE`, `MAXLENGTH=NUMBER`, `SRC=URL` (for background image), `ALIGN=TOP`|`MIDDLE`|`BOTTOM`|`LEFT`|`RIGHT` (image alignment), `TABINDEX=NUMBER`, `NOTAB` (tabbing order), `onClick`,

`onFocus`, `onBlur`, `onSelect`, `onChange` (associated with scripting).

`<INS>`

Words recently or provisionally inserted (*see also* `<DEL>`). Contains text. Has standard HTML 4 attributes, plus `TITLE`.

`<ISINDEX>`

In document head, indicates that a searchable index to the contents of the HTML page or related material already exists on the server, and provides an input field and button to start a search on the server. It does not create such an index. Netscape allows a customized prompt for the field. Empty.

`<KBD>`

Keyboard input: denotes text to be typed in by the user. Often a typewriter font such as Courier. Contains text. Has standard HTML 4 attributes, plus `TITLE`.

`<LABEL>`

Clickable piece of text within a `<FORM>`, for instance for a radio button. Contains text. Attributes include `FORM=ID_REFERENCE` (matches `ID` of a field), `ACCESSKEY=CHAR`, `TITLE`, `onClick`, `onFocus`, `onBlur`, `DISABLED` (control is unavailable in this context). Has standard HTML 4 attributes, plus `TITLE`.

`<LEGEND>`

Text caption to head a `<FIELDSET>`. Contains text.

`<LI>`

List item within an `<OL>` or `<UL>` list. Contains text or blocks. Attributes are: (list item style), value (reset sequence number). Has standard HTML 4 attributes, plus `TITLE`.

`<LINK>`

`LINK` has been part of HTML since the early days, although few browsers as yet take advantage of it. Relationship values can be used in principle:

For document-specific toolbars/menus when used with the LINK element in document head

To link to a separate style sheet (REL=STYLESHEET)

To link to a script (REL=SCRIPT)

By stylesheets to control how collections of HTML nodes are rendered into printed documents

To link to a printable version of this document; for example, a PostScript or PDF version.

Attributes are standard HTML 4 attributes, plus TITLE, also: HREF, REL (forward link types), REV (reverse link types), TYPE (advisory Internet content type), MEDIA (for rendering on these media), TARGET (where to render linked resource).

<MAP>

Client-side image map. Contains <AREA> elements. Has a single attribute, NAME.

<MENU>

Included in HTML 4 for historical reasons and not widely supported. Menu list. Contains text. Attributes include COMPACT.

<META>

In document head, supply name and value pairs for any purpose. Empty. Attributes are LANG and DIR for use with content string, HTTP-EQUIV (HTTP response header name), NAME (meta information name), CONTENT (associated information required) and SCHEME.

<NEXTID>

Identifier of the next item in a pre-planned path through a document. Empty.

<NOFRAMES>

Within a <FRAMESET>, text for use by browsers not capable of frames. Contains text.

<NOSCRIPT>

Within a <SCRIPT>, text for use by browsers not capable of scripts. Contains text.

<OBJECT>

Multimedia object of various possible kinds; for example, a static image, a sound, a movie clip. Contains bodytext. May contain the PARAM element. Attributes are as follows:

Has standard HTML 4 attributes, plus TITLE. It also has the following:

DECLARE – declare but do not instantiate flag

CLASSID – identifies an implementation

CODEBASE=URL – some systems need an additional URL

DATA=URL – reference to object's data

TYPE – Internet content type for data

CODETYPE – Internet content type for code

STANDBY – message to show while loading

ALIGN – positioning inside document

HEIGHT – suggested height

WIDTH – suggested width

BORDER – suggested link border width

HSPACE – suggested horizontal gutter

VSPACE – suggested vertical gutter

USEMAP – reference to image map

SHAPES – object has shaped hypertext links

NAME – submit as part of form

ALT – textual alternative

TABINDEX – position in tabbing order

<OL>

Ordered list; a list numbered in some way, by default in arabic numerals (*see also* <UL>). Contains <LI> list items. Attributes include TYPE=DISC|SQUARE|CIRCLE, START=NUMBER, COMPACT. Has standard HTML 4 attributes, plus TITLE.

<OPTION>

Menu item within a <SELECT> list inside a <FORM>). Contains text strings. Attributes are SELECTED, DISABLED (control is unavailable in this context), VALUE. Has standard HTML 4 attributes, plus TITLE.

`<P>`

Paragraph. Contains text. End tag usually omitted. Attributes are `ALIGN`, standard HTML 4 attributes, plus `TITLE`.

`<PARAM>`

Named property with a value, for use in applets (*see also* `OBJECT`). Empty. Attributes are as follows: `NAME` (required: property name), `VALUE` (property value), `VALUETYPE` (DATA| REF|OBJECT) (how to interpret value), `TYPE` (Internet media type).

`<PRE>`

Pre-formatted text; instructs browser to accept any spaces and carriage returns literally so as to copy the layout as closely as possible. Normally, the result is in a fixed-pitch font. Contains literal pre-formatted text without images or font-size changes. Has standard HTML 4 attributes, plus `TITLE`.

`<Q>`

Inline quotation. Symbols used are language-dependent. Contains text. Attributes are `HREF` (the URL for the source of the quotation) and the standard HTML 4 attributes, plus `TITLE`.

`<SAMP>`

Symbols to be displayed literally instead of being interpreted. Contains literal text. Has standard HTML 4 attributes, plus `TITLE`.

`<SCRIPT>`

In document head, script statements, typically in Java, forming a small application program able to run on any suitable browser regardless of platform, and taking `<PARAM>` element values as parameters. Attributes are: `TYPE` (Internet content type for script language), `LANGUAGE` (predefined script language name), `SRC` (URL for an external script).

`<SELECT>`

Menu for selection from a predefined list of option items, within a `FORM`. Contains any number of `<OPTION>` elements. Attributes include `NAME` (required), `SIZE=NUMBER`, `MULTIPLE`, `TITLE`, `TABINDEX`, `DISABLED`, `onFocus`, `onBlur`, `onChange`.

`<SMALL>`

Smaller font than usual. Contains text. Has standard HTML 4 attributes, plus `TITLE`.

`<SPAN>`

Use to achieve a local stylistic or language effect within a paragraph or other block-level element. Contains text. Has standard HTML 4 attributes, plus `TITLE`.

`<STRIKE>` or `<S>` (This tag is now deprecated)

Strike-through text. Contains text. Has standard HTML 4 attributes, plus `TITLE`.

`<STRONG>`

Strongly emphasized (often boldface). Contains text. Has standard HTML 4 attributes, plus `TITLE`.

`<STYLE>`

In head or body, a description of styles to apply to document elements. Attributes are `LANG` and `DIR` – for use with title string, `TYPE` (Internet content type for style language), `MEDIA` (designed for use with these media), and `TITLE` (advisory title for this style).

`<SUB>`

Subscripted text. Contains text. Has standard HTML 4 attributes, plus `TITLE`.

`<SUP>`

Superscripted text. Contains text. Has standard HTML 4 attributes, plus `TITLE`.

`<TABLE>`

Table, structuring its contents into rectangular cells. Tables contain an optional `<CAPTION>`, `<TR>` table rows which in turn contain `<TH>` table header cells and/or `<TD>` table data cells. Borders may be drawn; cells may be separated by `CELLPADDING` or `CELLSPACING` attributes. Rows may be grouped with `<THEAD>`, `<TBODY>`, `<TFOOT>`. Columns may be identified with `<COL>` and grouped with `<COLGROUP>`. Display may be accelerated by hinting to the browser the width of the table and the number of columns in advance, as attributes.

`TITLE` – title for table
`ALIGN=LEFT|CENTER|RIGHT` – table position relative to window
`BGCOLOR` – background color for cells
`WIDTH` – table width relative to window
`COLS` – used for immediate display mode
`BORDER=VOID|ABOVE|BELOW|HSIDES|LHS|RHS| VSIDES|BOX|BORDER` – controls frame width around table
`FRAME` – which parts of table frame to include
`RULES` – rulings between rows and cols
`CELLSPACING` – spacing between cells, in pixels
`CELLPADDING` – spacing within cells, in pixels

`<TBODY>`

Optionally groups some table rows into one or more table bodies. Contains `<TR>` elements. End tag usually omitted.

`<TD>`

Ordinary `<TABLE>` data cell. Contains bodytext. End tag usually omitted. Attributes as follows: `AXIS` (defaults to cell content), `AXES` (list of axis names), `NOWRAP` (suppress word wrap), `BGCOLOR` (cell background color), `ROWSPAN` (number of rows spanned by cell), `COLSPAN` (number of cols spanned by cell), `HALIGN` (horizontal alignment in cells), `VALIGN` (vertical alignment in cells). Alignment can be: `HALIGN=LEFT|CENTER|RIGHT|JUSTIFY|CHAR` and/or `VALIGN=TOP|MIDDLE|BOTTOM| BASELINE`. Has standard HTML 4 attributes, plus `TITLE`.

`<TEXTAREA>`

Multi-line text field for use within `<FORM>`. Contains text strings. Required attributes are `NAME=NAME_OF_TEXTAREA`, `ROWS=NUMBER`, `COLS=NUMBER`. Other attributes include `TITLE`, `TABINDEX`, `NOTAB`, `onFocus`, `onBlur`, `onSelect`, `onChange`, `DISABLED` and `READONLY`. Has standard HTML 4 attributes, plus `TITLE`.

`<TFOOT>`

Groups some table rows into a single optional table footer. Has standard HTML 4 attributes, plus `TITLE`. Also: `HALIGN` (horizontal alignment in cells) and `VALIGN` (vertical alignment in cells).

`<THEAD>`

Groups some table rows into a single optional table header. Contains `<TR>` elements. End tag usually omitted. Attributes as for `<TFOOT>`.

`<TH>`

Table header cell. Contains bodytext. End tag usually omitted. Can align contents, attributes as in `<TD>`.

`<TITLE>`

In document head, records the title of the document to be displayed in the browser's title bar or page header. Often used as source of keywords when creating indices to HTML pages. Contains a text string (not part of the flow of document text). Mandatory.

`<TR>`

Table row within a `<TABLE>`. Contains `<TH>` or `<TD>` elements. Can align contents of all cells in row, attributes as in `<TD>`. End tag usually omitted.

<TT>

Teletype: a fixed-pitch font, usually Courier. Contains text. Has standard HTML 4 attributes, plus TITLE.

<U>

Underlined (if the display device is capable of doing that). Contains text. Has standard HTML 4 attributes, plus TITLE.

<UL>

Unordered list; a list of items bulleted in some way (*see also* <OL>). Contains <LI>.

Attributes are standard HTML 4 attributes, plus TITLE, COMPACT, and also TYPE to specify the type of bullet (DISC|SQUARE|CIRCLE).

<VAR>

Program variable (placeholder) within fragment of computer program (*see also* <CMD>). Contains text. Has standard HTML 4 attributes, plus TITLE.

Appendix C
CHARACTERS

HTML allows you to refer to all Latin-1 characters by their numbers as listed here, bracketed by & ; symbols. For example, you can get the Cent sign ¢ by inserting the string &162; into your text.

The characters which are in the Added Latin-1 Entities (ISO 8879:1986) *also* have mnemonic HTML names, which you will probably find more convenient than their numeric references. For example

Á for Á instead of &192; and

á for á instead of &224;

Notice that (as this example illustrates) the HTML names are case sensitive. Most characters from 32 to 126 can simply be typed in directly, though spaces, tabs and line breaks may be ignored by browsers. Special care is needed with angle brackets < > (their codes are < >) since if inserted literally they are interpreted as tag boundaries.

Char	English name	Latin-1	HTML
	Characters 0–8 are unused.		
	Horizontal tab	9	(normally set and use tabs with `<TAB>`)
	Line feed	10	(normally use `<P>` or ` `)
	Characters 11–31 are unused.		
	Space	32	
!	Exclamation mark	33	
"	Quotation mark	34	`&quot;`
#	Number sign	35	
$	Dollar sign	36	
%	Per cent sign	37	
&	Ampersand	38	`&amp;`
'	Apostrophe	39	
(	Left parenthesis	40	
)	Right parenthesis	41	
*	Asterisk	42	
+	Plus sign	43	
,	Comma	44	
-	Hyphen	45	
.	Period (full stop)	46	
/	Solidus (slash)	47	
0	*Digits*	48	
1		49	
2		50	
3		51	
4		52	
5		53	
6		54	
7		55	
8		56	
9		57	
:	Colon	58	
;	Semicolon	59	
<	Less than	60	`&lt;` useful when *explaining* HTML
=	Equals sign	61	
>	Greater than	62	`&gt;` useful when *explaining* HTML
?	Question mark	63	
@	Commercial at	64	
A	*Upper case letters*	65	
B		66	
C		67	
D		68	
E		69	
F		70	
G		71	
H		72	
I		73	
J		74	

Char	English name	Latin-1	HTML
K		75	
L		76	
M		77	
N		78	
O		79	
P		80	
Q		81	
R		82	
S		83	
T		84	
U		85	
V		86	
W		87	
X		88	
Y		89	
Z		90	
[	Left square bracket	91	
\	Reverse solidus	92	
]	Right square bracket	93	
^	Circumflex	94	
_	Horizontal bar	95	
`	Grave accent	96	
a	*Lower case letters*	97	
b		98	
c		99	
d		100	
e		101	
f		102	
g		103	
h		104	
i		105	
j		106	
k		107	
l		108	
m		109	
n		110	
o		111	
p		112	
q		113	
r		114	
s		115	
t		116	
u		117	
v		118	
w		119	
x		120	
y		121	
z		122	

Char	English name	Latin-1	HTML
{	Left curly brace	123	
|	Vertical bar	124	
}	Right curly brace	125	
~	Tilde	126	

Characters 127–160 are unused.

Char	English name	Latin-1	HTML
¡	Inverted exclamation	161	
¢	Cent	162	
£	Pound	163	
¤	Currency	164	
¥	Yen	165	
¦	Broken vertical	166	
§	Section sign	167	
¨	Umlaut/diaeresis	168	
©	Copyright	169	©
ª	Feminine	170	
«	Left angle quote	171	
¬	Not sign	172	
-	Hyphen	173	(­ denotes a soft hyphen)
®	Reg. trade mark	174	®
¯	Macron	175	
°	Degrees	176	
±	Plus/Minus	177	
²	Superscript 2	178	
³	Superscript 3	179	
´	Acute accent	180	
µ	Micron	181	
¶	Paragraph sign	182	
·	Middle dot	183	
¸	Cedilla	184	
¹	Superscript 1	185	
º	Masculine	186	
»	Right angle quote	187	
¼	One quarter	188	
½	One half	189	
¾	Three quarters	190	
¿	Inverted question mark	191	
Á	A Acute	192	Á
À	A Grave	193	À
Â	A Circumflex	194	Â
Ã	A Tilde	195	Ã
Ä	A Diaeresis	196	Ä
Å	A Ring	197	Å
Æ	AE Diphthong	198	Æ
Ç	C Cedilla	199	Ç
É	E Acute	200	É
È	E Grave	201	È
Ê	E Circumflex	202	Ê

Char	English name	Latin-1	HTML
Ë	E Diaeresis	203	Ë
Í	I Acute	204	Í
Ì	I Grave	205	Ì
Î	I Circumflex	206	Î
Ï	I Diaeresis	207	Ï
Ð	Icelandic eth	208	Ð
Ñ	N Tilde	209	Ñ
Ó	O Acute	210	Ó
Ò	O Grave	211	Ò
Ô	O Circumflex	212	Ô
Õ	O Tilde	213	Õ
Ö	O Diaeresis	214	Ö
×	Multiplication	215	
Ø	O Slash	216	Ø
Ú	U Acute	217	Ú
Ù	U Grave	218	Ù
Û	U Circumflex	219	Û
Ü	U Diaeresis	220	Ü
Ý	Y Acute	221	Ý
Þ	Icelandic Thorn	222	Þ
ß	Small sharp S	223	ß (sz ligature)
á	a Acute	224	á
à	a Grave	225	à
â	a Circumflex	226	â
ã	a Tilde	227	ã
ä	a Diaeresis	228	ä
å	a Ring	229	å
æ	ae Diphthong	230	æ
ç	c Cedilla	231	ç
é	e Acute	232	é
è	e Grave	233	è
ê	e Circumflex	234	ê
ë	e Diaeresis	235	ë
í	i Acute	236	í
ì	i Grave	237	ì
î	i Circumflex	238	î
ï	i Diaeresis	239	ï
ð	Icelandic eth	240	ð
ñ	n Tilde	241	ñ
ò	o Grave	242	ò
ó	o Acute	243	ó
ô	o Circumflex	244	ô
õ	o Tilde	245	õ
ö	o Diaeresis	246	ö
÷	Division	247	
ø	o Slash	248	ø
ú	u Acute	249	ú
ù	u Grave	250	ù

Char	English name	Latin-1	HTML
û	u Circumflex	251	`&ucirc;`
ü	u Diaeresis	252	`&uuml;`
ý	y Acute	253	`&yacute;`
þ	Icelandic thorn	254	`&eth;`
ÿ	y Diaeresis	255	`&yuml;`

Entities for special symbols (added to Latin-1 for HTML/EN)

English name	HTML
Em space	` :`
En space	` `
Em dash	`&mdash;`
En dash	`&ndash;`
Non-breaking space	` `
Soft hyphen	`&shy;`
Copyright sign	`&copy;`
Trade mark sign	`&trade;`
Registered sign	`&reg;`

Entities added in HTML 4 to support language directionality

English name	HTML	
Thin space (1/6 em)	` `	
Zero width non-joiner	`&zwnj;`	forces gap where join expected
Zero width joiner	`&zwj;`	forces join where gap expected
Left-to-right mark	`&ltr;`	
Right-to-left mark	`&rtl;`	

Appendix D
HOW TO NAME COLORS

HTML names colors in two quite different ways. A few familiar colors are given English names; all the rest are described in a way that looks very technical, but is in fact quite easy to understand and use with a little practice.

The description uses the idea of organizing colors by the relative amounts of the three basic colors of light (such as of the beams in a television monitor tube) which you would need to mix to make up each displayed color. The colors are arranged in what is called the Red-Green-Blue color space, or sRGB for short. This is in contrast to competing (and equally useful) schemes which use the perhaps less familiar combination of hue, saturation, and luminance to identify colors.

Colors are given in the sRGB color space as hexadecimal numbers, or as one of the 16 color names listed below. These were originally picked as being those supported by the Windows VGA palette. Each pair of colors, such as Green and Lime, consists of one dark and one light version of the same hue. This can be seen by comparing their RGB values.

The sRGB colors are written "#" followed by two hexadecimal digits for each of the red, green, and blue components respectively. Hexadecimal digits range through the values:

0, 1, 2, 3, 4, 5, 6, 7, 8, 9, A, B, C, D, E, F.

(It is just like decimals from 0 to 9, but you need 16 fingers to count on!) 00 is therefore the smallest component value, FF the largest. If you are familiar with mixing paints, the combinations will seem counter-intuitive, as you are mixing lights, which works the opposite way. So, the maximum of red gives you the **brightest** possible red, not the darkest. Similarly, the maximum (FFFFFF) of all three components gives you the brightest of all possible mixtures of colored lights, white. Once you are used to this idea, you can work out what a desired color should be in sRGB, but it is easier to use the palette of a graphics editor such as JASC's PaintShop Pro® to mix the color, and then to copy down its component values.

Predefined color names with equivalent sRGB values

```
Black  ="#000000"          Green ="#008000"
Silver ="#C0C0C0"          Lime  ="#00FF00"

Gray   ="#808080"          Olive ="#808000"
White  ="#FFFFFF"          Yellow="#FFFF00"

Maroon ="#800000"          Navy  ="#000080"
Red    ="#FF0000"          Blue  ="#0000FF"

Purple ="#800080"          Teal  ="#008080"
Fuchsia="#FF00FF"          Aqua  ="#00FFFF"
```

Try experimenting with values around these fixed points and see what you get. Notice, for instance, that Navy is darker than Blue as its values are closer to 000000. If you want an even darker blue-black, you could use #000040, halfway between Navy and Black. At the other end of the scale, a bright sky-blue can be obtained with #DDDFF, intermediate between Blue and White.

Color-capable HTML elements

Colors can be specified in the following attributes of the BODY element:

```
BGCOLOR    document's background color
TEXT       document's text color
LINK       color of unvisited hypertext links
VLINK      color of visited hypertext links
ALINK      color of hypertext links at the moment they are clicked on.
```

For example:

```
<BODY BGCOLOR=white
      TEXT  =black
      LINK  =red
      VLINK =maroon
      ALINK =fuchsia>
```

Colors can be assigned to text using the **color** attribute of the BASEFONT and FONT elements:

```
<BASEFONT COLOR=fuchsia   SIZE=4>
<BASEFONT COLOR="#CC0000" SIZE=5>

<FONT     COLOR=green    >
<FONT     COLOR="#C0FFC0">
```

Colors can also be specified in a few other contexts, for example within table cells:

```
<TD BGCOLOR=red>          <!-- a cell's background color -->
```

Finally, colors can be specified in style sheets:

```
<STYLE>                   <!-- embedded style sheet -->
   DD {COLOR    : green;
       FONT-STYLE: italic}
</STYLE>
```

Appendix E
URL SUFFIXES

Who's at that URL? This appendix lists the three-letter suffix codes which are generally used. We can't help you with the rest of the URL, but luckily most companies and organizations are only too happy to announce themselves, so you shouldn't have too much trouble guessing whose pages are at www.microsoft.com, for instance. As you can see from the list, the codes mainly distinguish American institutions.

.com   American or international commercial venture (but many non-US firms use '.co.xx' where xx is their country code)

.edu   American educational institution (in contrast, non-US ones mostly use '.ac.xx')

.gov   American government agency

.int   International

.mil   American military (for example, US Navy)

.net   Network facilities company

.org   Non-profit organization (mostly American)

The International Ad Hoc Committee (IAHC) which is revising the Internet's Domain Name System (the DNS your browser uses to look up real addresses from URLs) has proposed (early 1997) to add the following suffixes:

.arts   Artistic, cultural and entertainment website

.firm   Business firm of any kind (*apparently a rival to '.com'*)

.info   Information service

.nom   Personal (nominal) website

.rec   Recreational organization

.store Store offering goods for purchase on the Web

.web   Web activity group

Appendix F
COUNTRY CODES

Addresses in URLs that do not use organization codes generally end with a two-letter country code. For example, the company `easynet.co.uk` is seen to be based in the United Kingdom. The country codes in common use are listed here. Country codes can also be used in Language Codes, such as `en.uk`, as described in Appendix G.

am	Armenia	fi	Finland
ar	Argentina	fr	France
at	Austria	gb	Great Britain
au	Australia		(most Brits use 'uk')
be	Belgium	gr	Greece
bm	Bermuda	hk	Hong Kong
br	Brazil	hr	Croatia (Hrvatska)
ca	Canada	hu	Hungary
ch	Switzerland	id	Indonesia
cl	Chile	ie	Ireland
cn	China	il	Israel
co	Colombia	in	India
cr	Costa Rica	is	Iceland
cz	Czech Republic	it	Italy
de	Germany	jm	Jamaica
dk	Denmark	jp	Japan
ec	Ecuador	kr	Korea
ee	Estonia	kw	Kuwait
eg	Egypt	lt	Lithuania
en	England	lv	Latvia
es	Spain	mx	Mexico

my	Malaysia	si	Slovenia
nl	Netherlands	sk	Slovakia
no	Norway	su	Soviet Union (yes, we know)
nz	New Zealand	th	Thailand
pe	Peru	tr	Turkey
ph	Philippines	tw	Taiwan
pl	Poland	uk	United Kingdom
pt	Portugal	us	United States
ru	Russia	uy	Uruguay
se	Sweden	ve	Venezuela
sg	Singapore	za	South Africa

Appendix G
LANGUAGE CODES

The codes used to identify languages are described in the Internet RFC 1766 at `ftp://ds.internic.net/rfc/rfc1766.txt`. The list below is extracted from it. The language tag is composed of a primary language tag and zero or more subtags, as in 'en.uk'. All tags are case insensitive.

In the first subtag:

- All 2-letter codes are interpreted as ISO 3166 2-letter Country Codes (see Appendix F) denoting the area in which the language is used.

- Codes of 3 to 8 letters may be registered with the IANA by anyone who feels a need for it.

- The information in the subtag may be:
  - Country identification, such as `en-us` (this usage is described in ISO 639);
  - Dialect or variant information, such as `no-nynorsk` or `en-cockney`;
  - Languages not listed in ISO 639 that are not variants of any listed language, which can be registered with the i- prefix, such as `i-cherokee`;
  - Script variations, such as `az-arabic` and `az-cyrillic`.

In the second subtag:

- Anything may be registered.

Additional language codes (1989 is the latest year with registrations):

ug	Uigur
iu	Inuktitut, *also called* Eskimo
za	Zhuang
he	Hebrew, *replacing* iw
yi	Yiddish, *replacing* ji
id	Indonesian, *replacing* in.

Unregistered examples for illustration purposes only:

Both official versions of Norwegian:	no-nynorsk, no-bokmaal

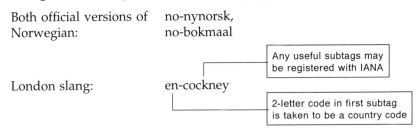

London slang:	en-cockney

North Sami ('Lappish'):   i-sami-no

Appendix H
TAGS THAT DID *NOT* MAKE IT INTO HTML 4

`<TRANS LANG=RFC1766_language>...`
`</TRANS>`

Instructs the browser to translate dynamically from the language used in the HTML source, generally English, into the indicated language, such as Japanese, as specified in RFC 1766.

`<MARCH PRESENT>...</MARCH>`

The enclosed text or graphic moves to the left, the right, the top, and the bottom, and then marches smartly off the left of the screen. The optional `PRESENT` parameter makes the item present arms and flick its head and eyes briskly to the right as it marches off.

`<ACC DELAY=seconds>...</ACC>`

When the pointing device hovers over the enclosed text for more than the time specified in the delay attribute, `ACC`ompanies the browser's visual display with suitable themes,

for example suspenseful B-movie program music.

`<REC>...</REC>`

Causes the document to act `REC`ursively as its own style sheet, using definition-by-example. For instance, if the first paragraph is written inside `<FONT SIZE=6><B>...</B></FONT>`, then all paragraphs in the document are typeset in size 6 boldface by default. Known bugs: if there is a `<FRAMESET>` in the document, the entire contents of the document are inserted as a nested frameset in the top left frame. This feature is being discussed by the task force which will report in 1999 with a preliminary draft describing possible remedies.

`<WARP SHAPE=%shape>...</WARP>`

Reshapes graphics-capable browsers according to the *shape* (`rect|circle|polygon|default`) specified in the **SHAPE** attribute. For example, with SHAPE=circle, the display is distorted like a fisheye-lens view into a circle. Default is browser-specific but is suggested to be the simplest polygon, an equilateral triangle. This does however make the first few lines of text rather small. Well, very small indeed.

<A HREF=url NOCLICK>

The **NoClick** attribute signals to the browser not to accept clicks on the marked link anchors. Behavior if the user attempts to click on any such tag is browser-defined, but a conventional default is to download a 20 Megabyte UNIX core dump, saving the context so that the download continues next time the user logs on, in case the user attempts to restart the machine before the download is completed.

<SHADOW TIME=hours>...</SHADOW>

Causes the enclosed text to cast a shadow as if illuminated by the sun at the specified time of day; if the time attribute is omitted, the current time is used. When displaying shadowed text at night, browsers should make the shadow pale and wobbly, with the occasional owl and bat flitting across the shadowed areas. On Windows 95, the shadow angle should be date- and latitude-specific, so the user should see a longer shadow in winter than in summer, and in far northern countries than on the equator.

<FRAME TEXTURE=%texture>...</FRAME>

The **TEXTURE** attribute causes the frame to be drawn with the specified texture (tortoiseshell|woodgrain|ormolu| beatencopper|soapstone). If neighboring cells have different textures, the more costly frame texture is drawn for their common boundary.

<DOOM LEVEL=number>...</DOOM>

Enlivens home pages by responding to joystick firing-button clicks. Graphics enclosed by the tags are highlighted in yellow and black. If pressed within 1/10 second of display, enclosed graphics (or text) respond by exploding noisily in a shower of red and yellow sparks. If not pressed within 2 seconds, whole screen erupts into boiling lava and the message 'Game Over – You Lost' is displayed. The optional level setting configures the timings between easy and impossible.

<MARQUEE>...</MARQUEE>

Makes the enclosed text scroll horribly ... ahem. Sorry. That one is in already.

Appendix I
COLOR ON THE WEB

We are grateful for this contribution to John Weise, Digital Media Solutions, Office of Instructional Technology, University of Michigan, http://www.oit.itd.umich.edu/projects/DMS/answers/colorguide/index.html.

- 'Clock in Window' was taken in Mikulov, Czech Republic in 1996.

- 'Horse Barn' photo was taken at Barothy Lodge, Walhalla, Michigan in 1995.

The problem

Many, if not most, Web users have computers that can display only 256 colors at once. Some PCs are limited further to 16 colors. Yet, it is very easy to create digital images that contain as many as 16.7 million colors. How good an image looks on the Web depends entirely on the capabilities of each user's hardware and software. Netscape Navigator, NCSA Mosaic, and Microsoft Internet Explorer actually use only the 216 colors that are common to Macintosh and Windows operating systems to display images. Lynda Weinman has dubbed this 216 color palette the Browser Safe Palette.

When a Web browser displays an image on a 256 color system, the image is drawn using the browser's palette of choice (most commonly the Browser Safe Palette). The results can be less than desirable, and will vary from browser to browser and platform to platform. Most seriously affected are images with broad areas of a single color, or flat color. Photos and other types of continuous tone images tend to look better.

The solution

There is no universal solution, though use of the **Browser Safe Palette** to create images goes a long way toward achieving predictable results. In general, if the Browser Safe Palette is used when preparing images for the Web, the images will look good, at least on Macintosh and Windows machines. Unfortunately, it is not quite as simple as that. It is not always appropriate to use the Browser Safe Palette.

The Browser Safe Palette

The Browser Safe Palette contains the 216 colors that are common to the system palettes of the Macintosh and Windows operating systems. It is used by Netscape Navigator, NCSA Mosaic, and Microsoft Internet Explorer. The 216 colors of the Browser Safe Palette are shown in the color section of this book.

You can download the Browser Safe Palette for Mac or Windows. The palette can be loaded into Photoshop's swatches so that the colors can be used while creating images.

The scary truth

Truth is, very few images actually use all 16.7 million colors, and usually a reasonable job of image display can be done with 256 or fewer colors.

When to use the 216 color Browser Safe Palette

- Use the Browser Safe Palette when creating logos or illustrations that have large areas of solid color. Load the Browser Safe Palette into your paint program and when creating the artwork, select colors only from the 216. If you are working in RGB mode, do not dither the image when switching to indexed color. Use the GIF file format.

- Use the Browser Safe Palette when reducing the colors of a pre-existing logo or illustration that has large areas of solid color for use on the Web. Most often, do not dither the image. Use the GIF file format.

- Photographs and other types of continuous tone images should generally use an adaptive palette. However, some types of continuous tone images, when viewed on 256 color Windows displays, will look better with the Browser Safe Palette. In any case, be sure to dither the image and use the GIF file format. Please see the section about adaptive palettes for more information.

Example

The images below (color equivalents are shown in the color section of this book) were created originally without using the Browser Safe Palette. After the fact, the image colors were reduced. The first two images approximate the background color the best, but are dithered on a 256 color display. The third image is not dithered, but the color is not very accurate. On a display capable of thousands or millions of colors, the first image looks just like the original (accurate color, no dithering), and the last two look just like they do on a 256 color display.

256 color adaptive palette without diffusion.

Browser Safe Palette with diffusion.

Browser Safe Palette without diffusion.

Again, the key with this type of image is to use Browser Safe Palette colors from the start. This eliminates surprises when the image is moved to the Web.

When to use an adaptive palette

- Use an adaptive palette with continuous tone images such as photos. Some types of continuous tone images, when viewed on 256 color Windows displays, look better with the Browser Safe Palette (for example, the first set of images below). An adaptive palette image, when viewed on a 256 color Macintosh, will look at least as good as the same image using the Browser Safe Palette. In any case, be sure to dither the image and use the GIF file format.

- When reducing an image to 256 or fewer colors, the image can be remapped to an adaptive palette which uses the most common 256 colors of the image. When the image is displayed by a Web browser on a 256 color system, the image is redrawn using the browser's standard palette (most likely the Browser Safe Palette). It seems logical that if the browser is going to remap the image anyway, better color could be achieved by using the 216 color palette in the first place and never using an adaptive palette. However, this is generally not the case.

The biggest advantage to using an adaptive palette is that users with computers capable of displaying thousands or millions of colors will see an image far superior to what would be seen if the 216 color palette were used.

It is often possible to reduce an image to an even smaller number of colors, perhaps 128 or 64, and still get a great image with an adaptive palette. The benefit is a smaller image file size.

Example

On a 256 color display, the following sets of images will be of similar color quality. However, the first and third image of each set, which use adaptive palettes, will look much better on computers that can display thousands or millions of colors. And if you are concerned about file size, consider the third image of each set which uses only 64 adaptive colors. The adaptive palette images likely look better on a Macintosh than on a Windows computer, especially for the first set of images. Keep this in mind if preparing images on a Macintosh – 64 colors may not do the job of a 256 color Windows display.

256 color adaptive palette with diffusion (24K).

Browser Safe Palette with diffusion (16K).

64 color adaptive palette with diffusion (16K).

Browser Safe Palette with diffusion (18K).

256 color adaptive palette with diffusion (32K).

64 color adaptive palette with diffusion (22K).

In case you are wondering what a continuous tone image looks like without diffusion, here is the first photo, prepared with the Browser Safe Palette and no diffusion.

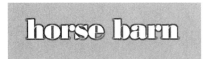

When to use thousands or millions of colors

Use thousands or millions of colors (16 bit or 24 bit color) when color accuracy is crucial. For example, art historical images that have been color balanced and are of exceptional quality need 24 bit color. This assumes that most of the users, or at least the most important users, have displays capable of displaying millions of colors. 256 color displays can still show the images, but they will be dithered much like the adaptive palette images are. Use JPEG compression (JFIF file format).

When to use the Windows 16 color base palette

Use the Windows 16 color base palette if you really need to cater to the lowest common denominator and you know that the majority of your users have computers that only display 16 colors. When using the 16 color palette, it is really necessary to design from the start with those colors.

Gamma for the Web – why things come out darker or lighter on different machines

Gamma can be intimidating, but really it is just brightness control. How bright or dark an image appears on a computer display depends on several factors including the software gamma setting on the computer, the physcial brightness setting of the monitor, and ambient light (the light in the room, or on the beach if you are one of those non-existent, virtual-office-on-the-beach people that can only be seen on TV). So, gamma for the Web is a pretty tricky issue since you cannot adjust everybody's viewing environment.

In general, it is known that images prepared on a Mac will look too dark on a PC, and images prepared on a PC will look too bright on a Mac. One option is to shoot the gamma gap and use a brightness that is right in the middle. This way, images will only be a little too bright on the Mac, and a little too dark on the PC. The common gamma setting on the Macintosh is 1.8. And on a PC it is 2.5. So, shooting the gap would be about 2.2. Monitor gamma can be set to 2.2 before preparing images for the Web. Photoshop 3.0 allows the global gamma to be adjusted. Select from the File/Preferences menu the Monitor Setup... menu item, and set the gamma to 2.2. Do not forget to set it back when you are done if you will be doing non-Web image work. With the gamma set to 2.2, adjust images so that they look good, and save them.

Photoshop for the Macintosh comes with a gamma control panel that allows the gamma to be adjusted at the system level for all applications. It is worth installing and using because it allows the gamma setting to be tweaked visually for the physical working environment. Images can also be adjusted after the fact, but this is a bit more complicated.

Making Good-looking WWW GIFs or JPEGs for Multi-platforms with Photoshop, provided by the Computer Graphics Systems Development Corporation (CGSD), goes through the steps for using Photoshop to retroactively adjust the gamma of images that are going on the Web.

Other colorful Web resources

- *Lynda's Homegurrrl Page and the Browser Safe Palette.*

- *I am Curious Yellow* by John MacDemott, New Media Specialist at the University of Pennsylvania.

- Victor Engel's *No Dither Netscape Color Palette.*

- *The 256, Oops, 216 Colors of Netscape (Which do not Dither)* by Bob Cunningham.

Appendix J
APPLET

If the OBJECT element seems too complex for your purposes – you have no need to manipulate numerous pieces of data within multiple confines of different object systems – if you have simply downloaded or coded a Java applet that you wish to include in your Web page, then the APPLET element is for you.

APPLET is one of the tags initially proposed by Sun Microsystems in order to specify the usage of a Java applet within a Web page. The tag and its syntax subsequently folded into the HTML specification, and most Web browsers know how to interpret the element.

Keep in mind that the APPLET element works only with objects created in the Java programming language. If you try to use the APPLET syntax with another type of object, you may wind up disappointed, and no one wants that.

The APPLET element has the following attributes:

- CODE
- OBJECT
- WIDTH
- HEIGHT
- CODEBASE
- ARCHIVE
- ALT
- NAME
- ALIGN
- VSPACE
- HSPACE

The APPLET element also makes use of an associated PARAM tag, to specify parameters for the applet. The APPLET element only requires that you use the labels for **CODE** (or **OBJECT**), **HEIGHT** and **WIDTH**. The other attributes are optional for the element.

A basic example of the APPLET element in action:

```
<APPLET CODE="PlayerPiano.class" WIDTH=250 HEIGHT=100></APPLET>
```

CODE

In this example, the compiled Java class file referenced by **CODE** exists in the same directory as the HTML file. This attribute is necessary for the applet to run, since without it, the browser does not know of the existence of the applet. Instead of **CODE**, you may use the more complicated ...

OBJECT

Not to be confused with the OBJECT specification described in Chapter 15, the use of the **OBJECT** attribute with APPLET allows you to use a serialized applet. This means that rather than displaying the compiled applet, the reference is to a stream of bytes that essentially comprise a copy of the applet. When using this attribute, the applet's init() method is not called, but instead, it calls the run() method. Once the applet starts, it references any other of the APPLET attributes in a normal fashion.

Serialization can come in handy if you want to pass Java applets among machines to be restored remotely or to create state-persistent objects. The

Sun documentation on using **OBJECT** with serialized applets rather seriously calls for control when using the attribute, so we recommend sticking with **CODE**.

WIDTH and HEIGHT

The **WIDTH** and **HEIGHT** for the applet are specified above as well, so the browser knows to allocate 250 pixels for the width of the applet and 100 pixels for its height. These measurements only describe the initial composition of the applet; if the applet creates any new windows, they do not adhere to these limitations. **WIDTH** and **HEIGHT** are both measured in pixels.

CODEBASE

The **CODEBASE** attribute is intended to reference Java code that resides in a location other than the base URL of the HTML document. This can merely be in a different directory on the same machine, or a wholly separate computer. For example:

```
<APPLET CODEBASE="/code/java" CODE=AngryMob.class WIDTH=150 HEIGHT=150>
</APPLET>
<APPLET CODE="http://world.server.net/~chauncey"
        CODE="lawnmower.class" WIDTH=300 HEIGHT=280>
</APPLET>
```

The first example references the AngryMob.class that resides on the same server, in the java subdirectory of the code directory, which is located off the Web server root, from which all HTML and related files are served. The second example contacts a different server, world.server.net, to get the lawnmower.class that resides in the directory of a user named chauncey.

While remote referencing as seen in the second example is perfectly legal, it may have the negative result of slower network access for the end user.

ARCHIVE

ARCHIVE serves to reference an archive file that contains Java classes and possibly other files needed by an applet. These are preloaded by using an instance of the built-in Java class AppletClassLoader in your applet code. You may specify multiple archives by using a comma to separate the archive file names.

```
<APPLET CODE=MusicStore.class WIDTH=100 HEIGHT=150
       ARCHIVE="guitars.jar,drums.jar,keyboards.jar">
<PARAM NAME=picture VALUE=stratocaster.jpg>
</APPLET>
```

In this case, the `MusicStore.class` makes use of three separate archives: `guitars.jar`, `drums.jar` and `keyboards.jar`. The applet also makes use of a `PARAM` tag that references a file named `stratocaster.jpg`. This JPG file could be part of the `guitars.jar` archive, and the image could preload for faster access.

ALT

The **ALT** attribute will show text as an alternate to displaying the applet. This is in case the browser understands the syntax of the `APPLET` tag, but is unable to run Java, as is the case if the user shuts off the Java interpreter in the browser.

```
<APPLET CODE=BarkingDog.class WIDTH=80 HEIGHT=80
       ALT="My dog says 'woof'.">
</APPLET>
```

In the case of browsers that do not understand the `APPLET` element at all – as with older, text-based browsers – you can circumvent the issue of displaying text by nesting 'normal' text within the `APPLET`.

```
<APPLET CODE=MooingCow.class WIDTH=80 HEIGHT=80>
<I>I am not a steak.</I>
</APPLET>
```

In a non-`APPLET` supporting browser, the user will see the poignant message enclosed in the italic tags.

NAME

The **NAME** attribute is included so if necessary, other applets or client–side scripts may reference the instance of the applet by name. This enables communication between applets and scripts, allowing for a greater method of control.

```
<APPLET CODE=mannequin.class NAME=dummy WIDTH=100 HEIGHT=500>
</APPLET>
```

Here another applet or a script may reference and possibly manipulate the `mannequin.class` applet merely by using its name, `dummy`.

ALIGN

ALIGN allows you to specify the alignment of the applet on the page. Alignment of an applet follows the same guidelines as that of an image; it may reside `left`, `right`, `top`, `texttop`, `middle`, `absmiddle`, `baseline`, `bottom` or `absbottom`.

```
<APPLET CODE=socks.class WIDTH=60 HEIGHT=80 ALIGN=baseline>
</APPLET>We stock an attractive array of foot coverings.
```

In this example, the bottom of `socks.class` will align with the baseline of the text.

VSPACE and HSPACE

The **VSPACE** attribute determines how many pixels of space appear above and below the applet. **HSPACE** controls the number of pixels to the left and right of the applet. Like the applet's **ALIGN** attribute, **VSPACE** and **HSPACE** work in the same fashion as the corresponding attributes for images.

```
<APPLET CODE=chessboard.class WIDTH=80 HEIGHT=80 VSPACE=20 HSPACE=30>
</APPLET>
```

The PARAM tag

APPLET has an accompanying tag in PARAM. PARAM specifies additional parameters for the applet. The applet will attain the **VALUE** of the parameter by accessing the **NAME** through the applet method `getParameter()`. The advantage of using PARAMs instead of making these changes in the Java code is the ability to reuse the same applet for different purposes.

For instance, suppose you use a Java applet named `TextDisplay` that formats a text file for display according to a certain style. The applet uses `getParameter()` to determine the headline and text, as well as the size and style of font to use. You can use the applet to show a news story:

```
<APPLET CODE=TextDisplay.class WIDTH=80 HEIGHT=150>
<PARAM NAME=headline VALUE="Man Bites Dog">
<PARAM NAME=text VALUE=dognews.txt>
<PARAM NAME=fontsize VALUE=12>
<PARAM NAME=fontstyle VALUE=Times>
</APPLET>
```

or to format your latest work of poetry:

```
<APPLET CODE=TextDisplay.class WIDTH=50 HEIGHT=50>
<PARAM NAME=headline VALUE="Roses Are Red">
<PARAM NAME=text VALUE=roses.txt>
<PARAM NAME=fontsize VALUE=14>
<PARAM NAME=fontstyle VALUE=Helvetica>
</APPLET>
```

Appendix K
THE CYBERIA CAFÉ

Whitfield Street is a quiet backwater off Tottenham Court Road. It has Georgian brick terraces, a distant rumble of traffic, the sun glinting off the British Telecom Tower.

I sit on a gaily painted bench in a square by a playground to take a few notes and absorb the atmosphere. Connor from Dublin is sitting under a spread-out sleeping-bag with a banana and a couple of cans of Carlsberg lager. He leaves me about 10 seconds before engaging me in conversation.

'I used to play the computer machines constantly, before I came to London eight years ago', he says.

'Since I came to London, I stopped playing them ... and now when I go towards a computer, they are so advanced now, compared to when the first machines were, they're completely alien to me, I can't play them .... I dunno, some of the easier machines I can play, but the more up-to-date ones, I lose it completely. I used to live in snooker halls, arcades, things that were open 24 hours a day. It's changed now – most of the machines are that much more advanced now....'

Connor trails off into repetition, is happy to speak into the tape-recorder.

'I got married, got a kid, got divorced, a lot of things. Also did a lot of drugs where we played. The drugs used to enhance your performance on the machines ... at times your fingers got tired pressing the buttons ... you'd miss a move, lose, take a break, have a bit of snooker to take you down a bit, then of course you'd be back on the machines. Some of me friends were constantly on the machines – it was like taking a drug.'

Connor used to spend up to £500 a day on his 'habit', a cocktail of pool, snooker, games and 'real' drugs. The games made up £250-worth per day.

His favourite? '*Space Invaders*. As I say, this was 10 years ago.' What did he want?

'To beat them! Beat your mates at it! That was before you could buy home computers, tap in and get going. Once you're sucked in, you're in.' A police siren howls in the background.

I wonder if the Cyberia boys are doing the same thing.

'Yeah, it gets into your brain, it's an addiction thing, same as anything. It's the same as taking a drug. You get so spaced into the machine, as you do taking a drug. You can get so hyped out on that machine and wanting to beat it ... you can't let go, you have to stay, you have to beat it, you have to be best, and you know, you're not prepared for the machine to beat you.'

But the boys now are not playing a game, they can break into other people's machines, I suggest.

'I'm sure if they have home computers and good software, they can do what they want to do. What[ever] is possible through a machine, but they are just playing a game, they want to beat the system [like me]', Connor speculates.

I leave Connor on his bench and walk down the street to the Cyberia Café to see what they are really doing in there. Car parks and new concrete buildings have replaced some of the terraces, but they have evidently been controlled by the planners, as they are a similar height to the old houses of Fitzrovia, this area between Oxford Street, Fitzroy Street and Marylebone Road in London's downtown West End. There are little pubs like the Carpenter's Arms with flowers around their doors. The London Plane trees are fresh and green in the sunshine. There is a motorcycle park, showing how much money is about: a Honda Revere, a Polaris CX500, a Kawasaki Twin-Cam 16-valve, and more. Some prosperous-looking businessmen are having a smoke in their sleek Granadas and Sierras; it is an impromptu conference in the street. Down below the level of the road, there is a hobo's hostel, full of down-and-out men with coffee in paper cups. Next door is a fish bar and 'kebab with rice and yoghurt', dolmades and ratatouille. The Hope public house has an advertisement for Murphy's Stout: 'Buy 6, get one free, so like the Murphys there is no need to be bitter'.

Opposite is Pollock's Theatrical Print Warehouse, Pollock's Toy Museum, gaily painted like Victorian toys on the outside, inside play with puppets, coloured dominoes, magnetic kit moving toys, the tubes full of Spillikins pointed wooden sticks (remember those?). Masks and disguises. Then, across the road on the corner of Scala Street, W1, is the Cyberia.

The Cyberia Café, Internet Access, announces the window.

I sit down at the back. Half a dozen workstations along the front window, another inside. Windows workstations, all with big screens, comfortable and discreetly coloured. They have stereo loudspeakers.

Surprise, there are some women here. One of the machines has three women conversing (among them Ewa Pascoe, I discover), they are not punching buttons at all; two youngish men at machines by themselves, two older men dressed in check shirts, a sheepskin jacket over the chair, and all by himself a businessman in a dark suit punching away with his right index finger, bashing away very intently at something called Easynet.

At a table in the café, three men, two in white shirts, open-necked, one in a blue denim jacket, drinking coffee, portable phone, a bundle of papers, pen-computing tablets; they are gesticulating, I catch the word 'distributing', some form of computing is plainly being discussed.

The women are having something explained; they are doing very little on the machine but it is obviously the focus of attention. It looks like Mosaic on there . . . .

The rest of the café is rather sparse. There is rather an attractively stripped floor, not varnished. A small bar, painted a dullish grey-green. A few cups of coffee, a few bottles of lemonade, tea, a few small buns, but food does not seem very important.

Cyberia's current artwork is by Alex Berka on a Mac, digitally repro-duced by *The Colour Desk*, according to an art-gallery notice on the wall. 'The first quarrel' is a 36×38 inch colour inkjet print. A maiden in a flowery dress and the head of a gorilla in front of a French eighteenth-century four-poster bed with red, heavy gold velvet curtains, gold-and-plaster ceiling, tapestries, and on the maiden's head an enormous sunburst golden crown decorated with a Christ and saints' figures in niches among the rays. That seems to be a symbol of the Cyberia Café, the sunburst. The staff sport T-shirts with the word Cyberia in all four points of the compass, the four intermediate points marked with flashes.

Some rainforest plants, and to my surprise quite nice cut irises, tiger lilies and orange daisies brighten up the cerebral atmosphere. The first edition of the *Internet Magazine* is on sale at £1.50. The prices are low here for London: real espresso coffee is just 80p, cappuccino £1. The décor is sober with metallic greys, a little Cybernetic but not intensely so. Some soft piped music trickles out of the modestly sized speakers. Round glass tables, steel chairs with black plastic slats, silver paper in the office windows, white blinds, white bobble lights, pale sand-coloured walls complete the décor. It is rather a quiet harmonious café.

Some people go up to the bar and ask about a machine; they make a booking for a time-slot about an hour ahead. I join them to try a coffee. It's long and strong from the espresso machine, which is a home-style portable 'until we get one plumbed in', says **Donna** behind the bar. She wears a black T-shirt with the Cyberia starburst, and explains that in a perfect world, coffee would be free to journalists, but that: 'We've had a lot of press attention and we'd be broke if . . . ' – she trails off with a dizzy wave of the head, conveying the hordes of hyped-up hacks who have packed the bar in the past few weeks.

Phil comes behind the bar too, chats about the pricing, is astonished that Connor on the bench outside used to have a £250 habit on his space invaders.

'How did he get all that? At the most you'd spend £50 for a full day here, and if you were that interested, you would subscribe £57.34 including VAT for two months or (better) £168.97 for the year. Then you could download practically anything you wanted to play with!' Phil gives me the café's address, which is http:\\www.easynet.co.uk and their home page is home.htm – what could be simpler. I just have time to sip my coffee when

Ewa Pascoe, slim, pretty, self-possessed, comes briskly along to show me around. She was the woman doing the talking in the group at the workstation: 'I've been doing a lot of training this morning', she announces. It's easy to believe she has just done a couple of hours of weights and circuits, like the go-getting young women of Wall Street in sharp pinstripes worn over training shoes. But no:

'I was showing some customers around the Internet', she laughs. She is wearing a black miniskirt and a leopard-spotted shirt under a purple top.

'It's my normal work gear', she disclaims at once. She has a slight Central European accent, is blonde, and is, as I guess, Polish. She gestures calmly at the ruby-red lips in the bitmapped image:

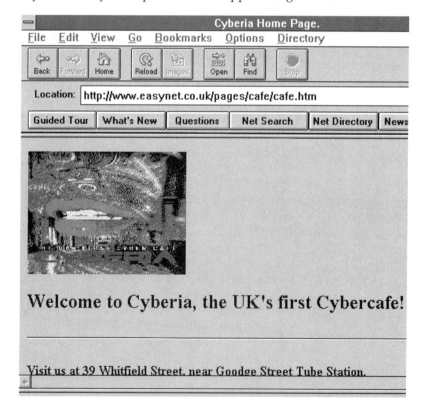

'Those are meant to be my lips', and indeed there is some resemblance. It seems she is rather the café's mascot: 'because my nickname is Europa'. She is still hoping to be carried away by Zeus in the guise of a bull, she says. She specializes in Human–Computer Interaction at the City University, where she is working on expert front-ends for psychologists with Imperial Cancer Research. She claims not to spend much time in the café, but all the press cuttings show her, the warm photogenic face of the chilly-sounding Cyberia.

She tells me about the band that played here on Friday; a 4-minute 'radio' program is available on the Internet, for those with the ability (or the patience) to download the 5-megabyte file for 3 minutes, 51 seconds worth of music and chatter.

'Ok, so we use the home pages for current event information, on Friday we had a live broadcast of a band, the *Charles Dexter Ward Experience*, and we wanted to have, at the same time, information about the band, so that people who were receiving the broadcast in Texas, Finland or Scandinavia, they could see the menu of what the band was playing with a little description of the music, and the people, so the broadcast is a little bit more than just pictures (via CUCM, the video conferencing system of the Internet), explaining the context of the event. The camera here, the band there....' Ewa rattles on, confident in her very human corner of cyberspace.

The café's network bandwidth is a business secret, Ewa says, with a smile. It is plainly ample, there is a huge file of the broadcast's music.

'We wanted to make sure that the full music from the whole album is there; commercial companies only provide a sample of 30 seconds of something-or-other, which is very annoying.' The Cyberia staff (and friends) know where they want to go, and they mean to get there. 'This is basically cutting the record label company out of the deal', she grins maliciously.

'We are trying to use the Internet to see how can we change other people's smart little businesses, and annoy them as much as possible, and use the technology to engineer what could be done. I don't think people mind paying; I mean, from what I've noticed, people are saying, well, we could contribute to the band, a fair amount, but that doesn't mean £11 per CD.'

They use the home page also for campaigns. 'All the current things going on like Green Screen Festival, which we are sponsoring, an environmental festival; so if anybody has anything interesting, non-profitmaking, at the foot of the pages we will do that.'

There are titles like *No More Hiroshimas*, *The Internet Now* (the radio programme), 'On a lighter note, you wouldn't believe what you can find on the Web', *Guide to the UK* ('here is a sensitive map guide to the sights and sounds of Britain'). We take a look. Ewa explains: 'As a lot of visitors to the café are tourists, the French are used to Minitel for local information; and we have to tell them, uh-huh, there isn't any!'

So the café commissioned people all over Britain to make hypertexts of their local history, geography, pubs, restaurants, hotels: the Domesday Book as the BBC did not make it. Ewa has an opinion on that too.

'This is a role which the Tourist Board should be playing', says Ewa sourly. I chide her on her cynicism. 'Well, I'm an academic, so I'm cynical by definition!', she snorts.

I click on Winchester; a kilobyte of HTML later, we are in the city of King Arthur and King Alfred, with an attractive colour bitmap of the cathedral close (87 kbytes). There is a long list of pubs: I track down the Royal Oak Passage, a nice secret place I used to frequent as a boy – the narrow alley outside reduced the risk of being detected by the school authorities, or the police. The information is very detailed and accurate, but Ewa quickly chips in: 'Not everything is represented, some parts of the country are not so well covered.'

'It's a virtual trip, you don't really have to go to Winchester', she jokes: at least she still knows she is joking. We look up St Cross monastery, where you can still be offered a welcoming glass of free beer as a passing traveller. 'You get a virtual beer here', laughs Ewa. She steers me to the CyberCafé guide, the Home Page of which the café is plainly proud.

'There are still places for people to meet their friends, read the newspapers, discuss the important events of the day, and to read and answer their snail-mail correspondence', announces the Home Page. Those who still put inky pen to cellulose paper are evidently nostalgic oldies who like the bard to sing them stories by the fireside in the mead-hall before bedtime. For those more up-to-the-minute, there is an email address: easynet.co.uk.

There are a couple of dozen Cybercafés around the world, listed online.

'Although none of them are as good as ours, because we have the best connection and full access to the Internet, including Mosaic', trumpets Ewa. 'The workstations get a 64-kilobit line, while the other cafés have one little terminal with text-based bulletin boards and charts.'

Keith Teare (a director) and David Roe (the MD) created the Easynet company, sister to the Cyberia, which works upstairs from the café, Ewa explains.

'We wanted to create something which would be very easy, even for children. The idea was to build a powerful and consistent system which was learnable and reliable, but which did not discourage people. Technophobes welcome!' The human-interface designer in Ewa shows through, the enthusiasm apparent.

'The email, the FTP, all the packages in our system are very similar, so once you learn on one, you can use another. Not too much transfer.... We selected purely Windows-based interfaces, and we are continuously trying to make it even more consistent in terms of what you see in the graphics, how you operate it.... One of the worst nightmares on the Internet is FTP-ing ... it never happens, basically. So we are using Archie for that.'

We go to archie.dot.ic.ac.uk, Imperial College, London. The file we want comes back into a single temporary directory on the Cyberia server, but Ewa is not impressed: 'So you see, it is still five more steps than it should be'. Ewa is striving for perfect simplicity on-screen. I notice only that it all seems much easier and faster than usual; a large bitmap arrives within a minute. Ewa immediately starts to paint it in bright colours. Then she rushes off to another appointment.

Andrew Blackburn works in the back office for Easynet. He could not be more different from Ewa Pascoe: slight, shy, inconspicuous, British, discreet. He quietly admits to having made the Internet Radio programme himself; he recorded some of the music onto tape from the mixing desk, some directly to disk, then edited it with the rather basic sound tool that comes with Windows. 'It was a bit difficult, but it's free and it works.' The end result: an HTML document full of music on the World Wide Web.

Under questioning, he says the clientele has changed from mainly journalists at first, to the general public now. There are plenty of regulars. 'At £168 per year, it is cheap, say some', he whispers. Andrew seems to find the antics of the press and public a little exaggerated. The phone rings and he excuses himself. He does have a proprietorial pride in the firm: 'We are just like any other Internet provider; but we pride ourselves on being easier than some of the others.'

Alexa Thomas is an actress over in England for six months from Florida State University. She's with the Study Abroad programme, which 'doesn't offer email to their students. It's a common problem, so a lot of foreign students come here to pick up their email and talk to their friends, that's what I do.' She works just down the street in London University.

'I'm not a techie at all, it's my first experience of computers beyond word-processing', she says in her nasal Florida drawl. 'This is really kind of a bit of an eye-opening experience as far as computers go. I'm afraid I've become addicted, I'm gonna have to have email when I get back home.' How long did it take to get addicted?

'God, a couple of weeks, then I realized, oh, it's great, even from the East Coast it takes a couple of weeks for a letter to get here; email is a lot quicker.' She has experimented with Mosaic, but email to friends in almost every university is why she comes into the café.

'I spend a lot of time here. A little less than half an hour every day, on Sundays a little longer.' She says that is probably how long she would spend writing to her friends if there wasn't a café here. She has a special rate for her email service, she comes in only at off-peak times.

'It's been wonderful to be able to talk to all my friends back home, I was worried ... phone calls are so ridiculously expensive and mail is so slow.' To Alexa, the short utterances and quick replies of email are more like talking than writing.

'You do get a lot of American students, a lot of businessmen in the lunch-breaks ... some do serious work, but often they just play around. There's definitely a variety of people here, not just computer junkies. Before I came here I said, oh, that's so nerdy and so difficult, I don't know if I can do it; but when I came here and found out how easy it was, I got really into it. The Internet is a wonderful idea. We had a performance by a rock group the other week ... it's crazy to think they can perform here in Cyberia and be seen all over the world. Back in the States they had an Internet dance concert where they had one dancer in one city, another in another city, doing a dance together.' I inquire if she would like to act on the net.

'Maybe! I don't think the Internet or virtual reality will make the real thing obsolete. It's gonna be an addition to what we have already. A very interesting medium with a lot of possibilities. It's special function is that nothing else allows so many people from so far distant to talk together. The ability to see things and hear things at the same time. I joined the performance of the band, I was talking to and looking at a young man in California, it's a lot of fun, also educational. The Internet is a great way to casually experience whatever you choose to do, it kind of fits in with the whole relaxed atmosphere of the café, definitely a relaxing and enjoying experience.' Perhaps the Cyberia is for the Internet what the intellectual Viennese fin-de-siècle cafés were for Chess.

Alan Newton is a freelance Physics consultant, middle-aged, suited, solidly professional, with a Home Counties English accent. He works from home, needs to access data, and wonders if the Internet might help him. 'I've read about it in the literature, and I think that if I just log on, on my own without any help, it's a black hole into which I pour money. I saw an article about this place, and I thought, half an hour here will allow me to decide where to go and give me some pointers to go there. I've used CompuServe which is fine for fun stuff, but the impression I've got is that Internet has got much more real technical stuff, and hopefully somebody will confirm that for me in the next half hour or so.' We use Mosaic to find CERN, the European nuclear research centre, in a few keystrokes. Alan writes down CERN's URL (http://info.cern.ch) and browses The Particle Data Group at Lawrence Berkeley, Experiments at Helsinki, General Physics via Info.desy.de, and more. The Superconducting SuperCollider 'the greatest ruin of all time', laments one heading. Alan is confused that we have leapt from Germany to the USA in a couple of clicks.... I leave him looking through a dozen bookstore catalogues. 'Thank you for taking our exit off the international data highway', intones one of them.

Nico Macdonald commissions the graphics for Easynet, deals with the designers, works with the icons on the Web pages. He is reviewing a CD-ROM on one of the workstations as it won't run on his own Mac. An Apple Newton is on the desk for notes, addresses and appointments. He is one of the white-shirted young men I noticed earlier. He talks enthusiastic-ally about the Net, graphics, business prospects. He is interrupted by Ivan Pope with an urgent question.

Ivan Pope publishes a magazine, *3W*, on the Internet. 'Since September 1993, first Internet magazine in the world. It's bi-monthly (every two months!), available internationally. Not a huge distribution, vaguely alternative.' Internet pages? 'www.3w.com/3w/ email to 3w@3w.com.' 'Shortest email address in the world!', I comment. 'Short and sweet!', he murmurs lovingly.

Geoff Turko from New Jersey is just calling up some things on a Skateboarding news net, surfing around the Net. He is short, young, fit, uses words economically, time is precious with the clock ticking away. 'I might find some things from my friends back home or something like that, finding out what's new, reading the messages.' Why?

'You can go down to the spots in London, but you're not gonna find out what's happening in the spots back home or in another part of the world.' Geoff is here for two years at the Architectural Association ... he breaks off to attend to a message. Today he has messages from Denmark. I thank him for his time. Another world.

Trystan Julliard is behind the bar, small, slight, blonde, but confident and energetic. She has been in the UK some years, comes from Silicon Valley of course, got married to an Englishman, has been with Cyberia since it started.

'I like computers, want to do something I enjoy, this is a really good place to grow in.' Her background? 'Silicon Valley, Dentistry, Travelling, Writing. Haven't gone to university.' Growth? 'The whole business will expand. I'm hoping to move up the ladder, into management.'

Trystan has taken on the soft-spoken air and idioms of the English-woman, but inside one quickly senses the excitement, the passion for technology, the boundless possibilities. She works behind the bar, helps to organize the Café.

'Neither of us, my husband or I, has any desire to go back to California. [England offers] a lot of growth, and a temperament I like. It's friendlier here; the cafés in the San Francisco area tend to be UNIX, text-only based. You have to be from the area, wearing an anorak to deal with that.' There are no anoraks in sight.

'No, that's just it, we're trying to get the normal people in, the everyday people, who have heard the hype, who want to try it out, find what all the hype has been about. Here's a place where they can do it without having a computer.' Soft, graceful piano music tinkles in the background as she reflects on the reality of a cyberspace café.

'The hype is starting to die down, it will go on for a little bit longer. If it doesn't there's going to be a big backlash, the Internet just can't deliver what the hype is promising. There are films where you just go tap-tap-tap and there is the information, and it just isn't like that.' What can the Net really deliver?

'A lot of fun, a lot of information if you really know how to look for it: that is the key thing, knowing how to look ... it's half pure logic and it's half pure intuition, knowing how to call something up, what somebody's going to call it. My own metaphor is trying to use somebody else's address book. Will it be under last name? first name? nickname? You've got to guess. The search engines are going to become even more sophisticated; they are already very clever. That is where the first AI is going to go.'

'I'm rarely behind the bar, usually I'm out as tech support, showing people around, most of the time.' How did she learn?

'You play. Ever since I was 16. Computers, the Internet, the whole culture, the mindset. I grew up with computers, in places where they were ubiquitous. The whole jargon around it ... it's not that different from growing up in surf country, it's just a part of knowledge and how things work.' A down side?

'I dunno. We'll find out as we go along. If you look at film as a metaphor: the Victorian Daguerrotypes ... and they had this technology starting, the film industry, they just didn't know where it was going to go. We just don't know. Can you imagine the Military [the DoD] imagining this when the ARPAnet got started? I'm not sufficiently prescient to imagine where all this is going to go.

'We get everything from little kids to grandmothers. We got one mom in who'd got no idea, but who wanted to email her son at university. The poor kid's gonna be shocked when he gets email from his mom!'

I.F.A.

GLOSSARY

This glossary lists a wide range of terms that readers may come across in the context of the Web. Most of the entries are serious definitions and discussions; we have included a few lighter entries but even those mostly make serious points.

Anchor A structure in **HTML** defining the start (or end – see description of the A tag) of a hypertext jump. Anchors generally use the A element with the HREF attribute, for example `<A HREF="target.html"> <IMG SRC="target.gif"> Target</A>`. Icons in the form of (small) IMG images can be included with the anchor text. The LINK, REL, and REV elements are also available to indicate various relationships between HTML pages. An alternative is to use an **image map**.

ANSI American National Standards Institute.

ASCII (American Standard Code for Information Interchange): the most common encoding of character data, using 7 bits (that is, 128 separate symbols) to represent the letters of the alphabet in upper and lower case, the digits, some control characters, and a very limited range of symbols such as $ and %. ASCII is used internally in most makes of computer (notably excluding IBM mainframes), and is essentially universally readable. It forms the lowest common denominator of data exchange, for instance by **email**. HTML provides a richer syntax but is itself written in ASCII,

though it can also reference binary files such as **GIF** or **JPEG** images.

ATM Asynchronous Transfer Mode, a newer and faster way of sending data on a network. It may catch on, or it may be overtaken by even newer and faster modes.

Attribute Ancillary building-block used to qualify **elements** in **HTML** so as to alter their properties. For example, identifiers can be added to many elements such as `<P>` with the ID attribute, as in `<P ID="example attribute definition">`.

Author (vb) To write, as in 'to author some HTML'. A better word is 'design', since **hypertext** is a structure containing text and other items (such as graphics and tables); most business sites in any case prepare HTML automatically by export from databases and other tools.

Block A chunk of HTML formed by an **element** which automatically starts a new line for itself in most browsers. For example, `<P>` and `<H3>` and `<UL>`.

Block-level element An element which terminates the preceding paragraph. Block-level elements include H1...H6, HR, P, TABLE, FORM, ADDRESS, DIV, PRE, BQ, NOTE, BR, FN, UL, DL, OL, CAPTION, FIG, MATH.

BoF Birds-of-a-Feather meeting of the **IETF**.

Browser A **client** program for the **Web**. Browsers are supposed to comply with the **HTML** standard, or at least with some version of it. Browsers are available for personal computers, Macintoshes, UNIX boxes, and other kinds of computer. Most browsers can display graphics as well as text; a few such as Lynx are intentionally text-only, typically for an 80×24 character screen; others such as EMACSpeak render text to speech or Braille.

CALS 'Continuous Acquisition and Life-Cycle Support', formerly 'Computer-aided Acquisition and Logistics Support', formerly ... a US Navy/ Department of Defense approach to handling data, with much influence on HTML's **table** model.

CD-ROM Compact disc – read-only memory. Disk exactly like audio CD but containing about 600 megabytes of computer data. A cheap and portable form of storing information which is not constantly needed and which needs to be updated only occasionally (by making new CD-ROMs).

CERN Centre Européen de Recherche Nucléaire, the European laboratory for nuclear particle physics at Geneva and the mother of the World Wide Web. She has now thrown her children out into the dark Massachusetts forests, as narrated in the Postscript to this book. *See also* **MIT**.

Character-level element An element which allows the text to flow on without causing a paragraph break. Character-level elements include character tags such as <I>, <SUB> and <STRONG>, link anchors <A>, and inline images <IMG>, all of which can be thought of as 'part of the text'. Special characters such as the em-space   and accented characters such as ü ü also work at this level.

Clickable Piece of text or an image, active in the sense that when the screen cursor is placed over it and a mouse or other pointing device button is clicked, something, generally a **hypertext** jump, takes place.

Client A program which can run on some computer in a network, giving access to data stored on a **server** (computer or program). The client– server model effectively shares out the work (distributes it) across the network, minimizing the processing needed at any one place, so it is becoming the dominant style of network opera-

tion in most computing systems. **Browsers** are **Web** clients.

Compression Reduction of storage and transmission bandwidth needed for data, especially images (which can become very large: a holiday photograph $3'' \times 5''$ might need 2 megabytes of storage when uncompressed to give anything like photographic quality). Compression can be lossy, as with **JPEG**, or loss-free, as with **GIF**. Lossy compression allows very large reductions in data volume, at the price of some loss of quality. Loss-free compression offers more modest reduction. Compression techniques are rapidly improving; for example, fractal compression can render photographs with little loss in 1% or less (100:1 compression) of their original volume, but requires great computational power for the encoding step. Decoding fractals is much easier.

Content model The logical structure which defines which elements can be included within a given element in a document. For example, a form is allowed to include 'body.content', meaning that anything which can occur in the body of an HTML page is allowed inside a form – headings, text, blocks (*see* **Block-level element**) and so on – without further explanation.

Context *see* **Permitted context.**

CSS Cascading Style Sheets: the mechanism chosen to permit HTML elements to be rendered in **styles** chosen by a page's author (rather than by setting up defaults in each browser). The cascade refers to the precedence hierarchy, which is quite complicated: basically, a page's styles are set by a style sheet for a whole Web site, but those styles can be overridden by a style sheet built into the page (in the document head), which in turn can be overridden by a style set for a specific tag (anywhere in the document body). The mechanism elegantly and powerfully allows authors to control exactly how each structure on each page will look, given that browsers have differing capabilities. Browsers capable only of, for example, teletype-style text or of speech necessarily ignore most style guidelines.

Delimiter Symbol with a specific meaning to HTML browsers; for example, the symbol sequence </ indicates the start of a closing tag, while the symbol > indicates the end of a tag.

DNS Internet Domain Name Server, a computer which returns to your machine the Internet

Address corresponding to some Internet Domain name.

Download (vb) To fetch files, such as **HTML** documents, over a network such as the **Internet**, from a **server**. *See also* **viruses**.

DSSSL Document Style Semantics & Specification Language, a candidate source for HTML style sheets. It is pronounced to rhyme with Thistle. Unfortunately it is horribly complicated.

DTD Document Type Definition, such as the formal description of **HTML**, written in **SGML**.

DTP DeskTop Publishing, the business of creating finished and attractive documents at home or in a small office with a computer and a laser printer.

Element Syntactic building-block in **HTML** able to stand by itself, unlike **attributes** which can qualify most elements. A typical element consists of a start tag, like <H1> or <FORM>, some text content, and a matching end tag, like </H1> or </FORM>. Some elements like <HR> have no content and hence do not require an end tag either. Many elements such as <P> do not require an end tag even though they have text content, as the start of the next similar element ends them implicitly.

Email Electronic mail. You can often send in replies or comments on **HTML** documents by writing email messages to their authors. Email is a much older service than HTTP and has its quirks, but is generally fast and reliable. No universally agreed way of encoding binary data or document mark-up exists for email messages, so it is wise to start transactions with plain **ASCII** text. The diverse encodings include BIN-HEX, UUENCODE, RTF and **MIME**; these depend for their success on your recipient's having the matching decoding software.

Embedding Putting objects (such as images, texts, tables, and data) belonging to application programs (such as image and text editors, spreadsheets and databases) into an HTML document as if they were just part of it. Embedding gives users a composite view of a system, with point-and-click access to any of the tools used to provide that view. The concept is already in wide use on personal computers and is likely to become very important on the Web.

Emoticons Emetic little symbols such as :-] for 'glum' or :-o for 'astonished', you tilt your head to the left or (Einstein and all that) the page to the right, to see rather bad **ASCII** drawings of faces expressing emotions. These are supposed to lend depth of feeling to otherwise cold communications, or to draw their sting. Their original and rightful place is in the Internet's Multi-User Dungeons (MUDs) where their terseness is part of the sport.

End tag The tag which closes an HTML **element**. The element name is preceded by an opening angle bracket and a slash, and is followed only by a closing angle bracket, for example </TITLE>. *See also* **Start tag**.

En units Originally the width of a letter N in the current font; now defined as half the width of the widest character in the font, generally the letter M. If you allow 20 ens for a piece of text, you can be confident that there is room for at least 10 characters, and usually about 15 in mixed text.

Entity A symbol specially defined for use in HTML documents. For example, & represents the ampersand &. The HTML entities are listed in the appendices.

ETP Egg Transfer Protocol, used as example to explain **HTTP**, **FTP**, and so on. Each kind of data has an appropriate protocol for its safe transfer over the Internet.

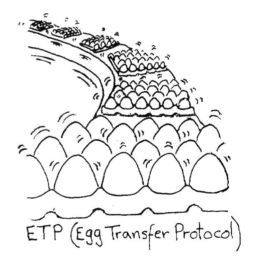

ETP (Egg Transfer Protocol)

FAQ (List of) Frequently Asked Questions; the rather repulsive term for a document which, like a scientific review, covers the field for newcomers to save everybody else from constant interruption by foolish questioning. Few FAQs are as well structured as reviews.

Fixed-pitch Font in which all characters have the same width, as on a typewriter. Common examples are Courier and Elite.

Flame To abuse aggressively, generally by **email** message. The practice is more dangerous than it looks, as messages, however hasty, can be stored permanently.

Floating Of an image, allowed to move to the left or right margin, with the (**marked-up**) text flowing around it, as opposed to having white space beside the image.

Form An HTML document structure which creates, in a browser, the appearance of a fill-in form such as those ceaselessly produced by bureaucrats; more loosely, also such a visible structure in a browser. HTML forms consist mainly of named fields, each of which consists of a text label and a mechanism such as a text box or radio button for obtaining input from the user. There are also predefined form controls for submitting the contents of a completed form to the server, and for resetting a form to its initial (empty or default) state.

Frame An HMTL document structure which creates the effect of a set of windows, each containing images or Web pages. A typical use of frames is to put an index in one more-or-less static frame, and the indexed documents in a scrollable frame which is updated when the user clicks on the index. Frames allow documents to be simple because the frame structure handles tasks such as navigation and presentation.

FTP (File Transfer Protocol) convenient, fast, and reliable method of sending or receiving files of any sort over the **Internet**. FTP sites can be accessed directly from the Web, or with a specialized FTP client on any computer attached to the Internet. FTP works well on virtually every kind of computer, and FTP clients are normally supplied free with UNIX boxes, for example. Program files **downloaded** with FTP or any other protocol may contain **viruses** and should be checked before use. *See also* **MTP**.

FYI For Your Information, a relatively informal document describing an Internet standard.

Generic attribute Property which can be applied to many different HTML elements. For example, the attributes ID, LANG, and CLASS can all be used to qualify paragraphs <P>, headings <H1> to <H6>, <TABLE> and so on.

GIF (Graphics Interchange Format) a lossless **compression** algorithm and data format, originating from CompuServe and now very widely used on the Internet for transmitting and storing graphics. It is especially effective for compressing diagrams and images prepared on computers. *See also* **JPEG**.

Gopher (from 'go for it', but also a pun on the burrowing rodents of that name) – a simple mechanism giving access to **ASCII** documents via an inordinate number of menus. Gopherspace was a precursor of the **Web**; it is now all but obsolete. As with the Web, Gopher menus could refer to each other in a simple way, so that the user could navigate rapidly around between Gopher sites with a few clicks of the mouse. Gopher searches are text-based, so they seem rather dull in comparison with **surfin'** the Web. As menu jumps are easily simulated by hypertext references, you can visit Gopherspace for yourself using your browser.

Home page(s) (1) HTML documents belonging to a person or an organization, and constituting his/her/its presence on the Web. (2) Top-level (index) HTML document of the set described in (1).

HoTMetaL A program made by SoftQuad, Inc., to edit **HTML** using paired symbolic tags. HoTMetaL is wise to the rules of HTML and can help you to avoid many types of error.

HTML HyperText Mark-up Language, the subject of this book. *See also* **SGML**.

HTTP: HyperText Transfer Protocol, the email- and **MIME**-based mechanism for transferring chunks of **HTML** across the Internet. *See also* **Secure HTTP, ETP**.

HTTP -ng A coming-real-soon-now New Generation of HTTP: which will not be based on plain old email.

Hypertext Text (but also graphics, tables, diagrams, sound clips, and other audio-visual media) represented in machine-readable form so that human users can move around from page to page by selecting predefined symbols with a pointing device. On the **World Wide Web**, the hypertext is written in **HTML** (the subject of this book), and jumps between pages are typically by means of underlined phrases, or by icons or buttons forming **anchors**. Broadly equivalent terms such as hypermedia and hypergraphics are sometimes used.

IAB Internet Architecture Board.

Icon Small image, often arranged as a button which can be clicked (that is, in HTML it is within a hypertext **anchor**). Icons are supposed to be instantly recognizable, but their general incomprehensibility is a stock joke.

IEEE Institute of Electronic and Electrical Engineering, a body responsible for promoting many standards in engineering.

IESG Internet Engineering Steering Group.

IETF Internet Engineering Task Force.

Image map HTML structure which enables an image to behave as a group of hypertext anchors. The map relates particular areas (such as rectangles) on the image to hypertext references. A click on a mapped area behaves exactly like a click on a normal hypertext anchor, taking the user to the file which is referred to in the anchor. There are two kinds of image map: (1) server-side, where the position of the click is sent back to the server, which can then use a script (typically CGI) to identify which file to fetch for the user; (2) client-side, where the browser determines what to fetch, and requests it (if necessary) from the server. This is often much faster, as the reference can be to another place in the current file, so that the job can be done entirely locally (with no messages across the Internet). Client-side image maps are suitable for use on Intranets, no scripts are needed.

Infobahn No, we don't know what this is either. It seems to be one or more of the following: (1) what the Internet will become when everyone who is rich is using it; (2) what the telecommunications and cable TV companies would like us to use, viz, a lot of bandwidth in our sitting rooms which we pay for by the second as our kids order and watch yet another porno video; (3) the techno-savior of western civilization as we know it, spreading electronic wisdom and knowledge from pole to pole and generally turning wicked savages into good Christians and white man's friends; (4) the death of family life, culture, the nuclear family and home-made apple pie, in which everyone will sit square-eyed in front of their monitors **surfing** the cyber-waves morning, noon, and night. We're sorry we can't help you further on this one.

Information super-highway *see* **Infobahn**.

Internet (1) The global network of computers based on the Advanced Research Projects Agency Network (ARPAnet), founded in the 1960s, and now exponentially increasing. (2) The physical home of cyberspace and the **Infobahn**. (3) Useful word to put in newspaper headlines when introducing any dull piece of research, for example, Internet Could Be Replaced By Brain-Implant Telepathy, Says Scientist.

Intranet By analogy with Internet, a network where files are accessed by hypertext references as if they were local. Since many companies already have private local (and sometimes global) networks where users can run browsers, the mechanism offers a quick and cheap way of organizing and distributing information.

IP Internet Protocol, familiar as part of **TCP/IP**.

ISDN Purely digital connection to the **Internet**, using a faster line (56 or 64 kbits per second; can be doubled-up to 128 kbits per second) than a normal telephone connection; offers very short setup times, unlike the slow dialling-in needed with phone lines; still generally too expensive for personal use, though this may change (if it does not, ISDN will probably disappear). ISDN seems likely to be overtaken by digital modems as soon as a standard for these is agreed. *See also* **Modem**.

ISO International Standards Organization.

ISOC Internet Society and its board of trustees.

Java (1) Central island of the republic of Indonesia, famous for coffees grown especially on the high volcanic plateaux such as Dieng, Ijen. Most coffee sold as 'Java', especially in the USA, actually comes from other islands including Sumatra (also a source of much fine coffee), or from other countries. (2) An interpreted programming language devised by Sun Microsystems, Inc.

Programs are translated (compiled) into a completely portable intermediate code, which is a convenient short form for transmission on the Web. A Java client (probably free), a small program available for many different types of computer, interprets and obeys the code line-by-line. Since Java programs can be included with HTML documents, Java opens the door to a wide range of services that cannot be built into standard HTML. Its use in both Netscape and Microsoft browsers and its ready portability are gaining it wide acceptance.

JavaScript An interpreted programming language designed to be used for short scripts inserted directly into HTML pages. JavaScript is the default script language and is interpreted by many browsers including both Microsoft's and Netscape's. The language has nothing in common with **Java** except its suitability for the Web. *See also* **VBScript**.

JPEG An internationally agreed standard for lossy **compression** of images, especially photographs. Some quality is lost (images become more blurred and edges become indistinct) at high compression ratios. Typical images can safely be compressed to 15:1 or more with little noticeable degradation. JPEG is currently the main Web format for photographs. *See also* **GIF** and **MPEG**.

Jump Relaxed way of saying 'use a hypertext link'. A local jump is made entirely within one HTML page; other jumps are to pages on the same or remote servers. *See* **Link**.

A local jump

⟨A HREF = "#2"⟩

LAN Local Area Network. If you are inside an organization which connects you to the Internet via a LAN, you get the **Web** for free, but at the

price of even more delay than usual, if the LAN is at all busy (or if 1000 engineers are sharing a 64 kbyte Internet connection).

Latin-1 A widely-used character set covering the letters, plain and accented, used in most European languages (except Greek and the Cyrillic alphabets), as well as a selection of common symbols.

LaTeX A sophisticated but not especially friendly typesetting language widely used on UNIX machines and considered as one possible basis for HTML. HTML to LaTeX filters are available to format output for printing from Web pages. Incidentally the 'X' is meant to be a Greek letter Chi (χ) and should be pronounced 'kh'.

Link Hypertext link, using <A> or <LINK> tags to connect a Web document to another document or image.

Mark-up By analogy with publishers' proof-reading signs, the set of symbols used to indicate how a document is to be treated for display or printing on any device. *See also* **HTML**, **SGML**.

MIME Multipurpose Internet Mail Extensions (Internet RFC 1590); a system to allow more complex types of file to be sent by email, including binary data, compared to the plain text supported by basic Internet mail.

MIT Massachusetts Institute of Technology, the not-quite-all-male institution which is now the stepfather of the World Wide Web. *See also* **CERN**.

Modem MODulator/DEModulator; a signalling device which converts either way between digital signals, such as those coming from a computer's serial data port, and analog signals (modulated tones) which can be sent on a normal telephone line. Most home users of the **Web** are connected to the **Internet** via a modem and telephone line. If you are buying a new modem for this purpose, the minimum useful speed is 14.4 kbps, and 28.8 is better. Ordinary phone lines can sometimes support 56 kbps for downlink, staying at about 28 for uplink; the limiting factor is the amount of noise, especially on older or longer local loops between homes and phone exchanges. Analog modems have thus reached their limit; digital modems, which convert between local and long-distance signalling patterns, do not have the same problem. Digital modems are therefore likely to supplant analog ones in the next few years. *See also* **ISDN**.

Mosaic *see* **NCSA**.

MPEG The video equivalent of **JPEG**. Most people's Internet connections (and most parts of the Internet itself) have too small a bandwidth to permit more than the smallest amount of video to be transmitted satisfactorily. This severe limitation will undoubtedly be attacked vigorously in the next decade (for example with digital **modems**), and the results will probably determine whether it is the Internet or some other network that achieves global dominance.

MTP Milk Transfer Protocol; *see* **ETP** for explanation.

MTP (Milk Transfer Protocol)

NCSA National Center for Supercomputing Applications, the American home of the first successful graphical **browser**, Mosaic, the application which made the Internet and the World Wide Web household names.

Nerd Person who is into things technical and out of social life. He is supposed to wear an anorak, but this hideous modern garment has nothing in common with the beautifully embroidered leather overshirt, *annoraaq*, worn by the Inuit of Greenland. The Web is rapidly becoming more practical and less nerdy.

Netscape Navigator The **browser** available on various types of computer made by Netscape Corp. Its concept derives closely from **NCSA** Mosaic, of which it is a more sophisticated re-implementation. It is currently available for free downloading and occupies about 70 or 75% of the browser market.

Object A term with many meanings in computing. In HTML, a structure which can contain a range of audio-visual components, together with associated information such as a caption.

Online (currently) Actively connected to the Web.

Page Loose term for an HTML document available on the Web. Documents can be much longer than the equivalent of a printed page, but the term is quite well established, as is the related **Home Page**.

Parse To analyse a construct in some language to determine its structure, in order to translate or represent it appropriately. Each **HTML** document has to be parsed by a Web **browser** for display on a computer screen.

Patch An *ad hoc* attempted solution to a software fault.

PC Personal computer (once made by IBM) based on an Intel 80×86 microprocessor chip and traditionally running DOS/Windows operating systems; though nowadays multi-chip sets, networking, other manufacturers' chips, and even other operating systems make the distinction between PCs and computers in general increasingly indistinct.

Permitted context Places in a document where you can use an element; for example, the table header cell TH is only permitted in (the context of) a table row TR.

POTS Plain Old Telephone System, the familiar mechanism using copper wires for the 'local loop', connected to different kinds of exchange (analog or digital) originally only for voice communications, but now used also for fax and Internet access. *See also* **modem**.

Publish To make available on the Web, generally in the form of HTML documents, though also as files of any other downloadable or executable type. The Web has already revolutionized the concept of publishing (paper and ink are no longer seen as essential ingredients, text does not have to be sequential, etc.). New arrivals like **embedding** and **Java** make the concept still more nebulous, as documents do not come into existence until viewed, and what comes into existence is probably different every time. The Web seems to be moving from broadcast publishing (everyone who visits a site sees some of the documents there) to narrowcast or even individual publishing (you see what you want to).

Pull Fetching of information on demand, driven by the consumer, as with use of a traditional library (or traditional Web browsing). Pull is highly specific and has, so far, been free apart from overheads like phone and **service provider** charges. *See also* **Push**, **Publish**.

Push Supply of information to people whether or not they requested it, driven by the supplier, as with traditional broadcasting. Suppliers who aim to make money from the Web advocate Push as a way of avoiding time-wasting surfing. Push services can typically be configured by the recipient, who may thus receive daily financial or sporting news, etc. *See also* **Pull**, **Publish**.

RFC Request for Comments, which sounds nice and vague, but is actually a virtually-definitive document describing a proposed Internet standard.

Router A computer which directs data on the Internet.

RTF Rich Text Format, a word-processing document interchange format created by Microsoft. It is notoriously complex and difficult to parse reliably.

RTFM Read The Flaming Manual. Generally the last resort.

Script A short computer program, such as one embedded in an HTML page. Scripts can do many kinds of job, such as verifying that a form's fields have been filled in consistently, or providing assistance with navigation among frame documents.

Secure HTTP: An updated version of **HTTP:** which includes encryption to protect sensitive data like credit-card details when transmitted over the Web; one of several competing protocols

for the potentially lucrative market of payment on the Web.

Server A program (or computer running such a program) which provides a (data) service of some kind to its **clients**. A **Web** server uses **HTTP:** to provide its own set of **HTML** documents to Web users. For example, an organization may advertise its products or services on the Web by making available a set of Web pages on its own server; people can **download** this information from anywhere in the world connected to the **Internet**.

Service provider Organization offering users access to the Internet. A typical package includes one or several email addresses, unlimited access to the **Web**, **FTP** and other services, and space for a personal Web site.

SGML Standard Generalized Mark-up Language, an international standard (ISO 8879:1986, Information Processing Text and Office Systems) for a method of describing the structure of a document of any type. The normal way to use SGML is to write a formal description (a **DTD**) in SGML syntax of how you want a particular type of document to be structured. SGML can also be used directly for unspecialized mark-up.

Shareware (1) Software which is available on free trial, and which can be freely distributed and copied provided the terms and conditions are also supplied; payment is usually required at the end of the trial period. Some shareware is issued commercially; other programs are written by individuals or places of learning. (2) Idiosyncratically configured software available free (if you ignore both your moral duty to pay for it, and your contribution to your telephone company's annual profits while you try to **download** it).

Smilies *see* **Emoticons**.

Sneakernet (across building with floppy disk in hand, sneakers on feet) A fast reliable network transfer protocol, capable of 1.4 megabytes in a minute or two. Works much better than frayed Ethernet.

Standard width units *see* **Width units**.

Start tag The tag which begins an HTML **element**. The element name is preceded only by an opening angle bracket, and may be followed by one or more **attributes**, each generally with an assigned value, for example, `<H2 ID=introduction>`. *See also* **End tag**.

Style sheet A document, not itself written in HTML, associated explicitly (by a declaration) with an **HTML** page, defining the way in which various elements and classes (using the CLASS attribute in various elements) in the HTML are to be treated for display. For instance, a style sheet might specify 11 point Garamond as the font for displaying <P> text on screen.

Surfing To spend time browsing around the **Web** or the **Internet**, generally for pleasure. The practice is deprecated by companies that want their technical staff to be productive. Surfing, like reading dictionaries (when you were trying to look a word up), is an addictively serendipitous way of gathering facts but is less fruitful at finding out anything in particular.

Table An arrangement of pieces of text or other data on a rectangular plan, possibly divided into a grid by horizontal and/or vertical lines and possibly surrounded by a ruled frame. Tables can have row and column headers, captions, a **table header**, and one or more **table bodies**.

Table body A group of table (data) rows treated as a unit, for example for bordering or alignment purposes. Tables can have any number of such groups.

Table header A single optional group of table rows at the top of a table, intended to be available to the user whenever table data are displayed, for instance by being fixed on screen while table data rows are scrolled.

Tag The mark-up structure in HTML which starts (**start tag**) or ends (**end tag**) an HTML element. A tag consists of a pair of angle brackets and whatever is inside them. Tags must contain at least the name of an element, for example, <P>, or; start tags can also contain attributes and their values, for example <P ALIGN=right>. *See also* **Element**, **Attribute**.

Tao and the Art of Server Maintenance, etc. The Way of Effortless Being; *see* **Zen** for explanation.

TCP/IP Terminal Communications Protocol/ Internet Protocol. Actually no one knows or cares about the expansion of this acronym, which like Radar has long since become a word in its own right. TCP/IP is the robust low-level means by which messages get sent on the Net.

Telnet A primitive mechanism for logging on to a remote computer (for example on the **Internet**) as if your computer was a terminal connected directly to it. Much early Internet work was conducted with nothing more sophisticated than cheap home computers, slow **modems** and Telnet.

URL Uniform Resource Locator, the form of name used by **HTTP:** to identify servers and resources uniquely.

VBScript Easy-to-use scripting language similar to Visual Basic, proposed and implemented by Microsoft as a rival to **JavaScript**. VBScript has many convenient and powerful features, especially the ability to call Microsoft's OCX interactive controls (widgets), but it is not supported by other browsers or non-Microsoft platforms. Portability is therefore a problem, in contrast to JavaScript or Java.

Veronica Supposedly 'Very Easy Rodent-Oriented Netwide Index to Computerized Archives'. This won *Byte* magazine's *The Really Stretching It Award* for worst acronym. A fairly useful companion in **Gopher**-space, Veronica is now fading into peaceful oblivion as the Web takes over the world.

Virus A program designed to attach itself to other (innocent) files such as programs, and to replicate itself when those programs are executed. Some viruses display offensive messages on screen; others are designed to destroy data immediately or at particular times. Viruses can readily be transferred over the **Internet**, most frequently when games or other free programs are **downloaded** with **FTP** from unofficial sites. The safest approach is to fetch software only from reliable sources, such as major mirror sites, and to check all incoming files with an up-to-date virus checker before use.

VRML Virtual Reality Markup Language, a supplement to HTML for low-bandwidth (that is, fast) transmission and representation of moving images of seemingly solid objects on client displays. For example, you might one day be able to steer your browser 'through' a shop, literally browsing through the books, records or clothes on sale there. We doubt you'll be able to sniff the different kinds of coffee-beans, though.

WAIS (Wide Area Information Server, pronounced 'ways') indexed databases on the Internet. WAIS databases can be searched very efficiently. Thousands of databases containing scientific, technical and government data are freely available from many countries. There are a few public gateways to WAIS from the Web; more convenient and less crowded access is available if your organization provides WAIS clients and a WAIS server or gateway.

Web *see* **World Wide Web**. We have deliberately used a range of commonly-used terms as synonyms for the Web: out there you will find all of them in use, so using only one is both artificial and monotonous.

Web page, Web site *see* **Page**, **Home pages**.

Width units Most **table** components can be sized either automatically or according to a specification supplied in a `WIDTH` attribute. This gives widths in a rich choice of units: pi – picas; pt – points; in – inches; em – em units; cm – centimeters; mm – millimeters; px – pixels (the awkward default). In some cases it is also possible to use percentages, for example the table's width as a percentage of the window or screen's. Finally, columns can be given relative widths by following their values with a star (*). No space is ever allowed between width values and width units; '3em' is right but '3 em' is not.

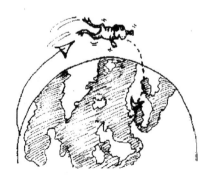

World, The The part of the world's human population rich enough to own or have access to a computer on the **Internet**.

World Wide Web The set of all **hypertext** documents written in **HTML**, transmitted by **HTTP:** and residing on Internet computers; the abstract space in which readers can navigate around such documents in search of knowledge. The Web is criticized for lack of structure, but in fact there are good general and specific indexes which are widely known and used, and which enable even inexperienced users to find almost anything in a few minutes.

WYSIWYG (1) What You See Is What You Get. This is undoubtedly true when choosing a spouse, being sold secondhand cars, or unwisely buying squashy peaches in your street-market, but no computer screen ever accurately portrays what you will really get when you print a document out, as there are too many imponderables. (2) What You See Is What You Get: claimed performance of various word processors and other software tools in depicting printable output.

Xanadu Ted Nelson's long-running and pioneering project, reflecting his 1960s vision of a truly global hypertext with all the world's literature, etc. The Web is a humble but practical successor to Nelson's vision. We are ashamed of the lack of recognition of this great man's achievement, and still more of the open abuse poured on him by *Wired*.

Yelnet Rapid and efficient information transfer protocol consisting of loudly enunciated data travelling from mouth to ear(s). Often much easier than **Telnet**. Quicker, too.

Zen and the art of... Zen is about being (part of) all that is. It is the opposite of separating reality into compartments, dealing electronically only with the most abstract of those. The Web could help bring people from all over the world together, or it could reinforce the separation of haves and have-nots. *See also* **Tao** ....

INDEX